GENDER, SEXUALITY, AND POWER IN LATIN AMERICA SINCE INDEPENDENCE

Jaguar Books on Latin America Series

William Beezley and Colin MacLachlan, Series Editors

GENDER, SEXUALITY, AND POWER IN LATIN AMERICA SINCE INDEPENDENCE

Edited by
William E. French and
Katherine Elaine Bliss

ROWMAN & LITTLEFIELD PUBLISHERS, INC.
Lanham • Boulder • New York • Toronto • Plymouth, UK

ROWMAN & LITTLEFIELD PUBLISHERS, INC.

Published in the United States of America
by Rowman & Littlefield Publishers, Inc.
A wholly owned subsidary of The Rowman & Littlefield Publishing Group, Inc.
4501 Forbes Boulevard, Suite 200, Lanham, Maryland 20706
www.rowmanlittlefield.com

Estover Road
Plymouth PL6 7PY
United Kingdom

British Library Cataloguing in Publication Information Available

Library of Congress Cataloging-in-Publication Data

Gender, sexuality, and power in Latin America since independence / edited by William E.
    French and Katherine Elaine Bliss.
    p. cm. — (Jaguar books on Latin America series)
    Includes bibliographical references and index.
    ISBN-13: 978-0-7425-3742-2 (cloth : alk. paper)
    ISBN-10: 0-7425-3742-0 (cloth : alk. paper)
    ISBN-13: 978-0-7425-3743-9 (pbk. : alk. paper)
    ISBN-10: 0-7425-3743-9 (pbk. : alk. paper)
    1. Sex role—Latin America. 2. Sex and history—Latin America. 3. Power (Social
sciences)—Latin America. I. French, William E., 1956– II. Bliss, Katherine Elaine, 1968–
III. Series: Jaguar books on Latin America.
HQ1075.5.L29G4617 2007
306.7098—dc22

                                                                              2006011357

Printed in the United States of America

⊗™ The paper used in this publication meets the minimum requirements of American
National Standard for Information Sciences—Permanence of Paper for Printed Library
Materials, ANSI/NISO Z39.48-1992.

"Sentimientos inosentes"

Vamos á amarnos pero sin promesas
Vamos a creer en nuestros momentos
llenos de amor y de iluciones
vañadas de fantacias y enbueltas
de inocencia, porque de tantos
libros que existen en ninguno
en ninguno se aprende
La felisidad ó el amor
es mejor vivirlo

Gerardo Navarro G.
28-VI-2002

"Innocent feelings"

Let's love each other but without promises
Let's believe in our moments
Full of love and hopes
Bathed in fantasies and wrapped
In innocence, because of all the many
Books that exist in none of them
In none can one learn
Happiness or love
It's better to live it

Gerardo Navarro G.
June 28, 2002

Note: The Spanish version of this poem appears on the front cover as part of the painting.

Contents

Introduction: Gender, Sexuality, and Power in Latin America since Independence

William E. French and Katherine Elaine Bliss

O UR FIRST TASK IN THIS INTRODUCTION is to explain what historians mean when they use the term *gender*. It was through the work of Joan Wallach Scott that gender became a useful category of analysis for many historians, in North America and elsewhere, including historians interested in Latin America. A historian of modern France, Scott moved from her initial interest in the labor history and political actions of the glassworkers of Carmaux,[1] in which she identified workers' experience of occupational change as the key to explaining their behavior, to a concern both with gender as a form of power and with discourse, that is, the production of particular kinds of knowledge about a subject through the use of language, images, spaces, and symbols. Writing nearly twenty years ago, Scott drew from feminist and poststructuralist theory to offer a two-part definition of the concept of gender.[2] In the first part, she explained how symbols, norms, and institutions helped to shape or construct male and female identities, in other words, how they made or created masculine and feminine subjects. For Scott and many others, gender is thus the social representation of perceived biological differences. Used in this sense, as it is by the editors and authors in this book, gender can be seen to be defined in different ways at different times and places. Gender is thus a problem for historical investigation rather than a given or something that can be taken for granted: in short, it has a history. This is what historians mean when they say that femininity and masculinity are socially constructed and historically contingent categories.

In the second part of her definition of gender, Scott makes a case for why she feels that gender must be included as a necessary component in any discussion of power. Scott argues that femininity and masculinity are not only socially constructed and historically contingent, but, as they are constructed mutually, they form a pair, or binary, that can be expressed in the form femininity/masculinity. Such a binary construction results in two negative consequences: first, it limits the possibility of other alternative constructions of gender, and, second, it makes the definitions of femininity and masculinity seem natural and not subject to change. The following examples may help illustrate this concept. When newspaper columnists in early-twentieth-century Mexico wanted to comment negatively on the increasing number of women working as wage laborers, they likened women working outside the home to women being able to grow hair on their chests. In other words, these journalists were suggesting that such behavior was not only different from women's previous roles but that it seemed to go against nature itself. Likewise, in the present volume, David Parker shows that male politicians in Uruguay at about that same time described statements made by journalists or politicians who then refused to back those statements up by dueling as the "insults of a woman." In this case, as you will see when you read Parker's chapter, the binary construction that is formed pits "responsible" gentlemen against women, assumed to be inherently incapable of dueling. In this manner, elite men not only constructed themselves as the opposite of women, they made women's full participation in politics unthinkable, even to seem to go against "nature."

These examples also illustrate the important point that the binary femininity/masculinity also supports other binaries by making them appear natural or legitimate as well. Other binaries that follow from our examples might read as follows: home/work, private/public, and passive/active. In each of these binaries, the first of the pair is gendered feminine while the second is gendered masculine. If turn-of-the-century Mexicans were then to go on and criticize their government (or any individual or institution) as being inactive or passive, this criticism became powerful because of the link between passivity and socially constructed ideas of femininity. It is in this way that gender serves as a means of organizing ideas of equality and inequality and becomes a crucial site or field where power is articulated.

The relationship among gender, power, and ideas about equality illustrates the most compelling reason for undertaking historical research through the lens of gender history: everything is gendered. Thus, although they don't always see it this way, historians interested in such things as political institutions, international relations, economic processes, and social groups, among others, can also find gender a useful category of historical analysis. Some skeptics, for example, have asked what a gendered analysis might reveal about the history of the Mexican Revolution, the violent phase which took place between 1910 and 1920. This is a tricky question, as, implied in its very asking is the assumption that studying gender means studying women. As women were not the main combatants (although they certainly participated in the violent phase of the revolution in many ways, including as combatants), then knowing more about women's activities, so the thinking goes, would not change our understanding of the origins, trajectory, or outcome of such an event. Also unstated in the question is the claim that some things are more important to study than others, such as politics, economics, and revolutions, for example, rather than women or even ideas about femininity and masculinity.

In our opinion, ranking subjects of historical inquiry in a hierarchy from greater to lesser importance (with gender at the bottom or left off of the list altogether) is a great mistake, as politics, economics, and, yes, even revolutions have been enacted within a field defined, at least in part, by gender. Indeed, an analysis of the Mexican Revolution from the perspective of gender history might help us to understand the reasons women, as well as men, from different classes and regions were motivated to participate in such a struggle. In other words, having a better understanding of official and popular ideas about masculinity and femininity might be essential to explaining the decisions people, both men and women, made, both during and after the decade of revolution. Moreover, political plans and the rhetoric of politics, such well-known parts of the story of the revolution, are often expressed in highly gendered language, as are the concepts of citizenship and national identity that grew out of the revolution. Even widely held and often unquestioned assumptions about who was even entitled to participate in politics and public discourse more broadly rest, as we will see in many of the chapters of this volume, on understandings of gender. While this introduction is not the space to write a history of the Mexican Revolution through the lens of gender history, many historians have taken up just that task, including Katherine Bliss and Ann Blum in their chapter in this collection. The growing body of work concerned with understanding the history of gender and the Mexican Revolution suggests that the origins, trajectory, and outcome of this complex process were indeed shaped by considerations of gender.[3]

Debating Gender

Delegates to the Fourth United Nations Conference on Women, held in Beijing, China, in the spring of 1995, spent weeks negotiating a definition of the term *gender* that could satisfy everyone present. Some participants argued that the term denoted differences between the sexes, while others insisted that it signified a wider range of meanings, including homosexuality or so-called permissive lifestyles. Faced with so many different interpretations and with the need to prepare the conference's final document and recommendations, the delegates deferred finalizing their definition of the term, instead forming a committee to come up with a working definition suitable for the international arena. Despite their disagreements, the conversations and debates at this and related conferences did reveal that those attending were of one mind when it came to one central idea: that gender, sexuality, reproduction, and power were all bound inextricably together. These conferences served to highlight the need to better understand terms such as gender, sexuality, and power in both their contemporary and historical contexts.[4]

Fortunately, the field of Latin American history has seen an impressive outpouring of scholarship related to the connections among gender, sexuality, and power. The authors contributing to *Gender, Sexuality, and Power in Latin America since Independence* have been among those at the forefront of this development. The central concern of their research—the interplay of gender and/or sexuality with ethnicity, nationality, class, and other aspects of identity—focuses on a specific period in a country or region within Latin America while paying close attention to the interaction and impact of local, national, and transnational contexts. Their writing has both built on and helped influence a wave of scholarly work in history, anthropology, and literary criticism on subjects central to the history of gender and sexuality in Latin America, including, among others, femininities, masculinities, homosexualities, honor, families, national identities, place, and ethnicities.[5]

The publication of *Gender, Sexuality, and Power in Latin America since Independence* also coincides with a period in which those working on the history of gender and sexuality in Latin America are debating both the manner and the extent to which the focus on gender and sexuality has reshaped our understanding of the past in Latin America and how it might continue to do so. Scholars are now exploring themes such as the relationship among gender, sexuality, and the state in Latin America over the last two centuries.[6] Review essays discussing recent works on gender in national and comparative contexts in Latin America have appeared with greater frequency over the past seven years, as have special editions of major journals, with both being devoted to the themes of gender and sexuality in Latin America.[7] In their dissertation research, graduate students are now exploring a variety of subjects through the lenses of gender and sexuality. Some recent work, for example, seeks to understand the relationship between gender and technology, especially as it relates to the development of the Internet in Mexico.[8]

Given this dynamism in the field, as represented by the increasing number of publications and conferences, and the sense that fundamental approaches to our understanding of the past are at stake, we have put together this book in hopes of accomplishing the following three goals: first, to assemble a unique collection of cutting-edge primary research in a form that is accessible to nonspecialists; second, to emphasize the many ways in which gender and sexuality have been centrally implicated in the workings of power in Latin

America; and, third, to participate in an ongoing interdisciplinary conversation that will trace where the field of the history of gender and sexuality in Latin America has been and help chart where it is going.

By this point, a number of questions will have suggested themselves to you. Why are so many scholars interested in the history of gender and sexuality in Latin America? How does studying gender and sexuality offer them new insights on the past and present in Latin America and elsewhere? What are the sources and methods they use to elicit information about gender difference, sexual practice, and power in historical contexts? Moreover, even though delegates to the Beijing conference couldn't agree on a definition, what do those contributing to this volume mean by the two terms gender and sexuality? Other questions might ask, Why talk about genders and sexualities in the plural? What do historians mean when they write about such issues as femininities, masculinities, and homosexualities? As for power, if it doesn't necessarily refer to armies, police, or other institutions of social control, what do we mean when we use this term? How has power been exercised, lived, and contested? Whereas all of these questions will be addressed in the course of this collection, perhaps we should begin with the most fundamental question: What is the difference between studying the history of gender and studying the history of women?

History of Women/History of Gender

The history of women and the history of gender, emerging out of similar circumstances and intertwined in many ways, need to be understood as two related, yet different, conceptual enterprises. Practitioners of the first have often been concerned with recovering women's voices and experiences, subjects often ignored or devalued by previous generations of historians, in order to add them to the historical record, often in order to provide evidence to support political change in the status and treatment of women in the present. Historians of gender, who are often in agreement with many of these goals, argue for a shift in the very categories used to evaluate and understand that historical past, problematizing the very existence of an all-encompassing category such as "woman." Instead, they focus on questions that we explain in greater detail later in this introduction, such as how discourses constitute subjects and how political documents and politics more generally, to take only two examples, are "gendered." Like historians of women, gender historians are also often committed to bringing about change in the present.

The dynamic development of both of these fields can be linked to at least two factors. The first is the growth in studies related to research programs on women in development and gender in development during the 1970s and

1980s, while the second is the more recent growth in the fields of the international and comparative history of women and gender, queer studies, and sexuality studies. Historians, anthropologists, and others working within the "women in development" model look at subjects such as women's social roles and their participation in labor processes, showing the ways in which major changes, including those associated with agrarian reform, revolution, and economic development projects, have frequently benefited men far more than women. Their focus has often been on the pervasiveness of the institution of patriarchy. Historians interested in gender have taken up many of these insights while reconceptualizing key categories, such as agency and identity, and rethinking all-encompassing terms like patriarchy.[9] Like many who have contributed to this volume, they have focused on societal expectations regarding appropriate roles for men and women and on how ideas about what constitutes feminine or masculine behavior structure hierarchies or relationships of power. For them, agency and identity are not fixed categories but, rather, are contextually defined and historically contingent.

As one scholar who has studied the interrelated development of these fields has observed, it was during the 1980s that many historians began to emphasize "gender," rather than "women," in their work, although this shift has been more pronounced in North America than in Latin America.[10] This helps explain why much of the work on gender, sexuality, and power in Latin America has been undertaken by scholars working in North American universities. An early example of the shift to emphasizing the history of gender in the study of Latin America can be seen in the work of one of the editors of this volume. Writing in the early 1990s, William French focused on the outpouring of concern, in the press and in official correspondence and reports, with morality, vice, work habits, and the figure of the prostitute in late-nineteenth- and early-twentieth-century northern Mexico. Those concerned with Mexico's development and progress could envision it taking place only if prostitutes could be regulated and all women became properly educated mothers and guardian angels of the home. Such rhetoric (or discourse, as we discuss it later in this introduction) created a binary pair, that of prostitute and guardian angel, that served to eliminate other possible roles for women. French's analysis highlights how the social construction of gender was central to the process of class and self-definition under way at that time.[11]

For a number of very good reasons, scholars in many parts of Latin America, until recently, have been more interested in the history, agency, and voices of women than in the history of gender. For some scholars in Latin America, the lack of attention to women in the writing of national histories has posed the most pressing problem in need of correction. A recent study of Brazilian historiography, for example, stressed that scholars in Brazilian universities working on the history of women have had difficulty getting their work recognized as belonging to a valid field of inquiry.[12] For some, establishing institutional space, that is, research centers that foster scholarship, academic exchange, and collaboration on issues related to women, has been the most immediate goal. Others have seen little reason to focus on gender, which they describe as a research agenda largely developed in North America and Europe.[13]

In just the same way, the work of North American scholars has also been influenced by the times in which they live. Broad changes and challenges stemming from the sexual revolution of the 1960s, the antiwar movement aimed at the war in Vietnam, the feminist movement of the 1960s and 1970s, gay rights activism beginning at about the same time, and the black civil rights movement prompted some academics, in the United States and Canada as elsewhere, both to ask new questions in their research and to search for different interpretive frameworks in which to find answers for them. Propelled by these and other developments, the field of Latin American women's studies grew in North America between the mid-1970s and mid-1980s. Much of this pioneering work has had a lasting impact on both the field of women's history to the present and the field of gender history, which emerged in the late 1980s.[14]

These examples illustrate that the researching and writing of the history of gender and sexuality, as with that of all history, takes place in many different national contexts and is shaped by those contexts in many fundamental and, at times, not-immediately-apparent ways.[15] In a provocative essay analyzing the main trends in the historical investigation of women and gender in Central America, Eugenia Rodríguez S. finds that 1995 marked the beginning of a boom phase in such studies there, although more in the history of women than in the history of gender. She observes that the process of pacification that took place in Central America in the 1990s, along with the work of a large number of nongovernmental organizations (NGOs) and international organizations dedicated to peacekeeping and social reconstruction, provided the impetus for much of the initial research into the study of women and gender.[16] Likewise, Thomas Klubock has argued that, in the case of Chile, three historical moments—the experience of the socialist government of Salvador Allende in the early 1970s, the military coup there in 1973, and the central role played by women in protests against the dictatorship in the 1980s—have shaped the recent boom in the writing of the history of women and gender in the Chilean context.[17]

In Mexico, the work of Carmen Ramos Escandón, Julia Tuñón, Verena Radkau, and others since the 1980s has helped create interest in, and the academic space necessary for, the development of the field of the history of women, gender, and sexuality in that country.[18] Writing about gender and history more than ten years ago, Ramos Escandón concluded that in Mexico, as in much of

Latin America, Marxist perspectives had been the most important in shaping social science approaches to the study of women, leading to an emphasis on relations of production within the family, often referred to as reproduction or social reproduction. Reflecting on the advantages and disadvantages of that approach, she argued for the need to develop the concept of gender and to use it as its own category of analysis, not as merely one aspect of the category of production. Ramos Escandón's identification of the questions that needed answering in the history of gender in the nineteenth and twentieth centuries continues to help orient the field of the history of gender.[19] Some of these questions have been taken up and addressed by authors contributing to *Gender, Sexuality, and Power in Latin America since Independence*, as the chapters by Pablo Piccato on sexuality and violence in Belem Prison in Mexico City, and by Katherine Bliss and Ann Blum on adolescent life during the Mexican Revolution, attest. Historians working in Mexico, however, have been less enthusiastic about taking up Ramos Escandón's call. Reflecting on the field of the history of gender for nineteenth-century Mexico, Gabriela Cano and Georgette José Valenzuela have recently concluded that the historical analysis of gender for nineteenth-century Mexico by historians in Mexico has only just begun.[20]

In the present book, Lara Putnam asks Why not combine the study of women with the study of gender? Her chapter illustrates how a focus on the patterned arrangement of social reproduction, that is, as she defines that term, the daily work carried out by women to keep body and soul together, can be combined with attention to the construction of gender and sexuality. Not only does this allow her to better understand the complex, yet previously ignored, participation of women in a Central American export enclave at the turn of the twentieth century, but it also enables her to illustrate the ways that family, kinship, and sexuality have served as arenas of struggle and as sites for the exercise and contestation of political power more broadly defined. Like many historians of gender, Putnam refuses to banish conflicts involving sex to the "private sphere," a place supposedly of little relevance to those interested in understanding how so-called real political power actually operates. One of the great contributions of her chapter is that, in drawing from and making connections between these literatures, she helps us understand the centrality of women, gender, and sexuality to the creation of an export economy.[21]

Scholars working in Brazil and Argentina have also developed substantial literatures treating women and gender. In the case of Brazil, as a recent reviewer has stressed, the term gender has been adopted to a much greater extent by social scientists than by historians, who, for the most part, have been more concerned with the need to recover the voices, experiences, and agency of women. Mary Del Priore dates the arrival of gender as a concept in Brazil to the beginning of the 1990s and maintains that as of 1998 the concept still had not been fully taken up by Brazilian historians. Argentine historiography has seen the development of an extensive body of work dedicated to the history of women and gender, in a field where Donna Guy's writing on prostitution, white slavery, and the history of childhood has been pioneering.[22] In Argentina, writing about gender has also meant writing about masculinities and homosexualities. Appearing in print beginning in the early 1990s, the books and articles of Eduardo Archetti, a contributor to this volume, Daniel Bao, and Jorge Salessi, among others, have explored topics that range from the role of soccer and tango in the construction of Argentine masculinities to the construction and dissemination of male and female homosexualities and their role in the imagining of the Argentine nation.[23]

These authors' works illustrate some of the factors that have led to differences from country to country in the timing of adoption and choice of research agendas. Rather than focusing on the deconstruction of discourses about women written by men, the task, for many historians in Latin America and elsewhere, remained (and often still remains) one of recovery, of both the voices of women and of evidence of their presence within the historical record.[24] This work also demonstrates that popular pressure and the organization of social movements have been central to providing an impetus to these studies.

New Directions: Gender in Latin American History

Just as the study of revolution has benefited from an analysis that includes gender, other political movements and events, along with processes of state formation, are now receiving attention from gender historians. Many historians of Chile's twentieth-century political history, for example, now insist on seeing gender not as an interesting addition to the existing literature on politics but as a key to understanding politics and historical processes there in general. In the case of Chile's Agrarian Reform, an expropriation of nearly half of that country's agricultural land between 1962 and 1973 that involved massive political mobilization on the part of the rural poor, gender expectations and ideals led women and men to participate in politics and political struggles in unequal ways. The reform process itself, premised upon specific and sometimes contradictory notions of appropriate feminine and masculine gender roles, led to arguments over the meaning of gender and left women hardest hit when conflict escalated.[25] Likewise, between 1936 and 1948, gender constructed, in part, the popular-front project of state building in Chile, just as it was reshaped by many of the actions of the state, like public health campaigns and welfare policies.[26]

In his work on Chile during the first half of the twentieth century, Thomas Klubock insists on the importance of gender to understanding the relationship between mine workers, their families, mining companies, and the state. Here, gender relations and ideals were central to attempts by the state and the companies to discipline a new work force, as well as to workers' responses to these efforts. By no means is this interest in rewriting the history of politics by focusing on gender limited to Chile. Writing about Venezuela in this volume, Arlene Díaz makes a convincing case that analyzing politics through the lens of gender does more than add missing voices or new stories; rather, it leads to a new understanding of politics itself.[27] Examining the controversy surrounding a mid-nineteenth-century death-penalty case involving a freed slave who was supposedly pregnant, Díaz exposes the ways those working to develop the laws and institutions of the new nation perceived social rights and responsibilities through a lens shaded by ideas about sexuality, gender, and reproduction.

As these authors also illustrate, new understandings of political conflicts and the dynamics of social revolution are only possible if, in addition to femininity, masculinity is made into a subject for historical analysis. In other words, studying gender cannot mean simply studying women, as the recent boom in the publication of studies dealing with masculinities in Latin America attests. Femininity and masculinity must be understood as relational categories, that is, as categories that are constructed at the same time and in relation to each other, as well as to other categories like sexuality, nationality, ethnicity, race, and class (discussed later in the introduction). Indeed, the importance of this idea of the interrelated and mutually constructed nature of identities has led some historians to criticize studies that focus separately on either femininity or masculinity, rather than on both together, as partial, incomplete, or flawed.

Work in this area over the last ten or fifteen years by anthropologists, literary critics, historians, and others has stressed the many ways that the social construction of masculinity is related to power in places as diverse as Nicaragua, Mexico, and Brazil.[28] Rather than a unitary masculinity characterizing Latin America or any single country, these studies have shown that multiple masculinities have been constructed in many parts of the region, with perhaps one, at times, being hegemonic and others subordinate. Of greatest significance, this new work stresses that class, ethnic, national, and gender identities, such as masculinity, are interrelated and, therefore, that masculinities need to be studied in relation to these other categories as well as to femininities.[29] David Parker's contribution to the present book, a study of dueling, masculine honor, and the ways that conceptions of masculinity limited female participation in the public sphere in Uruguay, builds on and contributes to this growing literature by highlighting the ways in which gender and understandings of political authority were mutually constructed. It provides another excellent example of why studying gender means studying masculinities as well as femininities.

As you might have imagined, extensive discussion and debate followed the appearance of Scott's work. Rather than finding gender a useful category of historical analysis, one of her critics called it a "postmodern category of paralysis."[30] Much of the criticism centered on the fundamental shifts that were involved in conceptualizing agency, identity, and experience (all discussed later) in this new approach and revolved around the fear that the switch from "women" to "gender" would be politically disastrous for the women's movement. Some also expressed concern that focusing on gender would obscure differences among women and privilege representation over women's agency. For nearly all of the authors discussed in this introduction, however, employing the theoretical tools advocated by Scott has not meant abandoning either women or history (or politics). Instead, they have abandoned the idea of a stable, unified, and autonomous subject, one that was often defined in such a way as to suppress differences and group all women into a single category.[31]

More recently, Scott herself has expressed reservations about the way that the idea of gender has been taken up and used by scholars. The problem of describing gender as a category, according to Scott, is that it seems to assume that knowledge about "men" and "women" is fixed or known in advance. Rather than describing actual people, these terms, she insists, are ideals that are used to regulate behavior. Attempting to understand the very production of the categories of "women" and "men" themselves, Scott asks, How are terms like men and women used in particular contexts? In what ways have boundaries between the sexes been enforced and why? And, how are relationships of power consolidated by appeals to sexual difference?[32] Scott's questions continue to inform the work of new generations of historians working on the social construction of femininities and masculinities in Latin American history as elsewhere. Scott, for example, was recently featured as one of the keynote speakers at the Second International Colloquium of the History of Women and of Gender in Mexico, held in September 2003 in Guadalajara, Mexico. Drawing from Scott's pioneering work, our understanding of gender and other facets of identity formation, like sexuality, ethnicity, nationality, and class, has been powerfully influenced by the concept of discourse.

Discourses

The importance of understanding the relationship between power and discourse, understood as a way of representing a particular subject through language, writing, symbol, or sign, in order to understand the significance of concepts like gender and sexuality is underscored by the use that feminist historians and others have made of the work of French philosopher Michel Foucault since the 1970s.

Professor of the history of systems of thought in Paris until his death in 1984, Foucault was chiefly interested in the question of power, its techniques, and effects. Instead of seeing power as something wielded only by armies, the police, or the state, with some exercising power and others without it, Foucault found power to be present everywhere, as in, for example, relations between parents and children, teachers and students, and doctors and patients. Rather than seeing power as purely repressive or restrictive, he found that it could be a mechanism of attraction, associated with, even productive of, pleasure and desire. Closely connected to power was knowledge, a way of ordering the world that was not absolute or "true" but, rather, a relative category for Foucault and one subject to many different interpretations.[33] Focusing initially on prisons, insane asylums, other institutions, and eventually on sexuality, he saw as his main task the construction of an "archaeology of knowledge," that is, an explanation of the conditions that led to the emergence of particular forms of knowledge at these and other sites and to the rules, or grammar, these forms of knowledge used to differentiate what was true from what was false. Connecting power to knowledge was "discourse."

Discourses are statements or groups of statements, as well as images, symbols, and built environments, that produce certain kinds of knowledge about subjects because they portray or represent these subjects in a specific manner. Discourses link power and knowledge because they position those speaking or deploying the discourse and those named by the discourse in important and related ways. Power circulates through discourses by creating various subject positions, locating some of those deploying the discourse as medical, scientific, or legal experts, while simultaneously bringing into being, or making known, those named by the discourse, such as the deviant, the hysteric, the criminal, the homosexual. For Foucault, discourses are not to be divided into those that are acceptable and those that are excluded or pigeonholed into the oppositional categories of dominant and subordinate. Nor are there discourses of power that oppose discourses of resistance. Rather, in Foucault's argument, a multiplicity of discourses operates and can be drawn upon at any given time, depending on the circumstances, strategies, and context. Moreover, while discourses produce, transmit, and reinforce power, they can also be a hindrance to power, a starting point for an opposing strategy.[34] The role of the historian, then, must not only be to ask how local relations of power made possible certain kinds of discourses and how these discourses were used to support power relations, but also to show how those named by the discourse used the same vocabulary to speak on their own behalf.

This is precisely what James Green does in his contribution to this volume. When you read his chapter entitled "Doctoring the National Body," you will see how medical doctors in Brazil used discourse to create a certain kind of knowledge about sexuality in that country between 1920 and 1945. These doctors, in their writings and speeches, named as "inverts" men who had, in their opinion, directed their "sexual instincts" erroneously. We see in this case an example of a medical discourse that positions these doctors as experts while at the same time bringing into being the very category that it names, that of "inverts." For the first time, "invert" became a subject position within a discourse. This discursive construction had very real consequences and effects for those occupying the subject position of "invert" and for others as well, as you will read. You may be interested in consulting Green's book, *Beyond Carnival*, where he develops these insights further. In that work, Green also reveals how dominant discourses of homosexuality were appropriated by homosexuals taking part in, and eventually transforming, Brazil's major celebration, Carnival, resulting in increased public awareness and expanded social toleration (to a point) of homosexuality.[35]

Similarly, in revolutionary Mexico City, political authorities, teachers, and physicians developed new understandings that led to the creation of a new discursive category, that of the "adolescent," who was now seen to represent a distinct stage in the life cycle. As Ann Blum and Katherine Bliss show in their chapter, these experts, mirroring parallel developments in Europe and North America, became increasingly preoccupied with "youth" in the first decades of the twentieth century. Widespread public debate and the proliferation of governmental and medical agencies concerned with various aspects of adolescent life followed in the wake of this new discursive creation. Blum and Bliss, however, concentrate instead on showing how young men and women claimed as their own this new category. Focusing on such topics of conflict between parents and youth as fashion and entertainment choices, the authors illustrate how adolescents embraced a new sexual culture that they experienced in fundamentally gendered terms. And, although adolescent rebellion did not challenge established structures of gender and power, it may have been a critical first step in that direction.

The emergence of a discourse concerned with youth culture at the turn of the last century eerily resonates with contemporary concerns in North America about the discursive association, through the discourse of "young offenders," of youth with crime. And, although the "invert" is a particularly striking example of a medical discourse from a different time and place, in the course of your daily activities, you are also being positioned and position yourself as the subject of many discourses. It is our hope that, as the various chapters of this book are discussed in class, your own use of and positioning in various discourses will be raised.

Sexualities

It was when he turned his insights concerning discourse, knowledge, and power to the history of sexuality that Foucault made his most important contribution to shaping the future direction of much historical research in this field. In *The History of Sexuality: Volume 1*, a book you may be reading along with this collection, Foucault rejected what he called the "repressive hypothesis," the idea that a Victorian silence had draped itself over sexual practices during the last two centuries. Instead, he proposed that a veritable discursive explosion around sex had characterized that same period.[36] Foucault was not interested in gender per se. Rather, he endeavored to understand why so many people and institutions were interested in making so many others tell the "truth" about sex, and he found sexuality to be an especially dense "transfer point" for relations of power, useful for the greatest numbers of maneuvers and varied strategies. Rather than build up a new theory of sexuality, his goal was to break down already existing theories of sexuality in order to destroy their claims to legitimacy, authority, and truth. He did this by approaching sexuality not as some inherent quality but from the perspective of the history of discourses, with his principal interest being in the ways that sex had been "put into discourse" at sites located in medicine, psychiatry, the criminal-justice system, schools, and the family, among others.[37]

The radical nature of Foucault's approach to sexuality cannot be stressed enough, given the implications of his work for those carrying out research in so many fields (as will shortly be set out). By "sexuality," Foucault did not mean a biological fact or reality that various societies in the past and present represented or described in different ways. Rather, his idea was that sexuality came into existence only in the eighteenth and nineteenth centuries as a new and unprecedented set of strategies for constructing human subjectivities.

Historicizing the body and desire and approaching subjectivity as something that is constituted by sexuality requires a major conceptual shift. If, in the past, "sex" was a given, the biology of the body upon which cultural constructions like gender, ethnicity, and class were imposed, then taking up the insights of Foucault and others means accepting that sex and even the body itself must also be seen as social and historical constructions. Pablo Piccato, in his chapter in this book, illustrates how these ideas can inform the work of a historian of Latin America as he explores the construction of sexuality and desire in Belem Prison in Mexico City at the turn of the twentieth century. His insistence that sexual behavior was not the product of a "simple, universal drive" and his focus on the institutional and cultural factors that helped shape "sex" underline its constructed nature. Excellent topics for you to discuss in class would be the relationship Piccato sees between sex and gender and his idea of the negotiation of power.

Approaching the body as a historical construction can only be accomplished by rejecting the assumptions upon which most discussions about the body and sexuality are premised—that is, that sex and nature are "real," therefore unchanging or eternal, whereas gender and culture are "constructed," therefore less "real." Some historians now point to the second half of the eighteenth century as the time during which the modern body, the one that we now all take for granted, began to emerge. They stress that beginning at that time, new discourses of science, especially the clinical, investigative gaze, called the modern body into being by conceptualizing it as an unchanging object of study.[38] Others, however, link the modern body and bodily differentiation to the development of manners that formed part of much longer-term processes of self- and class identification. They emphasize how the modern, or "bourgeois," body, with its emphasis on cleanliness and manners dating to the late eighteenth and nineteenth centuries, served as a powerful symbol, the means by which new social groups visibly distinguished themselves from the nobility, peasants, and the growing urban underclass.[39]

Thinking of the body as a symbol of class and other social divisions alerts us to the complicated relationship that exists between the body, especially the sexual body, and society. Thomas Laqueur, a historian of science and the body whose work has been central to shaping this field of study, asks us to rethink our understanding of the direction of historical causation when it comes to the relationship between the body and society. Analyzing what he considers to have been the most fundamental shift in the conceptualization of female sexuality—from a model that stressed the homologous nature of male and female reproductive organs with the female's being on the inside, accepted before the second half of the eighteenth century, to one of incommensurability between male and female sexuality after that time—Laqueur stresses that social needs rather than new scientific advances in biology brought this shift about. In other words, the end of the old social order associated with the changes brought about by the Enlightenment created an urgent need to use the body to represent and justify inequality in biological terms.[40]

Social relations and discourses shape sexuality and the body in other ways as well. Some scientists, for example, now assume that beliefs about gender affect the very knowledge that scientists produce about sex. Anne Fausto-Sterling, for example, a biologist with an interest in gender theory, argues that our bodies are too complex to provide clear-cut answers about sexual difference. For her, labeling someone a man or a woman is a social decision, regardless of how much scientific knowledge is brought to bear on the question. She shares with many theorists a rejection of the idea that the body exists prior to discourse about being male and female.[41] Those particularly concerned with determining the sex of specific individuals have come around to this point of view. After a number of highly controversial cases in the past concerning the sex of Olympic athletes, Olympic officials for the 2000 Sydney Olympics, finding biological science to be unable to differentiate reliably between males and females on the basis of specific chromosomes and genes, refrained from such testing.[42]

It may seem strange to you to think of something like the human body as having a history. Yet, historians of medicine interested in how people in the past understood such things as sickness, health, and their bodies have found that these very categories of analysis are premised upon contemporary assumptions and understandings very different from those held by the people they have sought to study. When Barbara Duden, for example, began investigating the complaints of women to their doctors in eighteenth-century Germany, she found it necessary to question her own deeply held assumptions about health and the body before she could carry out her task. She found words such as "health," "reproduction," and "sexuality" to be normative terms whose emergence dated to the second half of the eighteenth century; they were of little use in understanding earlier conceptions of birth, sickness, or the body. Such terms followed from the redefining of "nature" as a category of analysis, reinterpreted in the context of Enlightenment ideas of science and medicine and the assigning of the body, especially the body of women, to that category. Using the idea of discourse in the way outlined above, Duden argues that by describing the female body as belonging to nature, science fixed it as immutable and unchanging, inscribing upon it its supposed "natural" destiny, that of reproduction.[43]

Part of the process of inscribing the female body in this manner by science and medicine involved discrediting traditional knowledge about birth held by such specialists in the field as midwives, in both Europe and the Americas. In this book, Erica Windler looks at how one woman, a "man-woman" as she was known at the time, utilized her own body to bridge the gap between the masculine world of professional medicine and the world of female patients in Rio de Janeiro, Brazil, in the mid to late nineteenth century. The first woman admitted to the Faculty of Medicine to train as a midwife, Madame Durocher manifested her attachment to scientific medical knowledge and its concomitant professional and masculine authority by both disparaging folk remedies and practices and presenting herself in (mostly) male attire. At the same time, she reassured female patients by retaining some aspects of womanly dress, along with her title of "Madame" (she was of French origin). One wonders if she did not also mediate between very different constructions and understandings of the body that may have set doctors apart from some of their patients in much the same way as she did between genders. Although this is difficult to know, Windler does show that Durocher took great pains to distinguish herself from the practices and manners of those "common women" (defined not only as not possessing modern knowledge but as promiscuous as well), who had traditionally acted as midwives.

What is apparent is that historians are now exploring the historicity of the body from a number of different perspectives. While Duden seeks to understand the "reality-generating experience"[44] of the body that is unique to a given historical period, others are concerned with how gender, sexuality, ethnicity, and class are inscribed upon the body. For many, the task of making visible the historical dimensions of "the body," something previously thought to be universal and without history, is a compelling political necessity. In his insightful discussion of Foucault, David Halperin, who has written extensively on the history of sexuality, expresses what is at stake in the following manner: "there is no orgasm without ideology."[45] He means that bodies do not possess ready-made sexualities. Human subjects are attracted to other subjects, and that attraction depends on the institutions and discourses that inform human subjectivity itself. His concern, and that of many others, is to challenge the specific discourses that portray the body as without history, that make desire into something supposedly natural rather than socially constructed. Only in this way can "the body" be claimed as a site of cultural activism and political resistance.[46]

Queer Theory

Scholars contributing to the body of work that has come to be called queer theory have also made important contributions to our conceptualization of subjectivity and the body. Philosopher Judith Butler, dissatisfied with the idea of agency implied by the term social construction, which implies that a person or a subject is already in place to carry out the task of constructing gender, advances the concept of performativity as an alternative. When she talks about gender as performative, Butler does not mean that as individuals we get up in the morning and then decide which gender to perform. Rather, she means that through reiteration, discourse produces the very phenomenon of gender that it regulates and constrains. For Butler, neither the body nor one's anatomy provides a neutral ground from which to understand sexual difference. For her, as for Fausto-Sterling, the materiality of the body does not exist prior to discourse but has been constructed through a gendered matrix; the body is, rather, a system simultaneously productive of, and produced by, social meanings. The main question for Butler then becomes, Through what regulatory norms is sex itself materialized? At the same time, the subject herself is formed by having gone through the process of assuming a bodily norm, or a sex. In other words, norms associated with regulatory sexual regimes, like the regime of heterosexuality, are the condition for the very formation of the subject or selfhood.[47]

One of the political goals of queer theory is to destabilize or decenter the categories of heterosexual and homosexual. Many (but not all) historians of sexuality would agree with the statement the history of homosexuality dates only to the last two hundred years and that the term itself dates only to the second half of the nineteenth century. This does not mean that same-sex relations between men or between women did not occur before that time but, rather, that with the emergence of sexuality in the way that Foucault understood the concept and as we have explained it above, the terms homosexual and hetero-sexual date to the modern period and emerged as part of the development of discourses and the production of knowledge regarding sexuality. Many of the discourses of medicine and science at that time began addressing or naming certain men as homosexuals, subjecting them to this categorization. Hetero-sexual/homosexual became a powerful binary construction, with each term defining itself against the other, whereby the first connoted the "normal" and the latter its opposite, the supposed "deviant." Much of the homophobia that characterizes modern societies is premised upon just this binary.[48]

Queer theorists and many historians of sexuality intend their work to chal-lenge the idea of what has been called "heteronormativity," the entire structure of meanings and practices that makes sexual desire, something that is cultural and constructed, into something supposedly natural and inherent and only "normal" in its heterosexual variant.[49] They contest the claim that heterosex-uality is somehow natural and original, timeless and universal, and that other forms of sexuality are copies or deviant. For Butler, this is accomplished by re-jecting the idea that homosexuality is a copy of heterosexuality. To accept this, she argues, would mean that heterosexuality existed first as the natural cate-gory. Instead, Butler suggests that homosexuality is an imitation, another per-formance. This helps her demonstrate that heterosexuality, as well, is a per-formance, the reiteration of certain idealized norms rather than "natural." An analysis integrating this perspective, then, destabilizes the hierarchy of hetero-sexual over homosexual; it breaks down this binary construction.[50]

For many of those carrying out research in the history of sexuality, the po-litical edge to their work comes from the fact that interrogating past categories and dichotomies makes existing binary portrayals of gender and sexuality equally questionable, thereby making it possible to challenge current inequal-ities and to bring about change in the present. Many historians of sexuality, then, carry out their historical research in conjunction with political engage-ment in social and human rights movements, work in which some of the con-tributors to this book have been and are currently engaged in both North America and Latin America.

Such advocacy work has, at times, been based on identity politics that re-sulted in the drawing of boundaries, inevitably including some while exclud-ing others. This has led many historians of sexuality, including those in fields encompassing lesbian and gay studies as well as queer theorists, to reject the idea that stable categories of identity exist upon which institutions act or from whose perspective history can be told or actions taken. These historians now often focus instead on difference, on how seemingly coherent categories of identity, such as "women," "lesbians," "men," "heterosexuals," and many others have been constructed over time through the use of discourses and binary constructions like those we have outlined above. Work on the history of homosexuality in Latin America now seeks to break down rigid binaries and propose in their place the existence of multiple homosexualities and gender identities. Whereas, in the past, much of the literature presented homosexuality exclusively in terms of an active/passive binary in which the sexual role of penetrator corresponded to the "real" man and that of penetrated to the effeminate male, recent research is discovering a great deal more diversity and shifting sexual roles within the category of homosexuality.[51] Correspondingly, the interest of many of these historians has shifted from an interest in the social history of homosexuals to the narrative representation of categories such as homosexual and lesbian. Interesting work is now showing how these categories are, in fact, social fictions, covering over or hiding a diverse array of embodiments and sexual desires.[52]

More on Identity

Challenging binaries and destabilizing categories, in the past and in the present, necessarily means rethinking what we mean by identity. We have begun to outline how discourses work by fixing identity, that is, by limiting possible subject positions that "individuals" occupy and, also, through the formation of certain kinds of subjectivities. Up to now, we have limited our discussion to the role of discourses of gender and sexuality in the process of identity formation while, nonetheless, suggesting at a number of points in this introduction that ethnic, "racial," class, and national identities are also, like masculinities and femininities, discursive constructions. Moreover, like much of the recent literature concerned with "race" and national identity in Latin America, one of the main points being made by contributors to *Gender, Sexuality, and Power in Latin America since Independence* is that all these categories are simultaneously constituted, meaning that they come into existence only in relation to each other.[53]

In her chapter on social science and female criminality in Cuba, for example, Alejandra Bronfman points to the intersection of "race" and gender in the construction of female delinquency and the mapping of the body by criminologist Israel Castellanos there in the 1920s.[54] In the case she describes, the use of the most recent technologies available for the production of criminological knowledge, namely statistics and photography, actually undermine Castellanos's claims about the ways that race, gender, sexuality, and criminality intersect with one another. However, the inconsistencies in the "scientific" data created by Castellanos in no way diminished the importance of sciences like criminology to the imagining of Cuba both as modern and as a nation, often through the discursive construction of the "delinquent body" and the "Cuban body." Bringing "race," gender, sexuality, the body, and national identity into the same frame, Bronfman shows how the mutual constitution of these categories resulted in the writing of a social science text that undermines not only itself but also dominant assumptions about both "race" and gender, which linked criminality to skin color and racially mixed women to sexuality. Although we may never know what the subjects themselves thought of their portrayal as "criminal types," the chapter invites speculation as it explores women's acts of self-representation in photographs. Likewise, in his chapter in this book, a study of the writings of criminologists, doctors, and other medical professionals from Brazil at about that same time (into the 1930s), James Green points to the mutual construction of "race," gender, sexuality, and nationality. Green shows how medical and criminological studies framed race and homosexuality as interrelated "perversions" of the Brazilian body (leading to the writing of social science texts every bit as self-contradictory as in the Cuban case).

In her chapter in this volume, Lessie Jo Frazier also explores "perversions," specifically the kinds of perverse subjectivities created in the "space of death," the sphere of interaction between oppressor and oppressed characterizing military regimes in Argentina and Chile. Frazier is concerned about the limited possibilities for what she refers to as political subjectivity in those countries today, the consequence, she argues, of the failure of subsequent civilian rulers to address the link between authoritarian political structures and authoritarian relations in the domestic realm. In the first part of her chapter, Frazier focuses on how the mental-health system put into place after the return to civilian rule in Chile continued to perpetuate many of the assumptions and understandings that had structured military/civilian relations under military rule, especially the gendering of patients as "female" by seeing them as passive victims, while maintaining the idea that participation in politics somehow makes one suspect or tainted. In the second part, she looks for a way out of this "space of death" by analyzing the Argentine story *Other Weapons*. Frazier concludes that by adopting "perverse subjectivity" as a subject position from which to act, the potential exists for questioning authoritarian domestic relations and political structures simultaneously. As in the case of the appropriation of the subject position of "homosexual" discussed by Green, emancipatory politics may only be possible, Frazier argues, by embracing and acting from the subject position previously defined by the military as perverse or monstrous.

In addition to developing insights into the complicated ways that identity has been shaped in modern Latin America through the mutual constitution of gender, sexuality, ethnicity, national identity, and the sense of personhood, the authors contributing to *Gender, Sexuality, and Power in Latin American since Independence* provide persuasive evidence that the process of identity formation has taken place in the context of not only the national but also the global circulation of discourses producing "race," gender, sexuality, and national identity. In Lara Putnam's chapter, for example, it is clear that meanings of gender and class and many other categories were negotiated within the context of a dynamic export economy in turn-of-the-century Central America, which involved the circulation of workers from throughout the Caribbean. For Argentina in the first half of the twentieth century, Eduardo Archetti argues persuasively in his contribution to our volume that the association of the masculine gaucho with tango and the rise of both to their position as preeminent symbols of Argentine national identity were the result of both European demands for exoticism and Argentine needs for cultural continuity in the face of massive immigration and the social and economic transformation it brought in its wake. As Archetti puts it, Paris provided the mirror by which Argentines came to see themselves as Europeans saw them.

Similarly stressing the global context in which identity formation takes place, Cymene Howe uses interviews with advocates of sexuality rights and women's rights in contemporary Nicaragua to show the profound effect of international human rights discourses (acting in conjunction with Sandinismo, the ideology of the revolution) on identity and identity-based politics in that country up to the present. In addition to political ideology, the troubled history of Nicaragua's relationship with the United States conditioned local understandings of transnational discourses concerned with sexuality, health, and rights, making for a more inclusive identity politics that aims its message of toleration for sexual difference not at sexual minorities but at all Nicaraguans.

Yet, Howe's chapter must also force us to stop and ask if there may not be an inherent tension, even a contradiction, between the constructed and decentered concept of identity we are advocating as an analytical tool and that of identity politics, the appeal to deep-seated and supposedly essential identities. After all, if we are interested in destabilizing fixed notions of identity in an attempt to subvert binary constructions and challenge normative concepts, how then can people and groups make claims from the point of view of "women," or "homosexuals," or "lesbians," some of the very categories we seek to problematize? There is no easy answer to this question, and activists and theorists are divided on this issue. For some, making political claims on the basis of the supposedly natural or essential qualities that those making up these categories are said to possess, a practice that has a long history, is and has been a useful and productive strategy. For example, if all women are "nurturing," as dominant discourses in the past and present have often insisted, then perhaps this nurturing can be applied to the nation as well as to the home. Here, a purportedly essential quality that had been used to justify women's domesticity can be used to make a claim for women's participation in the public sphere, as Arlene Díaz's analysis of how women deployed the idea of motherhood in seeking expanded political rights and opportunities in early-nineteenth-century Venezuela demonstrates. Such a practice is often referred to as "strategic essentialism."

Other activists and theorists reject essentialism, strategic or not, for a variety of reasons. Some, like Howe, see no contradiction between viewing identity as dislocated, fragmented, unstable, and constructed, on the one hand, and as a useful political point of departure on the other. They do this by defining categories like "woman" as positions from which to interpret and act politically rather than as established or inherent sets of values or characteristics.[55] In a recent book, Roger Lancaster makes a compelling case against embracing essentialism, either as a political tactic or as a means of conceptualizing identity.[56] Concerned with the claims made by science about the supposedly natural basis of desire, reflected in such things as the search for a gay gene and for the purportedly genetic basis of personality differences between men and women (men as aggressive, women as coy), and the representation of these claims in the mass media, Lancaster shows how such claims rest on essentialist conceptions of gender that attempt to produce certainties in periods of great conflict about sex and the body. The great danger in resorting to strategic essentialism as a means of countering these arguments, argues Lancaster, is that in leaving in place one binary (homosexual/heterosexual, for example), strategic essentialism actually supports the idea that heterosexual desire is also "natural," thus reinforcing not only the binary construction of masculinity and femininity but also that of heterosexual/homosexual. As we discussed earlier in this introduction, these chains of mutually constructed and reinforcing binaries are essential in propping up the entire heteronormative system.

This debate, pitting, in its starkest terms strategic essentialism against a constructionist conception of identity, enables us to see some of the political stakes involved in defining and understanding identity, as well as the centrality of identity to struggles over power. Additional evidence of the contemporary importance of identity to political debate is readily at hand. During the course of writing this book, for example, it became possible for same-sex couples in Canada and, more recently, in Massachusetts to contract marriage legally. Some of the reasoning used by those opposed to recognizing same-sex unions as marriages, drawn from religious, legal, and scientific (among other) discourses, is premised upon an essentialist (and binary) understanding of male and female identity. Perusing local or national newspapers or reading websites dealing with same-sex marriage leads almost immediately to essentialist descriptions of the nature of men and women, as, for example, "two distinct parts of humanity" who are said to be uniquely suited to marriage because they are "sexually complementary." Or, in some religious discourses on this theme, homosexuality is often represented as learned behavior that keeps people from becoming the "real" men and women they were "created" to be. Like some gender and sexual rights activists, many of those opposed to same-sex marriage utilize a form of strategic essentialism, opposing such marriages by presuming to know the true nature of men and women. Analysts of gender and sexuality in historical perspective stress that such claims fail to recognize the great diversity of practices and desires that characterize the human experience and that are well documented in the archival record.[57]

This particular example also helps us to see some of the ways that the power of nation-states is linked to the ability to patrol the boundaries of identity. While the ongoing debate over same-sex marriage has prompted some leaders in the United States to call for a constitutional amendment to define marriage as being between one man and one woman, linking national identity and interests with specific and simultaneously constructed gender, race, and sexual identities is as old as the republic itself. In her book on marriage and the nation in the United States, historian Nancy Cott shows that political and legal authorities in the new republic saw marriages of the "proper sort" as essential to the formation of suitable citizens. As both marriage and the new form of government were premised upon mutual consent freely given, each served to reinforce the other.[58]

When you read the chapters in the present volume, we trust that you will note how authorities in Latin America over the last two centuries have similarly believed that certain constructions of gender, sexual, and racial identity were essential to the formation of the nation. In her chapter on early-nineteenth-century Venezuela, for example, Arlene Díaz argues that dominant conceptions of women—as either symbols of virtue or of uncontrolled lawlessness—were used to justified male control of women, both in the nation and in the home, while women used the trope of motherhood to argue for a more inclusive role in the polity. Jumping ahead to late-twentieth-century Nicaragua, Howe shows that while the Sandinistas were interested in creating a "new man" imbued with values deemed more suitable for a new revolutionary society, subsequent regimes in that country have seemed bent on reinstating the "old" one, seeing moral engineering and the reimposition of "traditional" patriarchal values as particularly useful means of establishing authority in the political realm.[59] While the authors of these two chapters describe some of the ways that political and legal/juridical discourses have constructed identities, other authors contributing to this book focus on the equally important effects of medical, criminological, social science, mental health and human rights discourses on identity construction.

The ways that discourses "fix" identities, the simultaneous constitution and policing of the categories and boundaries of identity, the national and global circulation of discourses concerned with identity, and the various debates concerning identity and identity politics all point to the complexity of this concept and its centrality for the contributors to this volume. A number of general conclusions concerning identity follow from their work. The first is that identity construction almost always involves differentiation and exclusion; that is, it takes place by establishing difference, by simultaneously identifying, or calling into being, some who belong to or constitute a certain category and others who do not. A second important conclusion is that identities are never singular and unified; rather, they are fragmented and multiply constructed through these numerous, often contradictory, discourses enunciated at different sites, such as in legal codes, doctors' offices, and prisons. Racial, class, gender, sexual, and national identities are not only mutually constituted, then; they are also adopted and asserted by individuals in different and contradictory ways.[60]

This is not to posit the existence of autonomous individuals who have the power simply to decide which of an unlimited number of subject positions they will occupy. Nor is it to deny the ability of individuals, conceptualized in however fragmented a manner, to exercise any agency at all in deciding how to take up or identify with the limited and contradictory subject positions to which they are subjected. The contributors to this book view the historical construction of identity not as an unproblematic and direct result of discourse but as the very subject that calls for historical analysis. They are interested in the ways that individuals in the past and present have made history, that is, how they have come to identify with certain subject positions (and not others) at different times and how they have spoken and acted from these positions, sometimes to challenge and change these very constructions. This has been especially problematic for women, and recent work on women's oral history and testimony in Latin America has shown that sometimes the only vehicles available for women's expression and self-representation have been official (and predominantly male) discourses.[61]

An Invitation

In the chapters that follow, twelve scholars of Latin America examine some of the most important interconnections that they see between constructions of gender and/or sexuality, on the one hand, and the imagining of race, class, and/or national identity on the other. The work presented in this volume spans, chronologically, the two-hundred-year period since the independence of much of Latin America from Spain and Portugal in the early nineteenth century and, geographically, the region spanning Mexico, Central America, and the Caribbean to Venezuela, Brazil, Uruguay, Argentina, and Chile. Taken together, their work invites you to participate in an ongoing discussion of the ways in which focusing on gender, sexuality, and identity might reshape the themes, categories, and periodization used in the writing of the history of Latin America. Attention to the legal, juridical, medical, social science, criminological, and human rights discourses (among others that we have discussed in this introduction) that have shaped understandings of identity, as well as the possibilities of exercising and contesting power, reveal complex and interrelated histories that are just beginning to be established. An examination of the ongoing preoccupation with, and occasional moral panics over, women's roles and the supposed threat posed by homosexuality, for example, helps us to see not only that such categories are constructed historically but the ways in which such constructions have been used to police all kinds of boundaries, to shape the body politic in particular ways. In short, the chapters that follow make apparent that when teaching and writing the history of Latin America, the history of gender and sexuality is not something that can be relegated to "gender week" or to a separate chapter, then conveniently ignored. Perhaps the most important point that those contributing to this book make is that rather than subfields, gender and sexuality are central to any analysis of history. We encourage all those reading this book to question the relationship between constructions of gender and sexuality, on the one hand, and the meaning of power, broadly defined, on the other. It is our goal that readers will consider the importance of gender, sexuality, and power not only in the past but also in the present, and not only as these issues pertain to those they study but also to their own lives.

Notes

This book is the result of a series of conversations. One set of conversations has been between the editors and the contributing authors, whom we thank for their willingness to participate in an ongoing exchange of ideas. The introduction has benefited from an additional set of conversations. We thank Nina Morgan, Geoff Spurling, Joy Dixon, Cymene Howe, and Mark Overmyer Velázquez for their comments on earlier drafts and Charles Heath, Susan Hogue, Miguel Angel Aviles Galán, Wendy Vogt, John Klingemann Franco, David Teklits, and José Barragán, graduate students at the Oaxaca Summer Institute, for the opportunity to present an earlier version of the introduction to their seminar. In fact, we would like to acknowledge the graduate student fellows and faculty who participated in the seven incarnations of the Oaxaca Summer Institute, especially William Beezley, its director, for their role in shaping this volume. Ann Blum, Pablo Picato, and both editors were able to present their work at that seminar. Many of the questions addressed in the volume arose in these sessions and in the informal conversations which that meeting in Oaxaca made possible. We are indebted to the participants in these conversations and hope to find a way to continue them.

1. Joan Wallach Scott, *The Glassworkers of Carmaux: French Craftsmen and Political Action in a Nineteenth-Century City* (Cambridge, MA: Harvard University Press, 1974).

2. Joan Wallach Scott, "Gender as a Useful Category of Historical Analysis," *American Historical Review* 91, no. 5 (1986). Scott sets out her definition of "gender" on pages 1067–70.

3. Bliss's insistence on the importance of gender to understanding the Mexican Revolution is more fully developed in her book; see Katherine Elaine Bliss, *Compromised Positions: Prostitution, Public Health, and Gender Politics in Revolutionary Mexico City* (University Park: Pennsylvania State University Press, 2001). Others contributing to this examination of gender and revolution in Mexico include Robert M. Buffington, *Criminal and Citizen in Modern Mexico* (Lincoln: University of Nebraska Press, 2000), and those participating in "Las Olvidadas,

Women's and Gender History" at Yale, 2001, and in the Second International Colloquium of the History of Women and of Gender in Mexico, in Guadalajara, 2003. A forthcoming edited collection deals specifically with this topic; see Jocelyn Olcott, Mary Kay Vaughan, and Gabriela Cano, eds., *Sex in Revolution: Gender, Politics and Power in Modern Mexico* (Durham, NC: Duke University Press).

4. The decision of whether or not to participate in the Beijing conference was also the subject of considerable debate among some Latin American feminist groups; for a discussion of these issues and of the impact of this conference, see Sonia E. Alvarez, Elisabeth Jay Friedman, Ericka Beckman, Maylei Blackwell, Norma Stoltz Chinchilla, Nathalie Lebon, Marysa Navarro, and Marcela Ríos Tobar, "Encountering Latin American and Caribbean Feminisms," *Signs* 28, no. 2 (2003): 551–54. See also Evelyn Leopold, "Beijing Women's Conference—What Is Gender?" *World Tibet Network News,* April 11, 1995, item 4. A related conference was the United Nations International Conference on Population and Development, which had been held the year before to chart a new course for population policies worldwide.

5. Sylvia Molloy and Robert McKee Irwin, eds., *Hispanisms and Homosexualities* (Durham, NC: Duke University Press, 1998); Matthew C. Gutmann, ed., *Changing Men and Masculinities in Latin America* (Durham, NC: Duke University Press, 2003); Robert McKee Irwin, Edward J. McCaughan, and Michelle Rocio Nasser, eds., *The Famous 41: Sexuality and Social Control in Mexico, c. 1901* (New York: Palgrave Macmillan, 2003). See also Rosario Montoya, Lessie Jo Frazier, and Janise Hurtig, eds., *Gender's Place: Feminist Anthropologies of Latin America* (New York: Palgrave Macmillan, 2002).

6. Elizabeth Dore and Maxine Molyneux, eds., *Hidden Histories of Gender and the State in Latin America* (Durham, NC: Duke University Press, 2000); Mala Htun, *Sex and the State: Abortion, Divorce, and the Family under Latin American Dictatorships and Democracies* (Cambridge: Cambridge University Press, 2003).

7. See, for example, Elizabeth Quay Hutchison, "Add Gender and Stir? Cooking Up Gendered Histories of Modern Latin America," *Latin American Research Review* 38, no. 1 (2003). See the seven articles and the major essay in "Gender and Sexuality in Latin America," *Hispanic American Historical Review* 81, no. 3–4 (August–November 2001), and also James N. Green and Florence E. Babb, eds., "Gender and Same-Sex Desire in Latin America," *Latin American Perspectives* 29, no. 2 (March 2002).

8. Wendy Vogt, a graduate student in the Department of Anthropology at the University of Arizona, is carrying out this research. For a list of Web sites that she has found central to her study, please see appendix 1. The websites themselves cover a wide range of organizations and issues and offer a variety of perspectives on the question of identity (as discussed later in this introduction).

9. See, for example, Donna J. Guy, "Parents before Tribunals: The Legal Construction of Patriarchy in Argentina," in Dore and Molyneux, *Hidden Histories of Gender and the State in Latin America,* and Susan K. Besse, *Restructuring Patriarchy: The Modernization of Gender Inequality in Brazil, 1914–1940* (Chapel Hill: University of North Carolina Press, 1996).

10. For an overview of this process with respect to studies of women and gender in Latin America, see Jennifer Abbassi and Sheryl L. Lutjens, "Introduction: Theory, Themes, and the Realities of Gender in Latin America," in *Rereading Women in Latin America and the Caribbean: The Political Economy of Gender,* ed. Jennifer Abbassi and Sheryl L. Lutjens (Lanham, MD: Rowman & Littlefield, 2002), 1–11.

11. William E. French, "Prostitutes and Guardian Angels: Women, Work and the Family in Porfirian Mexico," *Hispanic American Historical Review* 72, no. 4 (1992): 529–53. Other early examples of writing on gender include David McCreery, "'This Life of Misery and Shame': Female Prostitution in Guatemala City, 1880–1920," *Journal of Latin American Studies* 18, no. 2 (November 1986): 333–53, and Mary Kay Vaughan, *The State, Education and Sexual Class in Mexico,*

1880–1928 (DeKalb: Northern Illinois Press, 1982). For a discussion of some of the literature concerning gender in nineteenth-century Mexico, see William E. French, "Imagining and the Cultural History of Nineteenth-Century Mexico," *Hispanic American Historical Review* 79, no. 2 (1999): 249–67.

12. Mary Del Priore, "Historia das mulheres: As vozes do silencio," in *Historiografia brasileira em perspectiva*, ed. Marcos Cezar de Freitas (org.) (São Paolo, Brazil: Contexto, 1998), 226. See pages 225–31 for her discussion of the development of the field of the history of women in Brazilian historiography.

13. For a brief discussion of some of these issues by one scholar located in Latin America, see Sonia Montecino, "Understanding Gender in Latin America," in *Gender's Place: Feminist Anthropologies of Latin America*, ed. Rosario Montoya, Lessie Jo Frazier, and Janise Hurtig (New York: Palgrave Macmillan, 2002).

14. For a discussion of the broad social context within which the writing of the history of women and gender in North America has taken place since the 1960s, see Micaela de Leonardo and Roger N. Lancaster, "Introduction: Embodied Meanings, Carnal Practices," in *The Gender Sexuality Reader: Culture, History, Political Economy*, ed. Roger N. Lancaster and Micaela de Leonardo (New York: Routledge, 1997).

15. For a discussion of some of these differences, see Sueann Caulfield, "The History of Gender in the Historiography of Latin America," *Hispanic American Historical Review* 81, no. 3–4 (August–November 2001): especially pages 449–56. Mary Kay Vaughan makes the point that more dialogue needs to take place among scholars working on cultural history (including gender) in North America and in Latin America; see Mary Kay Vaughan, "Cultural Approaches to Peasant Politics in the Mexican Revolution," *Hispanic American Historical Review* 79, no. 2 (May 1999).

16. Eugenia Rodríguez S., "Género, historia y política en Centroamérica," in *Conferencias internacionales: Primer encuentro mesoamericano de estudios de género*, ed. Marcela Lararde (1: 2001 agosto 28–31: Antigua Guatemala) (Antigua, Guatemala: Editorial FLACSO, 2001). Please see her extensive bibliography as well.

17. Thomas Miller Klubock, "Writing the History of Women and Gender in Twentieth-Century Chile," *Hispanic American Historical Review* 81, no. 3–4 (August–November 2001): 493–96.

18. Julia Tuñón, *El Album de la Mujer III. Siglo XIX 1821–1880* (Mexico: INAH, CNCA, 1991), and Verena Radkau, *"Por la debilidad de nuestro ser": Mujeres del pueblo en la paz porfiriana* (Mexico City: Centro de Investigaciones y Estudios Superiores en Antropología Social, Secretaría de Educación Pública, 1989). More recently, see Rafael Sagredo, *María Villa, (a) La Chiquita, no. 4002* (Mexico City: Cal y Arena, 1996).

19. Carmen Ramos Escandón, "La nueva historia, el feminismo y la mujer," in *Género e historia: La historiografía sobre la mujer*, ed. Carmen Ramos Escandón (Mexico City: Universidad Autónoma Metropolitana, 1992), 17, 30–37. See also Ana Lidia García, *Problemas metodológicos de la historia de las mujeres: La historiografía dedicada al siglo XIX mexicano* (Mexico City: Universidad Nacional Autónoma de México, 1994), and the discussion of gender in Mexico in French, "Imagining and the Cultural History of Nineteenth-Century Mexico."

20. Gabriela Cano and Georgette José Valenzuela, "Introducción: Historia y género en el México decimonónico," in *Cuatro estudios de género en el México urbano del siglo XIX*, ed. Gabriela Cano and Georgette José Valenzuela (Mexico City: Programa Universitario de Estudios de Género, UNAM, 2001), 24.

21. Lara Putnam develops these ideas more fully in her highly acclaimed book *The Company They Kept: Migrants and the Politics of Gender in Caribbean Costa Rica, 1870–1960* (Chapel Hill: University of North Carolina Press, 2002).

22. Guy's work has been central to the development of the fields of women's history and gender history in Latin America; her subjects of investigation have been wide ranging and include the

centrality of gender to the process of state formation, sexuality, changing constructions of motherhood, the relationship of gender and sexuality to power, and the intersection of gender and public health. Her many publications include Donna J. Guy, *Sex and Danger in Buenos Aires: Prostitution, Family and Nation in Argentina* (Lincoln: University of Nebraska Press, 1991); *White Slavery and Mothers Alive and Dead: The Troubled Meeting of Sex, Gender, Public Health, and Progress in Latin America* (Lincoln: University of Nebraska Press, 2000); and with Daniel Balderston, eds., *Sex and Sexuality in Latin America* (New York: New York University Press, 1997).

23. Eduardo Archetti, "Estilos y virtudes masculinas en El Gráfico: La creación del imaginario del fútbol argentino," *Desarrollo Económico* 139 (1995); Daniel Bao, "Invertidos sexuales, tortilleras and maricas machos: The Construction of Homosexuality in Buenos Aires, Argentina, 1900–1950," *Journal of Homosexuality* 24, no. 3–4 (1993); Jorge Salessi, *Médicos, maleantes y maricas: Higiene, criminología y homosexualidad en la construcción de la nación Argentina (Buenos Aires 1871–1914)* (Rosario, Argentina: Beatriz Viterbo, 1995). See also Eduardo P. Archetti, *Masculinities: Football, Polo and the Tango in Argentina* (Oxford, UK: Berg, 1999).

24. See the discussion by Caulfield, "The History of Gender," 454–55.

25. Heidi Tinsman, "Good Wives and Unfaithful Men: Gender Negotiations and Sexual Conflicts in the Chilean Agrarian Reform, 1964–1973," *Hispanic American Historical Review* 81, no. 3–4 (August–November 2001): 587–619. The idea of gender's being argued over and defined in different ways by men and women is central to the work of Steve J. Stern; see *The Secret History of Gender: Women, Men and Power in Late Colonial Mexico* (Chapel Hill: University of North Carolina Press, 1995).

26. Karin Alejandra Rosemblatt, *Gendered Compromises: Political Cultures and the State in Chile, 1920–1950* (Chapel Hill: University of North Carolina Press, 2000).

27. See also Thomas Miller Klubock, *Contested Communities: Class, Gender and Politics in Chile's El Teniente Copper Mine, 1904–1951* (Durham, NC: Duke University Press, 1998); Eileen Suárez Findlay, *Imposing Decency: The Politics of Sexuality and Race in Puerto Rico, 1870–1920* (Durham, NC: Duke University Press, 1999). A recent collection on gender and the state in Latin America contains chapters on Costa Rica, Colombia, Nicaragua, Argentina, Mexico, Bolivia, Chile, Cuba, and Brazil; see Dore and Molyneux, *Hidden Histories of Gender and the State in Latin America.*

28. Roger N. Lancaster, *Life Is Hard: Machismo, Danger, and the Intimacy of Power in Nicaragua* (Berkeley: University of California Press, 1992); Ana María Alonso, *Thread of Blood: Colonialism, Revolution, and Gender on Mexico's Northern Frontier* (Tucson: University of Arizona Press, 1995); Matthew C. Gutmann, *The Meanings of Macho: Being a Man in Mexico City* (Berkeley: University of California Press, 1996); Peter M. Beattie, *The Tribute of Blood: Army, Honor, Race, and Nation in Brazil, 1864–1945* (Durham, NC: Duke University Press, 2001).

29. See the interesting introductory essays by Matthew C. Gutmann and Mara Viveros Vigoya in Gutmann, *Changing Men and Masculinities in Latin America.*

30. Joan Hoff, "Gender as a Postmodern Category of Paralysis," *Women's History Review* 3, no. 2 (1994).

31. For an excellent critique of Hoff, see Susan Kingsley Kent, "Mistrials and Diatribulations: A Reply to Joan Hoff," *Women's History Review* 5, no. 1 (1996): 9–18.

32. Joan Wallach Scott, *Gender and the Politics of History*, rev. ed (New York: Columbia University Press, 1999), especially ch. 10, "Some More Reflections on Gender and Politics." Questions are from pages 206–207.

33. Building on the work of Michel Foucault, Scott defines gender as knowledge about sexual difference. By knowledge, she means the "understanding produced by cultures and societies of human relationships, in this case of those between men and women." For Scott, the uses and

meanings of such knowledge are and have been contested politically and provide the means by which relationships of domination and subordination are constructed. See her discussion of knowledge in *Gender and the Politics of History*, 2.

34. David M. Halperin, *How to Do the History of Homosexuality* (Chicago: University of Chicago Press, 2002), 44–45. Halperin's insights have been especially useful to us, and we have drawn extensively on them in writing this section of the introduction.

35. James N. Green, *Beyond Carnival: Male Homosexuality in Twentieth-Century Brazil* (Chicago: University of Chicago Press, 1999). For discussion of the homosexual appropriation of carnival, see chapter 5.

36. Michel Foucault, *The History of Sexuality: An Introduction*, Vol. 1 (New York: Vintage Books, 1990). This book was first published in French in 1976 and appeared in English translation in 1978.

37. Foucault's work has been discussed extensively in print and online. The following works have been particularly helpful in the writing of this section of the introduction: Jeffrey Weeks, "Foucault for Historians," *History Workshop Journal* 14 (Autumn 1982); Jeffrey Weeks, *Making Sexual History* (Cambridge, UK: Polity Press, 2000); David M. Halperin, "Is There a History of Sexuality?" *History Theory* 28, no. 3 (1989); and Halperin, *How to Do the History of Homosexuality*, especially the chapter entitled "Forgetting Foucault."

38. See the discussion by Barbara Duden, *The Woman beneath the Skin: A Doctor's Patients in Eighteenth-Century Germany* (Cambridge, MA: Harvard University Press, 1991), especially ch. 1, "Toward a History of the Body." While Duden discusses the impact of medical discourses on bringing the modern body into being, she does not see the modern body as resulting from developments in medicine but, rather, as an integral part of the broader history of the nineteenth century, as woven from the same materials that created "economic man" and modern society.

39. See, especially, the work of Norbert Elias, *The Civilizing Process* (New York, 1978); for a discussion of the importance of manners, morals, and respectability to nationalism, see George L. Mosse, *Nationalism and Sexuality: Middle-Class Morality and Sexual Norms in Modern Europe* (Madison: University of Wisconsin Press, 1985), especially the introduction.

40. Thomas Laqueur, "Orgasm, Generation, and the Politics of Reproductive Biology," in *The Gender Sexuality Reader*, ed. Lancaster and de Leonardo. These ideas are further developed in Laqueur's book, *Making Sex: Body and Gender from the Greeks to Freud* (Cambridge, MA: Harvard University Press, 1990).

41. Anne Fausto-Sterling, *Sexing the Body: Gender Politics and the Construction of Sexuality* (New York: Basic Books, 2000).

42. Eric Vilain, "Which Sex? In Reality, It's Not All That Easy," *Vancouver Sun*, May 24, 2004, A6.

43. Duden, *The Woman beneath the Skin*; see especially ch. 1, "Toward a History of the Body."

44. Duden, *The Woman beneath the Skin*, 31.

45. Halperin, *How to Do the History of Homosexuality*, 103.

46. Halperin, *How to Do the History of Homosexuality*, 88–89, 102–103.

47. Judith Butler, *Bodies That Matter: On the Discursive Limits of "Sex"* (New York: Routledge, 1993); see the introduction, especially pages 1, 2, 10, and 15.

48. See the discussion in Jeffrey Weeks, "The Body and Sexuality," in *Modernity: An Introduction to Modern Societies*, ed. Stuart Hall, David Held, Don Hubert, and Kenneth Thompson (Cambridge, MA: Blackwell, 1996), especially pp. 380–88, and Halperin, *How to Do the History of Homosexuality*, 130–34.

49. See Roger N. Lancaster, *The Trouble with Nature: Sex in Science and Popular Culture* (Berkeley: University of California Press, 2003), 104–106, for a discussion of "heteronormativity."

50. Butler, *Bodies That Matter*, especially ch. 8, "Critically Queer," 223–42.

51. In addition to the previously mentioned work of James Green, see Mara Viveros Vigoya, "Contemporary Latin American Perspectives on Masculinity," in *Changing Men and Masculinities in Latin America*, ed. Gutmann; and Richard Parker, "Changing Sexualities: Masculinity and Male Homosexuality in Brazil," in Gutmann, *Changing Men and Masculinities in Latin America*.

52. On this point, see Jennifer Terry, "Theorizing Deviant Historiography," in *Feminists Revision History*, ed. Ann-Louise Shapiro (New Brunswick, NJ: Rutgers University Press, 1994).

53. To see this argument about the mutual constitution of categories of identity worked out in a specific case study in the Latin American context, see Diane M. Nelson, *A Finger in the Wound: Body Politics in Quincentennial Guatemala* (Berkeley: University of California Press, 1999); for an excellent discussion of some of the recent literature and of the issues involved in the mutual constitution of race, gender, sexuality, and national identity, see Nancy P. Appelbaum, Anne S. Macpherson, and Karin Alejandra Rosemblatt, "Introduction: Racial Nations," in *Race and Nation in Modern Latin America*, ed. Nancy P. Appelbaum, Anne S. Macpherson, and Karin Alejandra Rosemblatt (Chapel Hill: University of North Carolina Press, 2003).

54. In her recently published book, Alejandra Bronfman examines the ways in which state officials, social scientists, and black and mulatto activists made, changed, and legitimated the many meanings of "race" in Cuba between 1902 and 1940. See Alejandra Bronfman, *Measures of Equality: Social Science, Citizenship, and Race in Cuba, 1902–1940* (Chapel Hill: University of North Carolina Press, 2004).

55. See, for example, Linda Alcoff, "Cultural Feminism versus Post-Structuralism: The Identity Crisis in Feminist Theory," in *Culture/Power/History: A Reader in Contemporary Social Theory*, ed. Nicholas B. Dirks, Geoff Eley, and Sherry B. Ortner (Princeton, NJ: Princeton University Press, 1994).

56. Lancaster, *The Trouble with Nature*. For Lancaster's definition of identity politics and critique of strategic essentialism, see pp. 13–32.

57. It is also important to note that some queer theorists have also attacked same-sex marriage as "normalizing." For one example, see Michael Warner, *The Trouble with Normal: Sex, Politics and the Ethics of Queer Life* (New York: Free Press, 1999).

58. Nancy F. Cott, *Public Vows: A History of Marriage and the Nation* (Cambridge, MA: Harvard University Press, 2000), see especially pp. 3–23.

59. These example are meant to illustrate the importance of constructions of gender to all regimes in Nicaragua (as elsewhere); by pitting the "new" man against "traditional, patriarchal values," we do not intend to imply that the Sandinistas were without failings with regard to gender. See the discussion by Howe as well as the literature she cites.

60. See the discussion on the relationship between identity and identification by Stuart Hall, "Introduction: Who Needs 'Identity'?" in *Questions of Cultural Identity*, ed. Stuart Hall and Paul du Gay, 1–17 (London: Sage, 1996).

61. See the excellent book by Daniel James, *Doña María's Story: Life History, Memory, and Political Identity* (Durham, NC: Duke University Press, 2000), especially the chapter entitled "'Tales Told Out on the Borderlands:' Reading Doña María's Story for Gender."

1

Vicenta Ochoa, Dead Many Times: Gender, Politics, and a Death Sentence in Early Republican Caracas, Venezuela

Arlene J. Díaz

O N MAY 24 AND MAY 31, 1836, TWO FLYERS were distributed in the streets of the city of Caracas in Venezuela. Entitled "Vicenta Ochoa and Her Constitutional Rights" and "Vicenta Ochoa, Dead Many Times," the propaganda pleaded for the commutation of the death sentence against Vicenta Ochoa.[1] A poor, young, married mother who was expecting her second child, Ochoa was to be executed in the popular Plaza of San Jacinto because she had stolen from and murdered María de la Cruz, a female slave. In the opinion of the "constitutional friends of humanity" (as the publishers of the flyers called themselves), the eyes of civilization and of the new republic demanded that such a drastic act be discussed in a public forum. At the same time, cloistered nuns and another group of women calling themselves "mothers of Caracas" petitioned the president of Gran Colombia (as the republic comprising Colombia, Venezuela, and Ecuador founded in 1819 and lasting until 1830 was called) to commute Ochoa's sentence of death.

The voices of those participating in the debate over Ochoa's sentence reveal that, while in agreement as to the need to save Ochoa's life, women and men differed in their arguments and strategies as well as in their underlying political claims. Given that women's participation in politics in the new republic was not acceptable, Ochoa's death sentence created, intentionally or not, an opportunity to bring attention to women's plight. This chapter offers a gendered analysis, that is, a discussion of how some men and women may have experienced this event, the possible meanings of their arguments, and how, in that discussion, a definitive idea of unequal relationships of power among the sexes emerged out of their statements. In the arguments used to save Vicenta

Ochoa, women's reproductive capacity became a core issue, either to claim protection of the law or to justify the subordination of women to men.

How some women and men used the opportunity publicly to speak their opposition to the execution of Ochoa needs to be understood in the legal and political context of the early republic. By the 1830s, new constitutional defini-tions, combined with the continued use of Spanish colonial laws and a gen-dered political language that excluded women, made the legal and political identity of women ambiguous and thus extremely difficult to challenge. In Venezuela, the issue of women's rights was not part of the political discus-sions, nor did the constitution grant women any specific rights. The abstract granting of citizenship to "all Venezuelans" beginning in the first constitution of 1811, written before independence was fully achieved, made some women feel included in the rights and privileges granted to all inhabitants of the new republic. Still, in reality, the practical definition of "citizen" excluded women and nonpropertied men altogether from voting or holding office. Theoreti-cally, everyone but a slave was equal and a citizen, but only propertied males, most of whom were white, could be active citizens and therefore enjoy the full protection of their individual rights and property.

Upholding male power and control over the society was fundamental to the builders of the new liberal republic. Thus, it is understandable that ruling men did not address the paradox of supporting a liberal state that praised the au-tonomous individual, freedom, and less governmental restriction in the econ-omy, while maintaining a hierarchical colonial social structure. This precedent was established in the 1811 liberal constitution, the model for subsequent constitutions in Venezuela, which incorporated ideas of equality, liberty, indi-viduality, and citizenship. The constitution also protected property rights and provided some basis for the construction of a modern nation that followed the dictates of more economically developed countries in Europe and the United States.

In the constitution of 1811, the ruling elites established the continued use of Spanish legal codes like the *Siete Partidas*, a thirteenth-century code based on canon and Roman law that supported a hierarchical society. This was cen-tral for men; the *Siete Partidas* granted male heads of household parental rights that allowed them to control family property and impose their will on their wives and children by legal authority and, if necessary, by physical pun-ishment. The Spanish colonial church and state in Venezuela dictated that as *padres de familia* (male heads of household), upper-class men extended their authority over their dependents, including slaves and other subordinates. In this context, how could women claim equal protection under the law as citi-zens when the legal codes currently in force denied them this very status?

This dilemma was a reflection of how an egalitarian rhetoric so widespread in Venezuela concealed and denied formal equality in practice.[2] While politicians talked about equality and freedom for the *pueblo* (the people), a term intended to include every inhabitant, in reality this discourse of equality was specifically addressed to a much smaller portion of the population. The pueblo to whom the male politicians referred comprised the citizens, that is, the select group of propertied males who participated in the elections.

The rhetoric of equality for the pueblo had other gendered and racial connotations based on traditional ideas of the church and the state. Women hardly appear in the political writings of these decades, in part because the ruling men of the early republic considered this half of the population dependent and weak and not part of public history. Still, women were not completely absent from the intellectuals' sphere of imagination. Women generally were seen as innocent victims whose domesticity had been threatened by the violent wars and now must be reestablished by a caring, paternal republic.[3] Metaphoric uses of "liberty" in speeches and paintings as a value that had to be policed by the government paralleled ideas about women in this period. To be cultivated and enjoyed properly, "liberty" had to be conditioned and controlled; otherwise, anarchy could arise.[4] In the same way, women could also be a source of *pasiones*—hatred, vengeance, and lawlessness—that could corrupt both men and civilization. Simón Bolívar, the great independence leader and father of the nation, did not use the word "pasiones" in his speeches to refer to the "dangerous seductive powers of women," yet he did regard the vice of jealousy and emotions in general as feminine characteristics. Rather, Bolívar mostly identified "violent passions" and turmoil with mulattos and blacks.[5]

The church in Venezuela treated women in a similar manner, complementing dominant opinions about the need to keep women confined to the domestic sphere. Not unlike the colonial ecclesiastical discourse on lust and chastity, nineteenth-century religious publications dwelt on the consequences of women's devilish behavior. Not only did women's sexual desire drive men to stupidity and loss of common sense (as in the story of Adam and Eve), such sin robbed men of their youth and health. Equally importantly, it also led to the loss of property. In sum, women were the "ruin of the Christian people" and the "home of lust and administrator of the demons"; their powers could make men lose their domination in society.[6] If uncontrolled, women were to be feared.

Faced with such a threat, men advocated that all women receive rigorous male supervision. Women supposedly lacked intelligence, so they had to be enclosed in their homes, away from the exterior world, and be obedient to the guidance provided by men.[7] Following the civil wars of independence, which mobilized different races and both sexes for over a decade, it became imperative to create an order that would reemphasize female domesticity and the male role of protecting the nation and the home.

According to Bolívar, for men, virtue was to be gained in the service of the nation, whereas women's contribution was to be made in the home, where they were to raise the next generation of patriotic citizens. These assumptions about gender and nation denied women the possibility of becoming true citizens because their actions were to be confined to the home and not extended into the military or public sphere.[8] In this context, men from the ruling classes spoke for women, as well as for everyone else, and allowed women very little space to maneuver in the public sphere. However, the arguments and metaphors used by both men and women in what became a collective debate over Ochoa serve as illuminating examples of how much some women tried to accomplish, even within such a limited sphere, and the extent to which men would go to deny women a voice in politics. In this sense, what was seemingly one of many political debates in the 1830s reveals connections among gender relationships, the role of women's reproductive capacities, and relationships of power between both men and women and gender and the state in this new republic.

By studying how gender is understood and represented by women, politicians, and judges, for example, and how unequal power relations are built around this construct, we can arrive at a clearer comprehension of the logic behind the unequal distribution of power in society and how this situation is perpetuated in different historical periods. What started as a lawsuit can teach us the broader implications of the way different people envisioned the future of the nation and the place that men and women should occupy in it. This chapter consists of a gender-conscious analysis of the discussion that revolved around the death sentence of Vicenta Ochoa because this debate brought to the surface some life strategies used by women in the new Venezuelan republic to deal with, participate in, or even attempt to enter the public discourse traditionally dominated by males. Consequently, this chapter situates itself in the fields of gender, legal, and cultural history.

Women needed extreme caution and carefully guarded strategic advances if they desired to make a public claim without evoking accusations of being dominated by *las pasiones*. While attempting to make themselves heard and to have their ideas taken seriously, women had to maneuver in such a way as to avoid outright confrontation with males, yet without sacrificing their dignity. Even in these conditions, at least in Caracas, women struggled individually and in less conspicuous ways for a transformation of their rights during the early republic.[9] The revolutionary struggles had created many opportunities for eluding and reworking the gendered formulations expressed by the state and the church. Notwithstanding legal, linguistic, and ideological limitations and exclusions, women directly or indirectly claimed to have the protection the nation granted to male citizens. Their ideas about citizenship did not include their right to participate in the political sphere, as in Revolutionary France, but rather the right to physical and material protection under the law that would provide them with increased economic and physical security and simultaneously make men more accountable for their actions. Thus, women were directly and indirectly referring to the egalitarian rhetoric of the time by requesting that both men and women enjoy equal protection under the law.

For example, in Caracas, poor women pursued their quest for equality by challenging their husbands or partners at home and bringing their grievances to court. In their daily lives, lower-class women defended their individual liberties by questioning not the validity of the institution of marriage but the capacity and character of their husbands or lovers. They accused men of being alcoholics, lazy, or abusive and unresponsive to the reciprocal rights and duties implicit in their formal or informal marriage contract. Looking at their actions at home and in the courts, it is clear that these women felt they did not deserve to be abused, to be banned from working for a salary, or to be deprived of their liberties and that they wanted compensation for their services. Their in-court "performances" were consistent with some of the contemporary expectations of citizenship, such as equal protection under the law.

Upper-class women, however, spelled out more openly their claim for citizenship, while defending their property. In lawsuits pertaining to the upper classes, husbands consistently accused their wives of relying on the "subversive" principles of the constitution, that is, of citizenship and the equality of people before the law. Husbands claimed that such liberal views would lead to anarchy, since they directly affected male familial control, which was the basis of civil society. Moreover, such principles defied male authority and honor in society.[10] Both lower- and upper-class males responded to women's challenges with verbal and physical violence; however, only members of the upper class openly accused women of "subversion" when confronted with their demands for constitutional rights as citizens.

The strategy used by Ochoa and her female defenders became a public defense of motherhood, not a claim for equality and citizenship as in other lawsuits. Women's reproductive capacities became an irrefutable argument, a strategic metaphor, and a source of authority that women could use effectively to enter a public space that they were not expected to penetrate.[11] By appealing to motherhood, they could make a radical claim, yet, at the same time, limit confrontation and conflict and preserve the social order. This strategy becomes logical when contrasted with the impact that the upper-class women's claim of citizenship had on men, described above, in which some men, alarmed by women's presumed inclusion as citizens, thought these ideas would lead to anarchy and disorder. The Ochoa case is unusual because it motivated men and women to mobilize, even with different purposes in mind, during the early years of the republic. What independence failed to do politically, that is, to organize women collectively, the defense of motherhood achieved in 1836.

The Constitution, the Death Penalty, and Vicenta Ochoa

Vicenta Ochoa's case was under consideration during a period in which a new constitution was ratified, strategies for economic revitalization were implemented, and the use of the death penalty was under question. After Venezuela's separation from Colombia in 1830, Venezuelan president José Antonio Páez united with landowners, slave holders, merchants, and learned and notable citizens to invigorate the devastated economy and build a new Venezuela. Between 1830 and 1847 deep reflection about both the economy and the political situation took place, one that was characterized by a good degree of consensus. In particular, these notables, also referred to as the oligarchy, agreed to follow the dictates of liberalism and to consolidate a government that respected individual rights, especially to hold private property.[12] With this in mind, they implemented a number of measures designed to revitalize business and agriculture within a free market framework. Their idea was to help Venezuela become an important agroexporter, as it had been at the end of the eighteenth century. All hopes for the achievement of these plans hinged on obedience to the 1830 constitution, which seemed to have overwhelming support among the notable citizenry. The constitution was drafted to suit their interests, which they confused with those of every Venezuelan.[13] For the notables, it was imperative to follow the constitution in order to distance themselves from the Spanish past, which they linked to obscurantism, and to replace state control over the economy and politics (which they referred to as "state godparenthood" or *padrinaje estatal*) with free market competition. By promoting agriculture through the introduction of new laws, such as the controversial creditor law of April 10, 1834 (which provided liberty for contracts and easy credit transactions between planters and creditors), and through the importation of machinery and improvements in science and technology, the country, they believed, could join the ranks of the civilized nations that were illuminated by reason.[14] The use of scientific knowledge to solve issues ranging from determining the most productive seeds to plant to solving broader economic problems such as credit was highly valued at this time in Latin America. In order to achieve economic progress and success through free competition, freedom of the press was deemed necessary as the foundation of civil liberties.[15] To create their new Venezuela, social peace and protection for individuals and property were imperative. Thus, they enacted harsh criminal laws, such as the lash law (*ley de azotes*), which punished those convicted of committing a crime against private property with public lashing. This law was added to others established by Bolívar, including one imposed by decree in 1813 that mandated the death penalty for anyone who disturbed "public order, peace and tranquility."[16] This order was to be enforced by all civil and military courts. Another law, passed on May 3, 1826, extended the death penalty to those convicted of theft and robbery and even to government functionaries found guilty of corruption (Decree of January 12, 1824).[17] Finally, Bolívar also established by decree (November 24, 1824) the need to expedite the judicial procedure in criminal cases and cases in which civil servants were accused of stealing money from the public treasury. As a consequence, women accused of criminal offenses would not be excluded from receiving harsher punishments in the new republic. It was in this public space opened in 1830 that the debate over Ochoa's death sentence occurred.

When it came to the application of the law, a sample of cases taken between 1835 and 1840 reveals that most of those involved in the criminal lawsuits belonged to the lower classes, those more prone, according to the elites, to be overtaken by the *pasiones*.[18] Contrary to the results of other samples of lawsuits taken for the late colonial period and the late nineteenth century, most of the cases dealing with criminal acts in the early republic had a conclusion, many times one that found the accused guilty of a crime. This statement is especially true in cases of murder; in five out of six cases between 1835 and 1840, the tribunal pronounced guilty verdicts. Also, in five out of eleven cases of assault and battery, the accused was found guilty.

Determining whether death sentences were common for convicted females in the late colonial period and the early republic is difficult. This was the only death sentence I found for a female in the 1835 to 1840 sample. Yet this was not the only instance in which the death penalty was mentioned in cases involving female felons. Juliana López, a woman from Curaçao, owner of a lodging house in Caracas, was accused with Guadeloupean Félix Ouvré of murdering and robbing a guest, Miguel Muñoz.[19] According to the sentence, the death penalty could not be applied in this case because there were still some doubts in the case, and "for the imposition of the death penalty, the evidence must be as true and clear as the light of the day at noon time."[20] Instead, the judge sentenced both to ten years in a penitentiary. The records do not indicate where the defendants were sent, and there was no penitentiary for women in Caracas. However, it is telling that in this case, which occurred a year after Ochoa's, the punishment was harsher. All in all, women were not excluded from punishment for criminal behavior. Women were also sent to jail for crimes such as knifings and assault, for instance.[21]

In the early republic, criminal acts such as murder were treated with special interest in an effort to curtail the excesses promoted by the period of wars for independence. To attain peace and order, and since there was no penal code at that time for the new republic, the tribunals used both Spanish and early republican laws to support their decisions, even though it seems that in the colonial period, sentences such as the death penalty were not prevalent. The severe sentencing pattern of the early republic did not discriminate in terms of gender, and, indeed, women's crimes were treated as seriously as men's. This was reminiscent of the wars of independence during which time women's actions became more visible, and hence were deemed as dangerous as those of men.

The murder of the *samba* (a person of Indian and black descent) slave María de la Cruz by Vicenta Ochoa resulted in the death penalty, the kind of stern sentence that was not out of place in the early republic. As narrated in a report on the case, Ochoa owed money to de la Cruz, a peddler who sold different items, such as veils and skirts, in the streets of Caracas. From the records, it is clear that Ochoa did not get along with the slave; according to Ochoa and many others, de la Cruz had a "haughty, bold, and peevish character."[22] While racial categorization was common when providing the identity of litigants in the colonial period, this practice formally ended with independence. However, litigants and judicial officials tended to point out the race of litigants who were not considered white. As the records make no mention of Ochoa's race, it can be inferred that the authorities did not regard her or those defending her as people of black ancestry. From the trial records, the events of October 28, 1834, can be pieced together. María de la Cruz went to Ochoa's home with her suitcase of goods to collect the money Ochoa owed her. When she arrived, Ochoa called Corporal Manuel Bastardo (or Cabo Bastardo) to help her tie up the insolent slave. Ochoa, it seems, hit de la Cruz several times and suffocated her with a piece of cloth, killing her. According to the court transcripts, Ochoa, with the corporal's help, placed the dead body in a sewer close to her house. She then gave Bastardo a pair of earrings as compensation, and during the night, she sold the goods that María de la Cruz had carried in her luggage. Five days later, the authorities located the corpse.

In June 1835, after much investigation, sentence was passed in the case. Based on the laws of the Spanish colonial legal codes, such as the *Novísima Recopilación* and the *Siete Partidas*, and on the republican law of May 3, 1826, Ochoa was sentenced to death in a public plaza of Caracas. She had not only murdered a slave but had stolen from her as well. Although the sentence was appealed, it was ratified by the executive power and by the court again on May 16 and 17, 1836, respectively. Eight days later, Ochoa was placed in a chapel for spiritual preparation before the execution, where she spent many tormented hours and was even said to have lost her mind. While in the chapel, Ochoa claimed to be in the early stages of pregnancy. This discovery incited significant public interest in her sentence, or, rather, in her plight. Soon, flyers were distributed in the city of Caracas. While the case of Vicenta Ochoa was but one of many issues circulating in the city, it was different. This time, in place of expressing political and economic grievances, headlines announced the impending death of an expectant mother.

However, the extent of interest in Ochoa's sentence, as measured by the willingness of individuals and groups to prepare, print, and circulate flyers in her defense, also stemmed from the political climate in Venezuela at that time. The 1830s witnessed the most prolific political debate in the history of Caracas, especially through newspapers, pamphlets, and flyers.[23] Freedom of the press abounded, and publishing houses like Valentín Espinal, A. Damirón, and Tomás Antero assured quick and good circulation in the city.[24]

The debate over Ochoa's death sentence occurred at a moment of emerging opposition against the government as well as increased public debate over executions. On July 8, 1835, a coup took place against elected president, José María Vargas. By August 20, 1835, Vargas was back in the presidency with the military and political support of José Antonio Páez. Military leaders and landowners who participated in the *revolución de las reformas* (revolution of the reforms), as the revolt is called, sought major reforms from the government, including the abolition of the free contract law of April 1834, which led to the increasing ruin of a number of landowners. While Vargas supported the imposition of severe punishment on those involved, many congressmen supported the exemplary execution of the reformist conspirators, a move that would essentially eliminate opposition to their economic policies. Although Páez, as the chief of the armed forces, favored pardoning the conspirators, Congress did not. This stance of the government in favor of cruelly punishing the conspirators provoked a heated a debate that circulated in printed form in 1836.[25] Although the debate against the death penalty continued until its abolition in 1849, it is very likely that opponents of that policy used the execution of Vicenta Ochoa to further their claims. The arguments used by these males suggested that the authors of the flyers, the so-called constitutional friends of humanity, and even the priests who wrote to the president were part of a growing opposition to certain policies of the regime.

Male Arguments

The two flyers mentioned above and a letter sent by the priests of Caracas serve as examples of male arguments in the case of Vicenta Ochoa. The authors of those documents went to great lengths to expound their vast constitutional knowledge in her defense.[26] As in the 1811 and 1819 constitutions, the revised version of 1830 symbolized the recently acquired and much heralded liberties upon which the establishment of a civilized humanity was predicated. Hence, their defense was imperative. The documents' authors claimed, for example, that Ochoa's execution violated the individual rights guaranteed by the constitution of 1830 because the events leading up to this judgment did not follow due process. According to Article 117, Number 21, the pardons in cases of death sentences had to be decided by the executive in consultation with the cabinet (*Consejo de Gobierno*). However, in Ochoa's case, the decision to continue with the execution was made solely by the vice president of the republic, who was acting as the executive at the time.[27] According to one flyer, if the execution order continued, it would further violate the constitution because Articles 186 and 187 mandated that no government official execute orders that were against the constitution or its formalities. Clearly, the "constitution refers to every official without exception," and although past governments approved of death sentences, Article 206 of the 1830 constitution sought to curb death sentences as much as possible.[28] If the constitutional discussion were not enough, centuries-old laws coming from the Spanish codes, the *Siete Partidas* and the *Recopilación de Castilla,* which were still in operation in Venezuela, were recalled in the flyers. Using those codes as supporting evidence, the flyers raised doubts about Ochoa's guilt, especially since there were no witnesses to the crime and because some thought that the medical examination of the victim was inconclusive. Thus, in this case, they argued, the death sentence should not have been given because there was no certainty that Ochoa was the killer. In addition, they argued that Ochoa was acting in self-defense in her own house and, according to the old codes and the new constitution (Art. 191), "no one may impunitively intrude into the home of a citizen, nor insult him while on the premises, nor provoke him in his castle [*castillo*] of repose and security."[29] As with the ardent defense of private property made by ruling elites since independence, the flyer asked the government to respect the family and the home as a private domain.

In Argentina, male immigrants made a similar argument when defending an allegedly pregnant murderer, Clorinda Sarracán from the death penalty in 1856. According to Ricardo D. Salvatore, "The liberal state . . . ought to respect families in the same way it respected private property. To violate the bodies of women was an inadmissible intrusion of the state in the male private domain."[30] In other words, like those involved in the case in Argentina, the flyers were arguing that state officials had extended their powers too far into the domestic sphere when they sentenced a pregnant woman to death. Yet, it is telling that during this period, the family and the home were understood to be the private domain of male, not female, authority. The argument made in the flyers did not note this contradiction; nor did it mention the rights of Ochoa's husband, who, incidentally, was not an active citizen. Were these men defending Ochoa because they felt that she was entitled to be treated equally as a woman under the constitution, or were they defending themselves from the presence of the state in the private sphere that they ruled?

The consistent argument men made about the privileged status of the female sex makes it doubtful that they were thinking about treating women equally in legal terms. It is revealing to note that even though the constitution embodied ideas of equal rights for "the people," these writers did not refer to women's equality before the law but consistently alluded to centuries-old Spanish concepts of female privilege based on the supposed inherent weakness of the female body and mind. The argument repeatedly went that the female sex had a distinct set of privileges and that "the laws of all times have viewed men in a different manner in the application and execution of punishment, even when in regard to equal crimes."[31] Thus, although the constitution of 1830 had been "modernized" to guarantee civil liberties to the "people," the antiquated expectation that the application of these laws would vary from one sex to another was still very much alive.

To further the claim that Ochoa had a privileged status based on her sex, she was described as a *madre de familia*—defined by the jurist Joaquín Escriche as a woman who lives virtuously in the home, even if she does not have children—and not a female head of household as one would be led to believe. The status of household head was reserved for the *padre de familia*, who governed and ruled the home.[32] Indeed, as Tomás Lander, the future leader of the opposition, wrote in 1835, the most significant role for someone to play in Venezuela was that of "*hacendado* [landowner] and male family head."[33] The term *madre de familia* was used to argue that Ochoa was bringing up new citizens and servants of the republic, and her life therefore was worth saving for the benefit of the new nation. While in the late colonial period female litigants did use motherhood as a defense strategy in court, it was not until the early nineteenth century that the argument of motherhood as a social function was widely used. In the case of Ochoa, it was claimed that she was a faithful wife "whose example in matrimony is very useful to society,"[34] evoking the pedagogical function of the female figure in bringing up citizens and in serving as an example of domestic virtue to society. As Ochoa belonged to the "privileged" sex, the argument went, she was a valuable figure in the family whose life had to be preserved.

Because of Ochoa's status as a woman, what in the government's view should have been a spectacle of death to instill terror actually had the opposite effect on the population. Rather than inciting better conduct from society, the execution could be interpreted as an act of inhumanity on the part of the government. As one flyer stated, her death would be "of no use to the order of society, because society only feels pity, and does not remember the crime, nor the law, but rather those who suffer from a lack of humanity." The execution of a woman would make people forget the crime that was being punished, especially in a city that "has no memory of a punishment of this sort," referring to the circumstances of Ochoa's case and to the fact that executions had not taken place in Caracas for decades.[35] All three writings agree that her execution would inspire compassion for her among *caraqueños* (people of Caracas), while at the same time generating a feeling of horror against the government.

Along those lines, the propaganda and the letter emphasized how Ochoa's death would besmirch the good character of the executive. This was a major concern if Venezuela was to enter into modernity. Since the agenda of the government was to distance itself from what it deemed a backward and barbaric Spanish government and to become a "civilized" nation guided by reason, with an economy inspired by the capitalistic principles of the most developed countries, a public statement such as that made by the execution of an expectant mother would not be appropriate. One has to recall that the massacres and sanguinary acts attributed to the Spanish Boves (a figure of the wars of independence responsible for the massacre of republicans in 1814) and the killings of patriots by the Spanish authorities were still fresh in the collective memory, even though the patriots had exhibited similar behavior. More importantly, the high degree of political stability enjoyed in the 1830s cautioned against returning to a bloody past.[36] When, after much consternation, Páez enacted a decree of immunity for the conspirators of July 1835, he showed how the fear of another civil war outweighed the probability of repercussions and harsh criticism from members of the cabinet:

> The decision to dictate this decree was based on the clamor of my feelings and horror at the disasters of civil war and not on the desire to conserve my popularity, to increase the affection of my fellow citizens, and fortify the influence of my services.[37]

The male argument demonstrates that publicly condoning leniency in Ochoa's sentencing was not an act on behalf of a woman per se, but that her cause was used as a pretext to further the political and personal concerns of the notable male citizenry. Men defended Ochoa not because they cared about women's political condition but because they could use it to defend their own privileged rights. In the closed male conversation taking place among judges, lawyers, politicians, landowners, and the clergy, women's claims would not be heard easily because, from the men's perspective, especially among those who felt responsible for ruling the rest of the people, women's ideas or issues were not important or even pertinent—women's place was in the home, and men ruled there, not the government. This was another way that the rhetoric of equality was articulated in daily practice, which had the result, whether deliberate or not, of strengthening male rights while avoiding dealing with women's issues in public discussions.

Men used the case of Ochoa to further a political claim against a regime that they believed intended to revert to barbarism and violent passion by condemning a pregnant woman to death.[38] Opponents of the regime sought to contradict the ruling oligarchs, who affirmed a superior masculinity, prided themselves on being the protectors of individual property, and claimed to be bringing progress and modernity to Venezuela. Yet these men were not necessarily acting on behalf of the female sex per se, nor did they publicly acknowledge in their writings that they were persuaded by the individual and collective actions of women who were mobilized to save the life of Vicenta Ochoa. These men's sensibilities may have been touched by these women's pleas, but, as in the wars of independence, they would not publicly validate the effects that women's activism had on politics. It cannot be denied, however, that even though women were used to further a male political agenda, the use of the female figure here opened a space for women to participate in this debate.

Female Responses

The first participant to employ what might be called a "female response" was Ochoa herself. On July 21, 1835, thirteen days after the military revolt that briefly ousted president José María Vargas, she wrote to the insurgent government seeking clemency from the executive. It is not clear whether Ochoa wrote the letter herself, but it is intriguing to observe that she or whoever wrote the letter (the handwriting did not match her signature) strengthened the arguments made by her lawyers. Ochoa took the opportunity brought by the revolt to call for reforms in the administration of justice and to plead for clemency:

> The reforms that Caracas proclaimed as necessary to different branches and above all to the administration of justice, are the same ones that have moved me to address your Excellency with the hope that, dignifying us by receiving my solicitation . . . will bestow all the honor that is owed to one of the most grandiose eras of Venezuela. The constitution that ruled the old system, and that has provisionally remained in use . . . concedes the president of the state the authority to grant favors like the one that I implore today of your Excellency who, while simultaneously occupying one of the highest positions, is interested above all in my favor, in an event as dignified as it is necessary.[39]

Ochoa, or her writer, did not hesitate at every available opportunity to praise the personality of the new executive, appealing to the "grandeur of your soul," to the revolutionary moment as "one of the most grandiose eras of Venezuela," and to the sensibilities "of your Excellency the first example of kindness in this era of triumphs . . . and with justice all will herald you as the hero of the greatest magnitude," in order to adulate the masculinity and political agenda of the executive.[40] Moreover, she possibly thought that her case would serve as benevolent propaganda in favor of the new regime. Indeed, the letter suggests that public opinion was on her side and that the "popular clamor" would hinder any attempt to take her life. To further assert the veracity of her claims, she argued that the Superior Court had moved to Puerto Cabello to escape the opposition to their death-sentence ruling. It was more likely, however, that the court members were hiding from the turmoil created in the city of Caracas by the revolt.

In her letter, she not only insisted upon her absolute innocence, but she also expressed indignation that while the criminal charges against her were going through the tedious legal process, the "true killer" (*Cabo Bastardo*) was at large. As such, the letter suggested that Ochoa had been the victim of a system that still privileged the military, even though such privileges had been formally abolished by the 1830 constitution. As part of the liberal agenda pursued in Venezuela at that time, special privileges that the Spaniards granted the military and the church during the colonial period were to disappear in the abstract spirit of equality and as a means of centralizing the control of those major institutions under the new nation's government. With this insinuation, Ochoa or her writer attempted to call attention to the need for changes in the reigning administration of justice. However, these arguments might not have sat well with the revolutionary government because that group sought, as part of the reforms they wanted to implement, to reestablish military privileges.[41] That the argument appears inappropriate under the circumstances could be the result of a coup that was highly heterogeneous in its rank-and-file and in its agenda. Hence, the goals of the reformists might not initially have been manifest to the general public.

Before ending the letter, Ochoa informed the reader about the child to whom she had given birth while in prison, and whom she was breast-feeding at the time, emphasizing the latter fact to express the extent of her bodily commitment to her maternal and patriotic duties. There is no mention in the court transcripts about the identity of the father, nor did the letter emphasize that this was her second child. Critical was the appeal for compassion that the image of a woman breast-feeding a newborn could convey to the president of the republic.

But her strategy and arguments failed. By August 20, 1835, Vargas was back in the presidency, and her letter was filed with a note: "As this request is not addressed to the government it appears to be a random plea."[42] She had addressed her grievances and requests to the wrong people; hence, her letter was simply filed away.

By the time the court denied her appeal and the executive had ratified her execution on May 17, 1836, there was little she could do. Eight days later, she was taken to the chapel in preparation for the execution as was customary in such cases, and it was there, after many tormented hours, that she communicated to the authorities that she was expecting another child. Doctors were sent immediately to examine her and found that, according to Ochoa, she had stop menstruating three months before and that her belly and breasts were enlarged. Doctors recommended that the execution be postponed for two additional months to confirm her pregnancy. Despite the doctors' recommendation, the judge by law had to continue with the plans for execution until he received orders to the contrary from the executive or the high court.

To expedite the orders, the lower court judge wrote immediately to his superiors to suggest that Ochoa's execution be postponed until her pregnancy was confirmed. To make these officials aware of the growing public support for the commutation of her sentence, copies of the printed flyers that were being circulated in Caracas were attached to the letter.

The prompt attention that Ochoa received from both the courts and the public after announcing her pregnancy point to the receptivity that motherhood engendered in the cultural milieu of Caracas. It seemed as though there were an implicit understanding that women's reproductive capacities were a "private property" that society had a duty to protect. Indeed, the pregnancy plea became the most effective strategy to evade execution, at least temporarily. In Roman law, infants could not be harmed if their mothers were going to be executed, and according to the reigning laws in Venezuela, even if claims of pregnancy were used as a strategy to postpone a death sentence, the execution had to be put off.[43] Therefore, it can be surmised that Ochoa used her pregnancy to manipulate judges and public opinion in order to postpone her execution. The attention that she was unable to obtain through the courts and written petitions to the executive was quickly obtained by her ability to bear children.

Indeed, the city seemed to have been disturbed by the prospect that the death sentence would be carried out against a pregnant woman. Printed flyers were distributed and letters were signed and sent to the president of the republic soon after the announcement of her pregnancy. Even though these documents do speak of the commotion that existed in Caracas over the death sentence, which could be interpreted as a way to strengthen their case by appealing to broader support, it is unquestionable that the flyers and letters, especially those written by women, testify to the deep public concern over this execution. Most Venezuelan women and men at this time were illiterate, and while women did not have much experience in dealing directly with the government, they did use this opening in the public sphere to seek understanding within their limited space of action and to give their unsolicited opinion on the need to abolish capital punishment. In their letters, they incorporated language and images that emphasized their irreproachable modesty and their strict adherence to the cultural and social norms regarding female domesticity and motherhood. The desired outcome was to foster an unquestionable consensus around the plight of a mother.

Even Ana Salias, owner of the murdered slave, wrote to the executive, "I must unite my voice with those of the majority of the habitants of this city who desire the commutation of the death penalty."[44] Salias asked the acting president to give life to Ochoa, even if the tribunals sentenced her to death. It is possible that Salias wrote the letter herself, as her signature resembles that of the handwriting in the document. Ana Salias stated that there were many serious and powerful reasons for pardoning Ochoa, the most persuasive being that she was pregnant. Furthermore, Salias claimed that Ochoa's suffering while in the chapel had nearly propelled her into a state of dementia. All this suffering had made this unfortunate mother nothing more than "an object of compassion for the sensitive caraqueños."[45] Her letter ultimately alluded to the constitutional right that permitted the executive to pardon individuals that were sentenced to death (Art. 117, Item 21). Finally, Salias did not argue for the innocence of the murderer of her slave but requested an alternative punishment compatible with her sex, state, and circumstances. Thus, as with all the writings by women and men in this case, Salias's letter does not indicate any deliberation over the conflict between the constitutional dictum of equality before the law and a call for continued protection based on women's sex: Are women "equal to men," or should they receive special protection and privileges based on their sex, as in the colonial period? Yet, it can be argued that some women went beyond this dichotomy. These women were demanding protection that they felt society owed to motherhood as a way of claiming or obtaining the equal protection of the law that was not otherwise practiced or granted in the tribunals. Motherhood provided a strategic pretext to enter into a public, male sphere.

On May 24, 1836, in a letter signed by twenty-seven married mothers, the "madres de Caracas" also requested the commutation of Ochoa's sentence.[46] Contrary to the previous two letters, this one began by defining motherhood as a respectable title that touches "sensitive souls." It was because of that noteworthy title that these mothers were encouraged to write to the president of the republic as the person in charge of guarding the "codes of our sacred rights." They appealed to the "heart of a tender father and loving husband" to engage his attention in this case. Following a preamble in which the writers explained their basis for claiming his attention, they began stating how anomalous it was to apply a death sentence in Venezuela to the "weak sex." They regarded such a sentence as anomalous because, in Caracan society, proper and delicate treatment of the female sex was considered a noble and humanitarian attribute. By commuting the death sentence of a mother, "Your Excellency will add to the glory of your illustrious name by your virtues, the surname of HUMANE and PHILANTHROPIC, always desired by just men."[47] Thus, in the latter instance, saving a weak mother from death would bestow greatness upon the president and his name.

While, on the one hand, it was motherhood that united them and gave them the power to write to the president and make a request, on the other hand, they were also making a personal appeal to his honor as a man when they emphatically stated that pardoning Ochoa would lead to the recognition of his important personal qualities. Adulating the president seemed to have been an approach that helped them to avoid the impression of a possible confrontation with male power, while simultaneously making him more receptive to their claims.

To these petitions can be added that of the nuns from the cloistered convents of *Concepción*, the Carmelitas and Dominicans, who wrote directly to the vice president requesting that Ochoa be spared from execution.[48] Discovering that a woman had been sentenced to death by the tribunals of justice caused them great anguish, and knowing that the government cabinet had the power to forgive her, they requested such commutation "so that in Caracas an execution so horrible as that of a poor woman is not seen, and so that the Republic conserves a mother and a good wife." The nuns, situating their discussion within a religious framework, stressed motherhood as a social function. They relied on the Scriptures that spoke of forgiveness as being more important than punishment. "It is always more glorious to forgive than to punish." Yet, pardoning a woman, a member of the weak sex whose brain does not account fully for her actions, is even more glorious. Although they acknowledged the importance of a madre de familia to society, they nonetheless requested forgiveness for a woman who, by means of her sex, did not inspire the fear that her mistakes would be repeated: "What is lost in pardoning one who because of her sex does not inspire the fear that she repeat her errors? A great deal would be lost by punishing a married mother who could be so useful to society."[49] In the letter, the nuns combined the argument of women's inherent weakness and their pivotal role in society but added to it a religious tone of forgiveness. And, as in the other letters, the nuns did not forget to praise the executive as well: "That she not die, Sir, that this unfortunate woman not die. This is what we hope from your Excellency's generosity."

Whether or not these women perceived their actions as a conscious political statement is not completely clear, especially when their arguments are examined in contrast with those of the litigants from the late nineteenth century (1875–1880) who explicitly saw motherhood as a generator of rights. However, their boldness and courage to make a collective plea in the context of their ambiguous political and legal situation is important. That they sought ways in which to make a claim and to get the attention of ruling males points to how women, and people in general, maneuvered within a limited margin of action while covertly challenging the subordination expected of them. That these women used motherhood as their argumentative avenue or "strategic metaphor" is understandable, since their reproductive capacities needed no further justification; culturally, the idea that society had to protect motherhood was unquestionable.[50] If that image was used in a way that did not evoke the idea of disruption to the social order or male power, it could help women obtain some receptivity to, and support for, their demands. While the uses of the social function of motherhood in the feminist movements of the early twentieth century have been interpreted as conservative because they reaffirmed women's domestic roles, which is a legitimate argument, Ochoa's case in the early nineteenth century helps us understand the logic of that strategy.[51]

In the end, Vicenta Ochoa's sentence was commuted from death to exile to the island of Margarita for six years. Since no prison existed on the island at that time, it was expected that she would live there in relative freedom. The courts did not wait to confirm whether or not she was pregnant to make their decision, reaffirming that society and the law respected motherhood deeply. Ochoa's case may not have been decisive in convincing the government of the need to abolish the death penalty, but it served to invigorate the debate that led to the gradual decline by 1849 of the use of the death penalty for murder cases. In addition, it may have been an important step toward the use of motherhood to claim legal and political rights, a development that characterized the late nineteenth century. Thus, while the successes may look slim by today's standards, the strategic use of motherhood contributed, in the long run, to creating more awareness among women of their need to participate in the political sphere.

No one, however, remembered María de la Cruz, the strangled slave. A *samba* slave, de la Cruz was also considered a woman with a bold and peevish character. In the minds of the ruling classes, this type of characterization may have been uncomfortably similar to the violent passions and lack of submissiveness of the wars of independence, characteristics with which they did not want *their* Venezuela to be associated. It is ironic, however, that while Ochoa's pasiones had provoked her to kill, it was her image as a useful mother to society that ultimately saved her. Ochoa may have been dead many times according to the law, politics, and the exclusionary language of the ruling classes, but it was motherhood that, in the end, kept her alive.

Notes

An earlier version of this chapter was published in Arlene J. Díaz, *Female Citizens, Patriarchs, and the Law in Venezuela, 1786–1904* (Lincoln: University of Nebraska Press, 2004).

1. "Testimonio de la sentencia pronunciada en la causa criminal seguida de oficio contra Guillermo Castell, su muger Vicenta Ochoa y sirvienta Manuela Benavides por el homicidio

cometido en la persona de María de la Cruz, sierva de la señora Ana Salías el dia 28 de octubre del año pasado de 1834" (hereinafter "Testimonio de la sentencia"), Archivo del Registro Principal del Distrito Federal (hereinafter ARPDF), Criminales, 1836, Letra O, exp. 3, f. 26, 33–33v.

2. See Elías Pino Iturrieta, *La mentalidad venezolana de la emancipación* (Caracas: Eldorado Ediciones, 1991).

3. Julie Skurski, "The Leader and the 'People': Representing the Nation in Postcolonial Venezuela" (PhD dissertation, University of Chicago, 1993), 18.

4. Mariano Picón-Salas and Fundación Eugenio Mendoza, *Venezuela independiente, 1810–1960* (Caracas: Fundación Eugenio Mendoza, 1962), 213.

5. Skurski, "The Leader," 18; Elías Pino Iturrieta, *Ventaneras y castas, diabólicas y honestas* (Caracas: Editorial Planeta, 1993); Sarah Clark Chambers, "Gender in Bolívar's Virtuous Republic" (paper presented at the Meeting of the Latin American Studies Association, Guadalajara, México, 1997).

6. Pino Iturrieta, *Ventaneras,* 16–17.

7. Pino Iturrieta, *Ventaneras,* 69.

8. Some scholars have discussed the implications of the influence of this idea by the eighteenth-century French thinker Jean-Jacques Rousseau on the elites in Europe, the United States, and Venezuela. See Chambers, "Gender"; Linda G. Zerilli, *Signifying Woman: Culture and Chaos in Rousseau, Burke, and Mill* (Ithaca, NY: Cornell University Press, 1994); Olwen H. Hufton, *Women and the Limits of Citizenship in the French Revolution* (Toronto, Ontario: University of Toronto Press, 1992); Darline Gay Levy and Harriet B. Applewhite, "Women and Militant Citizenship in Revolutionary Paris," in *Rebel Daughters: Women and the French Revolution,* ed. Sara E. Melzer and Leslie W. Rabine (New York: Oxford University Press, 1992), 79–101. For a discussion on how these ideas affected women in the United States, see Linda K. Kerber, *Women of the Republic* (New York: Norton & Company, 1986).

9. Arlene J. Díaz, "Gender Conflicts in the Courts of the Early Venezuelan Republic, Caracas, 1811–1840," *Crime, Histoire and Sociétés [Crime, History and Society]* 2, no. 2 (1998): 35–53.

10. See "Juan José Espinosa solicitando que Micaela Ravelo se restituya con los hijos que ha ocultado a la casa de su madre donde aquel la tenía," ARPDF, Civiles, 1836, Letra E, exp. 15, fol. 18r.

11. See the article by Arcadio Díaz Quiñones, "De cómo y cuándo bregar," *Palique* (22 de enero de 1999), for a provocative discussion on the use of language as a mode of daily-life resistance.

12. Elías Pino Iturrieta, *Las ideas de los primeros venezolanos* (Caracas: Editorial Tropykos, 1987), 23. As in the 1811 constitution, in 1830, Article 188 guaranteed all Venezuelans equality before the law, civil liberty, personal security, and security of property. All the ecclesiastic and military privileges were abolished since they were contrary to the liberal ideas of equality of the new republic. Mary Watters, *History of the Church in Venezuela, 1810–1930* (New York: AMS Press, 1971), 130–31.

13. Pino Iturrieta, *Las ideas,* 44, 47.

14. For the reasons for its promulgation and the economic and political impact of this law, see John V. Lombardi, *The Decline and Abolition of Negro Slavery in Venezuela, 1820–1854* (Westport, CT: Greenwood Publishing, 1971), 19–20, 99–100; Stephen Joel Friedman, "City of Caracas, 1830—1846" (PhD dissertation, New York University, 1976), 120–30; Francisco González Guinán, *Historia contemporánea de Venezuela,* 15 vols. (Caracas: Tipografía El Cojo, 1909), vol. 2, 329–32; and Mary B. Floyd, *Guzmán Blanco: la dinámica de la política del Septenio* (Caracas: Instituto Autónomo Biblioteca Nacional and FUNRES, 1988). Other laws that were enacted include the manumission law of 1830, the abolition of the *alcabala* tax (*alcabala de tierra*) on goods for internal consumption (1831), the elimination of all export duties (*alcabala de mar*) on cotton, indigo, and coffee, and the reduction of duties for hides and cattle. Planters welcomed

these measures, which were followed by the abolition of church tithe in 1833 and the abolition of the tobacco monopoly (*estanco*) in 1833. Fundación Polar, *Diccionario de historia de Venezuela* (Caracas: Editorial Ex-Libris, 1992), s.v. "Páez, José Antonio, Gobiernos de" and "alcabala"; Watters, *History of the Church*, 146.

15. However, by 1839, a board was created to censor criticism against the government. See Pino Iturrieta, *Las ideas*, 55.

16. Decree of September 6, 1813. Sociedad Bolivariana de Venezuela, *Decretos del Libertador 1828–1830*, 3 vols. (Caracas: Imprenta Nacional, 1961), 1:12.

17. Tulio Chiossone, *Formación jurídica de Venezuela en la colonia y en la república* (Caracas: Universidad Central de Venezuela, 1980) 149; *Decretos del Libertador*, 1:283.

18. These include cases of theft, bodily harm, cutting and wounding, murder, and poisoning. All the victims and people accused of these crimes belonged to the lower classes. In the cases of theft, however, four out of seven plaintiffs belonged to the upper classes.

19. "Sobre averiguar los autores y cómplices en el asesinato perpetrado en la persona del extranjero Miguel Muñoz, la noche del 19 de enero del presente año," ARPDF, Civiles, 1835, Letra H, exp. 7.

20. "Sobre averiguar los autores," fol. 350r.

21. Lee Michael Penyak observed a similar pattern for Mexico City in his study of criminal sexuality between 1750 and 1850. Specifically, he finds that men and women accused of adultery received comparable sentences See Penyak, "Criminal Sexuality in Central Mexico, 1750–1850," PhD dissertation, University of Connecticut, 1993, 144–47.

22. "Testimonio de la sentencia," fl. 5.

23. Pino Iturrieta, *Las ideas*, 17.

24. See the excellent collection published by the Presidencia de la República, *Pensamiento político venezolano del siglo XIX* (Caracas: Ediciones Conmemorativas del Sesquicentenario de la Independencia, 1960).

25. Pino Iturrieta, *Las ideas*, 62–63; Presidencia de la República [Venezuela], *Pensamiento político*, vol. 4.

26. Nancy Levit, *The Gender Line: Men, Women and the Law* (New York: New York University Press, 1998), 54–57.

27. Due to José María Vargas's resignation as president in April 24, 1836, vice president Andrés Narvarte was in charge of the government until 1837.

28. "Testimonio de la sentencia," fl. 26.

29. "Testimonio de la sentencia," 33–33v.

30. Ricardo D. Salvatore, "Death and Liberalism: Capital Punishment after the Fall of Rosas," in *Crime and Punishment in Latin America: Law and Society since Late Colonial Times*, ed. Ricardo D. Salvatore, Carlos Aguirre, and Gilbert M. Joseph (Durham, NC: Duke University Press, 2001), 333.

31. "Vicenta Ochoa pide al Jefe de las reformas que le conmute la pena de muerte a que ha sido condenada por delitos comunes" (hereinafter Vicenta Ochoa pide al jefe), AGN, Secretaría del Interior y Justicia, Tomo CVII, fl. 146v.

32. Joaquín Escriche, *Diccionario razonado de Legislación civil, penal, comercial y forense* (Caracas: Valentín Espinal, 1840), s.v. "madre de familia" and "padre de familia."

33. Pino Iturrieta, *Las ideas*, 27.

34. "Vicenta Ochoa y las garantías constitucionales," ARPDF, Letra O, Exp. 3, fl. 26.

35. "Conmutación de la pena de muerte impuesta a Vicenta Ochoa, en la de seis años de confinación en la Isla de Margarita" (hereinafter "Conmutación de la pena"), Archivo General de la Nación, Secretaría del Interior y Justicia, Tomo CXXXIII, 1836, fl. 146.

36. "Conmutación de la pena," fls. 146–47.

37. Chiossone, *Formación jurídica*, 174.

38. In 1848, the execution of Camila O'Gorman and her priest lover when she was allegedly eight months pregnant also produced much political discussion in Argentina. According to Donald Fithian Stevens, the executions "were meant to warn others not to keep secrets from him [dictator Juan Manuel de Rosas], not to doubt patriarchal authority, and not to accept passion as an acceptable guide to choosing a mate." See Donald Fithian Stevens, "Passion and Patriarchy in Nineteenth Century Argentine: María Luisa Bemberg's 'Camila,'" in *Based on a True Story: Latin American History at the Movies*, ed. Donald Fithian Stevens (Wilmington, DE: Scholarly Resources, 1998), 98.

39. "Vicenta Ochoa pide al Jefe," fl. 105.

40. "Vicenta Ochoa pide al jefe," fl. 106.

41. *Diccionario de Historia*, s.v. "revolución de las reformas."

42. "Vicenta Ochoa pide al jefe," fl. 107.

43. Stephanie Brown, "The Princess of Monaco's Hair: The Revolutionary Tribunal and the Pregnancy Plea," *Journal of Family History* 23, no. 2 (April 1998). *Diccionario de Legislación*, s.v. "muerte."

44. "Conmutación de la pena," fl. 140.

45. "Conmutación de la pena," fl. 140.

46. It is important to note that most of the women who signed the letter included their husbands' last names to acknowledge their married status. Since this was an upper-class convention, it can be surmised that these women belonged to or identified themselves with that group of people.

47. "Conmutación de la pena," fl. 142v. The words *humano* and *filantrópico* were written in larger letters in the original.

48. "Conmutación de la pena," fls. 111–60; "Vicenta Ochoa pide al jefe," fls. 105–7.

49. "Conmutación de la pena," fl. 144v.

50. See Asunción Lavrin, *Women, Feminism and Social Change in Argentina, Chile and Uruguay, 1890–1940* (Lincoln: Nebraska University Press, 1995), 5.

51. For a discussion of how the emphasis on motherhood undermined a redefinition of women's social role, see, for example, Susan K. Besse, *Restructuring Patriarchy: The Modernization of Gender Inequality in Brazil, 1914–1940* (Chapel Hill: University of North Carolina Press, 1996), 109, and Lavrin, *Women, Feminism and Social Change*.

2

Madame Durocher's Performance: Cross-Dressing, Midwifery, and Authority in Nineteenth-Century Rio de Janeiro, Brazil

Erica M. Windler

IN 1916, BRAZIL'S ACADEMY OF MEDICINE CELEBRATED the life and career of Maria Josephina Durocher by holding a conference commemorating the centennial of her arrival in Rio de Janeiro. Madame Durocher, as she would come to be known, was a French immigrant who practiced midwifery in the city between 1834 and 1893. The official *parteira* (midwife) for the imperial family, Durocher was the first woman to be inducted into Brazil's Academy of Medicine in 1861 (an event that would not be repeated for another five decades). Her devotion to providing charitable assistance to the free poor brought Durocher respect from the city's popular classes. Madame Durocher also published extensively in the major medical journals of the period. Her writings focused on issues ranging from obstetrics to abolition.[1]

Physicians who attended the 1916 conference in honor of Durocher spoke at length about the midwife's career. However, they did not limit their comments to Durocher's professional accomplishments. They also remarked on her role as *homen-mulher*, or man-woman. In doing so, they placed her within a tradition of *figuras* or public characters in nineteenth-century Rio, characters who embodied the influence of Enlightenment practices that celebrated the individual or individuality by embracing the eccentric. From their words, it is clear that they considered Durocher to be more than a quirky and beloved character. In his testimonial to the homen-mulher, Dr. Alfredo Nascimento, who practiced alongside Durocher during the final years of her career, recounted,

> Durocher was a public character in this city for more than a half a century, well known among us all. At first sight, one could not know to which sex this origi-

nal personality belonged. From physical attributes and dress, she was a poorly defined mixture of man and woman. Tall, muscular, speaking in gruff tones, hair cut short like a man, a hairy upper lip. . . . She dressed in a black skirt, with which she wore men's boots on her large feet, a pocket watch, a tie, an overcoat and a large black umbrella.[2]

Nascimento's words highlight two important elements of Durocher's significance for the study of gender, sexuality, and power in nineteenth-century Brazil: her public persona embodied in her identity as homen-mulher, and her manipulation of masculine and feminine attributes to claim authority as a midwife during a period in which women were not welcomed into the medical profession.

Durocher lived during a time of unprecedented change in Rio de Janeiro. She witnessed rapid urbanization, attempts to transform the port into a "modern" and "civilized" urban center, the gradual abolition of slavery, Brazil's transition from monarchy to republic, and the social tensions that resulted from these transformations. Durocher's life span similarly encompassed intense transformations in the field of women's health. It was a time when traditional gender roles associated with childbirth and obstetrics were being contested and redefined, as male physicians attempted to establish their authority in an area that had traditionally been the domain of free-poor and slave women who worked as midwives. This chapter explores how Madame Durocher embodied these broader societal transitions through her cross-gendered persona as homen-mulher and through her expression of a complex gendered authority that enabled her to win the trust and confidence of her female patients as well as the respect of her male colleagues in the medical profession.

To suggest that Madame Durocher's role as homen-mulher was a performance has implications for the understanding of both sex and gender. Gender is now commonly understood to mean the fluid or culturally constructed roles linked to the masculine or feminine, while sex has more often been associated with the natural or biological and bodily state of being male or female, a state that is static or fixed, regardless of time or place. However, envisioning gender as performance, as I do here, has important consequences for our understanding of both gender and sexuality. Here, I consider gender to be constituted through the constant repetition of bodily gestures and movements and through the shaping of the body in ways that come to be defined by both the individual and society as either male or female (examples that come to mind include the flipping of a woman's hair or a man's flexing of a muscle). By defining gender as a performance located on the body and acted out through the body, sex and gender become more closely intertwined, allowing us to consider how both categories are shaped within different contexts. Through the constant repetition of mundane gestures, gender is given what Judith Butler refers to as the "appearance of substance." As it comes to be accepted as natural, the scripted nature of such acts is overlooked. Butler states, "if the ground of gender identity is the stylized repetition of acts through time, and not the seemingly seamless identity, then possibilities of gender transformation are to be found in the arbitrary relation, in the possibility of a different sort of repeating in the breaking or subversive repetition of that style."[3]

As homen-mulher, Durocher represented a different sort of repeating. She was an individual who encompassed elements of what her society defined as both male and female; as Nascimento noted, "one could not know to which sex this original personality belonged." She was a woman, but one who wore boots and a tie, who expressed her masculinity through her body, "tall and muscular," who spoke in gruff tones and had a hairy upper lip and large feet like a man. In this chapter, I assert that being identified as both masculine and feminine enabled Durocher to assert her influence in two often disparate worlds: the homes of her patients and the halls of the academy. In the pages that follow, we explore how her position between these two spheres simultaneously contested the norms of her society while, perhaps unexpectedly, contributing to the fortification of its social hierarchies.

"One is not born, but rather becomes, a woman":[4] Durocher's Early Years

In Paris in January 1809, Anne Nicolli Colette Durocher gave birth to an illegitimate daughter, Maria Josephina Durocher.[5] In 1816, the single mother and her daughter departed France for Rio de Janeiro. After the long transatlantic journey, their new-found home probably astonished them. The city's tropical climate and its slave and racially mixed population would have stood in stark contrast to those of their homeland. The intense transformations that were occurring during their early years in the capital also likely made an impression on the mother and her young daughter. In 1808, the entire Portuguese court and several thousand of its followers, fleeing the Napoleonic invasion with the help of the British, had left Lisbon for Brazil, establishing Rio de Janeiro as the new imperial capital. This transmigration and the subsequent opening of Brazil's ports to free trade brought thousands to Rio. Slaves were brought from Africa in greater numbers, and the city quickly became the largest urban slave center in the nineteenth-century world. Free migrants came from Europe and, to a lesser extent, the United States. Rio's population swelled over the course of the century. In 1799, it had a mere forty-three thousand inhabitants; by 1889 that number had reached nearly four hundred thousand. In 1822, Brazil achieved its independence, and Rio de Janeiro became the economic, political, and intellectual center of the nation. When Durocher and her mother arrived in Rio, they found a city that was undergoing the growing pains of these transitions.[6]

Members of Rio's expanding French immigrant community offered friendship and support to the mother and daughter as they adjusted to life in the tropical port. Most French immigrants to Brazil arrived in search of economic opportunities following the conclusion of the Napoleonic wars. Anne Nicolli opened a shop specializing in French imports on the Rua dos Ouvires in the newly fashionable area of downtown Rio. As an adult, Durocher would speak fondly of her childhood years, emphasizing the strong role her mother had played in her rearing and education. As a single mother, Anne Nicolli made constant sacrifices to ensure that her daughter received exemplary instruction in languages, history, and math. Such an education would have been rare for a female child of the period. Most elite and middle-class girls received limited instruction in reading and writing. Their education typically emphasized religious practices and the domestic skills needed to be good wives and mothers.[7] As an adolescent, Durocher temporarily ended her formal schooling and worked as a cashier in her mother's store. In 1828, Anne Nicolli took ill, and, at the age of nineteen, young Durocher was placed in the city's Recolhimento, an orphanage and depository for women in the city run by the Santa Casa de Misericórdia,[8] a powerful religious lay brotherhood with chapters throughout Brazil and the Portuguese Empire. The brotherhood was responsible for providing assistance to the impoverished and infirm and to widows, orphans, and prisoners in need of defense. In Rio, the Misericórdia directed the city's charity hospital and cemeteries, as well as its insane asylum, the foundling home, and the Recolhimento.

Durocher remained in the Recolhimento for nearly a year. During her time there, she likely witnessed the comings and goings of the city's medical community and the dire state of health conditions in the city. The Recolhimento was on Santa Luzia Beach beside the Castello Hill in downtown Rio, directly beside the Misericórdia's charity hospital. Beginning in 1813, the hospital served as a teaching facility for students from Rio's medical school who offered care to the city's slave and free-poor population.[9] It is possible that Durocher's proximity to this environment during her time at the Recolhimento ultimately led to her dedication to health care and assisting the needy.

After leaving the Recolhimento, Durocher experienced numerous life-changing tragedies. Her mother died in 1829, and the young woman took over the import business. Between 1830 and 1831, Durocher had two sons with her lover, the French merchant Pedro David. However, David only legally recognized his paternity of the second child. The first son remained illegitimate throughout his life. In 1832, an assailant murdered Pedro David, Durocher's common-law husband, in front of the couple's home, leaving her alone with two small children. His death marked a turning point in Durocher's life. Confronted with the struggles of being a single mother at the age of twenty-four and the failure of her business, she had to make a decision that would enable her to provide security for her family. She closed the store and turned to Dr. Xavier, a member of Rio's French immigrant community and a longtime family friend. At his insistence, Durocher entered medical school in 1833 to begin a special program that had been created for training in obstetrics and midwifery.

Midwifery and Medicine in the Growing Capital

After finishing her certification in 1834, Durocher became the medical school's first woman trained in obstetrics. While a woman training in medical school was unusual, a woman attending births was not. During the early nineteenth century, a few women had come to Rio from Paris who held French certification in midwifery.[10] However, these women served only a small circle of elite patients. The majority of births in nineteenth-century Brazil were attended by slave women (particularly on plantations) or members of the free poor. In the city, a midwife's residence could be identified by a cross painted over the door. These women developed their skills by witnessing childbirths over the course of their lives and through the passing on of skills and traditions from one generation to the next. They learned remedies for inducing labor, techniques including the application of animal fats and oils to help ease the baby out of its mother, and the practices of giving *cachaça* (cane alcohol) and special soups to reduce birthing pains and give their patients needed energy. The midwives also learned how to use appropriate religious relics and ornaments to ensure a safe and tranquil birth for both mother and child.[11]

The midwives' experiences and knowledge included far more than just attending to women in labor. After a child was born, the midwife often gave advice to new mothers regarding how to care for their infants. Midwives were entrusted with the very private aspects of their patients' lives. In cases of unwanted pregnancies, they gave remedies to bring on miscarriages and even performed abortions.[12] When a woman needed to abandon an infant, it was typically the midwife who delivered the baby to the city's foundling wheel, or *roda*, a large rotating wooden cylinder with an opening on one side that was lodged in the window sill of the city's orphanage. The child to be abandoned was placed in the wheel. The parent or midwife would then rotate the wheel so that the infant faced the inside of the institution. Between 1730 and 1889, more than thirty-five thousand babies were left in Rio de Janeiro's foundling wheel alone. The mechanism provided anonymity. However, to ensure that the parents' identity was not disclosed, mothers often requested that their midwives take the baby to the wheel.[13]

In cases where a young woman's virginity was in question, public authorities also called upon the midwife to determine if she had been "deflowered."[14] All of these responsibilities placed a great deal of power regarding family life and honor in the hands of the midwife. However, over the course of the nineteenth century, as in other parts of the world, in Brazil the official medical community came to view midwives as competitors, as male doctors were working to establish respect and confidence among women in the communities with which they worked.

At the time Durocher began practicing midwifery, Rio de Janeiro's medical community was still in its early stages of development. Prior to the arrival of the Portuguese court in 1808, the city had no printing press or institutions of higher learning. In 1809, Rio de Janeiro's School of Anatomy, Surgery, and Medicine was established. In 1832, the institution underwent state-mandated reforms inspired by French models. The new Faculty of Medicine incorporated three courses, or programs, in general medicine, pharmaceutics, and obstetrics.

European and U.S. practices greatly influenced Brazilian doctors in the country's nascent medical community. Following the lead of physicians in these regions, Brazilian practitioners began to assert the establishment of their authority over female and family-health issues to affirm their own legitimacy and, they argued, to promote the advancement of Brazil as a modern and civilized nation. This is demonstrated by the above-mentioned creation of a specialization in obstetrics at the Faculty of Medicine in 1832. The importance doctors placed on women's health can be linked to nationalistic Enlightenment ideals regarding the mother's central role in raising a society's children, its future citizens.[15] During the first decades of the nineteenth century, doctors in the United States and Europe published numerous treatises on women's health and began to develop surgical techniques for feminine disorders. It should not be surprising that by the mid-1800s, Brazilian doctors and medical students followed suit. Students wrote theses on issues including the selection of wet nurses, the foundling home, abortion, female masturbation, and menstruation. Doctors also began publishing guides on childcare aimed at educating mothers on proper practices.[16]

Central to the success of the official medical community's goal of transforming female health practices was the male doctors' ability to gain the confidence and support of the female population, which was not an easy task. Many Brazilian women (and their husbands) distrusted male doctors when it came to such private issues as childbirth and the examination of the genital area, which many may have perceived as a threat to family honor.[17] Traditional practices of using female midwives were hard to break, due to the confidence or trust that women placed in their *parteiras*. Women seeking abortions or purgatives may have feared that male doctors would report them to the authorities.[18] The difficulties male practitioners confronted in gaining the acceptance of female patients is evidenced by the fact that, at the time of Brazil's 1872 census, there were still only 50 men listed as practicing midwifery in comparison to 1,147 women.[19] This figure may also reflect men's initial reluctance to embrace a profession that had traditionally been associated with poor women.

Faced with the difficulties of gaining the trust of female patients and transforming obstetrics into an arena of "official" medicine, the medical communities in Rio de Janeiro and other urban centers in Brazil began to attack the practices of those women, whom they referred to as charlatans or ignorant *comadres* (a term that signified both "godmother" and "midwife" and that held negative connotations, suggesting the antiquated and uneducated character of the women). In his text on the medical care of infants and children published in 1860, Americo Hypolito stated, "The abandonment and neglect of doctors made it so that this important part of medical practice was left subject to the damages of certain *matrons and midwives.*"[20] Although Hypolito shames the medical community for not taking an earlier interest in the health of infants, his disapproving stance regarding the "matrons and midwives" and the damages they caused is clear. Doctors like Hypolito claimed that such midwives were illiterate and often prostitutes whose backward practices brought about the unnecessary illnesses and deaths of infants and mothers. Such tragedies, they claimed, could have been avoided with the modern techniques of trained physicians.[21]

The medical community's attacks on the traditional midwives should be understood as a lens through which to view the larger social tensions of the time rather than a simple commentary on doctors' beliefs regarding the incapacity of midwives. As Rio de Janeiro grew during the nineteenth century, perceptions of the poor were altered. Once a tolerated, if not accepted, part of society, by the mid-nineteenth century, the poor were being labeled as the *clases perigosas*, or dangerous classes.[22] Elites and the state not only blamed the popular classes for their own condition of poverty but also for the increasing problems of crime and disease in the urban center. These class tensions were compounded by fears of the abolition of slavery looming in the distance. Abolition did not occur in Brazil until 1888. However, with the effective termination of the slave trade in 1850, complete manumission was understood to be inevitable. As a result of the city's chaotic urbanization and its gradual transition from a slave- to a wage-labor economy, those in power feared a disruption of traditional social hierarchies and searched for ways to maintain order. Midwives, who were typically members of the free-poor and slave community, held what came to be seen as a threatening degree of power within the Brazilian family and society. Furthermore, they were often single women on their own, who represented a break with the norms of the patriarchal society that held the traditional family to be the building block of an orderly nation.[23] The attacks of the reform and medical community on the midwives' practices can be interpreted as a part of broader attempts to fortify race, class, and gender hierarchies at a time of uncomfortable transition, a time when such shared understandings that underpinned the social order seemed to be breaking down.

Authority in Performance:
Durocher as Homen-Mulher, Madame, and Midwife

In the midst of this struggle over the territory of women's health, we find Madame Durocher, neither a typical female midwife nor one of the city's many newly trained medical doctors. Yet, it was precisely her position on the margins between these two communities that enabled Durocher's success. Blending qualities associated with the usually opposed categories of traditional/modern, male/female, and foreign/native, Durocher was able to gain the trust of female patients while legitimizing herself in the eyes of the official medical community. As homen-mulher, Madame Durocher performed an identity that can be understood as a contestation or combination of these usually binary roles. The choices she made in the construction of her identity exaggerate and therefore accentuate how she and her society defined normative characteristics. Here I will consider how the many facets of Madame Durocher's persona were interwoven in a performance that at once allowed for her authority and highlighted her own and her society's perceptions of gender, race, and class hierarchies.

In the introduction to this chapter, we gained insights on how Durocher was perceived by members of the medical community as expressed in the words of Alfredo Nascimento. Although Nascimento recognized Durocher as a woman, he emphasized the aspects of her appearance that were masculine, perhaps out of a desire to accentuate her eccentricity or perhaps due to his perception that it was those masculine traits that gave Durocher the celebrated position within the medical community that was being honored at the 1916 centennial conference. However, his description leaves us wondering how Madame Durocher viewed herself.

That Durocher saw her appearance as an important part of her identity is confirmed by a speech that she gave to the Imperial Academy of Medicine in

1871, in which attire was a central theme. In this speech, Durocher describes the life events that led her to choose the profession of midwifery, her practices, and her decisions regarding attire:

> As the first trained Brazilian midwife, impressionable as one is at twenty-four, I decided that I was authorized, or better stated, obliged to serve as a model for those who would come after me. I adopted clothing that would not only be most comfortable, but that was also decent and characteristic of what a *parteira* should be. I determined that my exterior should inspire proper morals in my female patients, giving them confidence and distinguishing the midwife from common women; and I was not mistaken, for over the years many of my patients confessed that my dress alone gave them faith . . . the tendency that women have to dress in frivolous clothing is prejudicial to their health, taking away the courage to confront the challenges of work in the clinic.[24]

Durocher emphasizes that her decision to dress in masculine attire was a choice made for practical reasons. It was clothing that allowed her to do her job more easily. However, her words suggest more than practicality. She describes herself against the backdrop of other women, "common women," whose frivolous nature prevents them from being respected as midwives. It would seem that Durocher envisioned her manly appearance as giving her authority. In effect, by making such statements, she equates masculinity with power and legitimacy in the field of medicine.

The contrast between Durocher's discussion of her choices regarding her attire and the description provided by Nascimento quoted at the beginning of this essay are striking. Although Durocher must have been aware that she was referred to as homen-mulher, she does not emphasize that she sees herself as manly. Instead, she describes her choices regarding appearance as based on a rationality that she equates with masculinity. Her performance of gender was likely one that seemed natural for her, as natural and normal as the performance of any man or woman. For Nascimento, however, little seemed normal in the appearance or persona of Madame Durocher. While he accepted that she was a woman, he underscored her masculine physique and demeanor. It is possible that Durocher envisioned herself as feminine, as a woman making necessary choices, while the male physicians and her community chose to emphasize her masculine attire as an expression of their belief that to have authority in the field of medicine, one needed to be a man. Such a contrast highlights the ways in which gender performance is not an act of the individual but rather a negotiation between the individual and his or her society. It is the product of both a person's actions and the way that those actions are understood or interpreted by the surrounding community.

Durocher's use of attire brings into question how the term *cross-dressing* is defined. The documentation on Durocher's life does not suggest that she wished to become a man or manly in a sexual sense, other than the fact that she wished to express a degree of modesty that she interpreted as masculine by defining it against the behavior or appearance of "common women."[25] By attempting to pass as a man, Durocher might have helped herself gain fuller acceptance and respect from the male-dominated medical community. But in practicing midwifery in nineteenth-century Rio, being a woman seems to have been essential in attaining the confidence of patients. Durocher's cross-dressing was a reflection of her gendered performance and her persona that incorporated markers of both male and female identity. Whether it was a conscious decision or not, her adopting the role of homen-mulher aided Durocher in negotiating a position of prominence in the community. Furthermore, by encompassing both the masculine and feminine, Durocher's persona was representative of the transitions obstetrics was undergoing during her lifetime as it moved from a field dominated by women to one overseen by men.

That Durocher saw her appearance as an important part of her identity as midwife is further confirmed in the 1871 speech, when she speaks of a young woman of ancient Greece who had disguised herself as a man in order to attend classes in surgery. After passing the coursework, the young woman began practicing medicine and developed an enormous clientele. However, after a short time, the young doctor was accused of seducing the married women whom she served. Upon disclosing her true identity as a woman to officials, she was absolved of the charges, and the society began to accept the idea of female practitioners. Durocher cites this as the beginning of the centuries-long tradition of midwifery, a practice she claimed fell quickly into the hands of untrained women and became the domain of charlatans.

Durocher's discussion of the woman from ancient Greece might appear to be a simple explanation of the history behind the development of midwifery, from her perspective. The Western medical community commonly traced its traditions back to ancient Greece, an example being the Hippocratic oath. However, if we give the story Durocher told further consideration, it seems plausible that she selected the tale because it held another message, a message about her own identity. Like Durocher, the woman from ancient Greece lived in a society where education and legitimacy were associated with the masculine, while ultimately it was her identity as a woman that allowed her to gain the confidence of her patients.

Durocher was not solely defined by her performance of gender; other elements of her identity, including race, nationality, and class, were interwoven with her status as homen-mulher to shape the way she was perceived and contributed to her successes. Her French heritage, much like her role as homen-mulher, placed the midwife outside of the norm and in a position of privilege. Although ideas of white racial superiority were commonly accepted in nineteenth-century Brazil, whiteness alone was not enough to aid

Durocher in her achievements. In the 1800s, many of Rio's midwives were Portuguese immigrants, a factor that did not give them credibility in the eyes of the city's surgeons or protect them from attacks. The targeting of Portuguese midwives as charlatans, as common and ignorant as other, non-Portuguese midwives, was a reflection of anti-Luso sentiments of the time. To be French, however, was understood by both the medical community and *carioca*, or Rio de Janeiro, society as a marker of civilization and advancement. The medical school and hospitals, particularly in Rio, held French developments in medicine as the standard to be attained or imitated.[26]

Elites may have interpreted Durocher's French background as "civilized" or "modern." However, being French also had negative sexual connotations. In nineteenth-century Rio de Janeiro, single French women were commonly associated with upscale prostitution. The term *francesa* was often used interchangeably with the word for prostitute.[27] This may have contributed to Durocher's attempts to adopt a "modest" and masculine identity. Her desire to distance herself from the perceived "promiscuous" sexual nature of "common women" might have been intensified by her status as a single mother of an illegitimate child. Her education and place as a member of Rio de Janeiro's growing middle sector would have also worked to distance Durocher from the women she viewed as ignorant and immoral.

Despite the cachet of French medical practices, upon entering the Faculty of Medicine in 1833, Durocher became a naturalized citizen of Brazil. In an article entitled "Deve o não haver parteiras?" ("Should there or should there not be midwives?"), Durocher describes her reasons for becoming a citizen of Brazil. She states, "Enthusiastic as one is at twenty-four at the prospect of planning a new life, I understood that in gratitude to the nation, cradle of the second phase of my childhood, as the first female student to enroll in the faculty of medicine in Rio de Janeiro, I should be Brazilian."

Although she became a Brazilian citizen, Durocher could not (and perhaps did not wish to) escape her French identity. This is made clear by the fact that she was referred to throughout her career by the French title "Madame." Having come to Rio as a small child, Durocher's memories of, and associations with, France would have been few. It is therefore likely that Durocher chose to maintain this aspect of her identity because she and those who surrounded her interpreted her French background as a marker of status and sophistication. Much as she performed gender, Durocher performed nationality as a pastiche.

Authority in Text: The Writings of Madame Durocher

Madame Durocher's publications provide further insights into her role in Rio de Janeiro's medical community and her identity as *homen-mulher*.

While being a woman may have assisted Durocher in her practice, her writings primarily reflect the positions of the male-dominated medical community to which she officially belonged. This can be interpreted as a statement about Durocher's own assumptions equating (medical) authority with masculinity.

In similar tone to the writings of her male counterparts in the Academy of Medicine, Durocher's texts give little sympathy to the traditions of the slave and free-poor women who had long practiced midwifery in Brazil. She states,

> Indigenous, Portuguese, and black elderly women monopolized the practice of midwifery. . . . They were named *comadres*. They were completely illiterate, pertaining to the lowest class of society, the majority of them ex-prostitutes. . . . They performed abortions, committed infanticide and abandoned newborns on the streets. . . . Also, many ladies preferred to have their slaves assist them in childbirth, particularly on plantations. In this state of things, you can well see how the frequency of all types of disasters occurred, while the honor of families was far from guaranteed.[28]

By underscoring what she perceived to be the traditional midwives' inferior qualities, Durocher accentuates her own status as educated, French, middle-class, and sexually modest, characteristics that she felt placed her above the common midwife and gave her authority and legitimacy in her society and among her peers at the medical academy. From her perspective, the traditional midwives' gender, race, class, and morality combined to reinforce their inappropriateness for the profession and placed the honor of Brazilian families in jeopardy. That the midwives were women was not enough to protect the virtue of their patients.

In her series of articles "Deve ou não haver parteiras?" Durocher further criticizes the tradition of using untrained midwives in Brazil. Referring specifically to one incident involving the certification of a deflowerment that she witnessed during her first year of practice, she states,

> I cannot resist relating what happened to me in 1834, my first year working as a clinician. At the request of the *Juiz de Paz* [justice of the peace] I went to the Rua dos Ciganos to verify if a deflowerment had occurred. The night before, I did my best to review my books on legal medicine. After arriving at the home, a *comadre* appeared, and with an air of importance she showed me an egg, saying "here I have the teller of truth." I asked her what she intended to do with this egg. She responded, "Ah, you have studied and you don't know!!!—if the egg enters she is no longer a virgin, and if it doesn't, her honor is still intact." I was advised by the justice who was present to ignore the comments of the *comadre* and proceed with the exam. After I had finished, the *comadre* could not resist coming to me and stating "good that you didn't use the egg, for now I can have it for dinner."[29]

Durocher's story about the comadre and the egg is one of many incidents that she cites to illustrate her perceptions of midwives as ignorant and provincial. In much the same tone as her male colleagues, she discredits the women for their lack of "training" and knowledge, arguing that without an education, they could not be considered capable of performing the tasks required of them. To make her point, Durocher comically contrasts her own reliance on "modern" and "civilized" techniques that stem from the study of texts on legal medicine to the "ignorant" comadre's use of something so "backwards" and "traditional" as an egg that could just as easily be cooked for dinner.

Despite her repeated condemnation of the comadres, Durocher did not entirely envision midwifery as a profession suited for male doctors. Instead, she called for strict training programs for women wishing to practice. She argued that although registration of midwives had been required by law since the early nineteenth century (shortly after the arrival of the Portuguese court), enforcement was rare, and standards of literacy and training were typically overlooked. Durocher outlined a two-year training and examination process at the Faculdade da Medicina as the solution to these problems. While this program would leave midwifery in the hands of women, it placed regulation firmly under the supervision of the medical community, which was seeking to gain authority in the field. This plan would also have eliminated the majority of women who were practicing, since their humble origins would have left them without the education required to attend classes. From her comments, we might conclude that Durocher's criticisms of midwifery were not entirely based on the gender of the midwives but were instead heavily influenced by fears regarding the power held by those in a position of inferior social status, a potential threat to the fortification of social hierarchies and order in Carioca society.

The majority of Durocher's writings focused on midwifery and women's health. However, in 1871, just before the passing of the Lei do Ventre Livre, or Free Womb Law, which freed all children born to slave mothers, she presented her ideas regarding the emancipation of slaves in Brazil to the National Assembly.[30] The text highlights her beliefs regarding the role of the state within the sphere of the home and the necessity of its intervention for the progress and modernization of the nation, a theme that reverberates throughout all of her works.

In her publication on abolition, Durocher denounces slavery in a fashion similar to abolitionists of the time, stating that the institution was not only immoral and should have been demolished at the time of Brazil's independence, but that it was a "sore or wound (*cancro*) that tied the nation to its colonial past, retarding its chances for progress and development." Despite these strong words, Durocher did not envision complete and immediate abolition of slavery in 1871 as an appropriate step for Brazil. She feared that by allowing slaves to go free, a disorderly society, haunted by the slave population's vengeance on its former masters, would emerge.

Instead, Durocher envisioned a gradual process of emancipation where state institutions (including medical doctors) would play an interventionist role in establishing order and promoting the transformations necessary in the slave-master relationship for the successful transition from a slave- to a wage-labor economy. Durocher laid out a somewhat detailed blueprint for how this program would function. Laws regarding the limits of a master's power over slaves would have to be established, including appropriate work hours, food allowances, and monitoring of punishment. The physician's role would be one of monitoring the treatment slaves received. The slaves would also be monitored by a tutor appointed by the justice of orphans to oversee the behavior of both children and adults.[31] This tutor would assist the slave in learning what it meant to be a productive and orderly free member of society. Abolition, in Durocher's plan, would then be achieved through philanthropic donations to a lottery fund that would gradually pay masters to manumit slaves, beginning with those who would make the most productive and orderly members of society—in her estimation, the first to be freed should have been women, children, and those who were married men.

Durocher's text on emancipation would have placed authority over the master-slave relationship, once a matter of private domain, in the hands of Brazil's government and its institutions.[32] Despite her faith in the state, she did not refrain from criticizing the organization of the current government. She pointed out reforms that she deemed necessary not only for the successful transition to wage labor but also for the advancement of Brazil as a modern nation. Durocher pointed to the legislature's clientalistic practices of wasting time with the "banal petitions of people desiring exemptions and favors." In her eyes, if her fatherland were to achieve modernity, increased power would have to be placed in the hands of its institutions, moving away from the centralized, paternalistic, and awkward organization of power as it existed under the monarchy.

Durocher's text reflects more than her position on the subject of slave emancipation. That her words on a subject so distant from the world of midwifery, and on so contentious a topic, gained the attention of government representatives speaks to the authority she attained, not only within the world of male physicians but in the larger community. Her authority was made possible not only through her choice to adopt a male physical appearance but also through her acceptance of the ideas that men with authority supported.

Durocher's writings on abolition argue for the masculine and educated "modernization" that she embodied, one that she felt represented a break from the backwards world of Brazil's colonial past. The recurring theme in the midwife's texts is her unbending belief that for Brazil to progress as a nation, it would have to permit its growing professional classes the authority to shape and mold social relations ranging from childbirth to slavery. In her writings as in her life, she walked the line between the masculine and the feminine, the rich and the poor, and the "traditional" and the "modern."

In nearly every aspect of her identity, Durocher was a figure who contested the norms of her society and represented the embodiment of transition. Through her gendered performance as homen-mulher, she defied binary definitions of both gender and sex. As an educated woman in the health profession, she stood between the female midwives and the growing male medical community, representing the transformations resulting from nineteenth-century reform and modernization. She was a member of Rio de Janeiro's growing professional middle sector who broke with the society's longstanding dichotomy of elite and poor. And, as a French-born Brazilian, she stood on the ground between national identities.

As I stated in the introduction to this chapter, Durocher's performance represented a different sort of repeating. She broke from the traditionally defined scripts of her society and signified the possibility of something different, a different construction of sex and gender, in conjunction with her race, class, and nationality. However, Durocher's persona not only signified a break from the norm, it also accentuated the emerging ideals of a society in transition, ranging from manliness and the masculine nature of authority to the educated and "civilized" qualities of being French. Through a performance that was both individual and relational, Durocher highlighted the qualities desired in her society. In many ways, it was Durocher's position on the margins that made possible her exaggerated and stylized performance of such markers of the ideal and ultimately permitted her to rise to a position of authority in a profession and a society entrenched in the process of redefinition.

Notes

Numerous people have helped me with ideas on this essay at various stages. I would like to thank Tracy Alexander, Bert Barickman, Luciana Gondelman, Elizabeth Kuznesof, Susan Quinlan, and the members of my seminar on the biography in Brazil at the University of Notre Dame, Spring 2001. I would also like to thank Peter Beattie, Katherine Bliss, and William French for their extensive and helpful comments.

1. I first came across Durocher in Lycurgo Santos Filho, *História da medicina no Brasil* (São Paulo: Brasiliense, 1947), where he mentions her as a unique character in nineteenth-century Rio de Janeiro, making note of her masculine appearance. Durocher's practice is discussed in Maria Lucia de Barros Mott, "Parteiras no século XIX," in *Entre o virtude e o pecado*, ed. Albertina de Oliveira Costa and Cristina Bruschini (São Paulo: Fundação Carlos Chagas, 1992), 37–56. She is also mentioned in Julyan Peard, *Race, Place and Medicine: The Idea of the Tropics in Nineteenth-*

Century Brazilian Medicine (Durham, NC: Duke University Press, 1999). See also the entry on Maria Josephina Durocher in Ronaldo Vainfas, ed., *Dicionário do Brasil imperial (1822–1889)* (Rio de Janeiro: Objetiva, 2002), 522–23.

2. Speech by Dr. Alfredo Nascimento published in "Centenario de Madame Durocher," *Annaes da medicina do Rio de Janeiro* 82 (December–January 1916). The city of Rio has a long history of these types of public characters, or *figuras* (the exact word that Nascimento used, a word that has no exact translation into English). He gave a description of one other in particular, Dom Oba. Oba was a man of African descent who had fought in the Paraguayan War. He later went to live in Rio. Claiming to be an African prince, Oba dressed ceremoniously and attended all open ceremonies with Emperor Pedro II. He even on occasion attempted to give Pedro advice, from one royal figure to another. Dom Oba's role in the city was the subject of a detailed study: Eduardo Silva, *Prince of the People: The Life and Times of a Brazilian Free Man of Colour* (London: Verso, 1993). Dom Oba was also the theme for the Mangueira Samba School in Rio 2000. Nascimento listed numerous other figuras, including the Prince of Nature, the Philosopher of Dogs, Twenty-Nine, and the Father of the Children.

3. Judith Butler, "Performative Acts and Gender Constitution: An Essay in Phenomenology and Feminist Theory," in *Feminist Theory Reader: Local and Global Perspectives*, ed. Carole R. McCaan and Seung-Kyung Kim (London: Routledge, 2002), 415. Also, see Diane Taylor, *Disappearing Acts: Spectacles of Gender and Nationalism in Argentina's "Dirty War"* (Durham, NC: Duke University Press, 1997), 183–87.

4. Simone de Beauvoir, *The Second Sex*, trans. H. M. Parshley (New York, Vintage, 1974).

5. The identity of Durocher's father was listed as unknown on her birth certificate.

6. Brazil's ports were opened to free trade at the encouragement of the British, who had assisted the Portuguese in fleeing Napoleonic invasion. The British wished to benefit from open trade with the region. For more on this and the transmigration of the court, see Kirsten Schultz, *Tropical Versailles: Empire, Monarchy and the Portuguese Royal Court in Rio de Janeiro, 1808–1821* (London: Routledge, 2001), and Jurandir Malerba, *A corte no exílio: Civilização e poder no Brasil ás vésperas da independencia (1808–1821)* (São Paulo: Companhia das Letras, 2000).

7. For more on female education in nineteenth-century Brazil, see June Hahner, *Emancipating the Female Sex: The Struggle for Women's Rights in Brazil, 1850–1940* (Durham, NC: Duke University Press, 1990); Muriel Nazzari, *Disappearance of the Dowry: Women, Families and Social Change in São Paulo, Brazil* (Palo Alto, CA: Stanford University Press, 1991): Alessandra Frota Martinez, "Educar e instruir: A instrução popular na corte imperial, 1870–1889" (master's thesis, Universidade Federal Fluminense, 1997).

8. See entry for Maria Josephina Durocher in *Matriculas do Recolhimento da Santa Casa de Misericórdia do Rio de Janeiro, 1824–1834* (Arquivo da Santa Casa de Misericórdia do Rio de Janeiro).

9. On the Santa Casa de Misericórdia, see Laurinda Abreu, "O papel das misericórdias dos 'Lugares de Além-Mar' na formação do imperio portugues," *História, ciencias,saúde: Manguinhos* 8, no. 3 (September–December 2001): 591–611, and Luciana Gandelman, "A Santa Casa de Misericordia do Rio de Janeiro nos séculos XVIII a XIX," *História, ciencias, saúde: Manguinhos* 8, no. 3 (September–December 2001): 613–30; P. A. Almeida, "A Santa Casa de Misericordia do Rio de Janeiro," *Jornal do Comércio*, July 8, 1899.

10. See Sandra Lauderdale Graham, *The Domestic World of Servants and Masters in Nineteenth-Century Rio de Janeiro* (Cambridge: Cambridge University Press, 1988), 82. Lauderdale Graham also provides a general discussion of the role of midwives in nineteenth-century Rio. Durocher also mentions two French women, Madame Pipar and Madame Merthout. See speech from April 12, 1871, in "Centenario de Madame Durocher," *Annaes da medicina do Rio de Janeiro* 82 (1916).

11. Mary Del Priore, "O cotidiano da criança livre no Brasil entre a colonia e o império," in *História das crianças no Brasil*, ed. Mary Del Priore, 85–86 (Rio de Janeiro: Editora Contexto,

2000), and Mary Del Priore, *Ao sul do corpo: Condição feminina, maternidade e mentalidades no Brasil colonial* (Rio de Janeiro: Ed. José Olympio & Edunb, 1993).

12. On purgatives and practices of abortion in Brazil during the colonial period and nineteenth century, see Del Priore, *Ao sul do corpo,* and Joana Maria Pedro, "Aborto e infanticídio: Práticas muito antigas," in *Práticas proibidas: Práticas costumeiras de aborto e infanticídio no século XX,* ed. Joana Maria Pedro (Florianópolis: Cidade Futura, 2003), 19–58.

13. Durocher herself mentions this role of the midwife in a speech she gave on April 12, 1871, at the time of her induction into Brazil's Academy of Medicine. Speech reprinted in "Centenario de Madame Durocher," *Annaes da medicina do Rio de Janeiro* 82 (December–January 1916): 214. On the foundling wheel in nineteenth-century Brazil, see Renato Pinto Venancio, *Famílias abandonadas: Assistencia a crianças de câmaras populares no Rio de Janeiro e em Salvador—séculos XVII e XIX* (São Paulo: Papirus, 1999).

14. Although little has been written on the issue of deflowerment in nineteenth-century Brazil, there are two excellent studies on the twentieth century. See Martha de Abreu Esteves, *Meninas perdidas: Os populares e o cotidiano do amor no Rio de Janeiro da belle epoque* (Rio de Janeiro: Paz e Terra, 1989); Sueann Caulfield, *In Defense of Honor: Sexual Morality, Modernity, and Nation in Early Twentieth-Century Brazil* (Durham, NC: Duke University Press, 2000).

15. L. Santos Filho, *História geral da medicina Brasileira* (São Paulo: Hucitec, 1977). These ideals of "republican motherhood" are often linked both to the writings of Enlightenment philosophers such as Rousseau (who was very popular among reformers and medical professionals in nineteenth-century Rio) and to the building of new nations. Just a few examples from the literature that discusses this issue in greater detail within different historical contexts include Jean-Jacques Rousseau, *Emile, or On Education,* trans. Allan Bloom (New York: Basic Books, 1979); Doris Sommer, *Foundational Fictions: The National Romances of Latin America* (Berkeley: University of California Press, 1991); Christine Stansell, *City of Women: Sex and Class in New York, 1789–1860* (Champaign: University of Illinois Press, 1982). See also Jean Franco, "Sense and Sensuality: Notes on the National Period, 1812–1910," in *Plotting Women: Gender and Representation in Mexico* (New York: Columbia, 1989), 79–101.

16. Examples of these types of theses and texts are too numerous to list here. Theses can be found at the Archive of the Academia da Medicina in Rio de Janeiro. Two examples of guides for new mothers include Américo Hypólito, *O médico das crianças: Ou conselho as mães sobre a higiene e tratamento homeopático das moléstias de seus filhos* (Rio de Janeiro: s.ed. 1860), and J. B. A. Imbert, *Guia medica das mães da familia ou a infancia considerada na sua higiene, suas moléstias e tratamentos* (Rio de Janeiro: s.ed. 1843).

17. On women's distrust of male physicians, see Peard, *Race, Place and Medicine.* On the same issue in a European context, see Barbara Duden, *The Woman beneath the Skin: A Doctor's Patients in Eighteenth-Century Germany* (Cambridge: Harvard University Press, 1991).

18. In her work on late-nineteenth-century Argentina, Kristen Ruggiero has shown in that context that the authorities relied on the midwives themselves to provide information and testimonies regarding issues such as infanticide. See Kristen Ruggiero, "Honor, Maternity, and the Disciplining of Women: Infanticide in Late-Nineteenth-Century Buenos Aires," *Hispanic American Historical Review* 72, no. 3 (1992).

19. J. Silva, *Investigação sobre os recenseamentos da população geral do império e de cada província de per si tentados desde os tempos coloniais até hoje* (São Paulo: IPE/USP, 1986). Vainfas, *Dicionário do Brasil imperial (1822–1889),* 131–33, 522–23.

20. Américo Hypólito, *O medico das crianças: Ou conselho as mães sobre a higiene e tratamento homeopatico das molestias de seus filhos* (Rio de Janeiro: s.ed. 1860), 12.

21. One example is J. B. A. Imbert, *Uma palavra sobre o charlatanismo e os charlatões* (Rio de Janeiro: n.p., 1837).

22. On changing ideas of poverty in urban nineteenth-century Brazil, see Walter Fraga Filho, *Mendigos, moleques e vadios na Bahia do século XIX* (São Paulo: Editora Hucitec, 1996).

23. This issue of the power that women such as midwives and particularly wet nurses held is discussed in Sandra Lauderdale Graham, *House and Street: The Domestic World of Servants and Masters in Nineteenth-Century Rio de Janeiro* (New York: Cambridge University Press, 1988). On arguments regarding "women on their own" and the family as an order-promoting unit, see texts in Guido Ruggiero and Edward Muir, eds., *Sex and Gender in Historical Perspective* (Baltimore: Johns Hopkins University Press, 1991), and Guido Ruggiero, "Re-reading the Renaissance: Civic Morality and the World of Marriage, Love, and Sex," in *Sexuality and Gender in Early Modern Europe: Institutions, Texts, Images*, ed. James Turner (Cambridge: Cambridge University Press, 1997).

24. From the printed text of a speech she gave April 12, 1871, in "Centenario de Madame Durocher."

25. Another example of a cross-dressing woman in Latin American society is Carolina Erauso, who dressed as a man in order to participate in the Spanish Conquest. Erauso was, however, different from Durocher in the sense that she initially was mistaken for a man and was even said to have conquered women's hearts. Erauso was eventually discovered, but she ultimately received permission from the crown to dress as a man. As we see in the case of Durocher, cross-dressing gave Erauso a degree of legitimacy in a patriarchal society. See Catalina de Erauso, *Lieutenant Nun: Memoir of a Basque Transvestite in the New World*, trans. Michele and Gabriel Stepto (Boston: Beacon Press, 1996). Anne McClintock also provides ideas about the multifaceted ways in which cross-dressing can be used. She talks about dressing across classes and cultures. One primary example she uses is the dress practices of the young British character in Rudyard Kipling's novel *Kim*. See Anne M. McClintock, *Imperial Leather: Race, Gender and Sexuality in the Imperial Conquest* (New York: Routledge, 1995), particularly the chapter entitled "Imperial Leather: Race, Cross-Dressing and the Cult of Domesticity," 132–80, and the section on *Kim*, 66–71.

26. Peard's analysis of the medical community in Salvador focuses on the development of the Tropicalistas, who, unlike the physicians, attempted to develop the area of tropical medicine, asserting that Brazil was not inferior to European civilizations because of its tropical climate and disease, it was simply different and called for the development of different medical techniques than those used in Europe. Peard argues that while the Tropicalistas sought to develop different practices rather than just copying those of France and the United States, physicians in Rio were far more heavily influenced by their European counterparts. See Peard, *Race, Place and Medicine*, 109–37, for her discussion of midwifery and women's health.

27. Magali Engel, *Meretrizes e doutores: Saber médico e prostituição no Rio de Janeiro* (São Paulo: Brasiliense, 1989).

28. Maria Josephina M. Durocher, "Deve ou não haver parteiras?" *Annaes brasilienses de medicina* (Rio de Janeiro) 22, no. 9 (1871): 290.

29. Maria Josephina M. Durocher, "Deve ou não haver parteiras?" no. 10 (1871): 331.

30. Maria Josephina Mathilde Durocher, *Idéias por coordenar a respeito da emancipação* (Rio de Janeiro: Ty. de Diario do Rio de Janeiro, 1871). On the Brazilian *Lei do Ventre Livre*, or Free Womb Law, see Martha de Abreu Esteves, "Slave Mothers and Free Children: Emancipation and Female Space in the Debates on the Free Womb Law," *Journal of Latin American History* 28 (1996); Renato Pinto and Lana Lage de Gama e Lima Venancio, "Abandono de crianças negras no Rio de Janeiro," in *História da criança no Brasil*, ed. Mary Del Priore (São Paulo: Contexto, 1991).

31. The *Juiz de Orphãos*, or Justice of Orphans, was an institution developed initially by the Portuguese crown. Its initial purpose was to protect the inheritance rights of orphans and to appoint them with legal guardians. It was also responsible for placing poor orphans and aban-

doned children in homes where they could work until they reached the age of majority. The suggestion that the Justice of Orphans would be responsible for supervising adult slaves suggests that in Durocher's eyes adult slaves were initially not to be considered as full adult citizens. On the Juiz de Orphãos, see Timothy Joel Coates, "Exiles and Orphans: Forced and State Sponsored Colonizers in the Portuguese Empire" (PhD dissertation, University of Minnesota, 1993); Joan Meznar, "Orphans and the Transition from Slave to Free Labor in Northeast Brazil: The Case of Campina Grande, 1850–1888," *Journal of Social History* 27, no. 3 (1994).

32. This strengthening of institutions would represent a shift away from the norm in imperial Brazil, which placed a great deal of authority in the hands of the family, or, more specifically, elite patriarchs who ruled over their families, slaves, and often large networks of clients. It has often been argued that such a shift away from private authority occurred with the fall of the empire in 1889 and the creation of the republic. However, there are indications that such reforms were being discussed, and in some cases implemented, as early as the 1850s and 1860s. For a discussion of this issue, see Lauderdale Graham, *House and Street*, 3–4.

3

Mismeasured Women:
Gender and Social Science on the
Eve of Female Suffrage in Cuba

Alejandra Bronfman

I N 1929, A NEW BOOK ENTITLED *Female Delinquency in Cuba* (*La delincuencia fe-menina en Cuba*) presented to Cuban readers an unprecedented collection of photographs of incarcerated women. Its author, Cuban criminologist Israel Castellanos, had assembled four hundred images, from the front and in profile, of the faces of women convicted and serving their sentences in Havana's prison. In addition, he presented a series of analyses of female criminality: the frequency and type of crime, its regional concentration, and the correlation of crime with race, marital status, age, and national origin all fell under the study's broad scope. By all measures, this was a complex, labor-intensive text to assemble. It included three volumes, hundreds of pages of statistics, charts and graphs, discussions of major criminological theories, and an engagement with previous statistical analyses of Cuban criminality.[1] But it was well rewarded: Castellanos received one of the greatest honors for criminologists of his day; as the recipient of the Lombroso Prize for the best work in criminal anthropology sponsored by the Italian journal *Archives of Criminal Anthropology, Psychiatry and Legal Medicine* (*Archivio di Antropologia Criminale, Psichiatria e Medicina Legale*), Castellanos was the first author in the Americas to be so recognized.[2]

This text raises many questions, including why there was such interest in female criminals in Cuba at that moment. As in other Latin American criminologies, women had not traditionally received much attention.[3] The prolific Castellanos had already produced several studies of Cuban criminals, but he had not seemed particularly interested in women. Moreover, he and Fernando Ortiz, another prominent criminologist, had deemed what they called witchcraft, or *brujería*, to be a principally male phenomenon. Unlike other contexts in which witches were thought of as mostly female, Cuban witchcraft scares had resulted in the targeting mostly of men of African descent as the perpetrators of violence and cannibalism in the service of religious rituals. While very few of these men were actually proven guilty, the image of the male witch, or *negro brujo*, came to be widely disseminated in Cuban popular and scientific culture.[4] The new fascination with women as criminals demands some explanation. But these volumes, unusual for their relentless display of technologies of measuring and recording, also call attention to the very nature of the production of knowledge: On what basis did criminologists justify their claims? How did Castellanos "measure" female criminality? Upon closer examination of the text, however, a final question emerges: How did the contemplation of female criminals challenge the practice of criminology itself?

Historians of Latin America interested in exploring the relationships among state formation, the production of knowledge, and social control have recently focused their interests on studies of criminality and criminology. They have demonstrated the ambiguity of criminological discourse that both shapes and is changed by the society and criminals it purports to describe. Many have observed that criminological discourses are both analytical and normative, cobbling together insights from hereditary and environmental theories as they seek to explain criminality and offer prescriptions for the prevention of crime and the treatment of criminals.[5]

The introduction of gender into the historical study of criminology has yielded insights into the construction of masculinities, femininities, and sexuality. When historians have looked in particular at criminology's constructions of female criminals, they have examined the ways social science defined women, using gendered assumptions about their sexuality, responsibility for crime, natural virtue, and capacity for redemption.[6] They have also explored the ways ordinary people responded to, resisted, or redefined these discourses. Following the lead of historians who have used close readings of texts to excavate coexisting understandings of criminality, this chapter examines the text and context of *La delincuencia femenina en Cuba*, focusing in particular on Castellanos's use of statistics and photography.[7] I argue that he was more fascinated by the tools and their implementation than he was interested in the repression of criminality. In the end, however, statistics and photography proved insufficient tools, as they only revealed (for Castellanos) a bewildering array of criminal women, rather than serving to encase them into a series of well-defined categories or types.

Politics and Suffragettes

During the early 1920s, Cuban politics witnessed a period of heightened mobilization in the form of strikes, protests, and numerous oppositional publications. In the immediate aftermath of World War I, elevated sugar prices initiated the "dance of the millions," a period of unparalleled prosperity and heightened expectations. The dance was short-lived, however, as a crash in sugar prices in 1921 reminded Cubans of the fragility and danger of depending on sugar. The economic crisis gave rise to a political crisis, and by 1923, a growing number of oppositional groups began to express their discontent over continued dependence on the United States and rampant corruption. The Platt Amendment, adopted at the end of the first U.S. occupation and promising to intervene at the first sign of "instability," granted the United States, many believed, too much control over Cuban affairs. Student groups, veteran groups, and intellectuals articulated demands for nationalist reform. Gerardo Machado was elected in 1924, riding this wave of nationalist fervor, and he promised to relieve Cuba's dependence on the United States and to alleviate economic and social troubles.[8]

This was the context in which women's groups entered public debate. Women's organizations had become more visible with the founding, in 1917, of the Women's Club of Cuba (*Club Femenino de Cuba*), a group calling for social reforms, including the end of prostitution, the establishment of women's prisons, and attention to what they rather vaguely referred to as "women's rights." During the next decade, women's organizations became more visible as a result of the National Women's Congresses in 1923 and 1925, during which they initiated a series of projects and campaigns. Although they were all made up of white, middle- or upper-class women, women's groups were divided as to what kinds of policies they wanted to promote. While some thought the first priority ought to be legal and institutional reform, including the creation of women's prisons and juvenile courts, others, whom K. Lynn Stoner has identified as more conservative, were more interested in beautification of the city and contributing to charitable organizations. Their most violent disagreement was over the status of illegitimate children, as some women called for the legal recognition of all children, legitimate or not, while others were more prepared to defend traditional marriage structures and received notions of moral purity. Despite their ideological and cultural differences, one of the few issues upon which they agreed during the first congress of 1923 was the adoption of female suffrage.[9] Gaining access to the vote and to electoral politics had become, by this time, a central demand of most women's groups.

The campaign for female suffrage received a boost from political contingencies. Machado had been elected by appealing to many constituencies, even as he sought to repress others, such as labor. Once in office, he sought out traditionally marginalized groups and created new bases of mass support to counteract his alienation of organized labor. In 1925, during the Second National Women's Congress, he declared his support for female suffrage, promising that women would receive the vote during a second term, if he stayed on.[10]

Two years later, Machado convoked a constitutional assembly in order to extend his term and allow him to seek reelection. Critics, dismayed at what they perceived as a rapid transformation from liberal nationalist to autocratic dictator, raised vociferous protests. Machado, in turn, responded by both terrorizing opponents and insisting on his commitment to democracy: According to Stoner, "women's suffrage was touted as evidence that in 1934 Machado would hold elections in which all Cubans could participate."[11] Thus, as Machado drew the issue of women's suffrage into controversies about his own autocratic tendencies, it came to occupy a central place in political debate.

At the same time, women had become more publicly visible in the early 1920s as a result of a heightened campaign against prostitution. Prostitution in Cuba was not illegal during this period, but women engaged in the marketing of sex could be convicted of "public scandal" or "corruption of minors" if their activities were deemed too publicly disruptive or involved girls under eighteen years of age. For the most part, police had refrained from enforcing these regulations, while the departments of sanitation and welfare were more interested in controlling disease or "rehabilitating" prostitutes. Beginning in 1925, however, police chief R. Zayas Bazán initiated a campaign against prostitution, using the regulations against "public scandal," "moral offenses," and "lack of modesty" to arrest women throughout the city. Through electoral politics and policing, women had become objects and subjects of contention in the early 1920s.[12]

Social Science and the Cuban State

As part of his program to buttress nationalist sentiment and accelerate modernization, Machado supported and encouraged scientific and social scientific activity. In a speech delineating his ambitions for Cuba, the production of knowledge occupied a prominent role: "We must stimulate literary and scientific production. . . . Since we have received so much knowledge from the rest of the world, we must participate and reciprocate with our own contributions."[13] More specifically, he looked to those social scientific endeavors that had practical application and could be put to use as part of a particular modernizing project.

Of the social sciences, criminology enjoyed the most support from Machado's administration. Certainly part of the reason for this interest was criminology's utility in controlling and repressing political opponents. But criminology also met Machado's ambitions to propel Cuba into the community of modern nations. Criminology was one of the social sciences most engaged in developing new technologies and updating its theoretical foundations. As part of this project, he asked Fernando Ortiz, Cuba's most prominent criminologist of the day, to write a proposal to replace the penal code in use since the colonial era with one that incorporated all the newest scientific theories. Ortiz complied and created a proposal informed by the assumptions of Italian criminology and its recent shift of focus onto the criminal rather than the crime. More effective repression of crime required, according to Ortiz, thorough analysis of physical and psychological characteristics rather than (as had been previously thought) social factors. Ortiz's proposal laid out plans for the creation of new institutions in which these studies would take place. Ortiz envisioned a centralized National Committee for the Prevention and Repression of Crime (Junta Nacional de Prevención y Represión de la Delincuencia) staffed by government officials and experts whose role it would be to direct not just the repression of crime but also the acquisition of knowledge. Since the criminal was at the center of cutting-edge criminological theory, it would be necessary to study him or her carefully. A significant aspect of the proposal involved the collection and systematization of data, including statistics, measurements, and "psychological" data.[14] If Ortiz was the first to suggest these reforms in the penal system, his friend and colleague Israel Castellanos would become fully involved in their implementation as director of the evolving penal apparatus and devoted student of the delinquent body.

A Career in Crime

Israel Castellanos would eventually become the most powerful criminologist working in Cuba. In 1921 he was appointed director of the National Bureau of Identification, an institution that had been established in 1909 for the purpose of identifying criminals. By 1928 he was also director of the Laboratory of Penitentiary Anthropology created as part of Machado's project of penal reform and intended to gather, record, and analyze anthropological data from inmates. He would remain at this post, weathering the political turmoil of the 1930s (not without twice resigning after facing considerable opposition), until the end of 1958, when he was forced to flee the country as nationalist revolutionaries led by Fidel Castro brought Fulgencio Batista's regime to an end. He clearly supported and was supported by both Machado and Batista, for it was only when their power was imperiled that his faltered as well. He must have been deeply implicated in the attempts to control and repress persons deemed criminal or delinquent during these periods. His precise role and influence are difficult to gauge due to the difficulty of finding police or penitentiary records for this period. His prolific writings, however, demonstrate his lasting interest in the biological and measurable sources of criminality.[15]

At the age of seventeen, Castellanos had been introduced to the theories of Italian criminologist Césare Lombroso, which linked tendencies to criminality with biological traits. By his account, he was so taken with Lombroso's claims about discerning criminality through physiognomy that he immediately decided to dedicate his life to the study of positivist criminology. As part of this endeavor, he embarked on a series of empirical studies, somehow obtaining permission to work in jails, insane asylums, and juvenile correctional centers where, by his account, he managed to "weigh jaws, measure heads, collect photographs, study tattoos, take fingerprints and investigate every aspect of the human body."[16] His interest in criminal anthropology became a fascination with the possibility of using technology to thoroughly render and represent human bodies.

The organizing principle of Castellanos's long and variable career was an ambition, through statistics, measurements, fingerprints, and blood analyses, to map the Cuban body. Any piece of a body could be plumbed for the truths it might reveal. His efforts to create a system of racial classification, for instance, led him to the study of hair. Racial mixture, or *mestizaje,* had produced such a range of skin colors, he argued, that it had become difficult to read race (which he understood in biologically determinist terms) using only that criteria. It was necessary, therefore, to look beyond skin color to other physical characteristics that might reflect more accurately a person's racial origins. According to the recent claims of anthropologists, hair was one such physical trait: the color, thickness, and degree of curl could all be measured and "read" to reveal a person's racial origins. A study of hair, therefore, would produce the kind of certainty he sought. This became the impetus for his strange but thorough *The Hair of Cubans* (*El pelo en los Cubanos*) (1933), which includes hundreds of pages on hair classification, including diagrams, charts, and graphs.

This and other publications were well received by the Cuban, European, and Latin American scientific establishments. He was a member of scientific associations in Spain, France, Austria, Mexico, Peru, and Argentina, and he published in Spanish and Italian criminological journals. In Cuba, he became director of the journal *Vida Nueva,* to which he contributed articles on race, criminality, and degeneration, including "The Facial Muscles and Physiognomy of a Delinquent" ("Los músculos faciales y la fisonomía de un delincuente") (1916), "Witchcraft, Madness and Ancestor Worship" ("Brujería, locura y necrolatría") (1916), and "Physical Signs of Degeneration in the Races of Color" ("Los estigmas somáticos de la degeneración en las razas de color") (1927). Several of his book-length publications, including *Wizardry and Ñañiguismo in Cuba* (*La brujería y ñañiguismo en Cuba*) (1916), *The Height of Delinquents in Cuba* (*La talla de los delincuentes en Cuba*) (1926), *The Weight of Delinquents in Cuba* (*El peso corporal en los delincuentes de*

Cuba) (1927), and *The Hair of Cubans* (*El pelo en los cubanos*) (1933), received prizes from the Cuban Academy of Medical, Physical and Natural Sciences.[17] Political and professional conditions, then, proved auspicious for the study of female delinquency. The simultaneous campaigns for women's suffrage and against prostitution in 1920s Cuba lent an air of relevance to Castellanos's investigation. The state's efforts to modernize the penal establishment afforded him a distinct set of tools with which to proceed.

The Numbers

La delincuencia femenina en Cuba expresses much more interest in displaying the power of statistics and photography than it does in issuing prescriptions for repression or reform. Ironically, these technologies ultimately work against one another in the text and call into question the notion of objectivity, casting doubt on the possibility of knowing the women and bodies they scrutinize. Castellanos did not open his three-volume study of female delinquency with a discussion, or even a mention, of female delinquency. He did not invoke terrible crimes, bemoan a recent rise in evidence of criminality, or even note the absence of criminality with an invocation of female virtue. Rather, he filled the first volume with a torrent of data on female bodies, mapping, in his words, "their morphology, normal physiology and delinquent activity."[18] The second volume opens with an epistemological reflection on the history of statistics in Cuba, asking on the first page, "When did the quantification of things, persons and events concerning Cuba begin?"[19] His answer to this question is a narrative of haphazard, uneven information gathering. Castellanos laments the lack of a systematic approach to counting and classifying that characterized Cuba in both the colonial and the national periods. Without proper counting and codification, he argues, there can be no understanding of criminality.[20]

What then, did Castellanos's numbers reveal about female delinquency? According to all available data, Cuban women demonstrated very low delinquency rates when compared to both Cuban men and to women in other parts of the world. Castellanos included a number of ways to calculate female delinquency. He cited numbers asserting that between 1909 and 1913, for every five thousand inhabitants, less than 1 percent of women were sentenced. Of all the people convicted for assorted crimes in the years 1914 and 1915, women made up 1.78 percent of those sentenced in appellate courts (*Audiencias*) and 3.78 and 3.47 percent of those sentenced in criminal courts (*Correcionales*). Compared to those in Uruguay and Chile, Cuban women had much lower rates of criminality.[21] By all accounts, Cuban women retained their position as virtuous, or at least not criminal. Castellanos's position at the head of the penal establishment and the efficacy of his methods rendered him the obvious person to announce this to the world:

> This is why, when we began our work at the head of the Central Laboratory of Penitentiary Anthropology . . . we decided to dedicate our first work to female delinquency in Cuba, to prove, with all the resources of positivist and experimental science, that Cuban women are rarely delinquent, and that they commit crimes with greater rarity than in any other part of the planet.[22]

Briefly extending his domain to the political debates of the day, he suggested that such numbers provided a justification for female suffrage. Citing and clearly supporting another social scientist who believed that low levels of criminality justified granting women the vote, he articulated what could almost be called a feminist viewpoint: "Perhaps that would be the solution to many of our problems."[23]

But this incursion into politics, surprising as it is in its use of criminological discourse to advocate the extension of suffrage, is a muted aspect of the text. Furthermore, Castellanos was not particularly interested in pondering an explanation for these remarkable numbers. While he did assert that low levels of female criminality demonstrated women's well-developed moral capacity and their "immunity to the criminal virus that . . . attacks and germinates even amongst the most refined social classes," he backed away from elaborating an extended theory. After briefly invoking the conclusions of prominent French and Italian criminologists, including Césare Lombroso (women are inferior physically), Gabriel Tarde (women are superior morally), and Napoleone Colajanni (economic and social conditions are most important), he dropped the discussion and returned to his "resources of positivist and experimental science." What was needed, he argued, were more and better statistics.

In great detail, he described the nature and utility of the three types of documents he had used as sources, the *ficha dactiloscópica*, the *prontuario u hoja histórico penal*, and the *ficha inquisitiva*.[24] The *ficha dactiloscópica* recorded all inmates' fingerprints. The *hoja histórico penal* was a sheet filled with very specific biographic and physical data, including race, civil status, age, profession, level of education, and "anthropological data," including descriptions of hair, nose, ears, "complexion," and tattoos. This sheet also listed all previous infractions. Finally, the *ficha inquisitiva* included a photograph and some of the same data as the *hoja histórico penal*. Castellanos proudly argued that his was the most thorough collection of data in the Spanish-speaking world. "We believe also that this is the first work of its kind published in Spanish America, and that none of the other works of this kind, either in Europe or the Americas, has used such complete data or used better techniques for gathering exact numbers and attaining the most realistic reproduction of female delinquency in a country."[25] The documents were useful not just for their thorough accounting of criminal bodies but also for their utility as signals, to the outside world, of the accomplishments of Cuban criminology.

Despite his enthusiasm for his statistics and data-gathering enterprises, the more deeply he probed the possibilities of recording female criminality, the more he expressed doubts about the power of those methods to provide an accurate rendition of female criminality. This was especially true with regard to creating a fixed set of racial classifications. The question of race and its relationship to criminality, he argued, was unique to the Americas (and something from which Europe was happily exempt) and ought to be studied in a comparative context. It was thus the responsibility of Latin American criminologists to provide accurate information about the racial underpinnings of delinquency. But race proved elusive.

In other works, such as *La brujería y ñañiguismo en Cuba* and many articles, Castellanos had demonstrated his conviction of the connection between race and criminality. In *La delincuencia femenina en Cuba*, he introduced his arguments about the "scientific truth" of mestizaje. Resisting what he deemed North American racial puritanical tendencies, which tended to hide scientific truths by denying mestizaje and relying on a binary racial system, he insisted on including the *mestiza* (woman of mixed European and African heritage) in his racial categorizations. Moreover, the mestiza was important to his scheme because she had the highest rate of criminality: Cuban *mulatas* (Castellanos used this term interchangeably with mestiza), he argued, were the "priestesses of native love" (*sacerdotisa del amor criollo*) and so displayed the highest rates of crimes related to sexuality. Yet, attempts to classify women's bodies rendered his theories contradictory. He argued, for instance, not only that mulatas had the highest rates of criminality but that criminality increased in proportion to darkness of skin color. Both of these could not be true at the same time, because mulatas have lighter skin than people solely of African ancestry. He solved this (or made a greater mess) by arguing that the Cuban "race of color" was actually moral but that foreign blacks were not. In the end, racial determinism broke down in the face of gender stereotypes (the sexualized mulata) and national chauvinism.[26] Ultimately, the confrontation with women's bodies led to an acknowledgment of the limits of statistics and the statistical method. Although mestizaje was a scientific truth, he argued, people weren't properly trained in identification, and women who were marked as mulata showed up as "black" (*negra*) in subsequent files, or women marked as "white" (*blanca*) showed up later as mulata. The *hojas*, or statistical documents, he had to admit, weren't always reliable with regard to race.

Putting race aside and turning to female bodily functions, he again acknowledged that statistics and hojas had proved particularly limited. If pregnancy, menstruation, and menopause might explain incidences of criminality, then the statistics were inadequate, as they didn't reflect those conditions.

Castellanos's faith in numbers and their capacity to fix and demonstrate so many truths faltered with his admission of their failure to capture the entirety of female bodies. The second volume ends on an ambiguous note. Statistics could demonstrate incontrovertible evidence of Cuban women's aversion to delinquency, but they could neither provide a reason for this phenomenon nor totally encompass that which they purported to count.

The Pictures

The final volume of *La delincuencia femenina en Cuba* was dedicated to photography, another technology about which Castellanos expressed a great deal of enthusiasm. The publication of four hundred photographs of female criminals is remarkable for a Cuban criminological text of this era. Other books of this type in circulation, including Rafael Roche y Monteagudo's *The Police and Their Mysteries in Cuba* (*La policía y sus misterios en Cuba*) and Fernando Ortiz's *Male Witches* (*Negros brujos*) (reissued in 1917), included photographs, but in far fewer numbers, and very few are of women. In fact, apart from passing references, women are quite absent from both texts. The sheer number of photographs raises the question of their role in this text and of their relationship to Castellanos's intentions. Susan Sontag and others have observed that when photography is placed in the service of science, the intention is to create an illusion both of objectivity and of possession. Photographs make objects that don't necessarily lend themselves to control suddenly collectable, therefore more controllable.[27] Historically, the introduction of photography to institutions of social control, including the police departments or prisons, allowed them to claim greater objectivity and neutrality in the representation of criminals or delinquents.[28] In addition, as the criminological theory to which Castellanos ascribed urged the analysis and differentiation of criminals into distinct types, classification and categorization were important goals.

Certainly these are relevant ways to understand the photographs. The women are caught in still photographs in a way that echoes the intentions of criminology and the penal apparatus. They have been "seized" and are made available to the viewer for surveillance, inspection, and, implicitly, judgment. The mere fact of their rendition both frontally and in profile, a precursor to the mug shot, labels them "criminal."[29]

Yet, if the intention was to represent female delinquents as somehow "controlled," or at the very least as objectively observed neutral "objects," the women themselves made such a reading difficult. Roland Barthes's observations about photographs raise two intriguing points. First, he argues that "whatever the origin and the destination of the message, the photograph is not simply a product or a channel but also an object endowed with a structural autonomy."[30] That is,

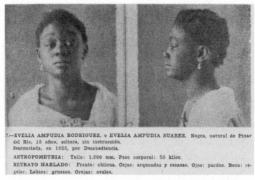

7.—EVELIA AMPUDIA RODRIGUEZ, o EVELIA AMPUDIA SUAREZ. Negra, natural de Pinar del Río, 15 años, soltera, sin instrucción. Sentenciada, en 1923, por Desobediencia.
ANTROPOMETRIA: Talla: 1.590 mm. Peso corporal: 55 kilos.
RETRATO HABLADO: Frente: oblicua. Cejas: arqueadas y escasas. Ojos: pardos. Boca: regular. Labios: gruesos. Orejas: ovales.

Figure 3.1.   Evelia. Source: Israel Castellanos, *La delincuencia femenina en Cuba* (Havana: Imprenta Ojeda, 1929).

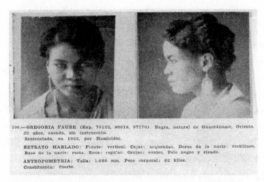

100.—GREGORIA FAURE (Exp. 79132, 80619, 97170). Negra, natural de Guantánamo, Oriente. 32 años, casada, sin instrucción. Sentenciada, en 1922, por Homicidio.
RETRATO HABLADO: Frente: vertical. Cejas: arqueadas. Dorso de la nariz: rectilíneo. Base de la nariz: recta. Boca: regular. Orejas: ovales. Pelo negro y rizado.
ANTROPOMETRIA: Talla: 1.680 mm. Peso corporal: 62 kilos. Constitución: fuerte.

Figure 3.2.   Gregoria. Source: Israel Castellanos, *La delincuencia femenina en Cuba* (Havana: Imprenta Ojeda, 1929).

299.—MARGARITA PEREZ o GREGORIA PEREZ LAGE o GREGORIA PEREZ PEREZ o GREGORIA PEREZ VALDES (a) CHANCHULLO o GOYA (Exp. 25219, 27474, 93577, 95750, 101776). Negra, natural de Güines, Habana. 50 años, soltera, cocinera, sin instrucción.
Sentenciada, en 1912, por Faltas, Hurto y dos veces por Resistencia; en 1919, por Resistencia y Escándalo; en 1920, por Alteración del órden; en 1926, por Hurto, Atentado y Lesiones.
RETRATO HABLADO: Pelo: lanoso. Frente: oblicua. Cejas: arqueadas. Dorso de la nariz: rectilíneo. Base de la nariz: recta. Boca: grande. Labios: gruesos. Orejas: ovales.
ANTROPOMETRIA: Talla: 1.629 mm. Peso corporal: 81 kilos.
TATUAJES: En el brazo izquierdo: SOY DE JUAN ROMEU. En el brazo izquierdo: ANGELITO CABRERA y otros.

Figure 3.3.   Margarita. Source: Israel Castellanos, *La delincuencia femenina en Cuba* (Havana: Imprenta Ojeda, 1929).

Figure 3.4. Ramona. Source: Israel Castellanos, *La delincuencia femenina en Cuba* (Havana: Imprenta Ojeda, 1929).

despite the assertions or intentions of criminological theory, photographs might or might not be in step with those conventions.

Look for example at Evelia Ampudia Rodríguez, sentenced for disobedience, or Gregoria Faure, sentenced in 1922 for homicide. Evelia looks down her nose, unflinchingly, at the photographer with an air of defiance, while Gregoria glowers at the camera. Others, like Cesarea Allende Fuentes from Spain, sentenced for robbery, look very contrite. Other images are more ambiguous. Margarita Pérez, for instance, looks out at her audience with a placid half-smile in the frontal photograph and modestly lowers her eyes in profile. Her hair is neatly braided, and her clothes and jewelry suggest a certain level of prosperity and concern for her appearance. Ramona Mercado Castillo looks pensive, if not lugubrious. Her glasses and upswept hair create a prim, schoolmarmish image, and her clothes are similarly proper. She may look somewhat forbidding, but she does not look "delinquent." Finally, María Coureaux's wistfully tilting head and serious, tired gaze suggest a soulful, almost moral character. Again, the ruffled clothes and fastidiously neat hair speak of bourgeois gentility rather than a propensity to violence. To be sure, without corroborating evidence, especially regarding the aims or intentions of the women themselves, these descriptions are decidedly speculative. The women may have intended for their expressions and attire to be interpreted in other ways, but that they took part in their own representation is clear. Thus, they call into question the ability of criminology, and specifically the photograph, to "capture" the female delinquent. The extent to which she can be fully disciplined is also called into question. Rather than displaying the female delinquent as a quantifiable, classifiable type, the photographs suggest that female delinquency is too diverse and too full of unique figures to be organized according to type. If a set of types were discernible, Castellanos might have dispensed with the hundreds of photographs and offered a few well-chosen examples in the volume. Instead, he made no effort to place them in distinct categories, creating the effect of a vast, disparate collection.

Here, Barthes's observations about captions are instructive. Captions, he argues, reverse the relationship between text and image. While usually the photo illustrates the text, in the case of the caption, the text offers an explanation of the photo. Thus, it is through the captions that we learn that Margarita has frequently been at the center of public scandal (and has probably been involved in prostitution), that Ramona has been convicted of perjury, and María of parricide. Furthermore, we also learn that Margarita has tattoos, which Lombroso associated with tendencies to criminality. In the case of María, specific details connote a less-than-genteel existence. The initials "s.o.a" (*sin otro apellido*, meaning "without a second surname") immediately after her name suggest that she is illegitimate. These initials were used in Cuba in two distinct situations, either after the name of a slave or former slave who had been given only one last name, that of his owner, or to denote illegitimacy. Either way "s.o.a" carried with it the taint of impropriety.[31] Her physical description betrays another potential source of criminality. The term *prognatismo* was very often used by Lombrosian criminologists to describe a prominent jaw, which in their view signaled an atavistic physical type prone to criminality. Since this was most often used to describe people of African descent, its use in this instance is particularly telling. These details allow for a very different "reading" of María than the photograph on its own. The caption not only offers information about her unhappy social status, but it also hints that her biological heritage is partly African, therefore, according to criminological theory, inherently criminal. As Barthes observes, "the text loads the image, burdening it with a culture, a moral, an imagination." Added to these innocuous, or at most ambiguous, images, the text created a system of connotation, constructing the language, both visual and linguistic, by which the female criminal could come to be spoken, and if not understood, at least recognized.[32]

Thus, the photographs and their captions suggest both that it is possible to "see" criminality and that it is very easy to hide it. In contrast to the statistics, which claimed that female criminality scarcely existed in Cuba, these photographs imply that it was everywhere. But *La delincuencia femenina en Cuba* is neither, in the end, a totalizing discourse about Virtuous Woman or Immoral Woman. It is rather a contradictory text that celebrates, through statistics, female virtue, even as it creates a gallery, in black-and-white photographs, of female vice. Swept up in his fascination with the tools of the trade, Castellanos sought to represent female delinquency in as many ways as were available. But by doing so, he inadvertently suggested how difficult it was to control. The photographs failed, in the end, to lend themselves to systems of neutral representation or typological classification. Castellanos assembled a text that cannot offer a coherent construction of "female delinquency." Instead, the examination of female criminals underscored the inadequacy of criminological categories and their inability to explain or contain contradictions. Together, the technologies of modern surveillance and the acts of self-representation by the women themselves wrought disorder on the discipline of criminology. Rather than producing an identifiable and controlled "female delinquent," Castellanos's *La delincuencia femenina* exploded the very categories it aimed to construct.

Notes

1. Israel Castellanos, *La delincuencia femenina en Cuba: Estadísticas judiciales, penitenciarias y clínicas, gráficas criminológicas* (Havana: Imprenta Ojeda, 1929).

2. Andrés Galera, *Ciencia y delincuencia: El determinismo antropológico en la España del s. XIX* (Seville: Consejo Superior de Investigaciones Científicas, 1991), 141–73.

3. Ricardo Salvatore, "Penitentiaries, Visions of Class, and Export Economies: Brazil and Argentina Compared," in *The Birth of the Penitentiary in Latin America: Essays on Criminology, Prison Reform and Social Control, 1830–1940,* ed. Ricardo Salvatore and Carlos Aguirre (Austin: University of Texas Press, 1996).

4. On Ortiz, see Thomas Bremer, "The Constitution of Alterity: Fernando Ortiz and the Beginnings of Latin American Ethnography Out of the Spirit of Italian Criminology," in *Alternative Cultures in the Caribbean,* ed. Thomas Bremer and Ulrich Fleischmann (Frankfurt am Main: Vervuert, 1993); Fernando Coronil, introduction to *Cuban Counterpoint* by Fernando Ortiz (Durham, NC: Duke University Press, 1995); Diana Iznaga, *Transculturación en Fernando Ortiz* (Havana: Editorial de Ciencias Sociales, 1989); Jorge Ibarra, "La herencia científica de Fernando Ortiz," *Revista Iberoamericana* 56 (1990); Stephan Palmié, "Fernando Ortiz and the Cooking of History," *Ibero-Amerikanisches Archiv* 24 (1998):1–21; Stephan Palmié, *Wizards and Scientists: Explorations in Afro-Cuban Modernity and Tradition* (Durham, NC: Duke University Press, 2002); Ricardo Quiza Moreno, "Fernando Ortiz y su hampa afrocubana," in *Diez nuevas miradas de historia de Cuba,* ed. José Piqueras Arenas (Castelló de la Plana: Universitat Jaume I, 1998); Aline Helg, "Black Men, Racial Stereotyping and Violence in the U.S. South and Cuba at the Turn of the Century," *Comparative Studies in Society and History* 42 (2000): 576–604; Alejandra Bronfman, "En Plena Libertad y Democracia: Negros Brujos and the Social Question in Cuba, 1904–1919," *Hispanic American Historical Review* 82, no. 3 (August 2002): 549–87.

5. The Latin American scholarship is extensive. Some examples of the North American literature include Salvatore and Aguirre, *The Birth of the Penitentiary in Latin America*; R. Salvatore, Carlos Aguirre, and Gilbert Joseph, eds., *Crime and Punishment in Latin America: Law and Society Since Late Colonial Times* (Durham, NC: Duke University Press, 2001); L. Johnson, ed., *The Problem of Order in Changing Societies: Essays on Crime and Policing in Argentina and Uruguay* (Albuquerque: University of New Mexico Press, 1990); C. Aguirre and Robert Buffington, eds., *Reconstructing Criminality in Latin America* (Wilmington, DE: Scholarly Resources, 2000); R. Buffington, *Criminal and Citizen in Modern Mexico* (Lincoln: University of Nebraska Press, 2000); Alexandra Stern, "Buildings, Boundaries and Blood: Medicalization and Nation-Building on the U.S.-Mexico Border, 1910–1930," *Hispanic American Historical Review* 79, no. 1 (February 1999): 41–81.

6. Donna Guy, "Girls in Prison: The Role of the Buenos Aires Casa Correcional de Mujeres as an Institution for Child Rescue, 1890–1940," in Salvatore, Aguirre, and Joseph, *Crime and Punishment in Latin America*; Pablo Piccato, *City of Suspects: Crime in Mexico City, 1900–1931* (Durham, NC: Duke University Press, 2001); Katherine Bliss, *Compromised Positions: Prostitution, Public Health, and Gender Politics in Revolutionary Mexico City* (University Park: Pennsylvania State University Press, 2001).

7. Buffington, *Criminal and Citizen in Modern Mexico*, ch. 3. See also Piccato, *City of Suspects*, ch. 3, on the use of visual imagery in criminology.

8. Louis A. Pérez Jr., *Cuba under the Platt Amendment* (Pittsburgh, PA: University of Pittsburgh Press, 1986); Alejandro de la Fuente, *A Nation for All: Race, Inequality, and Politics in Twentieth-Century Cuba* (Chapel Hill: University of North Carolina Press, 2001); Marifeli Pérez-Stable, *The Cuban Revolution: Origins, Course, and Legacy* (New York: Oxford University Press, 1993); Jorge Domínguez, "Seeking Permission to Build a Nation: Cuban Nationalism and U.S. Response under the First Machado Presidency," *Cuban Studies* 16 (1986): 33–48.

9. K. Lynn Stoner, *From the House to the Streets: The Cuban Woman's Movement for Legal Reform, 1898–1940* (Durham, NC: Duke University Press, 1991), ch. 3

10. Stoner, *From the House to the Streets*, 65–70. Machado also appealed to Cubans of color during this period, promoting many to prominent positions in his administration and receiving praise from many *Sociedades de Color*. See de la Fuente, *A Nation for All*, and Alejandra Bronfman, *Measures of Equality: Social Science, Citizenship, and Race in Cuba, 1902–1940* (Chapel Hill: University of North Carolina Press, 2004); Robert Whitney, *State and Revolution in Cuba: Mass Mobilization and Political Change, 1920–1940* (Chapel Hill: University of North Carolina Press, 2001).

11. Stoner, *From the House to the Streets*, 72.

12. Rafael Roche Monteagudo, *La policía y sus misterios en Cuba* (Havana: La Moderna Poesia, 1925), 589; Castellanos, *La delincuencia femenina en Cuba*, 2:83. My assessment of prostitution regulations and their enforcement is speculative and tentative. This subject requires further study. For a comparable phenomenon in Puerto Rico, see Eileen Suárez Findlay, *Imposing Decency: The Politics of Sexuality and Race in Puerto Rico, 1870–1920* (Durham, NC: Duke University Press, 1999).

13. Gerardo Machado y Morales, *Declaraciones del General Gerardo Machado y Morales* (Havana: Rambla y Bouza, 1928), 19–20.

14. "Ponencia a la Comisión Certificadora," Biblioteca Nacional José Martí, Colección Manuscrita Ortiz, Carpeta 356, *Proyectos de leyes*.

15. Galera, *Ciencia y Delincuencia*, 141–72; For Castellanos's frequent resignations and reappointments, see letters from Castellanos to August Vollmer, Bancroft Library, University of California, Berkeley, Collection August Vollmer, Box 7. On Castellanos, see also Palmié, *Wizards and Scientists*.

16. Castellanos cited in Galera, *Ciencia y Delincuencia*, 146.

17. Galera, *Ciencia y Delincuencia*; letters from Castellanos to August Vollmer, Bancroft Library, University of California, Berkeley, Collection August Vollmer, Box 7.

18. Castellanos, *La delincuencia femenina*, 3:5. This volume is unavailable in the United States. Although this analysis is of course incomplete, it is possible nonetheless to use the second and third volumes to make an argument about the nature of the tools Castellanos uses and their implications with regard to the production of social scientific knowledge.

19. Castellanos, *La delincuencia femenina*, 2:9.

20. For a history of the developing relationship between statistics and statecraft, see Silvana Patriarca, *Numbers and Nationhood: Writing Statistics in Nineteenth-Century Italy* (New York: Cambridge University Press, 1996). Castellanos's approach stands in contrast to that of Ortiz, who used anecdotal evidence, the citation of authoritative texts, and comparative ethnology to support his claims.

21. Castellanos, *La delincuencia femenina*, 2:24–27, 96.

22. Castellanos, *La delincuencia femenina*, 2:38.

23. He cites Cristóbal de la Guardia, 1914–1915 on criminality: 26 "la mujer cubana de todas las razas, lo mismo que en las salas de las Audiencias que en los patios de las cortes correccionales, se condenaron 288 mujeres, que venían a ser el 3.47% del total de condenados. Esto habla muy alto

en favor de la mujer cubana y nos hace reafirmarnos más en nuestra creencia de que tienen derecho a intervenir con sus votos en nuestras luchas políticas. Quizás si ahí estuviera el remedio de muchos de nuestros males."

24. Castellanos, *La delincuencia femenina*, 2:60.

25. Castellanos, *La delincuencia femenina*, 2:69.

26. Castellanos, *La delincuencia femenina*, 2:105–106.

27. Susan Sontag, *On Photography* (New York: Farrar, Straus and Giroux, 1973), 156.

28. Alison Griffiths, *Wondrous Difference: Cinema, Anthropology and Turn-of-the-Century Visual Culture* (New York: Columbia University Press, 2002), ch. 3, and John Tagg, "Evidence, Truth and Order: A Means of Surveillance," in *Visual Culture: The Reader*, ed. Jessica Evans and Stuart Hall (New York: Sage, 1999).

29. Tagg, "Evidence, Truth and Order," 253.

30. Roland Barthes, *Image, Music, Text* (New York: Hill and Wang, 1977), 15.

31. Michael Zeuske, "Hidden Markers, Open Secrets: On Naming, Race-Marking, and Race-Making in Cuba," *New West Indian Guide* 76, nos. 3–4 (2002): 211–42.

32. Barthes, *Image, Music, Text*, 26–28.

4

"Such a Strong Need": Sexuality and Violence in Belem Prison

Pablo Piccato

PRISONS OFFER A TEMPTING INSTITUTIONAL SETUP to study the interplay among sex, gender, and power. Forced to share the narrow quarters of cells, patios, and stigmatization, prisoners seem the perfect object for a detached study of the human soul. Late-nineteenth-century criminologists already claimed prisons as their "laboratory," and historians, at least in the case of Porfirian Mexico, have been all too eager to use the evidence produced by prisons to understand patterns of sexual behavior in general.[1] The goal of this chapter is not to restore the anomaly of prisoners (thus embracing positivist criminology's views of "the criminal" as a human subspecies) but to reclaim the institutional and cultural determinations that, as in any other context, shape sex, gender, and power in prisons.

A few precisions on the categories used in this text are in order. By talking about people's sexuality I refer specifically to an interconnected realm of sexual desires and behaviors. Yet behaviors and desires are not fixed in stone, nor are they naturally derived from the anatomical differences usually referred to, among other things, by the word *sex*. I will talk about sexual practices to emphasize observable, patterned actions people engage in when they interact with others. Gender refers to the cultural consequences of sex. Thus, gendered masculine or feminine bodies become more than just bodies; they can be, for example, thought of as "strong" or "sensual," respectively. The social consequences of these distinctions are enormous, of course, and they help in understanding the relations between women and men, young and old, and, in general, between groups and individuals with different degrees of power.[2] Gayle Rubin's words are particularly suggestive in this context: "Sex is sex, but what counts as sex is equally culturally determined and obtained. Every society also has a sex/gender system—a set of arrangements by which the biological raw material of human sex and procreation is shaped by human social intervention and satisfied in a conventional manner, no matter how bizarre some of the conventions may be."[3] The understanding of gender relations, in consequence, should never stray too far from that of bodies and sexual practices. Thus, in the realm of sexuality, we can see how social actors do and desire things that are not neatly organized as a dichotomy of male or female.[4]

Prisoners' sexual behavior cannot be considered the mere product of simple, universal drives. Sex was the object of one kind of exchange among others, like labor, commerce, or influence, although the one that best expressed how gender and political power shaped each other. The following pages will place sexual practices and gendered identities in the very specific context of prison life, with particular emphasis on the role of violence, and consider how, rather than looking at either men or women separately, looking at one to understand the other offers a more promising path of research on gender.

A considerable section of this chapter is devoted to the organization and everyday routine of prison life. Here, too, it would be useful to warn the reader that the prison is not modeled, after Foucault's works about the panopticon and other institutions, as a place where power was exercised and internalized in an overwhelming, univocal way that shaped the souls of inmates. Belem prison in turn-of-the-century Mexico City was not an exemplary institution. Thus, it would be erroneous to consider sexuality there as the simple expression of authority, as power itself was not the attribute of one actor or the institution's structure itself, but the product of negotiations, alliances, and resistances that undermined, as much as preserved, them. In more concrete terms, this means that to understand sexuality in Belem, we must also consider governance, labor, and personal relationships. As much as violence and exploitation marked them, sexual practices cast a "web of meaning" over the entire surface of everyday life and gave a comprehensive reach to the social construction of gender.[5]

Such an open-ended agenda demands a critical reading of sources that emphasized the isolation of prison culture and the supposed perversity of homosexuality. That is the case of Carlos Roumagnac's interviews with the prisoners of Belem jail and the San Lázaro Penitentiary, the origin of most of our knowledge about prison life before the revolution.[6] I have tried to complement Roumagnac's early works with additional information from the administrative records of the prison at the Archivo Histórico del Antiguo Ayuntamiento in Mexico City, only recently made available, and from Roumagnac's journalistic articles on Belem, published in *El Nacional* in 1933. This evidence, colored by criminological theories, supports the need to place questions and answers about sexuality in the context of the institution whence they emerged.

Going too far in the close reading of Roumagnac's interviews (i.e., reading them as a literary text, a self-contained artifact that can explain itself without reference to other texts much less to its author's and readers' reality) poses the risk of imposing circular interpretations that demonstrate the isolation of one practice, male homosexuality, precisely because they reproduce Roumagnac's voyeuristic fixation and his blindness to the structures of power that shaped all social and intimate relations in Belem.[7]

Criminology acquired great prestige in late-nineteenth-century Mexico as a method to understand urban society, even as it exhibited contradictory views held by educated writers and readers toward the urban underworld. The discipline (particularly under the positivist influence of the Italian school of criminal anthropology) resurrected and lent the strength of natural science to centuries-old prejudices about racial hierarchies and their moral symptoms, crystallizing them in the idea of "the criminal." Positivist theories about the shapes of criminals' heads and the determining influence of their family backgrounds fit nicely with old views of Indians and the urban plebe as backward and inferior. The notion of atavism, dear to Césare Lombroso and influential well into the twentieth century, condensed these attitudes: Criminals' bodies and behaviors were essentially anomalous throwbacks to those of primitive men and societies. Penology complemented this perspective.[8] Mexican lawmakers and political authorities undertook an aggressive program of penal reform and prison building in the latter years of the nineteenth century. Central to these strategies was the isolation of "criminals": They were to be separated from the rest of society in order to prevent crime and from each other in order to prevent their cultural and natural reproduction.[9] Contemporaries praised the San Lázaro Penitentiary, inaugurated by president Porfirio Díaz in 1900, as the first to establish a comprehensive regime over inmates' lives within a "kingdom of . . . solitude."[10] Work was to be an essential part of this regime, enabling the institution to combine profits with prisoners' rehabilitation.[11]

Paradoxically, Mexican prisons became the focal point of criminological observations because they revealed that isolation was not working. Official reports noted the intense and autonomous social life of prisoners. In 1863, inspector Joaquín García Icazbalceta found that gambling, drinking, and violence were rife in Belem jail. García Icazbalceta, like many later observers, considered Belem a "focus of corruption" and a "school of immorality."[12] Recidivism was indeed overwhelming.[13] Particularly troubling in this picture of corrupt contentment was clear and abundant evidence about sex. Yet, specialists hesitated about how far to go in observing prison life and homosexuality in general. This silence was the limit, it seemed, of Mexican criminology's ambivalent attraction toward the world of crime. One is left to wonder, however, whether the numerous foreign and national visitors who were taken for a tour of Belem were not thinking about the sinful activities recorded by the eyes of the prisoners lined up for their review.[14]

Against this silence appear Roumagnac's interviews with prisoners of Belem prison and the San Lázaro Penitentiary. Thanks to criminological ideas about the connection of sexual anomalies, inheritance, and criminal behavior, these documents give considerable importance to usually silenced aspects of prisoners' lives, thus offering a clear contrast with the reticence of other sources on prison life.[15] Having worked for Mexico City's police department and courts, Roumagnac shared their perspective regarding the lack of morality among the lower classes, the failure of jails to rehabilitate inmates, and the "degeneration" of criminals. At the same time, however, as a journalist he incorporated a good eye for detail and a persistent questioning in search of shocking statements.[16] The reporter's persistence was all the more necessary as silence was a central element of prison governance. Regulations limited inmates' ability to communicate with each other and with the world outside. Despite this, the prohibition of conversations after 9 p.m. and during work hours (an influence of U.S. penitentiary models) had almost no impact on Belem's routine, although authorities did exercise their privilege to open and censor prisoners' correspondence.[17] According to Federico Gamboa, a novelist interested in criminological themes, prisoners were reluctant to talk about their offenses, particularly when their cases were still under review, and they did not press others to talk about theirs.[18]

Even when they decided to speak to Roumagnac about sex, prisoners remained silent on certain matters. Sexual intercourse was considered dangerous, not least because of the prevalence of venereal diseases.[19] María Isabel M. stated that women, in particular, were able to resist long years without sexual intercourse because "we do not have such a strong need."[20] Most interviewees strongly denied their participation in homosexual practices but stated that the practice was common among their fellow inmates. María Villa (also known as "La Chiquita"), sentenced for the murder of another prostitute in 1897, acknowledged that she had had homosexual relations when she was a prostitute but denied continuing them in Belem. Emilia M. also recognized the option but favored heterosexuality: "Even if I desired a man," she declared, "I would not be so dirty [*tan puerca*] as to mingle with a woman like me."[21] Roumagnac noted that homosexual practices were indeed common in prison and that, in the case of María Villa, her denial was known to be false.[22] It is probably impossible to know how widespread homosexuality was outside prison. Some authors have argued that, at least during the nineteenth century, male homosexuality was there, yet literature and science simply did not have the means to see it or the words to describe it until it was "invented" as a crime by the raid against the famous dance of the forty-one in 1901.[23] Lying or keeping quiet about their participation in homosexual intercourse was not a practice exclusively of Porfirian prisoners[24]; yet, implicit behind their denials was the strongest reason for silence, the function of sexual exchanges in the prison's structure of power. Reluctance to talk about their own sexual lives corresponded to the same caution that inmates exercised regarding their own crimes: Disclosure could be interpreted as a confession of deviance and weakness.

A close look at Belem jail reveals the institutional conditions that dictated such caution. Established in 1863 in the building of a seventeenth-century convent for women, Belem housed the largest number of prisoners among Mexico City jails. Even after some of its inmates were sent to the San Lázaro Penitentiary, Belem remained overpopulated. In 1863, the prison guarded 780 men and 336 women. In 1887, there were 1,299 men and 313 women. By 1906, it had approximately 5,000 prisoners, many of them suspects waiting for trial. The former convent also housed criminal courts, connected with the prison through a barred window, called *el boquete* (the hole), where prisoners made their statements to the judge. There were multiple passages between sections and the building's 7 patios and 116 "big and small" rooms. Prisoners gathered in the patios, making surveillance even more difficult. Female prisoners had to cross the men's section, exposed to their admiring gazes, to work in the kitchen or present their statements at the boquete. Sanitary conditions were poor, and diseases were often fatal, even for prison staff.[25] In 1907, the *Diario del Hogar* described Belem with strong words: "It stands at the center of the city, like a cloister, infectious, revolting, spilling over its walls, like a glass filled with poison, its vapors harmful."[26]

The harsh conditions and baroque architecture of Belem caused prison governance to be based on close personal relationships. Authorities reasserted the basic inequality of power between them and prisoners, as if the divide itself were permanently challenged. Arbitrary decisions, such as the sudden prohibition of all visits in 1890, conveyed to prisoners their limited ability to influence decisions in certain areas of the prison's administration.[27] Employees, stated inmate Arturo Bonilla, proclaimed their disregard for the lives of inmates. It was not an empty threat. In 1902, a prisoner in the isolation cells died after the medical student in charge of the infirmary refused to respond to several calls for help.[28] Behind this appearance of duress, however, thrived many more nuanced interactions. The main resource for authorities to secure order was to manipulate divisions among inmates and to use a minority of them as delegates.

The structure of vigilance in Belem gave some prisoners the ability to use violence against their peers with the support of authorities, thus to enjoy a stronger social position. Penitentiary regulations authorized the delegation of prison authority to a small core of inmates. This was inevitable, given the limited resources available.[29] Each section or galley had a *mayor* (boss) and several *presidentes* (presidents) who were appointed by the warden. They were male inmates armed with clubs, in charge of subduing troublemakers, keeping track of behavior, and the delicate task of walking prisoners from one section to another (female presidentes had other tasks, such as organizing the kitchen). A 1900 regulation gave them the humbler name of *cabos* (corporals) and *ayudantes* (assistants), respectively, and established that they should be prisoners chosen for their good conduct. The former received ten pesos a month, the latter four, and they added to their salaries the product of their work in the workshops or their involvement in other business. Presidentes, for example, demanded a *mordida* (bribe) from all merchants selling goods to prisoners.[30] Mayor Germán Estrada gave loans guaranteed by other inmates' property, charging 50 percent after three days and beating those who complained about the terms. He and other mayores associated with guards without the knowledge of the warden, who, according to a prisoner in 1911, "never comes inside the prison to see how things work."[31]

If he had inspected things more closely, the warden would have found that money was a central element in the alliance between presidentes and staff. Guards' working conditions were similar to those of some inmates with power and money. Their contracts (called *enganche*, like those signed by indentured workers sent to plantations) forced them to work for at least two years and deducted a fifty-peso deposit from their salaries against the return of their clothes and gun after their service. A guard earned 1.5 pesos a day, about the same as a street policeman.[32] Thus, like street cops, they added to their income by informally taxing commerce among prisoners or charging fees in exchange for help in pushing suspects' paperwork through court. Closeness generated other concessions: guards customarily gave trusted prisoners the keys to galleys and cells in order to expedite their work.[33] Mayores' and presidentes' fear of retaliation from other inmates made authorities' patronage essential for their survival. Incrimination was formalized in a book where the inmates' behavior was officially recorded, but there were other ways to peddle information to authorities. Francisco R., a mayor, denounced the construction of a tunnel and, for his own protection, kept a list of male homosexual inmates. Being a *soplón* (informer) was no small matter. Francisco complained bitterly about his transfer to the penitentiary because he believed that prisoners there would harm him. In Belem, his power as a mayor was supported by the fact that his brother was a police agent.[34]

The structure of vigilance (the clearest expression of the alliance of power and violence) permeated all social relations but did not replace them. There were other ways to establish hierarchy among prisoners. The 1897–1900 legislative reform established a hierarchy among inmates based on behavior and time served. To move from one of the four "stages" to the next, with newcomers assigned to the lowest, inmates accumulated points for good behavior, and they could be demoted as a punishment.[35] A second layer of division referred to prisoners' legal status. The prison had separate sections for *encausados* (inmates waiting for the conclusion of their trials), for those condemned to *arresto* (up to three years), for those condemned to *prisión* (for more than three years), and for *separos* or *bartolinas* (those sent to isolation cells to punish bad behavior and those sentenced to death).[36] Administrators also classified new inmates according to their social standing and sent the better-off to a separate section. Following jurist Miguel Macedo's theory that distinct strata of the Mexican population could be distinguished by their clothes, a 1900 regulation determined that employees had to register the "personal qualities of entered individuals," including trade, education, and "social class." The three classes (first, second, and third) were distinguished by the use of *levita* (frock coats), *chaqueta* (jackets), and *camisa* (shirts), respectively.[37] Gender and age marked other divisions that seemed natural in everyone's eyes. Regulations stressed that the departments for men and women had to be "completely independent from each other."[38] Although penal legislation established that the correctional prison would be separate from the main prison, there was a minors' department in Belem for boys aged nine to eighteen. In fact, many boys in Belem had already gone through other related institutions, like the Poor House or the orphanage. As with the women's sections, the separation from adult males was not effective.[39] A *departamento de distinción* (special section) housed encausados "chosen by the authority," in other words, those whose social status officials rated higher. A special department for former policemen prevented them from having contact with their fellow prisoners. Journalists, often incarcerated by the Díaz regime, were confined in a special area and felt entitled to respectful treatment from prison officials.

Inmates themselves acknowledged and preserved differences, beginning with experience. When a newcomer entered the prison for the first time, he would face the collective aggression of more experienced "sharks," who stripped him of any valuable clothes.[40] Other distinctions were more subtle. María Villa enjoyed some benefits, such as a maid, and insisted on the social distance that separated her from the rest of the female prisoners: "They do not understand me, and I do not understand them."[41] Rafael Tagle, who had attended high school, told Roumagnac that another prisoner who attacked him was a *pelado*, a word used to refer to the urban poor.[42] Roumagnac and some other journalists imprisoned in the 1890s were able to circulate through other sections accompanied, in pleasant conversation, by prison officials.[43]

These social differences were buttressed by economic activity inside the prison and the surplus generated by prisoners' labor. The 1900 regulation prohibited money, newspapers, musical instruments, pornographic pictures, or alcohol in the prison. Food rations were inadequate, in some cases dangerously so. But there were many informal ways to improve life with some cash.

Prisoners played dice, organized a lottery, and stole things from each other. Commerce was a necessary, if illegal, practice that involved furniture, marijuana, bread, coffee, sugar, cigarettes, and even weapons. Guards sold tequila—in those days an accessible drink. It is not surprising, therefore, to see prisoners accumulating money and power. Victoriano A., who had been sentenced to twenty years, owned a loom at which other inmates worked.[44]

Labor was the clearest example of the contradiction between penitentiary models and reality. Penal reformers congratulated themselves on the benefits of work, including that done in forced labor colonies, as a modern tool for regeneration. Yet late-nineteenth-century reforms only gave a shade of scientific legitimacy to a colonial tradition of prisoners' exploitation in textile mills and tropical forced-labor camps. In 1886, Belem prisoners could work at a bakery, three shoemakers' shops, two carpentry shops, and one shop each for cigar making, weaving, tailoring, and the production of matches or hats. There were no workshops for women, but they could do laundry and embroidering, and their main role was to staff and run the prison's kitchen and to prepare food for inmates in other jails in the city, thereby emulating the distribution of tasks in the home. Prisoners sentenced to death made wooden toys. *Jotos* (effeminates) earned money doing the laundry for male prisoners and outside customers, a feminine occupation outside the prison. Not all of the income, however, stayed in Belem. Many prisoners used their earnings to maintain their families, thereby trying to counter the subordination imposed upon them by incarceration.[45] Labor in prison, in other words, responded to social perceptions about gender roles (where women were supposed to be fit for domestic labor and men for skilled, better-paid jobs), yet altered them out of necessity: Some men did women's chores or saw their familial status diminished, while some women, the presidentas, enjoyed a measure of authority and economic autonomy difficult to attain outside prison. Profits from inmates' work cemented the structure of governance. Authorities and guards retained 35 percent of the profits from commerce in and out of Belem. In this way, the warden and the administrator of the prison earned one-third and one-half, respectively, of their wages, while the percentage was smaller for lesser employees. The system, according to inmates who accused warden Wulfrano Vázquez of such practices, encouraged corruption and more abuse and probably came in addition to the customary bribes.[46]

Sex was both part of prison labor and the most prestigious way to profit from power. As noted earlier, this was not so much a product of prison society's radical subversion of prevalent mores as the consequence of the intertwined character of sex, gender, and power. Penal legislation and prison vigilance could not disentangle the connections (obvious to anyone who observed, for example, the organization of labor in prison) between the construction of gender roles and objects of sexual desire, on the one side, and the social practices and exchanges that made of sex a commodity and a perk of authority on the other. To further distinguish things from penitentiary models, sexuality, as we shall see, also involved affections that seemed oddly out of place in a situation where power was supposed to reign over all interactions. Disciplinary and spatial restrictions on sexual activity were not effective, least of all against those among prisoners and staff with resources and power. Victims and beneficiaries of such freedom saw no benefit in being explicit about it. Female prisoners were commonly besieged and sexually harassed by employees (who were all male), but there was little use in complaining, Catalina S. informed Roumagnac, because nobody paid attention, and it could lead to punishment.[47] Influential prisoners gained from the informality of their access to female prisoners. Mayor Francisco R. masturbated in the penitentiary but "had women to enjoy" in Belem, where he bribed employees who allowed him to meet partners after hours in the infirmary or the room where suspects made their statements.[48] Sexual relations, therefore, involved money and occurred in the context of the prison's structure of governance. Drawing on the same mechanisms as other interactions, as we will see, sex often could mean violence but also protection.

However strange this may sound, these unequal relationships were articulated, in many cases, as love. Violence could stem from jealousy, the clearest proof of male love. A man killed his friend in prison, reported journalist and inmate Heriberto Frías, because both shared a female lover. Another prisoner decided to kill his lover in the women's section because he knew that she was betraying him with another male inmate. Just before he killed her, he changed his mind and handed his weapon to the guards. He died two days later, according to Frías, of meningitis. Less predisposed than Roumagnac by scientific views of criminals as inferior beings, Frías saw these as crimes of passion.[49] Roumagnac nevertheless documented how love, or at least the yearning for stable relationships, mobilized prisoners' emotional and social resources. María Villa, who was in prison because of her own crime of passion (she had murdered another prostitute in a dispute over a lover), had successive relationships with two male inmates. They managed to enter the women's department to see her using bribes or disguises. With one of them, María hoped to establish marital life after they left prison. She broke off the relationship when she discovered that he had married another woman, also inside prison, and held firmly to her decision even though the suitor, Arnulfo P., went to her section to convince her with promises and threats. Although there are no further details about the suitor's marriage in prison, there is evidence, as we will see below, that prisoners were eager to formalize their relationships by the means available. Francisco R., mentioned above, sent María clothes, shoes, and messages through another female prisoner. At first, María rejected him with the argument that "his social sphere is too low for me," but she finally gave in to his

desires because she felt gratitude for his protection and help.[50] Her case illustrates the reasons that moved prisoners to establish affective relationships with
other inmates. María Villa had been a successful prostitute, but in Belem she
soon found herself on her own and powerless. She wrote in her diary, ex-
cerpted by Roumagnac, that friends had come to visit her during the process,
"but I understand that . . . they will flee from me scared, like one flees from a
leper or a disease." The lover who was the cause of her crime abandoned her
after the trial. She then attempted suicide and only slowly overcame her social
prejudices and joined the society of fellow inmates.[51]

Relationships like María's were not exclusive to heterosexual couples. Tim-
oteo A. acquired letters exchanged between "pederasts" (understood as men
who engaged in relations "against nature") in Belem, in which "besides words
of innocent love, they sent each other kisses, by printing their lips with lipstick
on the paper."[52] Same-sex love, however, is shrouded by an image of violence
between men that seems to reduce homosexuality to domination. In the men's
department, Manuel T. saw "savage rapes, against poor devils who were first
inebriated and then abused by ten or twelve men in front of everyone else in
the room!"[53] According to Roumagnac, homosexuals there were divided into
caballos (horses), or the "passive," and *mayates* (beetles), or the "active." Male
same-sex intercourse was commonly construed as the subordination of the
penetrated partner and as another means to obtain money from prisoners. In
1910, two guards were fired because they pimped a "well-known pederast"
(*pederasta conocido*) to other male inmates.[54]

Perhaps the clearest examples of the coincidence of governance, violence,
and homosexuality were present in the minor's section. The hierarchies there
were starker than in the adult male section, with age and size giving a clearer,
more "natural" advantage to some inmates. The organization of vigilance followed a military style, with "sergeants" and "corporals" commanding "pla-
toons," and an adult inmate was the mayor. Roumagnac and Frías recorded
disturbing cases of rape and prostitution. According to Juan D. I., older boys
had "two or three kids who would allow anyone to perform filthy things on
them in exchange for any trifle." They would form a large circle and have *niños*
(boys) masturbate them or endure their "doing it" to them.[55] But even here,
violence did not exclude consensual relationships. Juan D. I., fifteen years old
and with previous experience in the Correctional School, tried to *hacer caballo*
(make the horse) to José M., thirteen years of age. José, he claimed, resisted
but was forced to submit. A third minor informed Roumagnac, however, that
the relationship between Juan and José lasted a long time and that Juan
bragged of his being the mayate.[56]

Thus, testimonies about consensual heterosexual relationships could not
be very explicit because they implied passivity and exploitation and, more
importantly, inevitably recalled social and scientific views of homosexuality

as a disease. Their entrance into the judicial and penal system placed prisoners in a discursive space that accentuated their "anomaly" and the public nature of their intimacy. They were aware of the links between sexuality and deviance presumed by criminologists and implied by Roumagnac's questioning. It is not surprising, then, that Roumagnac failed to obtain confessions; he only gathered witnesses' depositions, so to speak, as his proximity to judicial and prison authorities only reinforced suspects' reluctance to confess. Admitting homosexual desire, in particular, could be costly. Pablo Esqueda, a prison guard, was arrested for a month and then fired after he was found to be a "pederast" and to have been keeping "intimate relationships" with several inmates. The regulation of 1900 established that "pederasts," regardless of their legal situation, would be isolated in the section of *separos* and would not be allowed to communicate with other prisoners.[57] Disregard of this basic rule could lead historians to posit mistakenly the same societal condemnation toward all homosexual men, either "active" or "passive." Such was not the case.[58]

Beyond a first look, however, historians' emphasis on violence and silence would miss the complexity of some relationships and the continuum of experiences and desires that characterized everyday life. Domination and sex were not linked by a blanket condemnation of homosexuality but, to quote Eve Kosofsky Sedwick, by "the power of cognitively dividing and hence manipulating the male homosocial spectrum."[59] Prisoners and guards could benefit from denouncing homosexuals, but they were able also to build stable, or at least affective, relationships, both heterosexual or homosexual, in which protection was one but not the only factor.

Male homosexual desire had multiple opportunities to assume a public character. Men spent long hours out in the patios, where washing and doing the laundry made nudity common.[60] Frías described the jotos with a mixture of moral condemnation and appreciation for the "rare comradeship" that characterized their relationships:

> There are many of these effeminate men in Belem . . . where others, however, despise them. . . . [They] live with entirely feminized habits. They have soprano voices and speak with the intonation of an affected and skittish woman. . . . They dress as much like women as they can; they bear prostitutes' nicknames, like *la Diabla, la China, la Pancha*, and devote themselves to ironing, doing laundry, knitting, embroidering and cooking.

According to Frías, feminine men showed great affection to each other, helped in difficult times, and even fought to defend their partners.[61] This defiant openness could not have survived without some degree of acceptance, perhaps favor, from the rest the of prison population. As noted above, men could exchange sexual favors for money. The open nature of homosexual desire

complicated the moral condemnation that seems to emerge from Roumagnac's reports. Isolating "known pederasts" only served to encourage the exhibition of transgender identities. Roumagnac recovered the reporter's touch
to describe the scene in the pederasts' section: "It was worth seeing that parade
of sexual degenerates, strolling in front of the arrested, without shame, making feminized voices and movements." Through the moral disgust, the image
betrays the success of those inmates in evoking desirable female bodies.[62]

Gender transgression was not exclusive to the adult men's department. Inmates acting "like a woman" were also seen in the minors' section.[63] In the
women's department, the signs of subversion were less scandalous. According
to Roumagnac, female homosexuals in Belem "who play the male role" parted
their hair on the right side, while the others did so on the left. The distinction
was less evident than that established by male inmates acting like women because prevalent views of female homosexuality did not stress a stark divide
marked by subordination. Much as men were supposed to, however, female
partners could express their love by taking care of their companions, fighting
for them "with as much fury, or maybe more, than men," as Roumagnac gal-
lantly admitted.[64] According to Catalina S., women sent each other love letters
and presents, protected their partners, and fought out of jealousy. Yet, in the
women's section, the link between sex and violence was weaker. Catalina had
read some of those letters. They were like those written between heterosexual
lovers, including the offer of protection, clothes, and money in exchange for
the other person's favors. They used affectionate names like *mi prietita, mi
flaquita* (my dark one, my skinny one). Some couples even spent their time
"kissing, hugging and biting" each other.[65]

Several factors in the department of women diluted the structure of governance mandated by the law and practiced by male inmates. The separation between the sentenced and suspects, for example, was not applied.[66] Women
were fewer in number, and their department enjoyed better hygiene, thus
avoiding cases of typhus and other epidemics common in the men's section.[67]
The 1900 regulation established that female prisoners could keep their babies
during lactation.[68] Social life seemed to follow a more consensual course than
in the men's department, and inequality was not so clearly linked to the use of
force. The evidence suggests that authority did not derive exclusively from official patronage. María Villa enjoyed a good night on May 5, 1900, when "they
gave me a ball with music."[69] Later, she became mayora of the entire department, only to be separated from her office when authorities discovered that
another prisoner (presumably Francisco R.) visited her. The removal of María
from her post prompted a rebellion among the female inmates, but the measure was sustained, and María Trinidad T., who had been presidenta of the
production of *atole* (a corn beverage served as breakfast) and mayora in other
sections, replaced her.[70] Holding a charge was related to economic activities

rather than vigilance. Like María Trinidad, María Villa was involved in commerce. Emilia M., the *presidenta* of the kitchen, had fifty-two female inmates under her orders, a salary of ten pesos a month, and responsibility for the daily meals of all prisoners.[71]

According to the testimonies of prisoners and the observations of Roumagnac, women made religious beliefs part of their relationships. Although the 1871 penal code provided for religious assistance to inmates, it was limited to "a piece of a sermon" delivered by a priest on Sundays. Carmen V. was a believer but judged confession useless: "here inside, what for? There are so many occasions to sin!"[72] Relationships between women were formalized through the practice of *madrinazgo* (godmotherhood). The *madrina* (godmother) would sponsor another inmate by placing a scapulary of the Virgen de la Soledad or a *medida*, a ribbon the size of a saint's face, around her neck and then reciting the Lord's Prayer three times. This ceremony was intended to protect the sponsored *ahijada* (goddaughter) before she was to appear in court. The bond thus formed did not exclude other relations between the inmate and her madrina, or madrinas, if she had several.[73] I did not find any evidence of a similar practice among men.

The institution of madrinazgo clearly illustrates the reasons for and characteristics of solidarity among female prisoners. Distant from the use of violence monopolized by men and from the penitentiary and judicial system, madrinazgo coded the respect of established and reciprocal bonds and reflected distinctive social perceptions of male and female homosociality.[74] Female homosociality and homosexuality were, in comparison with male notions of their own gender, less related to violence and less explicit in terms of the manifestations of gender roles. There was no "pederasts" section for women; nor, as far as the available evidence shows, was there the public and collective embrace of the other sex's identity, like that of the "effeminates" described by Frías and Roumagnac. Perhaps relieved from the social condemnation given to male transgendered identities, women seemed better able to avoid the linking of sexual desire with violence and pathological anomaly.

For most male inmates, by contrast, life in prison was not a shameless exploration of the possibilities of sexual desire but a constant defense of masculinity. Being in prison radically constrained a man's ability to control and exert his normative heterosexual identity. I noted above inmates' fears about sexual activity and disease. Having erections was "the main thing of being a man," according to Manuel T., who had lost that ability in prison.[75] More importantly, male identity was rooted in ideas and practices of masculinity that brought many of them to prison in the first place: Manhood obliged one to follow his desires while fulfilling the expectations of other people—the automatic obedience to violent impulses that was supposed to guide men's behavior in contrast with women's. "Coward—defined Francisco M.—is he who's afraid to hit."[76] Many were in prison because of a scrupulous concern about reputation: Juan D. I. killed a coworker who ridiculed him for returning one peso that he had mistakenly received over his salary. Juan A., who had raped a ten-year-old girl, justified his action saying that she had invited him, that he had not wanted to "avoid being a man," and that he had proposed marriage to her after they had had intercourse.[77] Incarceration undermined men's ability to protect other attributes of manhood, such as the active defense of women and property. A revealing example was a letter, found by the police in a raid against counterfeiters, in which a man who was in Belem warned his wife that he knew that she was "offending me with other men" and using his tools to produce coins. He promised that soon after his release he would take revenge.[78] Being cheated on was a disgrace that prisoners always feared, and it was held as a sign of weakness and stupidity in society in general.[79] Given the limits imposed on legitimate heterosexual relations in prison, most inmates were restricted in their means to be men.

As a result, male sexuality in Belem tended to express itself in violent ways, whether the object of affection was a woman or a feminized man, and to be closer to the structure of power. Leandro T. had to "fulfill his obligation" and stabbed an inmate who hit him.[80] Broad condemnation of homosexuality and the seemingly contradictory acceptance of the normal, yet secret, virility of active partners in homosexual relationships were reconciled in an ethical obligation to use violence. Placing these reactions in the context of notions of honor and shame offers little help, particularly if doing so means referring to general "paradigms" to understand the dichotomy active/passive and ignoring the specific social relations that inform cultural meanings.[81] Violence, I contend, provided male homosexuality in prison with meaning; it generated interpretations that prisoners, criminologists, and historians could use in order to make sense of reality.[82]

Male violence, however, introduces a deceptive sense of order into our effort to place sex in context. The distinctions between the modalities of sexual desire were not as neat as they should have been, and there were no clear lines between autonomy and obedience, between the dominant and the dominated. Annick Prieur's point about contemporary homosexual subcultures in Mexico City is worth bearing in mind here: Same-sex relations, even if unacknowledged, "may well provide a man with more pleasure than a woman does."[83] Lucia Zedner's study of women in English prisons offers an example of such contextualization. She found guardians and inmates to be closer, socially and emotionally, than both the traditional and revised history of Western prisons had managed to perceive. Their relationships, much like those in Belem jail, involved sexual intimacy and "a carefully placed dividing line between emotional attachment and lesbianism" that was "not always easy to discern."[84] As I have suggested, a careful look at the women's section of Belem could shed light on the role of desire and love in relations that, in the men's section, were distorted by violence and cultural views about the greater risks of sex and the restrictions imposed by prison on masculinity.

The evidence of homosexual and heterosexual relations in prison obsessed educated observers. In prison, transgressions of gender (understood, with Joan Wallach Scott, as the social construction of sexual difference and a primary signifier of power) were the most visible evidence of criminals' challenge to social norms outside the prison. This challenge was upsetting and attractive as it demonstrated the instability of the boundaries between intimacy and public life and between homosociality and homosexuality, both inside and outside the prison. Social observers saw the fact that "love affairs" were not covert but took place on the streets or inside crowded bedrooms as one of the symptoms of the lack of morality among the lower classes in Mexico City.[85] The institutional features of Belem accentuated the material conditions that imposed this public character on the urban poor's erotic practices and buttressed its threatening value.

In Belem, playing with power was a way of playing with gender. As a consequence, the use of gendered dichotomies (homosexual/heterosexual, active/passive) renders a mechanical image of sex and governance in prison. Instead of identifying "roles," I contend that looking for individual predispositions toward gender definitions, their conditions of possibility, and a nuanced view of sexuality offers a more promising path for research.[86] This chapter has noted the fuzzy limits between the authority of prison officials and that of powerful inmates. The indirect nature of the statements of interviewees about sexual life also blurred the distinction between observers and the observed. Roumagnac, at times, limited himself to editing written and verbal information that other inmates had collected. And, if the archives of Belem jail are to be believed, Carlos Roumagnac himself was again a prisoner at Belem jail in 1906, approximately at the time when he compiled some of his interviews. His name in the book that registered prisoners' admissions to Belem that year serves as evidence. However, his personal file has not been found, and there is no corroborative evidence in newspapers.[87] As a contribution to the history of Mexican sexualities, in sum, this chapter suggests that separate histories of men, women, prisoners, and homosexuals (with their implicit emphasis on identities rather than practices) erect artificial boundaries around phenomena that, inside and outside prison, involved broader cultural patterns concerning desire and power.[88]

Notes

1. Francisco Martínez Baca and Manuel Vergara, *Estudios de Antropología Criminal: Memoria que por disposición del Superior gobierno del Estado de Puebla presentan . . .* (Puebla: Benjamín

Lara, 1892), 5. Robert Buffington, *Criminal and Citizen in Modern Mexico* (Lincoln: University of Nebraska, 2000), ch. 6; Martin Nesvig, "The Lure of the Perverse: Moral Negotiation of Pederasty in Porfirian Mexico," *Mexican Studies/Estudios Mexicanos* 16, no. 1 (Winter 2000): 1–37. Other works include Rafael Sagredo Baeza, *María Villa (a) La Chiquita, no. 4002: Un parásito social del Porfiriato* (Mexico City: Cal y Arena, 1996); Robert Buffington and Pablo Piccato, "Tales of Two Women: The Narrative Construal of Porfirian Reality," *The Americas* 55, no. 3 (January 1999): 391–424; Pablo Piccato, "'El Chalequero,' or 'the Mexican Jack the Ripper': The Meanings of Sexual Violence in Turn-of-the-Century Mexico City," *Hispanic American Historical Review* 81, nos. 3–4 (2001); Elisa Speckman, *Crimen y castigo: Legislación penal, interpretaciones de la criminalidad y administración de justicia (Ciudad de México, 1872–1910)* (Mexico City: El Colegio de México, 2002); Robert McKee Irwin, "The Famous 41: The Scandalous Birth of Modern Mexican Homosexuality," *GLQ* 6, no. 3 (2000): 353–76.

2. We can understand power as the ability to determine other people's beliefs and actions, but we should avoid placing power in one place or in the hands of one actor (the state, the warden) and follow Michel Foucault's view of power as "the multiplicity of force relations inherent in the sphere in which they operate and which constitute their own organization; as the process which, through ceaseless struggles and confrontations, transforms, strengthens, or reverses them," or, in other words, "power is not an institution, and not a structure; neither it is a certain strength we are endowed with: it is the name that one attributes to a complex strategical situation in a particular society." Michel Foucault, *The History of Sexuality* (New York: Vintage Books, 1980), 92, 93.

3. Gayle Rubin, "The Traffic in Women: Notes on the 'Political Economy' of Sex," in *Feminism and History, Oxford Readings in Feminism,* ed. Joan Wallach Scott (New York: Oxford University Press, 1996), 111.

4. Against ahistorical binaries, see Denise Riley, "Does Sex Have a History?" in Scott, *Feminism and History,* 21. See also Caroline Walker Bynum, "Why All the Fuss about the Body? A Medievalist's Perspective," in *Beyond the Cultural Turn: New Directions in the Study of Society and Culture,* ed. Victoria E. Bonnell and Lynn Hunt (Berkeley: University of California Press, 1999).

5. For culture and gender, see Clifford Geertz, *The Interpretation of Cultures: Selected Essays* (New York: Basic Books, 1973), 5, and Joan Wallach Scott, *Gender and the Politics of History* (New York: Columbia University Press, 1988), 42–43. I would stress Scott's "third aspect of gender relationships," easily neglected given the cultural stress placed on the first two: "a notion of politics and reference to social institutions and organizations." See Michel Foucault, *Discipline and Punish: The Birth of the Prison* (New York: Vintage, 1979). To understand Foucault's changing perspective on power from one defined as juridical repression to that cited in note 2 above, see "Las relaciones de poder penetran en los cuerpos" [1977], in Michel Foucault, *Microfísica del poder,* trans. and ed. Julia Varela and Fernando Alvarez-Uría (Madrid: La Piqueta, 1979), 153–62. For critical views of the prison as a disciplining machine, see Michael Ignatieff, *A Just Measure of Pain: The Penitentiary in the Industrial Revolution* (London: Penguin, 1978); Peter Linebaugh, *The London Hanged. Crime and Civil Society in the Eighteenth Century* (New York: Cambridge University Press, 1992). See Irwin, "The Famous 41," 356.

6. Carlos Roumagnac, *Crímenes sexuales,* vol. 1 of *Crímenes sexuales y pasionales: Estudios de psicología morbosa* (Mexico City: Librería de Bouret, 1906); Carlos Roumagnac, *Los criminales en México: Ensayo de psicología criminal. Seguido de dos casos de hermafrodismo observado por los señores doctores Ricardo Egea . . . Ignacio Ocampo* (Mexico City: Tipografía El Fénix, 1904); Carlos Roumagnac, *Matadores de mujeres (Segunda parte de "Crímenes Sexuales y Pasionales")* (Mexico City: Bouret, 1910). The contemporary authors cited in note 1 draw from Roumagnac's information. In 1933, he wrote that his "attempts" at criminology were now out of print and forgotten. Carlos Roumagnac, "Recuerdos de Belem," *El Nacional,* July 23, 1933, 2nd sec., 2. Roumagnac (1869–1937) was born in Madrid and died in Mexico "in poverty." Alfonso Quiroz

Cuarón, *Tendencia y ritmo de la criminalidad en México* (Mexico City: Instituto de Investigaciones Estadísticas, 1939), 129.

7. For an example of the gratuitous use of positivist criminology's explanations, see the reference to an inmate's descendants' diseases in Nesvig, "The Lure," 32. See further discussion of these problems in Pablo Piccato, "Interpretations of Sexuality in Mexico City Prisons: A Critical Version of Roumagnac," in *The Famous 41: Sexuality and Social Control in Mexico, 1901,* ed. Robert McKee Irwin, Edward J. McCaughan, and Michelle Rocío Nasser (New York: Palgrave Macmillan, 2003).

8. Both have been the object of careful and critical research in recent years. Besides the works on Mexico cited above, see Carlos Aguirre, Gilbert Joseph, and Ricardo Salvatore, eds., *Crime and Punishment in Latin America* (Durham, NC: Duke University Press, 2001); Carlos Aguirre and Robert Buffington, eds., *Reconstructing Criminality in Latin America* (Wilmington, DE: Scholarly Resources, 2000); Julia Rodríguez, "Encoding the Criminal: Criminology and the Science of 'Social Defense' in Modernizing Argentina (1880–1921)" (PhD dissertation, Columbia University, 1999). For a general view, see David Garland, *Punishment and Modern Society* (Chicago: University of Chicago Press, 1995).

9. An influential statement of this belief was Enrico Ferri, *La Sociologie Criminelle,* 3rd ed. (1881; Paris: Arthur Rousseau, 1893). In México, see "Sobre el número y clase de presos que debe alojar la Penitenciaría de México," [1882] *Boletín del Archivo General de la Nación: La Penitenciaría de México* 5, no. 4 (1981–1982): 14.

10. Speech by Miguel Macedo, *Boletín del Archivo General de la Nación: La Penitenciaría de México* 5, no. 4 (1981–1982): 13–14; prisons had to be the worst place for potential criminals. See Joaquín García Icazbalceta, *Informe sobre los establecimientos de beneficencia y corrección de esta capital; su estado actual; noticia de sus fondos; reformas que desde luego necesitan y plan general de su arreglo presentado por José María Andrade* (Mexico City: Moderna Librería Religiosa, 1907), 165; Antonio Martínez de Castro, *Código penal para el Distrito Federal y Territorio de la Baja California sobre delitos del fuero común y para toda la República Mexicana sobre delitos contra la Federación [1871]. Edición correcta, sacada de la oficial, precedida de la exposición de motivos dirigida al supremo gobierno por el C. Lic. . . . Presidente de la comisión encargada de formar el código* (Veracruz and Puebla: La Ilustración, 1891), 15. See Dario Melossi and Massimo Pavarini, *Cárcel y fábrica. Los orígenes del sistema penitenciario (siglos XVI–XIX)* (Mexico City: Siglo Veintiuno, 1980), 60, 191; David Garland, *Punishment and Welfare. A History of Penal Strategies* (Aldershot, Hants, UK: Gower Publishing Company, 1985); Foucault, *Discipline and Punish,* 54.

11. José Ceballos, *Memoria presentada al C. Lic Manuel Romero Rubio Secretario de Estado y del Despacho de Gobernación por el . . . Gobernador del Distrito Federal y que comprende los años de 1886 y 1887* (Mexico City: Eduardo Dublan, 1888), 164–65; Martínez de Castro, *Código penal,* 15. A reform to the penal code of May 19, 1896, stated that the inmate "will occupy himself, according to the terms established by penitentiary regulation, in the labor assigned to him by the director of the institution where he is serving his sentence." *Código penal, Edición oficial* (Mexico City: La Europea, 1906), 272.

12. García Icazbalceta, *Informe sobre los establecimientos,* 71. For writers' perspectives, see Angel de Campo, *Ocios y apuntes y La rumba* (Mexico City: Porrúa, 1976), 298; Miguel Macedo, *La criminalidad en México: Medios de combatirla* (Mexico City: Secretaría de Fomento, 1897), 34; Federico Gamboa, *La llaga* (Mexico, Eusebio Gómez de la Puente, 1922), 38.

13. On recidivism, see the letter from Judge Manuel F. de la Hoz in Ignacio Fernández Ortigoza, *Identificación científica de los reos: Memoria escrita por. . .* (Mexico City: Sagrado Corazón de Jesús, 1892), 8, 11, 20.

14. On foreign visitors to prisons, see *Gaceta Policía,* August 12, 1906, 8; Eaton Smith, *Flying Visits to the City of Mexico and the Pacific Coast* (Liverpool: Henry Young and Sons, 1903);

Charles F. Lummis, *The Awakening of a Nation: Mexico of To-day* (New York: Harper and Brothers, 1899), 63–64; Roumagnac, "Recuerdos de Belem," *El Nacional,* August 27, 1933, 2nd sec., 2. Mexican upper-class visitors, although less publicized, were also common. On the reluctance to talk about homosexuality, see Martínez de Castro, *Código penal,* 44–45.

15. These include mainly official reports produced by the Junta de Vigilancia de Cárceles and letters written by prisoners to political authorities. On the latter, see Pablo Piccato, *City of Suspects: Crime in Mexico City, 1900-1931* (Durham, NC: Duke University Press, 2001), ch. 8. Reports from the members of the Junta de Vigilancia de Cárceles to political authorities can be found at the Archivo General de la Nación, fondo Secretaría de Justicia, and Archivo Histórico del Distrito Federal, Gobierno del Distrito Federal, fondo Cárcel de Belén.

16. Buffington sees these features of Roumagnac's interviews as an expression of Porfirian anxieties regarding ethnic and gender difference. Buffington, *Criminal and Citizen,* ch. 3. Roumagnac had been imprisoned in the past because of his writings. In 1933, he looked back at journalism as his "dearest trade" and spoke with detachment about criminology; see Roumagnac, "Recuerdos de Belem," *El Nacional,* May 28, 1933, 2nd sec., 2. See also Xavier MacGregor Campuzano, "Historiografía sobre criminalidad y sistema penitenciario," *Secuencia: Revista de historia y ciencias sociales* 22 (1992): 221–57.

17. Manuel González de Cosío, *Memoria que presenta al Congreso de la Unión el General . . . Secretario de Estado y del Despacho de Gobernación* (Mexico City: Imprenta del Gobierno Federal, 1900), 847–48; Archivo Histórico del Ayuntamiento, fondo Gobierno del Distrito Federal, Carcel de Belén, Reos Quejas (hereafter AHDF, CB), 140, 9.

18. Gamboa, *La llaga,* 36.

19. On prisoners' views of the risks associated with sex, see Roumagnac, *Los criminales en México,* 88, 304, 307, 339. On venereal disease, see the administrative archives of Belem Jail at the Archivo Histórico de la Ciudad de México. Luis Lara y Pardo, *La prostitución en México* (Mexico City: Bouret, 1908), 179–80.

20. Roumagnac, *Los criminales en México,* 153.

21. Roumagnac, *Los criminales en México,* 107–108, 127.

22. Roumagnac, *Los criminales en México,* 112. On María Villa, see Buffington and Piccato, "Tales of Two Women." Roumagnac also wrote a criminalistics handbook: Carlos Roumagnac, *Elementos de policía científica. Obra de texto para la Escuela Científica de Policía de México* (Mexico City: Botas, 1923).

23. Carlos Monsiváis, "The 41 and the Gran Redada," in *The Famous 41: Sexuality and Social Control in Mexico, 1901,* ed. Robert McKee Irwin, Edward J. McCaughan, and Michelle Rocío Nasser (New York: Palgrave Macmillan, 2003): 164–65.

24. This seems to be a common pattern in sources about homosexuality, given stereotypical views of penetrated partners as powerless and feminized. See Irwin, "The Famous 41," 366, 369. Learning that her informers lied, Annick Prieur recognized, "This is of course a methodological problem, but I believe it is also a finding, since I came to realize why they cannot admit it [being penetrated by male partners]: to be passive means to be *homosexual,* and this in turn means not to be a man." Annick Prieur, *Mema's House, Mexico City: On Transvestites, Queens, and Machos* (Chicago: University of Chicago Press, 1998), 199 (her emphasis).

25. *La Voz de México,* January 23, 1890, 2; Ceballos, *Memoria presentada,* 142–45, 146; *Gaceta de Policía* 1, no. 39 (August 12, 1906): 8. *Nueva Era* gives the same number in 1911: *Nueva Era,* August 15, 1911, 2; García Icazbalceta, *Informe sobre los establecimientos,* 68–69; Federico Gamboa, *Suprema Ley* in *Novelas* (Mexico City: FCE, 1965), 242. The organization of prisons in Mexico City derived from superimposed layers of state reforms and inertia. Besides Belem and the San Lázaro Penitentiary, since 1900 each municipality of the federal district had a jail, and there was a military prison in Tlatelolco. The police usually sent the wounded to the Juárez public hospital, and prostitutes were treated at the Morelos hospital. Belem was first called Cárcel

Nacional but was renamed Cárcel Municipal in 1887, when the city government took charge of it. The Cárcel de Detenidos, located in the central square for those arrested for misdemeanors, was incorporated into the building. In 1900, after the official inauguration of the San Lázaro Penitentiary, Belem became the Cárcel General del Distrito. For overviews of the penal system, see Martín Gabriel Barrón Cruz, "Bosquejo histórico: La cárcel de Belén y el sistema carcelario" (manuscript, Mexico City); Antonio Padilla Arroyo, "Criminalidad, cárceles y sistema peniten-ciario en México, 1876–1910" (PhD dissertation, El Colegio de México, 1995), 100–149; Raúl Carrancá y Rivas, *Derecho penitenciario: Cárcel y penas en México* (Mexico City: Porrúa, 1986). For the move of prisoners to San Lázaro, see *El Imparcial*, August 1, 1897, 2. According to Héc-tor Madrid, administrative archives show that many employees became sick or died after rela-tively short tenures. Personal communication, May 11, 2001. Dr. Ignacio Ocampo died after a ty-phus epidemic. Roumagnac, *Crímenes sexuales y pasionales*, 143. Heriberto Frías, "Crónicas desde la cárcel," *Historias* 11 (October–December 1985): 53–54. Porfirio Díaz reported to Con-gress the outbreak of an epidemic of typhus in the municipal jail in 1896: Informe de Díaz, Sep-tember 16, 1896, in *Diario de los Debates de la Cámara de Diputados. Decimaoctava Legislatura Constitucional* (Mexico City: Imprenta de "El Partido Liberal," 1896), 27–28; *El Imparcial*, Janu-ary 19, 1900, 1; "Informe del inspector Sanitario del Cuartel No. 7," in Consejo Superior de Salu-bridad, *Memoria* (Mexico City: n.e., 1905), 249.

26. *Diario del Hogar*, November 19, 1907, 1. Part of the building was destroyed in the 1913 military uprising against President Francisco I. Madero, but Belem continued to work until the early 1930s, when it was demolished to make room for a school. Miguel Macedo, "El Municipio. Los establecimientos penales. La asistencia pública," in *México, su evolución social*, ed. Justo Sierra (Mexico City: Ballescá, 1900), 1:698–99; García Icazbalceta, *Informe sobre los establec-imientos*, 65–66; Ceballos, *Memoria presentada*, 140; Archivo General de la Nación, Gobernación Período Revolucionario, box 81, folder 4; Luis Vázquez and Julio Baz to City Council, July 27, 1917, Archivo Histórico del Distrito Federal, Justicia Juzgados, expediente 2745, folder 1.

27. *La Voz de México*, January 25, 1890, 3.

28. After inmates had requested a doctor for one of them, employees stated, "we care little about the life of all these." Arturo Bonilla to governor of the federal district, July 22, 1911, AHDF, Gobierno del Distrito Federal, Carcel de Belén, Reos Quejas, box 140, file 9; Ignacio Ocampo to Secretario de Gobierno del Distrito Federal, July 12, 1902; box 140, file 9. The student was fired.

29. Ceballos, *Memoria presentada*, app. 16; González de Cosío, *Memoria*, 864, reports a staff of twenty-four; in 1905, the number had increased to seventy-five employees, including the war-den, cooks, doctors, teachers, and accountants, with guards usually divided in two shifts. Barrón Cruz, "Bosquejo histórico."

30. Guillermo Mellado, *Belén por dentro y por fuera* (Mexico City: Cuadernos Criminalia, 1959), 68. Roumagnac, *Los criminales en México*, 208n; González de Cosío, *Memoria*, 866. For conflicts stemming from movement of a prisoner from galleys to the area destined for interviews with lawyers, see AHDF, CB, 140, 2.

31. Pedro Cuéllar and others to Governor of the Federal District, June 10, 1911, AHDF, CB, 140, 12 and 140, 9; Roumagnac, *Los criminales en México*, 313.

32. Contract signed by Petronilo Palafox, AHDF, CB, August 20, 1910, 40, 1307; Barrón Cruz, "Bosquejo histórico." See also Enganche del celador de la Cárcel general Manuel P. Castillo, July 1, 1908, AHDF, CB, 25, 863. Similar contracts were signed by gendarmes: González de Cosío, *Memoria*, 752–54.

33. Statement signed by several inmates, March 22, 1909, AHDF, CB, 26, 893; unreadable sig-nature to Secretario de Gobierno del Distrito Federal, February 24, 1909, AHDF, CB, 29, 1003.

34. Roumagnac, *Los criminales en México*, 208, 357–62. See also *El Imparcial*, January 8, 1900, 3.

35. González de Cosío, *Memoria*, 866.

36. Martínez de Castro, *Código penal*, 264; Roumagnac, *Los criminales en México*, 228.

37. González de Cosío, *Memoria*, 855.

38. González de Cosío, *Memoria*, 850; Martínez de Castro, *Código penal*, 264.

39. Macedo, *La criminalidad en México*, 29.

40. *Diario del Hogar*, November 23, 1907, 1.

41. Roumagnac, *Los criminales en México*, 113.

42. Roumagnac, *Los criminales en México*, 219.

43. González de Cosío, *Memoria*, 846–47; Ceballos, *Memoria presentada*, 146; *La Voz de México*, October 8, 1897, 3. For a complaint by a journalist against a drunken warden who treated him with "vociferaciones solo comparables con los que emplea nuestro bajo pueblo cuando en demasía ingiere alcohol," see Alfonso Peniche to Governor of the Federal District, August 16, 1910, AHDF, 140, 2; Carlos Roumagnac, "Recuerdos de Belem," *El Nacional*, April 16, 1933, 2nd sec., 2 and April 30, 1933, 2nd sec., 2. For an account of the difficulties of imprisoned journalists and their relative autonomy, see Antonio Saborit, *Los doblados de Tomóchic: Un episodio de historia y literatura* (Mexico City: Cal y Arena, 1994).

44. González de Cosío, *Memoria*, 848, 864–65; *Diario del Hogar*, June 3, 1905, 2; Frías, "Crónicas desde la cárcel," 51–54; Roumagnac, *Los criminales en México*, 215–16, 246, 306; *Diario del Hogar*, June 24, 1905, 2; *La Voz de México* October 14, 1897, 3; Warden Wulfrano Vázquez to Secretario de Gobierno del Distrito Federal, August 14, 1911, AHDF, CB, 140, 10; Julio Guerrero, *La génesis del crimen en México: estudio de psiquiatría social* (Paris: Viuda de Bouret, 1901), 155.

45. Ceballos, *Memoria presentada*, 142, 145; García Icazbalceta, *Informe sobre los establecimientos*, 70, 162; Miguel Jiménez to Governor of the Federal District, August 6, 1911, AHDF, GDF, CB, RQ, 140, 10; Mellado, *Belén por dentro*, 31; Nicolás Trujillo to Governor of the Federal District, July 16, 1911, AHDF, CB, 140, 11.

46. Vázquez, they claimed, was becoming rich "a la sombra de los brazos del desgraciado preso explotado en su trabajo y no permitiéndole que le pase ni sal para sus alimentos para que la tenga que comprarla en el interior de la cárcel." Emilio Helgero to President Francisco I. Madero, November 14, 1911, Archivo General de la Nación, fondo F. I. Madero, 60, 242. Both Vázquez and Lazcano were fired by Madero in March 1912: Emilio Helgero to President Francisco I. Madero, November 14, 1911, Archivo General de la Nación, fondo F. I. Madero, 60, 211 and 212. See also Padilla Arroyo, "Criminalidad, cárceles," 172–80; Mellado, *Belén por dentro*, 29; Wulfrano Vázquez and Amador Lazcano to Secretario de Gobierno del Distrito Federal, August 12, 1911, AHDF, CB, 42, 1339.

47. Roumagnac, *Los criminales en México*, 191. Yet, for a guard fired for keeping "relaciones ilícitas" with a married female inmate at the boquete, see J. Dosamantes, August 10, 1901, AHDF, CB, 31, 1051, and W. Vázquez to Secretario de Gobierno del Distrito Federal, August 3, 1909, AHDF, CB, 31, 1067. On a guard's attempt to rape a female prisoner and his dismissal, see W. Vázquez to Secretario de Gobierno del Distrito Federal, November 14, 1905, AHDF, CB, 8, 282.

48. Roumagnac, *Los criminales en México*, 359.

49. Frías, "Crónicas desde la cárcel," 53, 56–60. For a straightforward testimony of same-sex love and violence in contemporary Mexico City prisons, see Prieur, *Mema's House*.

50. Roumagnac, *Los criminales en México*, 113, 121–23.

51. Roumagnac, *Los criminales en México*, 104–18. She established a school and was released sixteen years after her admission. Mellado, *Belén por dentro*, 131–32.

52. Roumagnac, *Los criminales en México*, 330. "Pederast" referred to male homosexuals in general. Adopting such vocabulary, as Nesvig does, misleadingly extends criminological generalizations to different patterns of relationships. Nesvig, "The Lure," 2n4. See, instead, Peter Beattie, "Conflicting Penile Codes: Modern Masculinity and Sodomy in the Brazilian Military,

1860–1916," in *Sex and Sexuality in Latin America*, ed. Daniel Balderston and Donna J. Guy (New York: New York University Press, 1997), 66.

53. Roumagnac, *Los criminales en México*, 210.

54. Roumagnac, *Los criminales en México*, 77–78n; unreadable signature to Secretario de Gobierno del Distrito Federal, February 26, 1910, AHDF, CB, 33, 1107.

55. Roumagnac, *Los criminales en México*, 88, 210; Frías, "Crónicas desde la cárcel," 50–51.

56. Roumagnac, *Los criminales en México*, 86, 95–97.

57. Letter signed by Dosamantes, April 19, 1911, AHDF, CB, 1329. Roumagnac, *Los criminales en México*, 13, 68, 268; Roumagnac, *Crímenes sexuales y pasionales*, 11, 24; also Roumagnac, *Matadores de mujeres*. Judges did not see confessions as an exculpatory factor in the sentences I examined in Mexico City judicial archives. See Pablo Piccato, *City of Suspects*, ch. 7; Gamboa, *La llaga*, 58; González de Cosío, *Memoria*, 862, 870.

58. See Nesvig, "The Lure," 15.

59. Eve Kosofsky Sedgwick, *Between Men: English Literature and Male Homosocial Desire* (New York: Columbia University Press, 1985), 86, 88–89.

60. Ceballos, *Memoria presentada*, 149; González de Cosío, *Memoria*, 847.

61. Frías, "Crónicas desde la cárcel," 61. See also Mellado, *Belén por dentro*, 32.

62. Roumagnac, *Los criminales en México*, 77.

63. Roumagnac, *Los criminales en México*, 88.

64. Roumagnac, *Los criminales en México*, 174.

65. Roumagnac, *Los criminales en México*, 190–91.

66. González de Cosío, *Memoria*, 871.

67. Ceballos, *Memoria presentada*, 149.

68. After that, if no other member of the family claimed the children, they would be sent to the orphanage. González de Cosío, *Memoria*, 844.

69. Roumagnac, *Los criminales en México*, 122–23.

70. Roumagnac, *Los criminales en México*, 131.

71. Roumagnac, *Los criminales en México*, 127.

72. Roumagnac, *Los criminales en México*, 132, 147. Many prisoners carried a scapulary or a medal of San Dimas, who was believed to help thieves. *La Voz de México*, September 1, 1897, 2.

73. Roumagnac, *Los criminales en México*, 136.

74. According to Eve Kosofsky Sedwick, "the diacritical opposition between the 'homosocial' and the 'homosexual' seems to be much less thorough and dichotomous for women, in our society, than for men." Sedgwick, *Between Men*, 2.

75. Roumagnac, *Los criminales en México*, 206.

76. Roumagnac, *Los criminales en México*, 81.

77. Roumagnac, *Los criminales en México*, 85; Roumagnac, *Crímenes sexuales y pasionales*, 116.

78. *El Imparcial*, January 22, 1900, 3.

79. *Don Cucufate* 1, no. 7 (September 10, 1906): 4.

80. Roumagnac, *Crimenes sexuales y pasionales*, 125.

81. Nesvig, "The Lure," 6–7; Martin Nesvig, "The Complicated Terrain of Latin American Homosexuality," *Hispanic American Historical Review* 81, nos. 3–4 (2001): 69. But see Annick Prieur, "Domination and Desire: Male Homosexuality and the Construction of Masculinity in Mexico," in *Machos, Mistresses, Madonnas: Contesting the Power of Latin American Gender Imagery*, ed. Marit Melhuus and Kristi Anne Stølen (London: Verso, 1996), 83–107. For critical views of the Mediterranean model of honor, see David Gilmore, "Introduction: The Shame of Dishonor," in *Honor and Shame and the Unity of the Mediterranean*, ed. David Gilmore (Washington, DC: American Anthropological Association, 1987), 3; Michael Herzfeld, "'As in Your

Own House': Hospitality, Ethnography, and the Stereotype of Mediterranean Society," in Gilmore, *Honor and Shame*, 75, 87–88.

82. In this regard, it can be considered "a paradigmatic human event," to use Clifford Geertz's term. Clifford Geertz, "Notes on the Balinese Cockfight," in his *The Interpretation of Cultures*, 450.

83. Prieur, *Mema's House*, 211.

84. Lucia Zedner, *Women, Crime, and Custody in Victorian England* (Oxford, Clarendon Press, 1991), 161–62.

85. Macedo, *La criminalidad en México*, 14–15.

86. On the "different, smaller" categories into which contemporary Mexico City gay communities break down and resist labeling, see Prieur, "Domination and Desire," 88. See Pierre Bourdieu, *Outline of a Theory of Practice*, trans. Richard Nice (Cambridge: Cambridge University Press, 1998), 73.

87. AHDF, CB, Libro de entradas, 1906, file 61. I owe this reference to Martín Gabriel Barrón Cruz.

88. Nesvig dismisses the questions raised by violence as part of homosexual practices as the result of "situational homosexuality" in prisons ("The Complicated," 717). But see Prieur, *Mema's House*. For a critique of sex-role theory, see R. W. Connell, *Masculinities* (Berkeley: University of California Press, 1995); Lynne Segal, *Slow Motion: Changing Masculinities, Changing Men* (New Brunswick, NJ: Rutgers University Press, 1990).

5

"Gentlemanly Responsibility" and "Insults of a Woman": Dueling and the Unwritten Rules of Public Life in Uruguay, 1860–1920

David S. Parker

T HE BIRTH OF INDEPENDENT NATION-STATES in Spanish America between 1808 and 1824 brought far more than the expulsion of the old colonial authority. Not only were the institutions of daily governance crippled (when not swept away altogether), but gone, too, were the fundamental principles of king, crown, and church on which the legitimacy of rule had once solidly rested. With absolute monarchy weakened or defeated in France and Spain as well, new channels of political debate and participation emerged to fill the void.[1] Over the course of the nineteenth century, political clubs and embryonic political parties became vehicles of competition for public office, while voluntary associations, places of sociability such as cafes and literary salons, the publishing industry, and the periodical press increasingly provided Spanish Americans with new ways of "speaking" publicly about matters of governance and the collective good. By the turn of the twentieth century, a vibrant and dynamic public sphere had become firmly established.[2]

Although recent research has greatly enriched our understanding of how this emergent public sphere transformed nineteenth-century Spanish America, the larger ramifications of the change, particularly for women, are only beginning to be studied.[3] The issue has received greater attention in Europe and North America, where several influential scholars have argued that the rise of a more open and competitive public sphere paradoxically contributed to women's greater marginalization, in part because these emerging arenas of debate were thought of as exclusively masculine spaces, while femininity (or at least respectable femininity) was ever-increasingly identified with hearth and home.[4] Tempting as it may be to assume a similar pattern for Spanish

America, the case study of Uruguay raises enough questions to give us pause, because it appears to offer a significant paradox. In some ways, Uruguay was among the most progressive of all the Spanish American republics, and by the early twentieth century, it had become a pioneer in the promotion of women's rights. It was among the earliest Latin American nations to permit civil divorce (1907), and in 1913 it became one of the first countries in the world to allow "no-fault" divorce at the wife's request.[5] Leaders of Uruguay's ruling Colorado Party, including José Batlle y Ordóñez (president 1903–1907 and 1911–1915) and Baltasar Brum (president 1919–1923), were noted advocates of equal rights for women and publicly came out in favor of female suffrage.[6] At the same time, however, Uruguay's political life remained a male-only preserve, and in many ways became more exclusionary rather than less so in the 1900s. Despite the emergence of new opportunities for women and the general rise of progressive thinking about "the woman question," Uruguay's public sphere was suffused with a deeply masculine style, where issues of manliness or cowardice entered the discussion almost as often as issues of policy and ideology. Polemicists of all stripes, Batlle y Ordóñez foremost among them, were not above ridiculing their opponents as effeminate, and they described "the words of a woman" as having little consequence.

This chapter argues that the increasing importance of dueling in the late nineteenth and early twentieth centuries goes far to explain the paradox. Throughout the period under study, insults traded among Uruguayan politicians and/or journalists led to duels with ever greater frequency; by the 1910s, an especially busy month might see three or four. Though the typical duel usually consisted of a fencing contest stopped at the first trickle of blood, a substantial minority involved the trading of pistol shots, and while fatalities were rare, someone did get killed every ten years or so. Dueling was a masculine ritual par excellence, one that supposedly tested the public man's bravery, valor, and willingness to die for an ideal. I hope to show, however, that Uruguayan dueling was in no way a throwback to some past age of Hispanic chivalry; nor was the duel primarily about constructions of masculinity, the defense of elite privilege, or the aspirations of middle-class would-be aristocrats.[7] In fact, dueling went hand-in-hand with the liberal, secularizing trend so well embodied in reformers like Batlle y Ordóñez and Brum. The duel flourished most where the press was most free, where political debates were farthest ranging, where opinions of all kinds competed in the spirit of democratic debate.[8] By understanding the complicated relationship between this peculiar masculine ritual and the genesis of Uruguayan democracy, I hope to show why it was possible for the public sphere to become simultaneously more open to women's issues yet less open to women themselves.

Dueling, Honor, and the Public Sphere

The purpose of the duel is frequently misunderstood. In theory, dueling was supposed to be a civilized alternative to brute violence, a means to prevent insults, to cool emotions, and to resolve interpersonal conflicts rather than provoke them. A highly controlled, ritualized affair, dueling was governed by a strict code of conduct, according to which no man had the right to act out of anger or momentary passion. Instead of striking back when insulted, a proper duelist was expected to restrain himself and respond by naming two representatives (known as seconds), who would calmly approach the offender and demand an apology. If unwilling to apologize, the antagonist named representatives of his own, and together the four seconds were expected to work toward a peaceful solution. Only when mediation failed did a duel ensue, in conditions of strict equality between the combatants, and structured to limit the risk of bloodshed to a level consistent with the severity of the original insult or offense. These procedures were carefully set out in a number of widely read dueling manuals or codes, the most famous being *Essai sur le duel* by the Count of Chatauvillard, first published in Paris in 1836.[9] Advocates firmly believed that the duel, as a deterrent against incivility in speech and action, had the power to make society less violent.

But the understood rationale for dueling and the reasons why people took part in actual duels were not necessarily identical. If asked why they fought, most Uruguayan duelists would have argued that they did so to defend their honor. The concept of honor was the keystone of dueling culture: dueling codes were also known as "honor codes," duels were fought on the "field of honor," and insults or heated exchanges were "offenses against honor." Yet the idea of honor does little to explain why dueling became so much more common in the late nineteenth and early twentieth centuries, why certain insults led to duels and others did not, why some men provoked duels with deliberate premeditation, or why dueling was endemic among politicians and journalists but rare among other members of the economic and social elite, who presumably shared the same cultural norms.[10]

Mexican historian Pablo Piccato hits closer to the target, arguing that turn-of-the-century political elites deliberately cultivated the duel and trumpeted their superior qualities as "men of honor" in order to distinguish themselves as a class and to legitimate their exclusive claim to represent public opinion.[11] This conscious invocation of honor and the duel as the price of admission to politics not only justified class privilege, but it equally justified gender discrimination. "Women," according to Piccato, "were excluded from high levels of politics because their participation would undermine the ritualized use of violence that supported the personal legitimacy of politicians. . . . Women had to be silenced in order for upper-class men to maintain their authority and their ability to speak freely."[12]

Piccato's analysis of Mexican dueling supports the contention that the emerging public sphere was not just an all-male club, but a club whose innate characteristics presupposed, and indeed were defined by, the essential fact of women's exclusion. He echoes scholars such as Joan Landes and Nancy Fraser, who have depicted a public sphere constituted by masculine power and female marginalization.[13] Landes in particular, writing about eighteenth-century France, argues that the public sphere functioned as a means of gender exclusion because its supposedly novel characteristics—rationality, critical thought, and publicness itself—were construed by eighteenth-century minds as exclusively masculine attributes, in opposition to increasingly naturalized "feminine" qualities of privateness and domesticity. Landes thus argues that the relationship between this newly won public sphere and the equally new cult of private life was not coincidental but essential; in her words, "the [French] Republic was constructed *against* women, not just without them."[14] For Piccato, however, it was not the rationality or publicness of the public sphere that defined women as inherently beyond the pale, but rather its potential for violence and its reliance on a ritual in which only men—indeed, only individuals accepted as gentlemen—were allowed to participate.

The focus on dueling as one key ingredient in a politics of women's exclusion has the great virtue of appreciating the aggressive competitiveness that so often underpinned elite males' preoccupation with honor.[15] Such a perspective helps us to explain why dueling became more widespread rather than less so in the late nineteenth and early twentieth centuries, the very moment when other, more traditional means of excluding women and the poor from political life were under attack and beginning to lose their effectiveness. However, by concentrating on the duel's role in forging elite male power and unity, Piccato underemphasizes the extent to which dueling, at its core, was a product and a symptom of intraelite conflict. Though the honor codes may have envisioned a civilized world in which men thought twice before raising their voices in anger and settled their differences in ways that fostered reconciliation and class unity, the reality of dueling was quite different. The duel and its attendant code of honor formed part of a complex and contradictory series of behaviors that sometimes brought peaceful resolution to political conflict, but just as frequently pushed those conflicts to the brink, often for the most self-serving of motives.

Although we will see that the duel did indeed contribute to the political marginalization of women and nonelites, the examples that follow force us to rethink the idea that the duel's primary purpose was to shore up the crumbling boundaries of aristocratic privilege or to maintain what Piccato calls "the masculine monopoly of public speech."[16] The story has far more twists and turns than we have heretofore imagined, and following those twists and turns will help us better understand why the rise of the duel—and the increasingly masculine tenor of public life—so often went hand-in-hand with the opening of the political system, with broader participation and greater representativity, and with social changes that gave more rights, more power, and more opportunities to women, not fewer.

The Pen and the Sword:
Politics, the Press, and the Idea of "Responsibility"

A newspaper, for the public man, is like a knife for the quarrelsome gaucho: it should always be close at hand.[17]

Whether or not the ideal of "public opinion as the expression of reason"[18] ever existed—or even could exist—there is ample evidence that late-eighteenth- and early-nineteenth-century Uruguayans, like their counterparts in France, the United States, and much of Latin America, believed that it could. At least they invoked such an ideal with enormous frequency, in defense of political projects from the noblest to the most venal. Nowhere was this discourse of illustrated, deliberative public opinion more evident than in Uruguayans' defense of press freedom. A free press, its champions argued, was society's best defense against ignorance and despotism, its best tool for building an enlightened populace and safeguarding responsible government. As one writer put it, "It has been said, and rightly so, that the press is the most powerful element of order, of liberty, and of civilization, fount of enlightenment for individuals and societies."[19]

But by the middle of the nineteenth century, the press had already proved itself less a beacon of reason and illustration than a vehicle for the diffusion of partisan bile. Even as people continued to pay homage to the ideal of rational, illustrated debate in a disinterested search for the common good, faction and the competition for political office had inevitably tarnished that ideal. Such a state of affairs was by no means unique to Uruguay or Latin America: Descriptions of nineteenth-century journalism in France, Italy, the United States, and many other countries have painted a very similar picture of newspapers as privileged weapons in the low-intensity war of political faction.[20] The same Uruguayan writer who praised the press's mission in theory wrote about the press in practice,

> Many of our journalists have turned into a School of sedition, of immorality, of hatreds and bloody acts of revenge.... Few if any of the excesses or crimes of the periodical press are committed in the name of the authors themselves, but rather in the name of *public opinion*, of which they presume to be the legitimate and exclusive voices.[21]

This tension between the ideal of the press and the perceived reality lay at the heart of Uruguayans' many and frequent debates about censorship and press freedom. By Latin American standards (indeed, even by European standards), Uruguay's press laws were liberal: The first national legislation, approved in 1829, set the principle of free expression without prior censorship.[22] The 1830 constitution confirmed press freedom as a fundamental right. According to the text of Article 141,

> The communication of thought, by means of the spoken word, private writings or published in any type of press, is entirely free, with no need for prior censorship; the author or publisher takes responsibility for any abuses that might be committed, in accordance with the law.[23]

At the same time, the constitutional text makes clear that newspapers could be held accountable, after publication, for any excesses that they might have committed. In other words, at the very moment that freedom of the press was enshrined as a right, also enshrined was the idea of responsibility, that the author, publisher, or owner of a newspaper could be held criminally liable for slanderous or incendiary language.

This constitutionally mandated idea of responsibility was not in any way unusual. Virtually every nation in the world limits freedom of the press by punishing libel. The problem for Uruguayans was the widespread perception—surely based to some degree in reality—that their libel and defamation laws were deficient and the institutional mechanisms to prosecute slanderers were ineffective. Evidence of this dissatisfaction can be found in the frequency with which legislators took up the matter of press freedom and responsibility. New press laws were proposed and debated on the floor of the House of Representatives in 1829, 1854, 1862–1863, 1881, 1886, and 1912.[24] In virtually every case, the debates were heated ones, pitting the defenders of press freedom against the defenders of a man's right to his reputation. (Cynics would say that the debate more typically pitted supporters of the regime of the moment, who sought stricter restrictions on the press, against the regime's opponents, who fought tooth-and-nail against laws designed to silence them.) More restrictive press laws were sometimes passed, sometimes defeated, but even when approved, they rarely survived for very long. The 1854 press law was repealed in 1869 after years of lax enforcement, while the 1881 law was struck down when the Máximo Santos dictatorship fell from power in 1886.[25]

In the absence of draconian controls on the press, individuals who felt they had been slandered sought redress in accordance with procedures first established in the 1829 press law and modified by the 1879 Código de Instrucción Criminal. Claimants were given a choice of either initiating a hard-to-win criminal prosecution in the regular courts or turning to so-called press juries (*jurados de imprenta*), a sort of small-claims court of honor comprising seven male citizens age twenty-five or older, chosen by lot from a biennially renewed duty roster.[26] The problem with the jurados, many Uruguayans believed, was that just about every possible jurist was likely to belong to one of Uruguay's two major political parties, the Blancos or Colorados. And since libel claims almost invariably stemmed from politics, this meant that press juries were highly politicized and consequently believed to lack validity. If a government-stacked press jury ruled against an opposition journalist, people rightly saw this as pure politics. If an opposition-stacked jury acquitted, this was seen as politics, too. In such a climate, many influential Uruguayans claimed, the majority of libel cases brought to press juries did not get anywhere.[27] And even if a jury did convict, the built-in legitimacy deficit tainted that conviction, meaning that the man who had been libeled received no real vindication. For these reasons, defamation cases were not nearly as common as they might otherwise have been, given the wide-open style of debate in the Uruguayan press.

So what was a politician who believed himself to have been defamed to do? Increasingly, people stopped bothering with the formal legal system and turned instead to the principles and procedures set down in the dueling codes, enlisting their seconds to confront the slanderer and demand gentlemanly "explanations." As the prospect of a duel became significantly more likely than the prospect of a legal accusation for defamation, journalists and politicians began, as a matter of course, to take fencing lessons, to practice their marksmanship, and to immerse themselves in the etiquette of dueling.[28] So, when a newspaperman contemplated whether or not to sign an editorial, whether or not to publicize an accusation for which he lacked proof, or whether or not to use a particularly inflammatory turn of phrase, he worried less and less about the legal consequences and more and more about the chance that he would be compelled either to issue a humiliating apology or to face his adversary at sword point or gunpoint.

The dueling codes covered much more than the combat itself; they also sought to define what constituted an offense against honor and what did not, when an apology had to be accepted or could be rejected, and the conditions under which men had the legitimate right either to demand or refuse a duel. In other words, the conventions of dueling—as written in the honor codes and as established by precedent in earlier duels—played a key role in establishing the norms by which the public sphere operated. Indeed, it was no accident that the rules set down in the dueling manuals, which Chatauvillard and his many imitators had quite deliberately crafted in the style of legal codes, came to be known as "gentlemanly laws" or the "laws of honor."[29] Dueling "law" therefore supplanted defamation law as the normal, everyday regulator of public discourse in Uruguay's young democracy.

As the dueling codes replaced the criminal code as the remedy of choice in cases of alleged defamation, the popular definition of "responsibility" changed as well. When the authors of the 1830 constitution referred to the author's responsibility for his words, it is reasonable to assume that they meant his legal responsibility, in accordance with libel and defamation statutes. But Uruguayan politicians and journalists by the second half of the nineteenth century had developed their own conception of responsibility, which they often called "gentlemanly responsibility." To be responsible meant to be willing and able to answer for one's words and actions in the manner dictated by the honor codes, and on the dueling ground if necessary. Irresponsibility, the converse, characterized the man who hurled insults or engaged in polemics but was unprepared to face the consequences that might ensue if his adversary took offense and demanded satisfaction. Following the rhetoric of the era, an irresponsible man was a man whose words lacked the proper "guarantee." To give one example of this idea of a guarantee, in 1880, military officer Alberto Chilabert published a string of violent insults against an opposition journalist in a deliberate effort to provoke a duel. The open letter began "Washington Bermúdez is a miserable coward and a scoundrel," and ended with the word "guaranteed" in lieu of a signature.[30] Anonymous or not, the meaning of "guaranteed" was clear to all: it signaled Chilabert's readiness to accept any challenge that Bermúdez might issue.

By the latter decades of the nineteenth century, it became formulaic for writers and speakers to declare publicly their readiness to defend their words *en cualquier terreno* (on whatever terrain), be it in the courtroom or on the so-called field of honor.[31] By most accounts, the field of honor was the terreno of choice, but what stands out is the way that public men saw the different fields as essentially two alternative venues for the airing of identical disputes. In 1923, for example, Police Chief Juan A. Pintos took Socialist Deputy Emilio Frugoni to court for abuse of press freedom, accusing him of having committed libel when he denounced Pintos's alleged corruption. Why did Pintos take this particular case to the courts? On this, the police chief's answer was remarkably candid:

> It would be futile for me to attempt to meet Dr. Frugoni on the terreno that men seek out when they wish to respond to offenses received; because it is public knowledge that Dr. Frugoni does not recognize that terreno.[32]

This idea that a journalist or politician might be called to account for his words in either of two arenas, one with lawyers and jurors, the other with seconds and swords or pistols, lay at the heart of the idea of responsibility. Elsewhere, I have compared and contrasted in detail the functioning of these two different terrenos.[33] For our purposes, two points are crucial to understand: first, that the dueling codes inspired enormous respect, virtually on the same level as formal legal codes, and second, that many politicians and virtually all political journalists saw dueling protocol as the preferred regulator of discourse, the preferred deterrent against slander, the preferred means of resolving the conflicts that inevitably arose in heated political debate. Slander trials might be an alternative for some, but they were an inferior alternative.

The doctrine of gentlemanly responsibility by no means demanded that everyone become a duelist; it did, however, call upon those who would not or could not duel to avoid the kinds of situations that might incite duels or challenges. There was a clear idea that if you couldn't stand the heat, you needed to stay out of the kitchen; those unwilling or unable to face a duel were expected to avoid the polemical world of politics and journalism, or at least politics and journalism as usually practiced in nineteenth- and early-twentieth-century Uruguay.

"Insults of a Woman" and the Gendering of Responsibility

Although the concept of gentlemanly responsibility first emerged as a practical means to police the bounds of acceptability in journalism, it is difficult to overstate its impact on Uruguay's public sphere. First of all, gentlemanly responsibility meant that in order to participate in political debate, one had to accept and abide by the so-called laws of honor, notwithstanding the fact that dueling was both anathema to the Catholic Church and, until 1920, technically a crime.[34] This contrasts with the situation in some of the more devout, conservative, tradition-bound societies of the region, where the church's condemnation of dueling carried more weight, and the practice was therefore less widespread. Second, the concept of responsibility ensured that those who were not allowed to participate in the culture of the duel found themselves excluded a priori from full participation in the forum. That is not to say that excluded persons could not write for a newspaper or hold public office, but it did mean that society's leaders refused to recognize their right to engage in the intensely heated interchanges that so often constituted the daily bread of politics. In other words, the idea of responsibility made sharp political conflict off-limits to women, the elderly, the weak or infirm, and at least some of the lower classes.

Because responsibility, now redefined as the ability and willingness to duel, became the price of admission to public controversy, the gentlemanly honor codes came to shape the culture and spirit of public life itself. Willingness to face death, at least hypothetically, gave one the right to speak; therefore, one could silence an adversary by successfully placing *his* courage, *his* virility, *his* willingness to die in doubt. Although dueling protocol was theoretically designed to prevent insults, deter personal attacks, and resolve personal conflicts as they might arise, Uruguayans misused that protocol with great frequency, at times deliberately provoking duels or challenges. Part of this was a clear politics of intimidation; after all, if a politician or journalist gained a reputation as a formidable duelist who was quick to take offense, he might instill enough fear in his adversaries that they would censor themselves rather than face the possible consequences. Or one man would challenge another in the deliberate hope that his interlocutor would back down and apologize. When successful, this kind of intimidation was viewed by some as a great victory, almost as if silencing the other side were the same as winning the debate. Others criticized this bullying use of the dueling ritual, and there were limits to how far a man bent on forcing an issue could go, but the idea of responsibility typically gave power and resonance to a duelist's words, while it wrested legitimacy from the words of a man who appeared reluctant to defend them *en cualquier terreno.* The nonduelist was irresponsible. His words lacked any guarantee and could be safely ignored.

On many occasions, Uruguayans referred to their allegedly irresponsible enemies in openly gendered terms. If a man used insulting or heated political language but proved unwilling to accept a challenge in response, his erstwhile adversary might publicly dismiss those words as *insultos de mujer* or *ofensas de mujer* (insults or offenses of a woman). The phrase implied that a woman's insults had no authority, that they did not pose any challenge to a gentleman's honor, and that they did not need to be answered in any forum, either legal or gentlemanly. As one man put it in a public letter to the newspapers,

> I cannot respond to offenses from one who knows not how to answer a gentlemanly challenge. . . . I consider his insults as if they were insults of a woman, slanderous remarks to which I cannot possibly pay any attention.[35]

By describing a rival's words as *insultos de mujer*, the man of honor was, at one level, making the obvious point that a refusal to duel demonstrated a lack of masculinity.[36] Some duelists spoke in almost biological terms about the manly qualities that compelled them to punish every affront to their dignity and implied that a man who responded differently must have a virility deficit. Police Chief Pintos, frustrated at Emilio Frugoni's refusal to duel, wrote in his legal deposition,

> For Dr. Frugoni, personal honor means nothing. . . . He pretends not to know where to go in order to defend that quality of a man that he seems to appreciate so little, but as I possess this quality in great measure, I ask for punishment of the vile slanderer.[37]

Indeed, by far the most effective way to force a reluctant adversary into a duel was to call his manhood into question. In 1886, for example, friends of dictator Máximo Santos issued the following challenge to José Batlle y Ordóñez, notable opponent of the regime:

If within two days that drunkard José Batlle y Ordóñez does not seek us out to go to the terreno where men go, we will look for him ourselves. If he has any shame and if he has what men have, let him seek us out.[38]

But the gendering of responsibility went far beyond the formulaic feminization of the alleged coward. The idea of gentlemanly responsibility and its opposite, insultos de mujer, held that the words spoken by a woman—the words themselves—could not carry the same weight as the "guaranteed" words of a "responsible" male (i.e., a male willing and able to duel). This was not primarily meant as a moral condemnation of women but was merely a statement of self-evident fact. No one was saying that women were less likely than men to tell the truth or that they were more likely to offend. They were pointing out what they believed to be obvious—that women were neither able nor free to defend their words with their lives, and, as a result, those words could not command the same degree of authority. What appeared to be a simple description of fact (that women could not duel) thus served as a powerful mechanism of political exclusion, proving the adage that ideologies function best when they seem to do nothing more than state commonsense truths.[39]

José Batlle y Ordóñez, J. A. Ramírez, and Presidential Responsibility "On Whatever Terrain"

Even when charges of cowardice were not especially credible, issues of responsibility or irresponsibility could drive political and journalistic debates to feverish levels of intensity. Nowhere is this better illustrated than by the decades-long polemic between José Batlle y Ordóñez, Colorado Party leader (and president, 1903–1907 and 1911–1915), and the leaders of the rival Blanco Party, most notably Luis Alberto de Herrera and Juan Andrés Ramírez.

Batlle y Ordóñez has been described as the most important figure in twentieth-century Uruguayan history, the architect of the modern Uruguayan state, and a social and political reformer of continental significance. Among other achievements, he is credited with transforming Uruguay's Colorado Party from a patronage-based political machine into a mass party representing the interests of urban workers and immigrants, with the establishment of the first welfare state in the Americas, with the creation of a highly innovative collegial executive not unlike that of Switzerland, and with having a social agenda that included women's rights, the curbing of the power of the church, and protection for labor unions.[40] As a born political insider who employed a radical reform agenda in order to perpetuate his party's domination of Uruguayan politics, Batlle y Ordóñez had numerous lifelong enemies.

Throughout his political career, Batlle y Ordóñez was also a newspaper editor, an occupation inextricably intertwined with his politics. His paper, *El*

Día, served as the mouthpiece of his political movement, and like most other Uruguayan papers, it spiced up the national and international news with aggressive editorials, snide satire, letters from supporters, and polemics with opponents. *El Día* was also the first Uruguayan paper to be sold on the newsstands at a price that a modest artisan, worker, or employee could afford.[41] This innovation was doubly successful, earning profits for the paper while spreading the gospel of Batlle y Ordóñez's reformist program to thousands of new voters.

By most accounts, Batlle y Ordóñez was never particularly enamored of the duel. According to biographer Domingo Arena, "He only accepted [the duel] as a barbarous necessity imposed by custom."[42] As president, Batlle y Ordóñez frequently ordered the police to intervene and stop duels before they occurred. Yet, despite his evident lack of enthusiasm for dueling, he fought at least five duels, one of them fatal to his opponent. He issued or received challenges on countless other occasions. Such seemingly contradictory behavior only makes sense when we keep in mind the all-consuming idea of responsibility. Put simply, a man who refused to duel forfeited his right to polemicize with credibility, and forfeiting the right to polemicize was the one thing that Batlle y Ordóñez would never, ever do.

Batlle y Ordóñez vehemently refused to place any such limitations on his freedom to speak. He could have opted, as did many nonduelists, to write and speak publicly in measured words, censoring himself and avoiding anything that might be construed as a personal attack. This highlights the fact that nonduelists could participate in public debate; they were simply not permitted to argue, insult, attack, accuse, or impugn the honor of others, lest they be called to account for their words and forced to back down in humiliation amid charges of cowardice and irresponsibility. Expressing in 1886 his refusal to so limit himself, Batlle y Ordóñez wrote,

> There are certain moments . . . when the events that occur are so monstrous that in all the Spanish dictionary there are only words that express clearly, albeit faintly, the enormity of the offense. For example, an assassination is committed by the political authorities, or public monies are stolen by those in power. How do we describe these events? Do we say that "a lamentable act" has been committed (as *El Siglo* did)? No, that is immoral and cowardly. The man protected by the public post he occupies, who in treachery strikes against the life of another, is called an *assassin*, just as the man who takes the property of others, be it public or private, is called a *thief*. . . . To use other words would be to falsify the truth, sacrificing the noble independence of thought at the altar of supposed decorum in language.[43]

Because Batlle y Ordóñez would not countenance self-censorship, the unwritten rules of Uruguayan public life left him no choice but to be a duelist, whether he approved of dueling or not. To act otherwise would have undermined his ability to speak as he saw necessary.[44]

When Batlle y Ordóñez became president, he continued to write for *El Día*, from whose pages he attacked his opponents with the same energy as always. He pressed his agenda, writing unsigned editorials himself, inspiring his followers, railing against his opponents, and engaging in the kinds of heated exchanges that could easily spark challenges or duels. His opponents were incensed at his insistence on wearing both hats (that of polemicist and that of president) at the same time. According to the logic of gentlemanly responsibility, Batlle y Ordóñez's enemies had a point. As a sitting president, he could not duel. After all, dueling technically remained a crime, and you could not ask the president to resign his post temporarily or slip out of the country in order to duel; nor could any opponent be expected to face the consequences of killing the president, even in a scrupulously fair contest. But a sitting president was also immune from prosecution in the courts for libel. What recourse did they have, then, his opponents complained, if they were personally insulted in the pages of *El Día*? How could they call Batlle y Ordóñez to account?

Blanco leader Luis Alberto de Herrera raised the issue in 1906 after a particularly violent exchange of words. Herrera had accused Batlle y Ordóñez of being afraid to appear in public without bodyguards. Batlle y Ordóñez responded in *El Día* with an attack on Herrera, so Herrera named his seconds and issued a challenge. Batlle y Ordóñez answered with the unusual offer to accept a duel nine months hence, after his period in office had expired. In a letter published in several papers, Herrera's seconds reported,

> [Herrera] considered Mr. José Batlle y Ordóñez's actions to be highly irregular, given that he who offends should put himself immediately in a position to face the personal responsibilities occasioned by his attack, thus placing himself within the terms of the laws of honor.[45]

Noted poet and Blanco militant Carlos Roxlo joined the criticism, arguing that Batlle y Ordóñez had to decide whether he was president or journalist. If the former, then he had to accept that he was not free to insult and engage in polemics. If the latter, then he had no right to invoke presidential privilege.[46] In sum, Herrera and Roxlo were complaining about Batlle y Ordóñez's irresponsibility: because Batlle y Ordóñez the president was both immune from legal challenges and barred from accepting gentlemanly challenges, Batlle y Ordóñez the journalist was free to say whatever he liked with no mind to the consequences. Offering to duel nine months later was not a solution; for Herrera and Roxlo, responsibility demanded that Batlle y Ordóñez refrain altogether from writing in *El Día*.

During Batlle y Ordóñez's second presidential term (1911–1915), an identical criticism was taken up on a regular basis by Juan Andrés Ramírez in the pages of *El Siglo,* at that time the most influential of several opposition papers. Ramírez, who came from a line of important politician/journalists, was also a self-styled expert in matters related to dueling and gentlemanly honor. (A few years later he would author the law that decriminalized the duel in Uruguay.) Although Ramírez sincerely disagreed with almost every policy that Batlle y Ordóñez proposed, their rivalry was also deeply personal.[47] Few things angered Batlle y Ordóñez more than the palpable disrespect that regularly issued from Ramírez's pen: Ramírez often refused to refer to Batlle y Ordóñez by name, calling him "S.E." (for *su excelencia,* "his excellency"), "Pepe," or sometimes merely "him." Batlle y Ordóñez gave Ramírez the nickname "Scorpion," presumably for the venom with which he wrote.[48]

But of all the things for which he took Batlle y Ordóñez to task, the one that upset Ramírez the most was Batlle y Ordóñez's alleged disrespect for the laws of honor. Like Roxlo and Herrera in 1906, Ramírez argued that Batlle y Ordóñez consciously and deliberately slandered his opponents from the pages of *El Día,* using his presidential immunity to avoid the consequences either in the legal arena (*terreno legal*) or on the dueling ground (*terreno caballeresco*).[49] On numerous occasions but most frequently between 1912 and 1914, Ramírez denounced Batlle y Ordóñez for his irresponsibility. In response to an editorial in which Batlle y Ordóñez accused *El Siglo* of advocating that the police shoot striking workers, Ramírez wrote,

> This . . . is the new version of an infamous falsehood that has been made several times before against us by His Excellency, protected by the irresponsibility that the law assures him before the courts, and that he has assured for himself in the terreno caballeresco.[50]

Batlle y Ordóñez, according to Ramírez, used his irresponsibility not only to lie and slander with impunity. When Batlle y Ordóñez himself felt insulted, Scorpion charged, he enlisted others to do his dirty work for him, sometimes inciting partisan mobs to attack *El Siglo*'s offices, sometimes allowing surrogates to provoke duels or otherwise issue threats on his behalf.[51] The implication was that Batlle y Ordóñez's actions were not only lacking in gentlemanly honor but also deliberately designed to muzzle and intimidate the independent press. In April 1913, when Batlle y Ordóñez's *El Día* ran a recurring column that brutally attacked opposition elder statesman José Pedro Ramírez, tension levels between the president and the anti-government papers reached such a height that even Argentine observers took notice. *La Argentina* of Buenos Aires editorialized,

> President Batlle y Ordóñez has not abandoned his journalist's pen, a pen he unfortunately wields, not for peaceful propaganda and conciliation between his country's political factions, but to sustain continuous polemics, made more acer-

bic by the use of highly charged language. . . . The Head of a State may not be a political polemicist, especially when it involves the kinds of matters that incite passions to an extraordinary degree. Even less may he, shielded by his immunity, hurl personal charges from the . . . columns of his paper, impugning the honor of others, as such offenses are unable to find satisfaction.[52]

But no matter what Ramírez, the opposition dailies, or even the Argentine papers might say, Batlle y Ordóñez made clear that he did not believe his presidential inability to duel or his presidential immunity from prosecution should deprive him of the freedom to speak out on matters of public interest.[53] On several occasions between 1912 and 1915, just as he had in the 1906 conflict with Luis Alberto de Herrera, Batlle y Ordóñez offered to accept a duel as soon as he left office. The problem with this solution, Ramírez and other critics pointed out, was that it violated a fundamental principle of the honor codes: that the offender, the man whose insult brought the challenge, was required to answer for his words without hesitation or delay. "He who cannot take immediate responsibility for his offenses may not offend, without placing himself outside of the laws of honor."[54] To postpone the duel (during which time the offender was presumably free to improve his fencing or marksmanship skills) would be to violate the very purpose of the honor codes, which was to prevent insults in the first place.[55]

When viewed solely from the perspective of the honor code, Ramírez's logic was difficult to assail, particularly if one accepted the proposition that *El Día* rather than *El Siglo* had been the first to cross the line separating legitimate debate from ad hominem attack. Batlle y Ordóñez's contention, however, was that the irresponsible one was Ramírez, who deliberately chose to defame the only man in the entire country who was not permitted to answer him in the *terreno caballeresco*:

> The Director of *El Siglo*, who prudently avoids personal polemics with other individuals, provokes them daily with the President of the Republic. One other person does the same thing. The game is clear: there is no danger in such provocations.[56]

Building on the implication that Ramírez, the supposed expert in dueling and matters of honor, was in reality a coward who only attacked those who lacked the freedom to defend themselves, *El Día* lampooned Scorpion in ways that most unsubtly questioned his masculinity. On May 28, 1913, for example, in response to weeks of *El Siglo* editorials entitled "Para El" ("For Him"), *El Día* published a response (the first of several) entitled "Para Ella" ("For Her") with the footnote, "We consider ourselves authorized to call her this, in light of her latest journalistic stances."[57]

Other factors, in addition to the dueling issue, inspired the attacks on Ramírez's manhood. For example, Batlle y Ordóñez had earlier accused

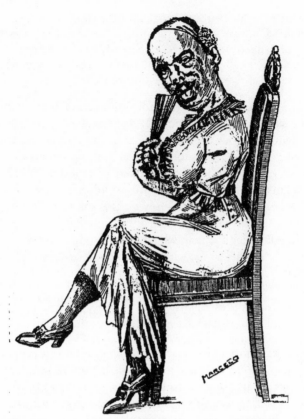

Figure 5.1.   "Para El" ["For Him"]. Source: *El Siglo,*
May 29, 1913, p. 1.

Ramírez of shutting down the offices of *El Siglo* when a pro-government march went by. A cartoon had depicted the paper's staff armed to the teeth, cowering behind a locked and barred door while a terrified Ramírez knelt and recited the Lord's Prayer.[58] In the case of the "For Her" articles, the context makes clear that the principal question at issue was precisely who was or was not responsible for his words. And the gendered insults in *El Día* did not stop. A piece appearing the following year, entitled "Escorpión en la Cámara" ("Scorpion in the Congress"), portrayed a seated Juan Andrés Ramírez in full drag.[59] The depiction of Ramírez was not in this instance related to dueling; *El Día* was repeating a comment Ramírez had made about another politician and implying an affection that exceeded the bounds of masculine propriety. But no matter what the issue, the pattern of insults was consistent, year in and year out.

Ramírez did not impugn Batlle y Ordóñez's masculinity in the same way. His response to the first "For Her" piece was to write yet another "For Him" editorial, copying the idea of a footnote:

"For Him"[1]

[1] As moral bankruptcy [*bellaquería*] is not the exclusive patrimony of either of the sexes, we see no reason to change that of Mr. Batlle y Ordóñez.[60]

Ramírez's approach was to treat Batlle y Ordóñez not as an effeminate coward but as an irresponsible *bellaco* (scoundrel), lacking the most elemental sense of honor, decency, morality, or fair play, a man who deliberately took advantage of the fact that no one could call him to account for his words. But even this seemingly opposite critique was delivered in gendered vocabulary. More than once, Ramírez pointedly ignored Batlle y Ordóñez's taunts with the refrain that insults lacking a proper guarantee were like "insults of a woman," words devoid of any authority, words requiring no answer.[61]

Conclusion

In Uruguay, where women's citizenship rights were seriously debated earlier than in most other Latin American countries, politicians did not hesitate to repeat the refrain that "women's words" deserved no response. In a nation where a feminist pioneer like public-health advocate Paulina Luisi could become a physician and rise to a position of genuine influence,[62] newspapers ran editorials entitled "For Her" and published cartoons depicting their opponent in a dress, legs demurely crossed. Considering the overall climate for women, one could ask, Was the discourse of "gentlemanly responsibility" and "insults of a woman" really that important in the larger scheme of things? At one level, it might be possible to answer in the negative. Women, like priests, socialists, and other nonduelists, were by no means excluded entirely from the public forum. Luisi, like other pioneering women of her era, published regularly in the press, held conferences of international scope, and found many other ways to influence public policy.[63]

Nevertheless, the gender-laden rhetoric of responsibility did restrict women's access to the public sphere, while intensely masculinizing the culture therein. Women remained free to speak, and speak they often did. But because they were not free to attack, accuse, denounce, insult, or otherwise engage in polemics, they found themselves pushed to the margins of a competitive political arena that was, for all intents and purposes, ruled by these very tactics. Worse still, the twin concepts of "gentlemanly responsibility" and "insults of a woman" not only marginalized women as potential political actors, but they also trivialized women's very words. Indeed, this kind of rhetoric implied that the unguaranteed words of a woman were by definition inconsequential.[64]

In all likelihood, most Uruguayan public men believed they were speaking figuratively rather than literally when denouncing each other's words as insultos de mujer. Certainly few people argued that women were more irresponsible than men or that they were less likely to adhere to the ideals of honor and decorum in public debate. Yet, the discursive trivialization of women's words did go beyond a mere figure of speech, or perhaps what I mean to say is that even figures of speech, when widely enough diffused, can have a genuine and profound impact on patterns of human behavior. They become culture. Uruguayans, incapable of imagining women as duelists, were incapable of imagining them as responsible, and hence were incapable of imagining them as involved in politics in the way that elite male Uruguayans understood politics.

Does the culture of gentlemanly responsibility and the resulting masculinization of political life provide evidence of a deliberate or systemic process of gender exclusion? Was the idea of gentlemanly responsibility, to paraphrase Joan Landes, the mechanism by which Uruguayan men constructed a public sphere "*against* women, not just without them"?[65] The question is straightforward; the answer is not. On the one hand, Uruguayan politicians and journalists embraced the duel not because they sought cohesion as a ruling class, or some kind of chivalric national ethos, or as a new masculine identity; they sought something much more immediate, mundane, and practical. In the duel and its accompanying code of honor, Uruguay's political elites believed they had found a more effective deterrent against libel, a way to resolve the conflicts that emerged in a rough-and-tumble political arena, and, above all, a sort of customary law policing the boundaries of speech at a time when speech could still launch revolutions.

On the other hand, with the dueling codes came the idea of gentlemanly responsibility, and with the idea of gentlemanly responsibility came the idea that women's words need not be taken seriously. Furthermore, the supposedly high-minded defense of honor did end up degenerating, with alarming frequency, into contests of masculine brinksmanship as each side sought to silence or humiliate the other by testing whether he was "man enough" to go to the wall (or to the terreno) in defense of his politics. Although these highly gendered games of chicken were perversions of the dueling code's intent, they were a direct consequence of the code's logic. It is easy to see, therefore, how something that started as a simple, practical dispute-prevention and -resolution mechanism could spawn a culture in which it made complete and utter sense to parade one's own virility and to call into question that of one's adversary. To that extent, Uruguayans did in fact construct a public sphere *against* women.

Notes

Research for this chapter was supported by a general research grant from the Social Sciences and Humanities Research Council of Canada. I wish to acknowledge the assistance of the Centro Latino Americano de Economía Humana (CLAEH), the Biblioteca Nacional, the Archivo General de la Nación, and the Biblioteca de la Cámara de Representantes in Montevideo, Uruguay. Special thanks go to Gerardo Caetano, Sandra Gayol, Pablo Piccato, and the editors of this volume.

1. François-Xavier Guerra, *Modernidad e independencias: Ensayos sobre las revoluciones hispánicas* (Madrid: Editorial MAPFRE, 1992), esp. chs. 7, 8.

2. Jürgen Habermas, *The Structural Transformation of the Public Sphere: An Inquiry into a Category of Bourgeois Society* (Cambridge: Cambridge University Press, 1989). Originally written in 1962, in this work Habermas argued that the public sphere was a unique product of the eighteenth century, for the first time creating the opportunity for private individuals to engage in reasoned debate, without deference to rank or privilege, thereby providing a new kind of mediation between civil society and the state. Craig Calhoun, ed., *Habermas and the Public Sphere* (Cambridge, MA: MIT Press, 1992), offers the most comprehensive introduction to Habermas's thought on the public sphere and the debates it has incited. Other critical overviews include Anthony J. La Vopa, "Conceiving a Public: Ideas and Society in Eighteenth-Century Europe," *Journal of Modern History* 62, no. 1 (March 1992): 79–116; Harold Mah, "Phantasies of the Public Sphere: Rethinking the Habermas of Historians," *Journal of Modern History* 72 (March 2000): 153–82; Dena Goodman, "Public Sphere and Private Life: Towards a Synthesis of Current Historiographical Approaches to the Old Regime," *History and Theory* 31 (1992): 1–20. The controversies raised by the Habermas thesis have been many. Geoff Eley has questioned whether the many diverse spaces and forms of participation constituted a single "public sphere," or whether they are better described as multiple, parallel, and *competing* spheres. Geoff Eley, "Nations, Publics, and Political Cultures: Placing Habermas in the Nineteenth Century," in Calhoun, *Habermas and the Public Sphere*, esp. 304–6. Nancy Fraser agrees and posits the simultaneous emergence of a hegemonic bourgeois public sphere and what she calls "subaltern counterpublics." Nancy Fraser, "Rethinking the Public Sphere: A Contribution to the Critique of Actually Existing Democracy," in Calhoun, *Habermas and the Public Sphere*, 123. Habermas's idea of the public sphere as a space of *reasoned* and *open* discussion has similarly been questioned. See Keith Michael Baker, "Defining the Public Sphere in Eighteenth-Century France: Variations on a theme by Habermas," in Calhoun, *Habermas and the Public Sphere*, 182–83; Eley, "Nations, Publics, and Political Cultures," 310; and Michael Schudson, "Was There Ever a Public Sphere? If So, When? Reflections on the American Case," in Calhoun, *Habermas and the Public Sphere*, 160. Schudson argues in the case of the colonial United States that it "does not appear that in any general sense rational-critical discussion characterized American politics in the colonial era. The politically oriented riot was a more familiar form of political activity than learned discussion of political principles." Harold Mah goes further to argue that the very idea of private individuals coming together in reasoned debate to formulate "public opinion" (in the process magically transforming themselves into a unitary "public") is not just an unrealizable ideal; far worse, it is a profoundly dangerous fiction, the kind of fiction that incited the violent excesses of the French Revolution. Mah, "Phantasies of the Public Sphere," esp. 170–72.

3. Carlos A. Forment, *Democracy in Latin America 1760–1900, Volume 1, Civic Selfhood and Public Life in Mexico and Peru* (Chicago: University of Chicago Press, 2003); Hilda Sábato, *The Many and the Few: Political Participation in Republican Buenos Aires* (Palo Alto: Stanford University Press, 2001), esp. ch. 2; Hilda Sábato, "Citizenship, Political Participation and the Formation of the Public Sphere in Buenos Aires, 1850s–1880s," *Past and Present* 136 (August 1992):

139–63; Sarah C. Chambers, *From Subjects to Citizens: Honor, Gender, and Politics in Arequipa, Peru, 1780–1854* (University Park: Pennsylvania State University Press, 1999).

4. Joan B. Landes, *Women and the Public Sphere in the Age of the French Revolution* (Ithaca, NY: Cornell University Press, 1988), provides the clearest articulation of this thesis, discussed in more detail below. For debate about the impact of nineteenth-century liberalism on Latin American women, see Elizabeth Dore, "One Step Forward, Two Steps Back: Gender and the State in the Long Nineteenth Century," in *Hidden Histories of Gender and the State in Latin America*, ed. Elizabeth Dore and Maxine Molyneux (Durham, NC: Duke University Press, 2000), 3–32. Christine Hunefeldt, *Liberalism in the Bedroom: Quarreling Spouses in Nineteenth-Century Lima* (University Park: Pennsylvania State University Press, 2000).

5. Asunción Lavrin, *Women, Feminism, and Social Change in Argentina, Chile, and Uruguay, 1890–1940* (Lincoln: University of Nebraska Press, 1995), 229–32. For a more general background to Uruguayan anticlericalism and the secularizing process, see Gerardo Caetano and Roger Geymonat, *La secularización uruguaya (1859–1919), Tomo I: Catolicismo y privatización de lo religioso* (Montevideo: Ediciones Santillana, 1997).

6. Lavrin, *Women, Feminism and Social Change*, 216, 332, and elsewhere. Baltasar Brum, *Los derechos de la mujer: reforma civil y política del Uruguay* (Montevideo: José Maria Serrano, 1923), cited in Lavrin, *Women, Feminism, and Social Change*, 451.

7. All of these explanations have appeared in the extensive literature on dueling in Europe and the United States. Some key texts include François Billacois, *The Duel: Its Rise and Fall in Early Modern France*, ed. and trans. Trista Selous (New Haven, CT: Yale University Press, 1990); V. G. Kiernan, *The Duel in European History: Honor and the Reign of the Aristocracy* (Oxford: Oxford University Press, 1988); Robert A. Nye, *Masculinity and Male Codes of Honor in Modern France* (New York: Oxford University Press, 1993); Robert A. Nye, "Fencing, the Duel and Republican Manhood in the Third Republic," *Journal of Contemporary History* 25 (1990): 365–77; William M. Reddy, *The Invisible Code: Honor and Sentiment in Postrevolutionary France, 1814–1848* (Berkeley: University of California Press, 1997); Ute Frevert, *Men of Honour: A Social and Cultural History of the Duel* (Cambridge, MA: Polity Press, 1995); Ute Frevert, "Honour and Middle-Class Cultures: The History of the Duel in England and Germany," in *Bourgeois Society in Nineteenth-Century Europe*, ed. Jürgen Kocka and Allen Mitchell (Oxford: Berg Publishers Limited, 1993); Kevin McAleer, *Dueling: The Cult of Honor in Fin de Siècle Germany* (Princeton, NJ: Princeton University Press, 1994); James Kelly, *'That Damn'd Thing Called Honour': Duelling in Ireland 1570–1860* (Cork: Cork University Press, 1995); Kenneth S. Greenberg, *Honor and Slavery* (Princeton, NJ: Princeton University Press, 1996); Bertram Wyatt-Brown, *Southern Honor: Ethics and Behavior in the Old South* (Oxford: Oxford University Press, 1982); Edward L. Ayers, *Vengeance and Justice: Crime and Punishment in the Nineteenth-Century American South* (New York: Oxford University Press, 1992). On Latin American dueling, see Pablo Piccato, "Politics and the Technology of Honor: Dueling in Turn-of-the-Century Mexico," *Journal of Social History* 33, no. 2 (winter 1999): 331–54; Sandra Gayol, "Honor Moderno: The Significance of Honor in Fin-de-Siècle Argentina," *Hispanic American Historical Review* 84, no. 3 (August 2004): 475–98; David S. Parker, "Law, Honor, and Impunity in Spanish America: The Debate over Dueling, 1870–1920," *Law and History Review* 19, no. 2 (summer 2001): 311–41.

8. The authors who have drawn the clearest link between dueling and nineteenth-century politics include Joanne B. Freeman, "Dueling as Politics: Reinterpreting the Burr-Hamilton Duel," *William and Mary Quarterly* 53, no. 2 (April 1996): 289–318; Mark G. Schmeller, "Imagining Public Opinion in Antebellum America: Fear, Credit, Law, and Honor (PhD dissertation, University of Chicago, 2001), ch. 6; and Steven Hughes, "Men of Steel: Dueling, Honor, and Politics in Liberal Italy," in *Men and Violence: Gender, Honor, and Rituals in Modern Europe and America*, ed. Pieter Spierenburg (Columbus: Ohio State University Press, 1998), 64–81. See also Sandra Gayol, "El honor de la política: usos y significados en la Argentina Moderna" (paper pre-

sented at the 2003 Meeting of the Latin American Studies Association, Dallas, Texas, March 27–29, 2003).

9. Comte de Chatauvillard, *Essai sur del duel par le cte. De Chatauvillard* (Paris: Bohaire, 1836): Parker, "Law, Honor, and Impunity," 326–28.

10. Some key English-language works on honor in Spain and Latin America include Julian Pitt-Rivers, "Honor," in *International Encyclopedia of the Social Sciences*, vol. 6 (New York: Macmillan/Free Press, 1968), 503–11; J. G. Peristiany, ed., *Honour and Shame: The Values of Mediterranean Society* (London: Weidenfeld and Nicolson, 1965); Frank Henderson Stewart, *Honor* (Chicago: University of Chicago Press, 1994); Peter Berger, "On the Obsolescence of the Concept of Honor," *Archives Européennes de Sociologie* 11 (1970): 339–47; Lyman L. Johnson and Sonya Lipsett-Rivera, eds., *The Faces of Honor: Sex, Shame, and Violence in Colonial Latin America* (Albuquerque: University of New Mexico Press, 1998); Ann Twinam, *Public Lives, Private Secrets: Gender, Honor, Sexuality, and Illegitimacy in Colonial Spanish America* (Palo Alto: Stanford University Press, 2001); Sueann Caulfield, *In Defense of Honor: Sexual Morality, Modernity, and Nation in Early-Twentieth-Century Brazil* (Durham, NC: Duke University Press, 2000); Gayol, "Honor Moderno." Also Pablo Piccato, "Salvador Díaz Mirón: The Limits of Honor and Violence in Porfirian Politics" (paper presented at the 2003 Meeting of the Latin American Studies Association, Dallas, Texas, March 27–29, 2003).

11. Piccato, "Politics and the Technology of Honor," 331.

12. Piccato, "Politics and the Technology of Honor," 346.

13. Landes, *Women and the Public Sphere*; Nancy Fraser, "Rethinking the Public Sphere," in Calhoun, *Habermas and the Public Sphere*, esp. 118; and Nancy Fraser, "What's Critical about Critical Theory? The Case of Habermas and Gender," in her *Unruly Practices: Power, Discourse, and Gender in Contemporary Social Theory* (Minneapolis: University of Minnesota Press, 1989), esp. 126–27.

14. Landes, *Women and the Public Sphere*, 171. For more critical perspectives on Landes's thesis and the idea that the public sphere presupposed women's exclusion, see Baker, "Defining the Public Sphere" in Calhoun, *Habermas and the Public Sphere*, esp. 200–202; Goodman, "Public Sphere and Private Life," esp. 14–20; Mary P. Ryan, "Gender and Public Access: Women's Politics in Nineteenth-Century America," in Calhoun, *Habermas and the Public Sphere*, 259–88; and Amanda Vickery, "Golden Age to Separate Spheres? A Review of the Categories and Chronologies of English Women's History," *Historical Journal* 36 (1993): 383–414, esp. 393–401.

15. See, for example, Gayol, "El honor de la política."

16. Piccato, "Politics and the Technology of Honor," 346.

17. Ramón Cárcano, 1883, cited in Tim Duncan, "La prensa política: 'Sud-América,' 1884–1892," in Gustavo Ferrari and Ezequiel Gallo, eds., *La Argentina del ochenta al centenario* (Buenos Aires: Sudamericana, 1980), 761. Original Spanish quotation: "Un diario para un hombre público es como un cuchillo para el gaucho pendenciero: debe tenerse siempre a la mano."

18. The quotation is from Habermas, *Structural Transformation of the Public Sphere*, 54, as cited in Baker, "Defining the Public Sphere," in Calhoun, *Habermas and the Public Sphere*, 194.

19. Facundo Zuviría, *La prensa periódica* (Montevideo: Imprenta de La Republica, 1857), 11. For similar arguments in Argentina, see Sábato, *The Many and the Few*, 43–44, 48–49.

20. William Reddy, "*Condottieri* of the Pen: Journalists and the Public Sphere in Postrevolutionary France (1814–1850)," *American Historical Review* 99, no. 5 (December 1994): 1546–70; Nye, *Masculinity and Male Codes of Honor in Modern France*, esp. 187–90; Hughes, "Men of Steel," 68–70; Mark G. Schmeller, "Imagining Public Opinion in Antebellum America," ch. 6. For Chile, Pilar González Bernaldo de Quirós, "Literatura injuriosa y opinión pública en Santiago de Chile durante la primera mitad del siglo XIX," *Estudios Públicos* (Santiago, Chile) 76 (1999): esp. 247–55; for Argentina, Duncan, "La prensa política."

21. Zuviría, *La prensa periódica*, 25, 39.

22. Benjamín Fernández y Medina, *La imprenta y la prensa en el Uruguay desde 1807 a 1900* (Montevideo: Imprenta de Dornaleche y Reyes, 1900), 69.

23. Carlos María Ramírez, *Conferencias de derecho constitucional*, 2nd ed. (Montevideo: Imprenta y Litografía "La Razón," 1897), 307–10.

24. Wenceslau Regules, *Breves consideraciones sobre la libertad de la prensa y de las distintas leyes que se han promulgado al respecto en nuestro país (derecho constitucional): tesis* (Montevideo: Imprenta a Vapor de El Heraldo, 1881), 30–34; Francisco Durá, *Del enjuiciamiento de los delitos de imprenta: tesis* (Montevideo: Establecimiento Tipográfico de El Telégrafo Marítimo, 1881), 9–29; República Oriental del Uruguay. Actas de la H. Cámara de Representantes de la 6a. legislatura. Tomo 5—años 1852–53–54 (Montevideo: Imprenta de "El Siglo Ilustrado," 1906), 364–65, 901–903, 921–22; República Oriental del Uruguay, Ley de Imprenta, 10 de Junio de 1882: Publicación oficial (Montevideo: Imprenta de la Patria Uruguaya, 1882); República Oriental del Uruguay, Diario de Sesiones del Honorable Camara de Representantes, 1863, 26–176; República Oriental del Uruguay, Diario de sesiones de la H. Cámara de Representantes, sesiones extraordinarias del 1o período de la 15a legislatura, v. 81 (1886) (Montevideo: Imprenta de "El Siglo Ilustrado," 1891), 192–234, 363–415, 479–504; Fernández y Medina, *La imprenta y la prensa en el Uruguay*, 70–83.

25. Fernández y Medina, *La imprenta y la prensa en el Uruguay*, 71, 76–77; Eduardo Acevedo, *Anales históricos del Uruguay*, vol. 4 (Montevideo: Barreiro y Ramos, 1934), 281.

26. República Oriental del Uruguay, Código de instrucción criminal de la República Oriental del Uruguay, promulgado por el gobierno provisional por decreto-ley de 31 de diciembre de 1879 (Montevideo: Imprenta a Vapor de "La Tribuna," 1879), 91–100; Fernández y Medina, La imprenta y la prensa en el Uruguay, 80–82; Francisco Durá, *Del enjuiciamiento de los delitos de imprenta: tesis* (Montevideo: Establecimiento Tipográfico de "El Telégrafo Marítimo," 1881), 10–23.

27. For critiques of the jury system in general and of press juries in particular, see *El Ferro-Carril*, February 12, 1870, 2, "Juicio de imprenta"; *El Ferro-Carril*, February 13–14, 1870, 1, "El jurado."

28. In neighboring Argentina, at least one major daily paper set up a fencing salon in its Buenos Aires offices so that writers could take lessons and practice during their off hours.

29. Parker, "Law, Honor, and Impunity in Spanish America," 327–29.

30. "Remitidos: permanente," *La Nación* (Montevideo), July 1, 1880, 1.

31. This language was so ubiquitous that citing specific examples may be unnecessary, but the phrase "en cualquier terreno" appears, for example, in "Para El Día," *La Democracia* (Montevideo), October 14, 1921, 1.

32. República Oriental del Uruguay, Archivo Judicial, Montevideo, Juzgado de Instrucción Segundo Turno, Expediente #236, Arch. #58, 1925, "Juan A. Pintos, Querella por abuso de la libertad de imprenta," fojas 126–27.

33. David S. Parker, "Parallel Codes: Criminal Law and the 'Laws of Honor' in Uruguay and Argentina, 1870–1930" (paper presented at the Latin American Studies Association [LASA] XXII Congress, Miami, FL., March 16–18, 2000).

34. Church denunciations of the duel as barbarous and against God's law date back to at least the thirteenth century, and Spanish law called for severe sanctions. Uruguay's 1888 Criminal Code continued to view dueling as a crime, though enforcement was lax and inconsistent. In 1920, a law was passed decriminalizing all duels carried out under certain specified conditions. See Parker, "Law, Honor, and Impunity in Spanish America," 322, 331–38; David S. Parker, "La ley penal y las 'leyes caballerescas': hacia el duelo legal en el Uruguay," *Anuario IEHS* 14 (1999): 295–311.

35. *Diario del Plata*, November 6, 1915, 3, "Personal." See also *Diario del Plata*, November 7, 1915, 3, "Personal."

36. See, for example, Domingo Arena's recollection of an editorial in which José Batlle y Ordóñez referred to adversary Leopoldo López Vago as "Doña Leopoldina." Domingo Arena, *Escritos y discursos del Dr. Domingo Arena sobre el Sr. José Batlle y Ordóñez* (Montevideo: n.p., 1942), 225.

37. República Oriental del Uruguay, Archivo Judicial, Juzgado de Instrucción Segundo Turno, Expediente #236, Arch. #58, 1925, "Juan A. Pintos, Querella por abuso de la libertad de imprenta," fojas 120.

38. *El Día 1886–1981: 95 años de la libertad* (Montevideo: Impr. Artegraf, 1981), 24.

39. Roland Barthes, *Mythologies*, cited in Dror Wahrman, *Imagining the Middle Class: The Political Representation of Class in Britain, c. 1780–1840* (Cambridge: Cambridge University Press, 1995), 18.

40. Some of the best-known sources in English are Milton I. Vanger, *The Model Country: José Batlle y Ordóñez of Uruguay, 1907–1915* (Hanover, NH: University Presses of New England, 1980); George Pendle, *Uruguay*, 3rd ed. (London: Oxford University Press, 1963); Goran G. Lindahl, *Uruguay's New Path: A Study in Politics during the First Colegiado, 1919–1933* (Stockholm: Library and Institute of Ibero-American Studies, 1962).

41. Walter Trías, *Batlle periodista* (Montevideo: n.p., 1958), 51.

42. Arena, *Escritos y discursos del Dr. Domingo Arena sobre el Sr. José Batlle y Ordóñez*, 225. See also Daniel Pelúas, *Batlle, el hombre* (Montevideo: Editorial Fin de Siglo, 2001), 181–94.

43. "El Siglo tiene razón en parte," *El Día*, September 20, 1886, 2.

44. See "Lance," *El Día*, June 10, 1914, 5, in which Batlle y Ordóñez communicated, through third persons, the following message: "The duel has never seemed [to Batlle y Ordóñez] to be a very reasonable thing; but despite that, he submits to all the laws of honor. . . . [And since] he cannot permit someone else [to take responsibility for words that are his], he considers himself fully obligated to respond at the proper moment for the editorial in question."

45. "Incidente personal," *La Democracia*, April 24, 1906, 1.

46. "De Carlos Roxlo: carta abierta," *La Democracia*, April 27, 1906, 1.

47. Some discussion of a few supposed reasons for their falling out appear in "Personalísimo," *Diario del Plata*, March 16, 1915, 3.

48. On one occasion Batlle y Ordóñez referred to "Scorpion" as "the toxic bug" (*el bichito tóxico*). "Escorpión en retirada," *El Día*, June 15, 1914, 5.

49. Echoing Carlos Roxlo's critique but using more direct language, El Siglo wrote, "If you cannot take responsibility for your insults, you are not allowed to insult." "El Siglo y el Jefe de Policía," *El Siglo*, June 11, 1914, 3.

50. "Personalísimo," *El Siglo*, March 12, 1913, 3.

51. For the first charge, see "Para El," *El Siglo*, April 16, 1913, 3, and "Escorpión y Batlle," *El Siglo*, July 12, 1914, 3. For the second, see "El Siglo y el Jefe de Policía," *El Siglo*, June 11, 1914, 3, and "Punto final," *El Siglo*, June 14, 1914, 3.

52. Reprinted in "Batlle juzgado en Buenos Aires: juicios severos," *El Siglo*, April 19, 1913, 3. See also "Batlle juzgado en Buenos Aires," *El Siglo*, April 18, 1913, 3; "'La Nación' de Buenos Aires y el Sr. Batlle y Ordóñez," *La Tribuna Popular*, April 18, 1913, 4. Batlle y Ordóñez's attack on José Pedro Ramírez can be seen, for example, in "Permanente," *El Día*, April 12, 1913, 7.

53. "Punto final . . . por ahora," *El Día*, March 17, 1913.

54. "Para El," *El Siglo*, April 16, 1913, 3.

55. "Responsabilidades a largo plazo," *La Democracia*, April 16, 1913, 5.

56. "Para El," *El Día*, quoted in *El Siglo*, April 16, 1913, 3.

57. "Para Ella," *El Día*, May 28, 1913, 6.

58. "Mientras pasan las manifestaciones populares . . ." *El Día*, April 9, 1913, 8.

59. "Escorpión en la Cámara," *El Día*, May 20, 1914, 5.

60. "Para El," *El Siglo*, May 29, 1913, 1.

61. For example, "Insultos de mujer," *El Siglo*, March 21, 1912, 3.

62. Lavrin, *Women, Feminism, and Social Change*, 321 and elsewhere.

63. Lavrin, *Women, Feminism, and Social Change*. Luisi wrote and published on eugenics, suffrage, and sex education, among other themes.

64. Nancy Fraser makes a not-dissimilar point about patriarchal disregard for the value and autonomy of women's words. Fraser, "What's Critical about Critical Theory," 127.

65. Landes, *Women and the Public Sphere*, 171.

6

Work, Sex, and Power in a Central American Export Economy at the Turn of the Twentieth Century

Lara E. Putnam

WHAT DOES IT DO TO OUR UNDERSTANDING of the export economies of Central America's Caribbean coasts when next to the classic image of West Indian men hefting bananas at a railroad siding, we place a new icon of enclave labor: women gathered around a communal water pipe in a boardinghouse courtyard, where laundresses stir cauldrons of manioc starch, girls peel vegetables for stew, and prostitutes fetch water to bathe? Women are rarely mentioned in traditional accounts of the economic "enclaves" from which U.S. companies exported millions of dollars' worth of tropical products in the late nineteenth and early twentieth centuries. This would not be particularly grave if one could simply extrapolate from men's experiences and still have an accurate picture of the functioning of the export regions. But, in fact, men's and women's roles were starkly differentiated, and for this reason, inattention to women and what they did has rendered whole categories of work, kinds of labor relations, and forms of struggle invisible.

All along the Caribbean coast, in ports like Santa Marta (Colombia), Colón and Bocas del Toro (Panama), Port Limón (Costa Rica), Bluefields and Puerto Cabezas (Nicaragua), Trujillo, Tela, and Puerto Cortés (Honduras), Puerto Barrios (Guatemala), and Punta Gorda and Belize (British Honduras), women manned the informal service economy that undergirded export production, an informal economy in which exporters like the United Fruit Company (UFCo) took little interest. Women traveled from adjacent lowlands, nearby highlands, and distant islands to provide food, clean laundry, shelter, sex, and companionship to the male migrants who labored in the diggings, on the rails, in the fields, or on the docks. Scholars call the kind of work these women did—the work that goes into keeping body and soul together day after day—the labor of daily social reproduction, differentiating it from generational reproduction, that is, childbearing and child rearing.

The export zones' cash service economy spread the wages male workers earned to highland cities in the form of fees paid to sojourning prostitutes, to homesteads in the plantations' interstices in the form of payments for meals delivered to plantation crews, and to Jamaican smallholdings in the form of remittances from laundresses, sweet sellers, boarding-house owners, and peddlers. Social reproduction was arranged in a patterned way across the region, not because it was centrally planned but because shared constraints (transport routes, price differentials, kin obligations, immigration laws) patterned individual choices in common ways. The patterned arrangement of social reproduction then had material consequences for actors large and small, from Jamaican schoolgirls to Colombian planters to UFCo managers. Thus, attention to gender and sexuality makes us reevaluate the causes and consequences of labor migration and the links between the banana enclave and the regional economy. Furthermore, attention to the arrangements through which reproductive labor was provided highlights the importance of kinship ties within the export zones and the significance of households as work sites. This in turn makes visible complex systems of labor relations not directly under plantation owners' purview and forces us to reevaluate long-standing assumptions about the extent and efficacy of UFCo domination.

The labor of daily social reproduction was often structured by kin ties and frequently linked to sexual activity and its consequences. Sex was often integral to young people's struggles for adult autonomy or economic independence. It became a flash point for power struggles within families, as well as those between men and women. Ideas about sex and sex acts themselves were also involved in conflicts much broader in scope, including the processes through which state power itself was constituted. Public authorities in the export region laid claim to the right to command by asserting a particular kind of masculinity, which included willingness to use physical violence and the right to be sexually active with multiple women. Once we stop assuming that all conflicts involving sex belong to a supposedly private sphere irrelevant to the functioning of "real" political power, we see how often collective and individual struggles over territory, property, authority, autonomy, and institutional access were connected to sexual boasts, sexual accusations, or sexual violence. If we ignore this, our portrait of political struggle in the export regions will omit some of its fiercest moments.

Academics, Exports, Empires, and Intimacy

In the 1970s, feminist anthropologists and sociologists studying Latin America were among the first academics to insist on the need to study gender roles and household arrangements in order to understand large-scale economic transformations. These pioneers of what came to be known as "women-in-development" studies put the gendered division of labor, the organization of social reproduction, and the informal economy at the forefront of their accounts. They analyzed these topics with close attention to the structure of power within families, asking who benefited from which changes under what circumstances. While the earliest work in this paradigm tended to focus on women to the exclusion of men and to treat subordination and empowerment as universal truths, subsequent efforts (often under the label "gender-in-development") examined both women and men as social actors whose experiences of hierarchy or conflict are culturally specific.[1]

In the same years that feminist pioneers were focusing on gender roles and the distribution of resources within peasant homes, another group of sociologists and historians was developing the concept of the "enclave economy" to describe certain instances of direct foreign investment in Latin America.[2] In the early twentieth century, U.S. investors created company towns across Latin America to facilitate the production and export of primary goods from oil to bananas. Exporters like United Fruit built internal transportation systems, barracks housing for workers, breezy residential zones restricted to white North American managers, hospitals, and sometimes schools. How could export enterprises create so much wealth for foreign owners and yet leave so much poverty behind when—as almost inevitably happened—declining yields led companies to close up shop and shift operations elsewhere? The answer lay in enclaves' isolation from the host nations and their tight connection to markets abroad. "The agroexport sector did not act as a growth multiplier," scholars argued. "The sum total of economic activity always remained in the thrall of the vicissitudes of the international marketplace."[3]

Such descriptions seemed to support the broader "dependency theory" Latin American intellectuals developed in the 1960s, which argued that political and economic problems in the region were the outcome of the particular nature of connections established with the industrialized economies, rather than proof of timeless backwardness or cultural pathology.[4] Dependency arguments provided a salutary critique of the modernization theory then guiding northern intellectuals' prescriptions for the Third World. However, subsequent historical reconstructions based on fine-grained sources have shown that enclaves were far less isolated from their surroundings than these authors assumed.[5] Research on foreign-owned mining and petroleum enclaves has shown that social, cultural, and political processes within these regions were continuously connected to those ongoing in the surrounding nations as a whole.[6] In the banana-exporting regions of Central and South America, researchers have found an interplay of proprietorship and wage labor within communities and over life cycles that undercuts earlier assumptions about the characteristics and role of the "rural proletariat" supposedly created by direct foreign investment.[7] These and other case studies have revealed multilayered systems of power in and around export zones, including both conflictive hierarchies among workers (often justified through racist ideologies) and cross-cutting alliances among foreign investors, local elites, and bureaucrats and politicians at the municipal, regional, and national levels.[8]

Recent developments in gender studies encourage us to bring these disparate scholarships together. Over a decade ago, feminist anthropologists began to formulate a research agenda that combined gender and political economy.[9] These authors take a "constructivist" approach to gender: rather than assuming that universal commonalities underlie women's condition, they argue that both manliness and femininity are social constructions that, however natural or eternal they may seem, in fact vary from society to society, as well as from group to group within societies, and change over time. Scholars unite this localized understanding of gender with a globalized perspective on power. They argue that processes of socioeconomic change have global, national, local, household, and interpersonal dimensions and are best understood by research that encompasses multiple scales of observation. A growing body of historical studies in this vein has explored the role of family labor and gender ideology in Latin American export production.[10] Meanwhile, recent work within colonial and postcolonial studies encourages us to take intimate practice even more seriously, highlighting connections among colonial administration, childrearing, sex, and the hierarchies of race that sustained imperial power.[11]

Each of the secondary literatures outlined here has come to insist on the importance of seeking out connections. This provides a particularly important corrective in the case of Central America's Caribbean export economies. When contemporary authors described the plantation regions, they buttressed their political agendas by creating exaggerated categorical separations, disguising real dilemmas as easy choices. They insisted there was a world of difference between "national" and "foreign" capital; between "native-born workers" and "West Indian Negroes"; between "modern, scientific" plantations and the supposedly "listless," "degenerating" aborigines who stood in the way of plantation expansion; between sexually "scandalous" women and the virtuous enterprise of economic growth; between state authorities and the "violence-prone" workingmen they governed.[12] As we shall see, significant similarities and material connections crossed all of these supposed divides.

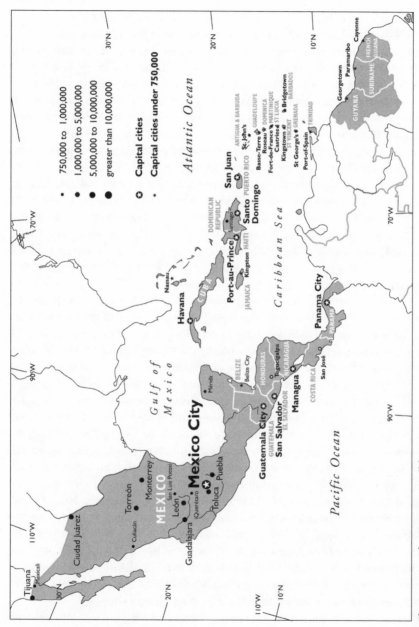

Figure 6.1. The Western Caribbean

Booms and Busts, Family Ties, and
Migration in the Western Caribbean, 1870–1930

Small-scale migration and trade had long linked the indigenous and Afro-Antillean populations of the Western Caribbean islands and rimlands.[13] Nineteenth-century infrastructure projects by North Atlantic investors acted as powerful magnets within these established circuits, disrupting some flows and creating new ones. Massive construction projects on the isthmus of Panama—the interoceanic railroad in the 1850s, the French canal in the 1880s, the U.S. canal in the 1910s—drew hundreds of thousands of workers from the Caribbean islands to the Central American coast, establishing social networks that facilitated migratory movements much larger than the projects themselves.[14] Thus, several thousand laborers from British Honduras, Curaçao, and especially Jamaica would labor on the Ferrocarril al Atlántico in Costa Rica between 1871 and 1890, while three or four times as many immigrants from these sites settled the surrounding province of Limón in the same years.[15] Some sixteen thousand workers were employed by the Compagnie Universelle du Canal Interocéanique each year at the height of construction (1884–1888), while more than eighty thousand men and women traveled from Jamaica to Panama in that decade.[16]

The massive influx of male workers to labor on the French canal created an intense market for reproductive labor in Panama—so much so that Jamaican laundresses routinely traveled back and forth carrying laundry from Colón (the Caribbean terminus of the works) to wash and press on the island.[17] Meanwhile, provisions from northwest Jamaica were exported to Colón, a trade that came to be the economic mainstay of peasant growers and "higglers," or market women, in the parishes of Hanover and St. James.[18] Smaller populations along the western Caribbean linked themselves to the nascent transnational market. A visitor to Isla de Bastimento in the Chiriquí Lagoon in 1883 described a large settlement where "potatoes, yucca, plantains, maize, and sugar cane" were grown, apparently for sale in Colón and Port Limón.[19] The constant flow of travelers and news meant that coastal traders could respond rapidly to unexpected shifts in demand. U.S. traveler A. Hyatt Verrill rounded the Caribbean on the steamer *Panama* in 1886. "At Cartagena we took on a deck-load of negroes and negresses, together with their chattels, livestock, fruit and vegetables which they were taking to the Colon market, for a disastrous fire had almost completely destroyed the Isthmian port, and the dusky Cartagena profiteers were taking advantage of their next-door neighbours' distress and intended to make hay while the sun shone."[20]

Peasant families in Jamaica's eastern parishes had long grown plantains and bananas for consumption and local markets. In the 1860s and 1870s, a number of Jamaican and U.S. shipowners began purchasing bananas from them for

Figure 6.2.   Women buying provisions from market boats, Panama City, Panama, ca. 1907. Source: Library of Congress, Prints and Figuregraphs Division, LC-USZ62-119655

sale on the U.S. eastern seaboard, a trade that proved immensely profitable. In the 1880s, banana cultivation for export began along the rail lines of Limón and in the hills around Bocas del Toro, at the hands of Jamaicans and other Caribbean islanders drawn to the coast by the construction booms. Local *poquiteros* (small producers) began growing bananas for export in northern Honduras in the same years, selling the stems to trading companies whose steamships called along the coast.[21] In Costa Rica, the bulk of early production came from land claimed by railroad entrepreneur Minor C. Keith, who was busy parlaying similar construction deals into land concessions and banana plantations in Colombia, Nicaragua, and Guatemala as well. In 1899, Keith merged his Costa Rican and Colombian holdings with the Jamaica-based

Boston Fruit Company, and the United Fruit Company was born. Other fruit traders and railway men like the Vaccaro Brothers and Samuel Zemurray followed a similar trajectory, leading to fierce competition to secure export monopolies from particular regions, often by means of illicit payments to the relevant government officials.[22]

Large-scale banana plantations were expanding in Jamaica in the same years, undermining rural households' economic foundations. The number of banana estates on the island more than doubled between 1900 and 1910, even as the average size of estates steadily increased. By 1930, banana estates covered six times the land they had held in 1893.[23] United Fruit aggressively defended its grip on banana purchase, and peasant growers found their profits shrinking even as land values—and related fees and taxes—grew.[24] Increasingly, the sons and daughters of the Jamaican peasantry sought opportunities abroad, looking to further their own fortunes and to send what they could to families back home. The resources such sojourners provided were considerable. The British consul in Port Limón wrote to his Foreign Office superiors in 1910 that "monthly some £3000 is known to be remitted by the labourers, in small sums, to their friends in Jamaica."[25] Remittances from Panama were even higher. Postal orders sent from the Canal Zone to Barbados alone totaled more than £62,000 in 1910.[26]

The rapid growth and just as rapid decline of logging, planting, and fruit exports at site after site along the coast spurred migrants to relocate repeatedly. Male migrants moved in and out of company employ; female migrants sold services and cared for kin, in combination or in turn. Branching migratory trajectories created transnational family ties and kin networks that spread across great distances and channeled the movement of people, resources, and support.[27] For instance, Belford Raines left Jamaica to seek work in Cuba in the late 1800s, then moved on to Panama where he met Armande-Marie, a St. Lucian immigrant. The couple's son Milford was born in Colón in 1897; Belford Raines died in Bocas del Toro a few months later. Milford and his siblings were sent to live with Armande-Marie's sisters and mother in Port Limón, while Armande-Marie sought work in Bocas del Toro. When Milford was ten, his mother brought him to Bocas to be schooled; seven years later, they returned to Limón, where Milford baked bread, and Armande-Marie took in laundry. At twenty-one, Milford married. He and his wife would have six children together, in spite of the fact that she spent much of their married life in Colón and he in Port Limón.[28] Such life stories foreground the role of kinship in structuring migration, production, and exchange for men and women alike. Salient kinship forms included not only "blood" ties but informal fostering, godparenthood, marriage, and temporary or long-standing consensual unions.

Extended household economies linked widely spaced sites of production and residence, connecting British West Indian parishes, Cuban sugar plantations, the Panama Canal, and the Central American coast, as well as rural hinterlands, junction towns, and port cities at each of those sites. In this way, family practices both shaped and were shaped by the intensifying U.S. involvement in the region. The accelerated expansion of U.S. direct investment in the Caribbean following the Spanish-Cuban-American War in 1898 created a transnational labor market that individuals moved into and out of repeatedly. Kinship ties and obligations shaped how people perceived the new opportunities and new constraints, under what circumstances they entered or abandoned wage labor, and how they combined it with other economic strategies. In doing so, kinship practice created opportunities and constraints for capital as well.

Gender, Geography, and the Labor
of Social Reproduction in Limón, Costa Rica

"What would become of us, in this burning climate, if the washerwomen declared themselves on strike even for a week?"

—Rafael Villegas, "Puerto Limón," *Páginas Ilustradas*, 1907[29]

In 1913, more banana stems were shipped from Port Limón than any other port in the world.[30] Vast tracts of lowland rainforest were cleared and planted in the province between the 1890s and the 1920s, first along the rail lines just west and south of the port, then later in the Estrella and Talamanca valleys farther south toward Panama, territory that had, until recently, been the sovereign domain of the Bribri and Cabécar indigenous peoples.[31] The regimented rows of identical plantings known as "banana walks" came to cover tens of thousands of acres held directly by United Fruit and at least twice that amount in the hands of individual planters. Over twenty thousand Jamaicans came to Limón in these years, accompanied by thousands of others from Barbados, St. Lucia, St. Kitts, and elsewhere in the Caribbean. Small groups of migrants from more distant lands crafted specific niches within the region's economy: Chinese men ran corner stores and bars; East Indian families grew vegetables for sale; Lebanese traders sold dry goods and sundries. Migrants arrived from highland Costa Rica as well, although in the first decades of the century, the easy availability of land in the western Central Valley meant that most highlanders found opportunities for waged or independent labor closer to home.

As laboring men poured into Limón (and poured out again, and poured back in) over the course of the 1870s, 1880s, and 1890s, women in smaller numbers traveled the same circuits. In rural Limón, especially in the jungle camps at the leading edge of plantation expansion, men might outnumber women by eight to one or more. Incoming women settled instead in the junction towns along the rail lines or in Port Limón, whose population was roughly one-third female in the 1880s and 1890s and just under half female by 1927.[32] This gendered division of residence shaped patterns of labor, accumulation, and consumption for both men and women. In the most remote settlements—the logging camps, rubber camps, and plantation frontiers—men cooked and cleaned for themselves or each other, or they paid UFCo subcontractors and saw room and board deducted from wages.[33] Elsewhere, though, the cash service economy was squarely in women's hands and beyond the company's purview.

Official documents of the era, such as legal depositions and censuses, give almost all women's occupation as *oficios domésticos* (domestic labors). The label homogenizes the variety of arrangements under which women worked, lumping together housewives who cooked and cleaned for their husbands and children, laundresses who charged by the piece, and meal sellers who earned monthly fees from steady clients. Yet, in another sense, the label is accurate. Working women in Limón earned their livings by offering for sale precisely those services otherwise subsumed into domestic economies: clean clothes, food, a place to sleep, sex. Furthermore, market and personal relationships were not sharply divided: while goods or services could be exchanged for cash, they were also bartered, loaned, and provided with the expectation of non-specific future returns.

In the earliest years of plantation expansion, women from the Costa Rican highlands seem to have been more likely than West Indian women to reside on the plantations themselves. A laborer on Minor Keith's Tropical Trading and Transport Company Jiménez plantation described one late night there in 1898: "Around one in the morning I went to the house of Josefa Ocampo to ask her to sell me some cigars for myself and for the three ladies who were taking care of a sick woman with me."[34] As the plantation frontier expanded southward in the following decade, indigenous youths were sometimes employed as domestic servants by engineers or managers in the camps. Orphaned around 1908 at the age of seven or eight, José Reyes was sent from Talamanca to work "in the house of a 'Mister'" in the Estrella Valley, where he hauled water and chopped and carried firewood. It is unclear whether he received any payment other than room and board. A few years later, he was promoted to field work and began earning five centavos a day—one-twentieth or less of what an adult laborer earned.[35]

As rail branch and feeder lines were completed and production intensified on the former frontiers, plantation populations grew. Established banana plantations had a complex built environment, with a spatial division that corresponded to different reproductive arrangements: there were barracks known as *baches* (from "bachelors' quarters") for laborers without female partners, semidetached houses for workers residing with families, and segregated neighborhoods (known as "white zones") for supervisors and their families. Low-level North American employees paid self-employed women by the piece to do their laundry and purchased their meals in a similar manner. Higher-ranking managers were provided with larger homes and full-time servants—houseboys, maids, cooks, and sometimes gardeners as well—as part of their employment contracts.[36]

The height of Afro-Caribbean travel to Central America was from 1904 to 1913, the period of most intense work on the Panama Canal. The same years were also the height of West Indian migration to Limón and those in which women and children made up the largest portion of arrivals.[37] Many of them—just like Milford Raines, his siblings, and his St. Lucian aunts and grandmother—reached Limón from Panama. Some women and children accompanied wage-earning men and confined their labor to household needs. Many others worked on their own in the plantation service sector described above. Simon Taylor, born in Jamaica in 1901, came to Limón with his mother in 1908 after his father's death. "When my mother first come here . . . she wash clothes for the timekeepers, the farm bosses, the commissaries, the overseers, right? I was helping her, in everything she needed I was helping. . . . The commissary chief pay her 7 pesos the dozen to wash clothes. Farm bosses pay the same. Timekeeper the same. Other people pay by the piece. Shirt 25 cents, pants 50 cents, so on."[38]

Women of every origin sold meals to *comensales* (steady boarders) or transients in the line-towns and port.[39] Others prepared candy, sweet and savory pasties, and sliced fruit, which were sold from trays along the streets of Port Limón. In 1913, Jamaican Emma Bailey, her fifty-five-year-old mother, and her eldest daughter sold fruit together every night outside the bar owned by Chinese merchant Juan José León.[40] Fifteen-year-old Adelaide Martin sold *pan bom* (sweet rolls) and *tosteles* (pastries) for an adoptive aunt on the streets of the port.[41] Caroline MacArthur, age nine, sold sweets prepared by Missus Catherine Parker, in whose home she had resided for the previous three years in Jamaica as well.[42]

Caroline and Adelaide would have been known within the West Indian community as schoolgirls, a Jamaican label for a growing daughter sent to live with relatives, friends, or social superiors to "help" in their homes and (supposedly) receive schooling or domestic training in return.[43] This role, which combined fictive kinship and labor obligations, seems to have linked many homes in Port Limón to families on the island. Just when demand for female services was booming in Port Limón, conditions for peasant families in Jamaica were worsening. "Child shifting" allowed idle hands to be put to profitable use, though the girls in question rarely received the profits themselves.[44] Thirty-year-old Rose Daniel brought her fourteen-year-old niece Jestina James to Costa Rica from Jamaica in 1910 "on the recommendation of [Jestina's] mother." The two lived in Siquirres with Rose's consensual partner and took in laundry "from the men along the [railroad] branch."[45] Miss Mariah Gordon had lived in Port Limón since 1888 and by 1914 was one of the busiest midwives in town. In 1913, she returned from a trip to Jamaica with twelve-year-old Olivia Brown, "entrusted to her by [Olivia's] mother," who for the next year did housework, cooked, minded Miss Mariah's daughter's children, and fetched medicines for Miss Mariah during difficult births.[46]

Among Costa Rican migrants in Limón, children alone or from families in need were likewise *recogido* (taken in) by others. As in the case of Jamaican schoolgirls, informal fostering among Costa Ricans carried elements of both kinship and servitude. Fifteen-year-old Marcelina Mora had lived with "la señora Alfonsina Sánchez" since she was two. When Alfonsina traveled, Marcelina was left in the home of Colombian Amelia Esquivel. A neighbor knew that Marcelina "ate, drank, and slept in that house for three weeks; [the witness] doesn't know whether *la Mora* received any wages or not for serving in that house." Other observers knew that Marcelina "owed obedience to *la señora* Esquivel, so that [Esquivel] punished her physically when necessary," but were likewise unclear on whether Marcelina was an employee, houseguest, relative, or foster daughter.[47]

Women of many origins, Amelia Esquivel among them, ran corner stores or bars in Limón in partnership with husbands or lovers. For Hermance Fontine, the venture did not end well. In 1902, her male companion, José Cuvillier de Brossard of St. Lucia, sold their bar and restaurant without her consent for 5,000 colones (U.S. $2,300) in cash and promptly helped the new owner initiate eviction proceedings against her. In a writ signed on her behalf by a local lawyer, Hermance declared that she and their daughter had been left penniless and homeless, hard thanks for the money she had loaned Cuvillier to maintain his business over their years together. Cuvillier would go on to thrive in real estate and commerce: his Casa Cuvillier became one of the most prominent brothels in the port. Of Hermance, no more is known.[48] Other unions were more enduring. Amelia Esquivel and her consensual partner, Colombian Jew Isidor Stein, ran a store together in Port Limón in 1900. Thirteen years later, they were still together and prospering, and by 1919, Esquivel had acquired a large plantation in the Estrella Valley, which their seventeen-year-old son administered on their behalf. The couple still had not married.[49]

In the port and junction towns, bars, brothels, billiard halls, and cheap hotels were often housed under a single roof. Such liquor-and-entertainment enterprises were among the most profitable in Limón. Often those renting rooms upstairs were women who earned a living from commercial sex. Along the second-floor balcony of a building like this in Siquirres in 1906, one could find a Jamaican woman entertaining a Jamaican laborer in one room, and a Nicaraguan woman with a Salvadoran carpenter next door.[50] It was not un-

Figure 6.3.   Afro-Caribbean female vendors alongside train in Limón, Costa Rica, ca. 1904. Source: Library of Congress, Prints and Figuregraphs Division, LC-USZ62-128703.

common for men to have ongoing relationships with the women they paid for sex. In 1909, Nicaraguan prostitute Conchita Cortés was living upstairs in a similar Siquirres establishment. She and a female friend were chatting in the room of Costa Rican prostitute Catalina Barquero when Nicaraguan laborer Jorge Oreamuno came to the door to invite Catalina for drink downstairs. Catalina answered "that since she was with *compañeras* [female companions] she couldn't accept. . . . Oreamuno said that it didn't matter, they all could go," and bought a round for the threesome downstairs.[51] The frequency of such vignettes suggests that what male workers sought from women in such settings was group sociability as much as sexual intercourse.

Dances as well as sex could be purchased by the piece in the export economy. As one participant explained about a dance held on Finca Catalina in
Sixaola in 1914, "It is the custom at those dances to pay one Panamanian
real, that is, ten cents of a colón, for each song that you dance to."[52] In Port
Limón, *bailes de contribución* (contribution dances) or *bailes de negocio*
(business-deal dances) were open only to men who paid in advance and to
women selected by the organizers. When Josefa Rojas, a prostitute from San
José, tried to crash one such dance in 1910 with several gentlemen friends,
"a Jamaican woman told her that the dance was not a pic-nic," that is, an
open gathering. They pushed in anyway. Elena Hawkins, the dance's "owner"
(*la dueña del baile*), tolerated their presence until, Elena explained, "a white
man I didn't know, who looked North American," asked Josefa to dance. At
that point, Elena called the police and had Josefa and her gate-crashing
friends ejected.[53]

Like the *americano del norte* who tried unsuccessfully to dance with Josefa
Rojas at Elena Hawkins's subscription dance, North American employees of
United Fruit sought out prostitutes in Limón just as other migrant workers
did. There was the dangerously inebriated *macho* (blond man), whom Delfina
Sáenz distracted with caresses so that her compañera María Pérez could slip
his loaded pistol out of his pants in 1911, or Robert Barton, railroad engineer,
whom Trinidad López Cabrera refused to let into her room one night in 1913
because he was too drunk.[54] Apparently, at the height of banana prosperity in
Port Limón, a pocketful of dollars and a Yankee accent were not always
enough to buy whatever you pleased.

The gendered division of residence in the province meant that those want-
ing to buy or sell sex often had to travel to do so. On bimonthly paydays, prostitutes traveled from Port Limón to plantations at the end of the rail lines.
After contracts were concluded, line-men traveled from the plantations, diggings, or forest clearings into the port to drink, dance, and pay for the privilege of sex. The mobility of prostitutes in the export zone meant that any
woman who traveled the rails frequently might be suspected of prostituting
herself. In general, it was Jamaican women who peddled in rural Limón, and
Jamaican community leaders, husbands, and neighbors who worried about
it.[55] Autonomous female commerce—higglering—had a venerable pedigree
throughout the West Indies.[56] But when female traders traveled the lines of
Limón, they were entering a territory far different from the Jamaican bush,
where aging matriarchs ruled from the fastness of their yards and children
tended roving goats. Rural Limón was a land of vast plantations and hard-
living men. How exactly did female traders earn their money in this realm
where single men were plentiful and settled families few and far between?
Which profitable opportunities did such women accept and what, if anything,
did they decline to trade?

In 1915, neighbors in Port Limón gave contradictory testimony about Vivian Black's travels along the *Línea de la Estrella*, the Estrella Valley rail line. Vivian's former lover James King reported that two of Vivian's friends, "women of bad conduct," had "told [Vivian] not to be a fool, that the salary she earned working in the Doctor's house was less than a man spent buying them beer in La Estrella." When Vivian repeated these comments to King, he said he had told her "that was only for bad women who spent their time traveling the lines." One of Vivian's female neighbors agreed with him, noting that "although [Vivian and her friend Etta Harris] used to take cigars along to sell no woman can enjoy a good reputation who goes to that place in the manner in which they did." Offering a contrasting opinion, this witness's own roommate, also a Jamaican woman, declared, "I've never heard anything bad about Etta Harris, and in my opinion she's an honorable woman because she frequently visits the lines to sell cigars, candy, and so on."[57]

Another neighbor defended Vivian and called King's version into doubt. "I am sure that [Vivian] was an honorable woman, in spite of the state of poverty I've described, and if she used to go [to] the *la Estrella* it was to sell vegetables, sweets, and other things on behalf of King, who told her that the money he invested in buying articles for her to make up the edibles she sold was borrowed on interest, and he said that so that she would see that he was without money and not ask for any money" for the expenses of their small child.[58] These conflicting stories about Vivian Black are a window into Limón's informal economy, in which production was financed by small-scale lending and commerce guided by kin ties; in which conflicts over profits earned intersected with conflicts over conjugal dues; and in which a man wishing to impugn a former lover could always call her a whore and be believed by some.

Struggles over Labor, Physical Integrity, and Autonomy

Just as kin ties organized resource distribution, labor obligations, and interpersonal authority, when individuals attempted to challenge such arrangements, the familial and the sexual became arenas of struggle. This was especially true for women and children, for whom work site and home were so often the same. The dynamic proved deadly in the case of James King and Vivian Black, introduced above, who had long been separated but remained linked by obligations of paternity and business. When a bitter argument culminated in Vivian's announcement that she had "a new man to cook for," King shot and killed her. Meanwhile, when the discontented women in question were female adolescents, like Jamaican schoolgirls Jestina James and Olivia Brown or Costa Rican Marcelina Mora, defiance of domestic authority often became intertwined with matters of sex.[59]

Rosa Chaves was a fourteen-year-old orphan from Cartago who had been placed as a nursemaid with a prominent Port Limón family. She decided to run away after "the wife of the doctor beat me because I didn't want to make the beds." Rosa made plans to meet former servant Juan José Quesada, who had promised to help her find another position. Yet, they had not gotten as far as the end of the garden path when "a policeman caught [Rosa]" and sent her back to the house and Juan José to jail, accused of illegal elopement (*rapto*). Rosa insisted nothing could be farther from the truth, that Juan José had never touched her, nor had any other man, "nor did [Juan José] make any proposals for me to go live with him, nor did he say any thing which an honorable girl like I am should not hear. As I have said I have always lived in honorable houses and I have never gone out onto the streets without accompaniment."[60] Her professions of feminine propriety were only partly successful. The case against Juan José was dropped, but Rosa remained honorably secluded in the home and the job she detested.

In 1907, fourteen-year-old Wilhemina Charles likewise tried to escape from an onerous position, one into which her mother had placed her. Unlike Rosa, Wilhemina felt no compunction about walking the streets alone. She went over a mile on foot, from downtown to Camp One Mile, looking for her elder sister, and when she got hungry, she stopped in a *pulpería* (corner store) run by a Chinese merchant to ask for work. He hired her as a maid at 5 colones a week. Recognized by a customer in the store ten days later, Wilhemina was taken back to her "guardian" by two local West Indian policemen. She immediately accused the merchant, Sing Li, of having raped her and held her against her will. But when the court doctor declared that her hymen had been ruptured long before, the case was dropped. Wilhemina's brazen grab for autonomy by running away on her own had proved no more successful than Rosa's demure departure and, if the rape accusation was true, had been far more traumatic.[61]

In each of these cases, as in a large minority of *estupro* (deflowering) cases that came before the Limón courts, the underlying conflict was between a female teen trying to switch residence in order to switch labor regimes and those who wanted to keep her where she was.[62] How did these end up as court cases pitting female supposed victims against male sexual aggressors? First, young women who demanded autonomy from parents or guardians were generally assumed to have been put up to it by men who wanted sex. Meanwhile, some young women in fact found that a willingness to have sex was one of the few kinds of leverage they had. Yet, their ability to control this strategy was undercut by a culture of male sexual privilege in which men accepted few limits on how they could get what they wanted. As one accused man declared, "It is more than proven by experience that a woman who resists cannot be 'overrun' by a man, because in these cases, if you'll pardon the harshness of the phrase, all she has to do is close her legs; and it is not possible to open her legs and at the same time have one's way with her, because wise nature has located those parts in a place where they can be defended."[63] Belief in the physical impossibility of rape was the ultimate proactive alibi—a blank check to use as much force as necessary to achieve penetration while insisting the victim had wanted it all along.

It is hard not to be cynical about court agents' and guardians' professed concern for the sexual protection of the girls involved. Such cases were easily begun, triggering police intervention to restore young women to the authority they had attempted to escape. But the standard of evidence needed to convict a man of sexual coercion or criminal seduction was in practice so high that it was almost never met.[64] It is clear from testimony in judicial and autobiographical sources and from the recorded results of vaginal exams that it was not uncommon for men to seduce, sway, pressure, bribe, or force underage girls into sexual intercourse. It is also clear that only a very few men ever paid a legal price for it.

Relations between men and women and parents and children were political in a broad sense, for they involved contests over power and resources. Such relations were also political in a more conventional sense because they came to involve state agents, from the policemen who enforced Rosa's and Wilhemina's domestic obedience to bureaucrats far more exalted. When Ethel Gibbs confessed to her mother in 1914 that she had been raped by her boyfriend and might be pregnant, Mrs. Gibbs filed criminal charges that very day. "I went immediately to the Governor of the Province, believing that he was the authority charged with vindicating my rights," she explained.[65] When a neighborhood policeman mentioned to Enriqueta Alvarez that he had seen her daughter María with Nicolás Mendieta by the seawall, Enriqueta immediately took María to be examined by the official port doctor, who reported that the fourteen-year-old was still a virgin. Yet, when María disappeared from the house several weeks later, Enriqueta had no doubts. She marched to the *alcalde*'s office, filed suit for rapto, and had Nicolás arrested.[66] In these cases, we see the impulse for action coming from "below," from popular actors focused on familial struggles, rather than from "above," from officials pushing policies of moral reform. In Limón, questions of sex came before the courts as a result of conflicts between girls, guardians, and suitors over kinship and obligation rather than as a consequence of politicians' or professionals' campaigns for virtue, eugenics, or progress.

Power, Authority, and Male Privilege on the Cusp of State Formation

The exercise of public authority and its impact on intimate lives was quite different at the fringes of plantation expansion. There, the fragile and fragmented nature of state power meant that the assertion of authority was personalized and often arbitrary and that the line between official and unofficial violence was tenuous at best. Claims to public authority and to masculine dominance frequently overlapped, were indistinguishable, or were simply one and the same. Officials asserted dominion through a classic repertory of manly insult and response, a repertory reiterated in payday brawls, machete duels, and conflicts between workers and bosses across early Limón.[67] State-designated authority was not enough to demand obedience: you had to make yourself respected "as a man."[68]

Benedicto Suárez, a Nicaraguan planter and pulpería owner, was justice of the peace in San Clemente de la Estrella. When Honduran laborer Salvador Pastora began to cause trouble at a payday dance in 1913, "saying every time they stopped singing that he wanted to fight, that it had been too long since he'd 'drunk blood'," Suárez told the commissariat, Nicaraguan Mario González, "Take this badge, now you're an authority, disarm that man to prevent *una desgracia* [a disgraceful occurrence; an irreversible act]." González warned Pastora, "Come, friend, I'm an authority," Pastora replied, "Better yet, if you're an authority, all the more reason to kill you," then slammed his machete down on González's hand.[69] Benedicto Suárez shot Pastora in the chest, and a riot ensued. As Pastora's companions were about to break down the door to the justice of the peace's home, Nicaraguan planter Hilario Esquivel came running "accompanied by several peones from [his] finca, whom [he] had armed with machetes," and broke up the crowd.[70] This happened in the Estrella Valley, two years before Vivian Black and Etta Harris would raise eyebrows by travelling to sell either cigars or sex along the rail line there. As lands closer to Port Limón became infected with Panama disease around 1908–1911, United Fruit and other planters shifted their attention south to the prime alluvial lands bordering the Estrella and Sixaola rivers. Hundreds of laborers crowded together in rough camps on the plantation frontier; families or resident womenfolk were rare. There was a huge demand for commercial sex, a barely incipient state apparatus, and a continuous need for actual violence to back up pretensions to command.

Banana plantations were not expanding in a vacuum. These were the homelands of the Bribri and Cabécar indigenous peoples, who now found themselves under simultaneous assault from adventurers, smugglers, UFCo agents, land speculators, and crooked officials. Most often, in fact, outsiders fit several of those categories at once.[71] Nonconsensual sex was one of the many ways outsiders took what they wanted by force in Talamanca, and those with power to demand sex were often state agents, present, past, or future. (As the image of Benedicto Suárez tossing Mario González a badge in the midst of a bloody brawl in La Estrella reminds us, the line between who was and who was not a state agent in these regions might be blurry indeed.) Carlos Luís Fallas's autobiographical novel *Mamita Yunai* includes a vivid account of election day in Amubre, as drunken Indians gathered by the *jefe político*, circled past official observers to vote—several times each. Afterward, the local planters and visiting políticos spent the evening drinking and enjoying indigenous women. "But how do you make yourself understood with the *indias?*" asked the narrator innocently. The local police chief guffawed. "You don't waste time talking to them. Just grab an arm and pull them into the woods. If they say 'ejem' it means they don't want to go with you, and if they say 'ejem' it means they do."[72]

Laughing, he went on to describe a recent conquest.

> "I got there, and without saying anything pushed the door open with my shoulder. 'No enter, no enter! *Indito* see!' screamed the *india*, holding the door from inside. 'What do I care about your indito?' I said, and with a big push got into the hut."
>
> "And what did the india do?" I asked.
>
> "What did she do? Just dropped to the floor crying and covered her face with her hands. . . ."
>
> "Where's the dance?" I asked, trying to change the topic.[73]

The anecdote serves Fallas's narrative strategy, which depicts indigenous Talamancans as the most degraded victims of the venal alliance between company and state. However, other evidence confirms the frequency of sexual coercion by public officials in the region. One man who worked for the St. Vincent de Paul missionaries in Talamanca from the 1890s to the 1910s described the state agents stationed at Sipurio as "*relajados, mujeriegos, egoístas, groseros* (loose-moraled, womanizing, selfish, and egregiously offensive)."[74] Whenever rivalries between different official actors in the region (*jefes políticos, agentes de policía,* and *regidores síndicos*) led one authority to lodge formal complaints against another, accusations of pilfering and smuggling were accompanied by descriptions of rape, kidnapping, and sexual abuse of indigenous girls. In a typical instance in 1913, the *agente fiscal* sent to investigate was told that "the Jefe Político positions himself along the paths where he knows there are young indias, he assaults them and takes them to the *jefatura política,* where he makes use of them by force."[75]

Such accusations took the physical expression of masculine power, which was admired in the everyday—indeed was a necessary component of the exercise of public authority—and placed it into a legal theater where the rules were different. By law, all women were supposed to be free from all kinds of sexual coercion.[76] Men in positions of authority (guardians, teachers, and priests) were considered to have particular responsibility for the virtue of women and girls under their control; thus, sexual abuse by men in these positions was punished particularly harshly.[77] But in practice, real men were supposed to be able to have their way, and men who wished to command others put their masculine power continuously on display. Formal accusations of sexual abuse used this disjunct between the judicial and vernacular definitions of the extent of male privilege in order to discredit authorities who, available evidence strongly suggests, were simply doing what many others did as well.

Nicaraguan trader Gordiano López and Honduran Valentín Urbina, jefe político of Talamanca, had been in the rubber business together, it seems, but had had a falling out. In 1898, López denounced Urbina for abuse of authority, accusing him of taking bribes to let contraband in from Panama, forcing indios to work without pay for his personal profit, and obliging the wife of Bribri king Antonio Saldaña "almost by force" to send her thirteen-year-old daughter Victoria to sleep with Urbina. King Antonio and all his family supported López's account, adding details regarding an attempt by Urbina to abduct Victoria after getting the family drunk (an attempt foiled by Victoria's older sister Cerafina, who attacked Urbina with a machete), and insisting that Urbina had eventually "deflowered [Victoria] with force and violence."[78] Urbina denied all, reporting almost as an afterthought that it had been his *agente de policía* who had abducted Victoria while he was out of town. Urbina clearly saw the accusation as a political intrigue. He wrote to former allies in Talamanca urging them to "talk Antonio out of this false accusation," threatening to sue Saldaña for libel, and boasting "you don't get me out of my post so easy as that."[79] But in fact Urbina was replaced as jefe político soon after the inquiry began. He fled the country in 1899 after the court of appeal refused to overturn his conviction for the rape of Victoria.

Gordiano López, whose testimony, perhaps at Saldaña's behest, had begun Urbina's downfall, would soon find himself similarly accused. Among the many witnesses against Urbina had been Pablo Molina, a Costa Rican migrant to Talamanca employed in the jefatura política. In January of 1900, Pablo Molina reported that five weeks before, Gordiano López had raped Molina's wife Gerardina Torres in the woods near the jefatura. Florencia Saldaña, a relative of King Antonio, testified through an interpreter that she had been with Gerardina at the time and seen it all. Again, shifting political fortunes seem to have been behind the timing of the accusation (which, of course, does not mean it was not true). López mentioned in his testimony that at the time of the alleged rape, he had been lodging in the jefatura itself "with the permission of the jefe político who was in office then."[80] It would seem that the departure of López's ally from that post in January left López vulnerable to accusation, likely with the support of Saldaña.[81]

One of Gordiano López's character witnesses was an *agrimensor* (land surveyor) from San José for whom he had once worked. Asked about Gerardina Torres's character, the surveyor declared "all he can say is that she has all the defects of the indigenous race, and therefore is of bad conduct." In his advisory opinion on the case, agente fiscal Jacinto Mora explicitly rejected the agrimensor's assumption that his "knowledge" about race and female vice would be shared by his audience. "It would not matter in the slightest in this case if the victim, Señora Gerardina Torres de Molina, really had 'all the defects of the indigenous race,' as the witness Don Francisco Alpízar opines without even explaining which those might be, because that would not diminish one iota the gravity of the deed." Mora insisted that Liberal justice protected all women without consideration of race or rank. "A public prostitute and the most honored wife should be equally sacred when it comes to rape, which is one of the most scandalous and grave crimes against general order and morality, and in this the law makes no *distinctions*."[82] Of course, this is not in fact how laws about rape were applied in Limón or anywhere else in Costa Rica; indeed, this case, like so many others, was eventually dismissed for lack of evidence. Yet, the wide gulf between the male privileges and female protections assigned by Liberal codes and those sustained in practice could become a political lever within factional conflicts like those ongoing in Talamanca.

In 1916, the particularly gruesome murder of four members of an indigenous clan in Mome de Estrella by two outside adventurers (one Costa Rican, one Honduran) drew national attention to the region. The two men, Ramón Salazar and Felipe Solís, had first come to Talamanca as *propagandistas políticas* (political party mobilizers), at least according to one local planter. Certainly, they were familiar with electoral practices of the sort Carlos Luís Fallas would later describe. Trying to discredit indigenous witnesses after the fact, Salazar argued, "I don't think, Mr. Judge, that any of those declarations can be true, because I'm a person who's used to dealing with those Indians and I know them and you can never count on a single word, as has been proved at the voting tables where they change their names three or four times, substituting it for another."[83] Salazar and Solís described themselves as rubber traders and farmers, but apparently they mainly acted as agents for outside speculators, acquiring titles to holdings long cultivated by specific clans. Salazar had also worked as a police agent in the region.

María Magdalena, a Bribri woman in her mid-thirties, and Graciela Pino, her thirteen-year-old daughter, lived with Salazar and Solís for some time in an arrangement that included both domestic servitude and sexual access. Both women were heavily pregnant at the time of the killings. Meanwhile, their extended family was involved in a lawsuit against Salazar and Solís over title to the clan's land. It is impossible to know from preserved testimony what benefits or pressures might have urged María Magdalena and Graciela into their relationships with the men. The pressures that kept them there, however, are suggested by subsequent events. María Magdalena and Graciela finally left Salazar and Solís and returned to their family compound, driven, in Graciela's words, by the *pésima vida* (extreme physical abuse) they had been forced to endure. Several days later, Salazar and Solís came to the *rancho* to try to convince them to return. In the ensuing argument, María Magdalena, her cousin (the compound head), his sixty-year-old mother, and another male cousin were stabbed to death. Graciela and the other children in the rancho at the time survived by fleeing into the surrounding banana groves.[84]

Three years earlier, in 1913, acquitted rapist Gordiano López had been working as a policeman in La Estrella (he arrested one of the laborers charged with assaulting planter Benedicto Suárez's house the night of the brawl). Now López was named as character witness by accused murderer Felipe Solís. López must have been in his late fifties by then: he was described as a "planter" and must have been respected or wealthy enough for his word to be worth something. He had come far in the twenty years since Jefe Político Valentín Urbina had written to his superior, "A 'celebrated' man by the name of Gordiano López has arrived here, a smuggler known all along the rail line who brings merchandise from San Juan del Norte [Nicaragua], and is known for bad deeds which he recounts from his own lips as if they were a source of honor. I have forbidden [López and his rubber tappers] to destroy the forests, which as you know is the trail everywhere left behind by this class of workers, whom I don't want here even as voluntary colonists. . . ."[85] But López had in fact stayed in the region, and others like him—such as Ramón Arroyo and Felipe Solís—followed. They had helped banana planters and the Costa Rican state extend real control over the Bribri and Cabécar domains. They had been small but integral pieces of the expansion of U.S. investment in Central America—harbingers of hardship for indigenous clans, and perpetrators of particular violations soon forgotten by the outside world.

Conclusion

In the preceding pages, I have tried to describe the role of service and succor within a particular economy—to place the reproductive work traditionally done by women alongside the productive work that both women and men have long done and continue to do, and to integrate the two kinds of work into a single story about how commodities, profits, labor markets, and regions are made. Along the way, we have examined intimate conflicts as both labor struggles and political contests. We have looked at the ways laws governing appropriate sexuality and the conditions of consent were applied, noting the gulf between Liberal pretensions to race- and class-blind protection for all women and the reality of widespread male impunity. We have seen how the assertion of state authority could depend on an individual's ability to "prove it like a man." Finally, we explored the role of sexual and other violence in the subjugation of the indigenous peoples of the southern valleys. Attention to gender, kinship, households, and sex has forced us to rethink fundamental assumptions about export economies in the early-twentieth-century Caribbean— about the determinants of labor migration, the variation of plantation labor regimes across the space they covered, the links between the banana enclave and the regional economy, the goals and efficacy of state and UFCo policies, and the very definition of political struggle.

Notes

1. Among many others, see Lourdes Arizpe, *Parentesco y economía en una sociedad nahua* (Mexico City: Instituto Nacional Indígena, 1973); Susan C. Bourque and Kay Barbara Warren, *Women of the Andes: Patriarchy and Social Change in Two Peruvian Towns* (Ann Arbor: University of Michigan Press, 1981); Carmen Diana Deere and Magdalena León, eds., *La mujer y las políticas agrarias en América Latina* (Bogotá: Siglo XXI Editores, 1986). For synthetic overviews, see Susan Tiano, "Women and Industrial Development in Latin America," *Latin American Research Review* 21, no. 3 (1986): 157–70; Susan Tiano, "From Victims to Agents: A New Generation of Literature on Women in Latin America," *Latin American Research Review* 36, no. 3 (2001): 183–203.

2. For the earliest formulations, see Fernando Henriques Cardoso and Enzo Faletto, *Dependencia y desarrollo en América Latina. Ensayo de interpretación sociológica*, 20th ed. (1969; Mexico City: Siglo XXI Editores, 1986); Edelberto Torres Rivas, *Interpretación del desarrollo social centroamericano*, 12th ed. (1969; San José: FLACSO, 1989). A pioneering analysis, which combined the study of an enclave economy from a dependency perspective with attention to kinship, gender, and household roles, was June Nash, *We Eat the Mines and the Mines Eat Us: Dependency and Exploitation in Bolivian Tin Mines* (New York: Columbia University Press, 1979).

3. Hector Pérez-Brignoli, *A Brief History of Central America*, trans. Ricardo B. Sawrey and Susana Stretti de Sawrey (Berkeley: University of California Press, 1989), 104.

4. Cf. Joseph Love, "The Origins of Dependency Theory," *Journal of Latin American Studies* 22 (1990): 143–68. For empirically grounded critiques of the economic arguments of dependency theory, see, among others, Victor Bulmer-Thomas, *The Economic History of Latin America since Independence* (New York: Cambridge University Press, 1994); Stephen Haber, ed., *How Latin America Fell Behind: Essays in the Economic Histories of Brazil and Mexico, 1800–1914* (Palo Alto, CA: Stanford University Press, 1997).

5. See David Hojman, "From Mexican Plantations to Chilean Mines: The Theoretical and Empirical Relevance of Enclave Theories in Contemporary Latin America," *Inter-American Economic Affairs* 39, no. 3 (1985): 27–53.

6. William E. French, "Prostitutes and Guardian Angels: Women, Work, and the Family in Porfirian Mexico," *Hispanic American Historical Review* 72, no. 4 (1992): 529–53; Thomas Miller Klubock, *Contested Communities: Class, Gender, and Politics in Chile's El Teniente Copper Mine, 1904–1951* (Durham, NC: Duke University Press, 1998); Miguel Tinker-Salas, "Relaciones de poder y raza en los campos petroleros venezolanos, 1920–1940," *Asuntos* [Centro Internacional de Educación y Desarrollo, PDVSA, Caracas, Venezuela] 5, no. 10 (2001): 77–103.

7. Catherine LeGrand, "Colombian Transformations: Peasants and Wage-Laborers in the Santa Marta Banana Zone," *Journal of Peasant Studies* 2, no. 4 (1984): 178–200; Aviva Chomsky, *West Indian Workers and the United Fruit Company in Costa Rica, 1870–1940* (Baton Rouge: Louisiana State University Press, 1996); Catherine LeGrand, "Living in Macondo: Economy and Culture in a United Fruit Company Enclave in Colombia," in *Close Encounters of Empire: Writing the Cultural History of U.S.–Latin American Relations*, ed. Gilbert M. Joseph, Catherine C. LeGrand, and Ricardo D. Salvatore (Durham, NC: Duke University Press, 1998); Steve Marquardt, "'Green Havoc': Panama Disease, Environmental Change, and Labor Process in the Central American Banana Industry," *American Historical Review* 106, no. 1 (2001): 49–80; Steve Marquardt, "Pesticides, Parakeets, and Unions in the Costa Rican Banana Industry, 1938–1962," *Latin American Research Review* 37, no. 2 (2002): 3–36; Steve Striffler, *In the Shadows of State and Capital: The United Fruit Company, Popular Struggle, and Agrarian Restructuring in Ecuador, 1900–1995* (Durham, NC: Duke University Press, 2002); Steve Striffler and Mark Moberg, eds., *Banana Wars: Power, Production, and History in the Americas* (Durham, NC: Duke University Press, 2003); John Soluri, *Banana Cultures: Agriculture, Consumption, and Environmental Change in Honduras and the United States* (Austin: University of Texas Press, 2005); and Ana Luisa Cerdas, "Vida y trabajo de los obreros bananeros. El caso del enclave en la región del pacífico sur de Costa Rica" (master's thesis in progress, Posgrado en Historia, Universidad de Costa Rica).

8. On hierarchies of race, ethnicity, and nationality among workers, see especially Philippe Bourgois, *Ethnicity at Work: Divided Labor on a Central American Banana Plantation* (Baltimore: Johns Hopkins University Press, 1989); Mark Moberg, *Myths of Ethnicity and Nation: Immigration, Work, and Identity in the Belize Banana Industry* (Knoxville: University of Tennessee Press, 1997); Marc Edelman, "A Central American Genocide: Rubber, Slavery, Nationalism, and the Destruction of the Guatusos-Malekus," *Comparative Studies in Society and History* 40, no. 2 (1998): 356–90; Aviva Chomsky, "Laborers and Smallholders in Costa Rica's Mining Communities, 1900–1940," in *Identity and Struggle at the Margins of the Nation-State: The Laboring Peoples of Central America and the Hispanic Caribbean*, ed. Aviva Chomsky and Aldo Lauria-Santiago (Durham, NC: Duke University Press, 1998); Frederick Douglass Opie, "Adios Jim Crow: Afro-North American Workers and the Guatemalan Railroad Workers' League, 1884–1921 (PhD dissertation, Syracuse University, 1999). On cross-cutting political alliances, see Paul J. Dosal, *Doing Business with the Dictators: A Political History of United Fruit in Guatemala, 1889–1944* (Wilmington, DE: Scholarly Resources, 1993); Darío A. Euraque, *Reinterpreting the Banana Republic: Region and State in Honduras, 1870–1972* (Chapel Hill: University of North Carolina Press, 1996); Ronny J. Viales Hurtado, *Después del enclave: Un estudio de la región atlántica costarricense, 1927–1950* (San José: Editorial de la Universidad de Costa Rica, 1998); Ronny J. Viales Hurtado, "Los liberales y la colonización de las áreas de frontera no cafetaleras. El caso de la región Atlántica (Caribe) costarricense entre 1870 y 1930" (PhD dissertation, Universitat Autónoma de Barcelona, 2000).

9. Micaela di Leonardo, "Introduction: Gender, Culture, and Political Economy: Feminist Anthropology in Historical Perspective," in *Gender at the Crossroads of Knowledge: Feminist Anthropology in the Postmodern Era*, ed. Micaela di Leonardo (Berkeley: University of California Press, 1991), 1–48; see also Aihwa Ong, "The Gender and Labor Politics of Postmodernity," *Annual Review of Anthropology* 20 (1991): 279–309.

10. In addition to books by Klubock and Striffler, cited in notes 6 and 7 above, see Verena Stolcke, *Coffee Planters, Workers, and Wives: Class Conflict and Gender Relations on São Paulo*

Plantations, 1850–1980 (New York: St. Martin's Press, 1988); Michael Jiménez, "Class, Gender, and Peasant Resistance in Central Colombia, 1900–1930," in *Everyday Forms of Peasant Resistance*, ed. Forrest D. Colburn (Armonk, NJ: M. E. Sharpe, 1989); Mario Samper Kutschbach, *Generations of Settlers: Rural Households and Markets on the Costa Rican Frontier, 1850–1935* (Boulder, CO: Westview Press, 1990); Verena Stolcke, "The Labors of Coffee in Latin America: The Hidden Charm of Family Labor and Self-Provisioning," in *Coffee, Society and Power in Latin America*, ed. William Roseberry, Lowell Gudmundson, and Mario Samper Kutschbach (Baltimore: Johns Hopkins University Press, 1995); Douglas W. Trefzger, "Making West Indians Unwelcome: Race, Gender, and the National Question in Guatemala's Banana Belt, 1914–1920" (paper prepared for the XXIII Annual Meeting of the Latin American Studies Association, Washington, D.C., September 6–8, 2001); Lara Putnam, *The Company They Kept: Migrants and the Politics of Gender in Caribbean Costa Rica, 1870–1960* (Chapel Hill: University of North Carolina Press, 2002); Heidi Tinsman, *Partners in Conflict: The Politics of Gender, Sexuality, and Labor in the Chilean Agrarian Reform, 1950–1973* (Durham, NC: Duke University Press, 2002).

11. Ann Laura Stoler, "Tense and Tender Ties: The Politics of Comparison in North American History and (Post) Colonial Studies," *Journal of American History* 88, no. 3 (2001): 829–65; Ann Laura Stoler, "Preface," in her *Capitalism and Confrontation in Sumatra's Plantation Belt, 1870–1979*, 2nd ed. (Ann Arbor: University of Michigan Press, 1995); Frederick Cooper and Ann Laura Stoler, "Between Metropole and Colony: Rethinking a Research Agenda," in *Tensions of Empire: Colonial Cultures in a Bourgeois World*, ed. Frederick Cooper and Ann Laura Stoler (Berkeley: University of California Press, 1997).

12. My formulation here is indebted to John Soluri, "Consumo de masas, biodiversidad y fitomejoramiento del banano de exportación, 1920 a 1980," *Revista de Historia* (San José, Costa Rica) 44 (2001): 57.

13. Cf. James J. Parsons, "English Speaking Settlement of the Western Caribbean," *Yearbook of the Association of Pacific Coast Geographers* 16 (1954): 3–16; Edmund Gordon, *Disparate Diasporas: Identity and Politics in an African Nicaraguan Community* (Austin: University of Texas Press, 1998), ch. 2.

14. G. W. Roberts, *The Population of Jamaica* (Cambridge: Cambridge University Press, 1957), 133–41; Elizabeth M. Thomas-Hope, "The Establishment of a Migration Tradition: British West Indian Movements to the Hispanic Caribbean in the Century after Emancipation," *International Migration* 24 (1986): 66–81.

15. Carmen Murillo Chaverri, *Identidades de hierro y humo: La construcción del Ferrocarril al Atlántico, 1870–1890* (San José: Editorial Porvenir, 1995); Lara Putnam, "Public Women and One-Pant Men: Labor Migration and the Politics of Gender in Caribbean Costa Rica, 1870–1960" (PhD dissertation, University of Michigan, 2000), 56–78.

16. Omar Jáen Suárez, *La población del istmo de Panamá del siglo XVI al siglo XX* (Panama: n.p., 1979), 455; Gisela Eisner, *Jamaica, 1830–1930: A Study in Economic Growth* (Manchester: The University Press, 1961), 147. Registered returns were over sixty thousand in the same era. Part of what these figures register is multiple round-trips by single individuals.

17. Olive Senior, "The Colon People," *Jamaica Journal* 11, nos. 3, 4 (1978): 62.

18. Roberts, *Population of Jamaica*, 282; Erna Brodber, "Life in Jamaica in the Early Twentieth Century: A Presentation of Ninety Oral Accounts" (unpublished mimeo, Institute of Social and Economic Research, University of the West Indies, Mona).

19. Charles W. Koch, "Ethnicity and Livelihoods: A Social Geography of Costa Rica's Atlantic Zone" (PhD dissertation, University of Kansas, 1975), 70–72. Bastimento was described by A. L. Pinart, whose report on his travels is summarized by Helmuth Polakowsky, "La América Central y el Canal de Panamá" [1886]; rpt. in Elías Zeledón Cartín, *Viajes por la República de Costa Rica,* vol. 2 (San José: Ministerio de Cultura, Juventud y Deportes, 1997), 303, 312n35; cf. Paula Palmer, *Wa'apin man. La historia de la costa talamanqueña de Costa Rica, según sus protagonistas,* 2nd ed. (San José: Editorial de la Universidad de Costa Rica, 1994), 35–46.

20. A. Hyatt Verrill, *Thirty Years in the Jungle* (London: John Lane the Bodley, 1929), 48.

21. Thomas C. Holt, *The Problem of Freedom: Race, Labor, and Politics in Jamaica and Britain, 1832–1938* (Baltimore: Johns Hopkins University Press, 1992), 347–53; Koch, "Ethnicity and Livelihood," 123–24n2; John Soluri, "People Plants, and Pathogens: The Eco-social Dynamics of Export Banana Production in Honduras, 1875–1950," *Hispanic American Historical Review* 80, no. 3 (2000): 463–501.

22. Charles Kepner and Jay Soothill, *The Banana Empire: A Case Study of Economic Imperialism* (New York: Vanguard Press, 1935); Lester D. Langley and Thomas Schoonover, *The Banana Men: American Mercenaries and Entrepreneurs in Central America, 1880–1930* (Lexington: University of Kentucky Press, 1995); Dosal, *Doing Business with the Dictators.*

23. Eisner, *Jamaica,* 203.

24. Charles Kepner, *Social Aspects of the Banana Industry* (New York: Columbia University Press, 1936), 46–48, 100–102; Eisner, *Jamaica,* 280–82; Kepner and Soothill, *Banana Empire,* 296–301; Holt, *Problem of Freedom,* 354–65.

25. Cox to Secretary of State, December 8, 1910, in British Public Record Office, Foreign Office, Ser. 288, Vol. 125, 267, cited in Chomsky, *West Indian Workers,* 160. The remittance system established by British Vice Consul F. M. H. Wood in Limón is described in Jeffrey Casey Gaspar, *Limón 1880–1940: Un estudio de la industria bananera en Costa Rica* (San José: Editorial Costa Rica, 1979), 181–82.

26. Bonham C. Richardson, *Panama Money in Barbados, 1900–1920* (Knoxville: University of Tennessee Press, 1985), 141.

27. Similarly, anthropologists suggest that the contemporary Caribbean household should be defined not as a residential unit but as "a tight network of exchanges of support" and that "migration [i]s thus less about people leaving the island to live and work elsewhere than about extending the domestic unit to include people working abroad, in some cases thousands of miles away." Karen Fog Olwig, "The Migration Experience: Nevisian Women at Home and Abroad," in *Women and Change in the Caribbean,* ed. Janet Momsen (London: James Curry, 1993), 166.

28. "Autobiografías Campesinas" (unpublished mimeo), Biblioteca Central, Universidad Nacional Autónoma, Heredia, Costa Rica [henceforth, AC], vol. 26, book 3, "Autobiografía de M. R. (entrevista)," 151. All names are pseudonyms.

29. Rafael Villegas, "Puerto Limón," *Páginas Ilustradas* 4, no. 167 (October 12, 1907), reprinted in *Crónicas y relatos para la historia de Puerto Limón,* comp. Fernando González Vásquez and Elías Zeledón Cartín (San José: Ministerio de Cultura, Juventud y Deportes, Centro de Investigación y Conservación del Patrimonio Cultural, 1999), 272.

30. Frederick Upham Adams, *Conquest of the Tropics: The Story of the Creative Enterprises Conducted by the United Fruit Company* (New York: Doubleday, 1914), 173. Total Jamaican banana exports were higher than total Costa Rican exports until 1915, when Jamaican plantations were devastated by hurricanes and wartime shipping disruptions; however, Jamaican exports

were divided among various ports. From 1917 on, Honduras's export totals surpassed Costa Rica's. See Eisner, *Jamaica*, 243; Reinaldo Carcanholo, "Sobre la evolución de las actividades bananeras en Costa Rica, *Anuario de Estudios Centroamericanos* 19 (1978): 145, 167; Mario Posas, "La plantación bananera en Centroamérica (1870–1929)," in *Las repúblicas agroexportadoras*, ed. Víctor Hugo Acuña Ortega, vol. 4 of *Historia General de Centroamérica* (Madrid: Sociedad Estatal Quinto Centenario and FLACSO, 1993), 152–53. For detailed descriptions of the formation of Limón's banana industry, see Viales, "Los liberales y la colonización"; Chomsky, *West Indian Workers*, 17–59.

31. Antonio Saldaña, the last king of Talamanca formally recognized by the Costa Rica state, died in 1910, according to oral tradition poisoned by an ally of the United Fruit Company. See Alejandra Boza Villareal and Juan Carlos Solórzano Fonseca, "El Estado nacional y los indígenas: el caso de Talamanca y Guatuso, Costa Rica, 1821–1910," *Revista de Historia* (San José, Costa Rica) 42 (2000): 62; Alejandra Boza Villareal, "Indígenas, afroantillanos, estado, misioneros y compañías en el sur de Costa Rica, 1840–1940 (Turrialba, Chirripó, Valle de la Estrella, Talamanca, Orosi y Pacífico Sur)" (master's thesis, Universidad de Costa Rica, 2004).

32. Koch, "Ethnicity and Livelihood," 136; *Censo General de la República de Costa Rica . . . de 1892*, facsimile ed. (San José: Ministerio de Economía, Industria y Comercio, Dirección General de Estadística y Censos, 1974), 49; Centro de Investigaciones Históricas de América Central, Universidad de Costa Rica, Base de datos del Censo de Población de 1927 (available to the public at www.censos.ccp.ucr.ac.cr): author's analysis.

33. Cf. Carlos Luis Fallas, *Mamita Yunai*, 2nd ed. (San José: Editorial Costa Rica, 1995), 109–58. On the meal ticket system used during railroad construction, see Murillo Chaverri, *Identidades*, 101; Watt Stewart, *Keith y Costa Rica*, trans. José B. Acuña (San José: Editorial Costa Rica, 1991), 96. On logging and rubber, see Lara Elizabeth Putnam, "Parentesco y producción: La organización social de la agricultura de exportación en la provincia de Limón, Costa Rica, 1920–1960," *Revista de Historia* (San José, Costa Rica) 44 (2001): 121–58, esp. note 52.

34. ANCR, Serie Jurídica, Limón Juzgado Civil y del Crimen [henceforth, LJCyC] 449 (incendio, 1898). Cf. domestic arrangements described in ANCR, Serie Jurídica, Limón Juzgado del Crimen [henceforth, LJCrimen] 924 (homicidio, 1904), LJCrimen 145 (homicidio, 1897); LJCrimen 47 (homicidio, 1902); LJCrimen 531 (homicidio, 1908).

35. AC, vol. 26, book 3, "Autobiografía de J. R. R. R. (entrevista)," 135–36. José Reyes is a pseudonym. The daily wage of an adult male laborer was roughly 1.50 to 2.15 colones (U.S. $0.70 to $1). It is unclear whether J. R. R. R. is recalling his wages in U.S. dollar/cents or in *centavos de colón*.

36. ANCR, Fondo INCOFER no. 241, "Copiador del Superintendente": Internal report on reduction of forces, October 2, 1929.

37. Putnam, *Company They Kept*, 62, 66.

38. AC, vol. 26, book 3, "Autobiografía de ST," 181. Simon Taylor is a pseudonym. A native English speaker, Taylor was interviewed in Spanish. The translation is mine.

39. ANCR, LJCrimen 111 (homicidio, 1900); LJCyC 466 (tentativa de incendio, 1903); LJCrimen 30 (incendio, 1910); ANCR, Serie Jurídica, Limón Alcaldía Unica [henceforth LAU] 667 (injurias, 1900); LJCyC 730 (injurias, 1903); LJCrimen 70 (homicidio, 1904); LJCrimen 125 (lesiones, 1903); LAU 3466 (calumnia, 1907).

40. ANCR, LJCrimen 1041 (violación, 1913).

41. ANCR, LJCrimen 41 (violación, 1902).

42. ANCR, LJCyC 266 (violación, 1901).

43. Patrick Bryan, *The Jamaican People: Race, Class and Social Control, 1880–1902* (Kingston, Jamaica: University of the West Indies Press, 2000), 112–14; Edith Clarke, *My Mother Who Fathered Me: A Study of the Families in Three Selected Communities of Jamaica*, rev. ed. (1957; Kingston, Jamaica: University of the West Indies Press, 1999), 134–35.

44. See Sally W. Gordon, "I Go to 'Tanties': The Economic Significance of Child-Shifting in Antigua, West Indies," *Journal of Comparative Family Studies* 18, no. 3 (1987): 427–43; Isa María Soto, "West Indian Child Fostering: Its Role in Migrant Exchanges," in *Caribbean Life in New York City: Sociocultural Dimensions*, ed. Constance R. Sutton and Elsa M. Chaney (New York: Center for Migration Studies of New York, Inc., 1987, 1992).

45. ANCR, LJCrimen 407 (estupro, 1911). See also LJCrimen 1065 (violación, 1907).

46. ANCR, LJCrimen 955 (estupro, 1914).

47. ANCR, LAU 460 (injurias, 1900).

48. ANCR, LAU 2480 (desahucio, 1902). See LJCyC 376 (homicidio, 1901) for a *cantina* owned by a Jamaican woman and Barbadian man in Zent Junction, and LAU 409 (injurias, 1898) for a similar business held by a Nicaraguan woman and her Colombian male partner in the port.

49. ANCR, LAU 460 (injurias, 1900); LAU 447 (inujrias, 1900); LJCyC 557 (estafa, 1913); LJCrimen 1235 (homicidio, 1919).

50. Specifics from ANCR, LJCrimen 156 (homicidio frustrado, 1906). On the rarity of cross-group commercial sex in Limón, see Putnam, *Company They Kept*, 102.

51. ANCR, LJCrimen 128 (homicidio, 1909). For more on prostitutes' female companions and steady male lovers, see Putnam, *Company They Kept*, ch. 3.

52. ANCR, LJCrimen 901 (homicidio, 1914). UFCo's Sixaola Division straddled the border between Costa Rica and Panama; bananas grown there were shipped through Bocas del Toro.

53. ANCR, LAU 3466 (calumnia, 1907); see also Policía 1484 (comunicaciones, 1906): letter, June 25, 1906.

54. ANCR, LJCrimen 689 (homicidio, 1911); LJCrimen 786 (hurto, 1913).

55. Cf. Biblioteca Nacional de Costa Rica, Hemeroteca, Limón *Searchlight*, February 1, 1930, 1.

56. Cf. Sidney W. Mintz, "The Jamaican Internal Marketing Pattern: Some Notes and Hypotheses," *Social and Economic Studies* 4 (1955): 95–103, reprinted as "The Contemporary Jamaican Marketing System," *Caribbean Transformations* (New York: Columbia University Press Morningside Edition, 1989), 214–24.

57. ANCR, LJCrimen 988 (homicidio, 1915).

58. ANCR, LJCrimen 988 (homicidio, 1915).

59. I illustrate this here with cases drawn from judicial archives. But exactly the same pattern appears in personal testimonies from women who were adolescents during the first decades of the twentieth century in Limón and elsewhere in Costa Rica. See autobiographies transcribed in AC, vol. 23.

60. ANCR, LJCrimen 663 (rapto, 1910).

61. ANCR, LJCrimen 930 (violación, 1907).

62. See, for instance, ANCR, LJCrimen 72 (estupro, 1906), LAU 3461 (estupro, 1910), LJCrimen 855 (estupro, 1913), LJCrimen 955 (estupro, 1914).

63. ANCR, LJCrimen 801 (violación, 1913).

64. Of the eighteen deflowering suits that have been preserved from this era from Limón, three ended in marriage. Fifteen were dropped by the plaintiffs, were suspended for lack of evi-

dence, or ended in not guilty verdicts. Of the twenty-seven preserved rape cases, five resulted in convictions and jail sentences ranging from two months to four years, three ended in not guilty verdicts, and the rest were dismissed for lack of evidence or simply abandoned. Rape case victims' median age was ten and a half.

65. ANCR, LJCrimen 978 (violación, 1914). The governor directed her to the judge's office to file suit.

66. ANCR, LJCrimen 328 (estupro, 1910). The young man argued that he had merely "done what any man would have done in the presence of a woman who he desires to possess," had met no resistance, and had made her no promises. The case was dismissed on a technicality.

67. See Putnam, *Company They Kept*, 180–84.

68. Cf. ANCR LJCrimen 252 (homicidio, 1912).

69. ANCR, LJCrimen 748 (homicidio, 1913). Witnesses confirm Pastora's words.

70. ANCR, LJCrimen 748 (homicidio, 1913). Suárez was absolved of all responsibility for Pastora's death. Criminal proceedings continued against Pastora's companions for inciting a brawl and attacking Suárez' home.

71. Boza Villareal and Solórzano Fonseca, "El Estado nacional y los indígenas"; Boza Villareal, "Indígenas, afroantillanos, estado, misioneros y compañías."

72. Fallas, *Mamita Yunai*, 63 and 47. A former banana worker and Communist Party organizer, Fallas served as election observer in Amubre in 1940. See Marielos Aguilar, *Carlos Luis Fallas. Su época y sus luchas* (San José: Editorial Porvenir, 1983), 119–20.

73. Fallas, *Mamita Yunai*, 63. Ellipsis in original.

74. Pablo Solano, "Los indios de Talamanca," *Tradición indígena costarricense* (mimeo, Departamento de Antropología, Universidad de Costa Rica) 1, no. 2 (1983): 7. Solano's account was written in 1953.

75. ANCR, LJCrimen 883 (malversación de fondos, 1913).

76. Rape was defined as "lying with a woman . . . by means of force or intimidation" or with a girl under twelve under any circumstances. *Código Penal de la República de Costa Rica* (San José: Imprenta Nacional, n.d. [1880]), Libro 2, Título 7, Capítulo 5: "De la violación."

77. *Código Penal*, Libro 2, Título 7, Capítulo 7: "Disposiciones comunes a los tres capítulos anteriores."

78. ANCR, LJCrimen 767 (violación, 1898). The local priest concurred with this testimony as well. The names of Urbina, López, Saldaña, and his family, as they are public figures, have been conserved here.

79. ANCR, LJCrimen 767 (violación, 1898). Original reads, "que a mi no se me quita del puesto así no más."

80. ANCR, LJCyC 432 (violación, 1900).

81. On conflicts and alliances between Saldaña, various jefes políticos, and agents of United Fruit, see Boza Villareal, "Indígenas, afroantillanos, estado, misioneros y compañías."

82. ANCR, LJCyC 432 (violación, 1900). Emphasis in original. This was one of only two rape accusations brought by adult women in Limón between 1880 and 1925 (at least among cases that have been preserved).

83. ANCR, Serie Jurídica, Juzgado Penal de Limón 1221 (homicidio, 1916). The case is mentioned in Solano, "Los indios de Talamanca," 20–21.

84. ANCR, Serie Jurídica, Juzgado Penal de Limón 1221 (homicidio, 1916). Solís and Salazar were sentenced to twenty-one and twenty-four years, respectively, on the island penitentiary of San Lucas; theirs were among the harshest sentences handed down for any homicides in Limón

in this era. It is worth noting that while the context of political manipulation and illegal territorial acquisition in which this case occurred was unique to the southern valleys, the interpersonal dynamics were anything but. As in the vast majority of homicide cases with female victims in Limón, violence was initiated by former lovers to whom women refused to return. See Putnam, *The Company They Kept*, 184–94.

85. ANCR, LJCrimen 767 (violación, 1898).

7

Dangerous Driving: Adolescence, Sex, and the Gendered Experience of Public Space in Early-Twentieth-Century Mexico City

Katherine Elaine Bliss and Ann S. Blum

That one was a driver,
A big jokester
Who to play a trick
Turned off his motor
At a "chic" dance
In a tenement house
He left them in the dark.
How scandalous!
One father gave him
A good hard whack
For getting intimate
With his daughter.
You should see him, yes,
Making a splash,
Showing up
At any old party. . . .
Sweet on all the girls
Attending the gathering
Kindly offering
To take them for a spin. . . .
Yes, there was one girl
Who took up his invitation.
Later he took her
With satisfaction. . . .
That's the driver
Who is the admiration,

Of even the most proper girls,
Of this population.[1]

THE LYRICS FROM THIS POPULAR *corrido*, or ballad, from the 1910s and 1920s, known as "El Chauffeur," depict the driver as a devil-may-care ladies' man who cruises around the Mexican capital in his Ford motorcar, "making a splash," seducing young women and leaving heartbreak and intrigue in his wake. In this song, at least, the driver can illuminate a party outside an apartment building by leaving the car lights on; similarly, he has the power to create the circumstances for a kiss or more extensive caresses between dancing couples by killing his motor and plunging the courtyard into darkness. For males, the lyrics suggest, association with the automobile gave the driver freedom of movement on the city streets, sexual attractiveness, and the opportunity to catch the attention of "even the most proper girls." For young women, the chauffeur and his motorcar offered somewhat different links to sexual adventure and risk, on the one hand, and to social protection and decency, on the other. The interior of the car, itself, could make a public street the intimate site of a willing sexual tryst or the venue for a young woman's deflowering and disgrace; conversely, by inviting her into his vehicle the male driver could provide a girl a safe haven from the otherwise dangerous streets.

The ballad of "El Chauffeur" points to the possibilities modern transportation offered *capitalinos* to move quickly through the urban landscape and to transgress more easily geographic and social boundaries that had previously separated districts dedicated to vice and entertainment from neighborhoods inhabited by *gente decente*. It also suggests the increased access to new venues for the pursuit of love and pleasure for the generation reaching their teens in the wake of revolutionary conflict. In celebrating the convergence of modern technology with the flaunting of convention and propriety, the song prefigured the growing influence on urban social life of entertainments like the cinema and public dance halls where socializing could lead to sexual liaisons. The image of the motorcar, powerful machine of the street, and its ability to create romantic and sexual opportunities also reflects the increasing importance of public venues of entertainment rather than home and family for the formation of new models of masculine and feminine behavior. But with the power of the automobile in the hands of its masculine driver, the song also forewarned that urban youth cultures of entertainment and sexual adventure would be shaped by unequal relations of gender and power.

The associations among youth, entertainment, public spaces, and sexual behavior were hardly new in 1920s and 1930s Mexico City; for example, public officials had long lamented the participation of young women—and, to some extent, of young men—in sexual commerce in the city's parks and public walkways.[2] However, parental and official concerns over adolescent sexual behavior reached new heights in this period of rapid cultural and demographic transformation of the capital. As the city shed its grim demeanor after ten years of revolution, food shortages, and repeated army occupations, bawdy theaters, dance halls, cinemas, and cabarets opened as if to celebrate the end of war.[3] These venues offered opportunities for entertainment to many young Mexicans and employment to others. Moreover, breaching prewar distinctions between contained districts for licensed prostitution and areas of respectable commerce, many of the new and enticing centers of public diversion opened in residential neighborhoods where their extended hours of operation mingled entertainment seekers with shop keepers, artisans, and families and confronted adolescents working at home or in small shops and restaurants with myriad opportunities to abandon work for play. City planners extended the networks of public transportation and erected new market centers, while workshops and services catering to new technologies like the automobile sprang up throughout the city. As merchants competed for customers with proliferating advertisements in print media and street display, unemployed and working adolescents sought increased mobility and access to tempting new products and fashions.

The presence of an unprecedented number of young people, thanks to rural-urban migration, made Mexico City in the 1920s and 1930s a visibly youthful urban center, as well. Census officials estimated that the district's population between the ages of ten and nineteen grew by nearly fifty-one thousand between 1910 and 1921, with the greatest growth shown among the group aged ten to fourteen. By 1921 the population between the ages of ten and twenty-four represented fully one-third of the entire metropolis.[4] City councilors, residents, and reformers keen to implement the social promises of the revolution routinely expressed concern regarding the visibility and vulnerability of the capital's youth and noted with alarm their prevalence on the street, freedom from parental vigilance, and frequent attendance at entertainments of "dubious propriety." Officials feared that these unsupervised adolescents were eager to spend their wages on, and free time in, venues associated in public discourse with sexual permissiveness. In this logic, girls who attended public dances or nightspots were destined for a life of prostitution, while boys drawn by the attractions of the automobile and the city's bars and brothels were headed to certain alcoholism and a life of degeneration and crime.[5] Although many parents of the urban popular classes put their children to work rather than in school, they nevertheless complained to public officials that they felt powerless to exercise control over the work habits or pastimes of their teenagers and routinely implored public authorities to intervene in family conflicts centering on dating, sexual behavior, and physical appearance, even if they did not always approve of the state's methods of intervention.

Struggles over parental authority, dating and sexual behavior, and family relations resonated both with adult complaints about unruly youth of earlier periods and with freshly articulated concerns over leisure and sexual activity that drew on new understandings of adolescent development gaining attention throughout the Atlantic world. In the first decades of the twentieth century, the category of the adolescent emerged in North American and European intellectual circles as a physically, psychologically, and conceptually distinct stage of life bridging childhood and adulthood and separating the formal institutional markers of schooling and married life; scholars, activists, and reformers actively debated the roles of work, leisure, and romance among this "new" social group.[6] In Mexico, where social revolution coincided with the influence of international trends in social science and Progressive Era reformism, politicians aware of the new thinking with respect to adolescent development attached great importance to the notion of youth as the revolution's future. The revolutionary constitution of 1917 had established universal public education as the cornerstone of the national program for social and economic development: constitutional limits to child and adolescent labor further reinforced the emphasis on education. Additionally, a new law of family relations issued the same year affirmed the values of parental authority and filial obedience in defining the family structure of the revolutionary order. Teachers, physicians, sociologists, and officials in the rapidly proliferating government agencies of education, corrections, and public health promoted programs and policies aimed at creating a healthier, better-educated, and more skilled generation to build a modern society and competitive economy.[7] Inspired by medical studies that suggested sexual promiscuity and the associated perils of sexually transmitted infections, such as syphilis, could threaten the quality of future generations through inherited and degenerative afflictions, reformers worried especially about the sexual behavior of Mexico's adolescents and sought to promote ideals of sexual restraint and prudence among men and women alike.[8]

Over this period, a variety of groups from diverse political and social perspectives joined reformers in calling attention to the need to investigate, analyze, and protect Mexico's adolescents. Women's magazines encouraged mothers to "be vigilant of their daughters" and pointed out that the physical and mental benefits of dancing and exercise could at any moment be offset when the young couple enjoying synchronized movement to music got too close or strayed too far from the supervisory gaze of the parents to enjoy unsupervised physical adventure.[9] Other ad campaigns targeted young women themselves. One pamphlet directed at young women warned, "at any moment you are in danger of being assaulted; on the street, at the movies, in the countryside, at the factory. Make sure your boyfriend is truthful to you, he may be sick."[10] Family-oriented magazines, like the biweekly review published by the Con-federación Regional Obrera Mexicana, featured cautionary fiction specifically for young women. One such story told of Matilde, a working-class girl known in her neighborhood for her beauty, who succumbed to temptation and left the security of her seamstress position in a private home to work in one of the expensive downtown department stores. There, the store owner showered her with gifts, seduced her, and raised her to director of the Fashion Department, until he tired of her and replaced her with another victim. The fate of Matilde, doubly betrayed by her seducer's favors and the lure of modern fashion, represented the pitfalls of youthful independence in the commercializing urban environment. The workplace threw adolescent men and women into close contact, and wages gave working youth the means to pursue potentially corrupting entertainments.[11] These conditions put male adolescents "at risk" as well. Educational tracts urged young men to learn how to identify "good girls" and encouraged them to forego trips to brothels or sexual experimentation with "loose" women in the neighborhood.[12] And popular magazines highlighted the risks associated with "the high priestesses of street love" or ran scandalous stories highlighting the tendency of the daughters of the city's elite to spend their free afternoons in discreet brothels in the metropolis's most exclusive neighborhoods.[13]

But as the lyrics of "El Chauffeur" suggest, the seductive nature of the street and its association with freedom, passion, and a possible sexual encounter were hard for many adolescents to resist. Our goal in this chapter is to show how the youth of Mexico City's popular classes, in whose very name the revolution was waged, crafted a sexual culture for themselves in public spaces in spite of vociferous adult remonstrations against it. We focus on youth, roughly the age group between eleven and eighteen, who, unlike their middle-class peers, were neither in school nor, in most cases, ready for marriage. Building on the considerable work dedicated to understanding the importance of education, reformism, and state formation in the revolutionary period, we offer an analysis of how the heirs of the conflict—those who were too young to have fought with revolutionary armies or to have participated in the constitutional phases—sought to organize their lives in the shadow of reformist institutions.[14] Our interest in this topic is inspired by a sense of sympathy for these adolescents who clearly struggled to make choices and lead lives of independence in the midst of personal dilemmas, family conflicts, and their transitional state between childhood and adulthood. In this chapter, we highlight the occupations that attracted youth when they sought financial and personal freedom, the public venues where young men and women met and developed sexual relationships, and the conflicts that ensued as the protagonists discovered that they held different understandings of where a sexual liaison might lead. The examples we present are drawn largely from case files of the Mexico City Consejo Tutelar para Menores Infractores, which was instituted in 1926 to articulate a system of juvenile justice and protection in the capital. The court adopted a reformist and actively interventionist agenda to remove Mexico City's youth from the domestic and occupational environments that led them astray, to reeducate them in the skills necessary to become productive adults, and to reintegrate them into the economic and social mainstream.[15] Although juvenile court documents reflect the preoccupations of reforming officials, who condemned adolescent sex as socially deviant on moral grounds or as undesirable from a public-health perspective and who equated many urban entertainments with moral ruin, the court's investigative process allowed adolescents to express their own perspectives on their motives for seeking independence, as well as their expectations of their relationships with peers of the opposite sex.

Drawing on the methods of social history, gender history, and the history of the family, our analysis, focused on intersections of adolescent sexual experimentation in public settings, illuminates ways that a social group identified by others as a special category made choices and constructed a social world and sexual culture distinct from their parents' in a revolutionary city undergoing political, economic, and social transformations. While their behavior was often reactive against structures of power and authority personified by parents, employers, or public officials, young capitalinos of the popular classes, we argue, rejected adult moralizing, evaded oversight, and claimed as their own the right of the adolescent to postpone adult commitments and responsibilities while nevertheless asserting independence and indulging in so-called adult pastimes, including flirting, drinking, dancing, and engaging in multiple and uncommitted sexual relationships with their peers. Mindful of the difficulties of using institutional and especially morally tinged reformist documents to glean information about subjects' beliefs and choices, we endeavor in this chapter to filter through the prejudices of scribes, social workers, and police authorities, who were the chroniclers of this new youth culture, to reveal and highlight the distinct voices of parents, reformers, and especially adolescents themselves.[16]

We also show that the consequences of frequenting the city's entertainments and acting on sexual inclinations were not equal for young women and men. Fashions and entertainments may have presented adolescent girls with alluring glimpses of cosmopolitan femininity that suggested an enhanced social freedom from constraining convention and a new assertiveness in romantic relationships, but such promises often proved illusory. While our analysis demonstrates that some young women did successfully negotiate romantic or sexual relationships of independence and satisfaction, many others did, as reformers often predicted, find themselves faced with an unanticipated pregnancy or trapped in an abusive sexual relationship. Young men, however, could frequently gain the upper hand in negotiating the outcome of their encounters because they could count on laws and regulations based on a sexual double standard that accepted male promiscuity but condemned young women who were sexually adventuresome. Yet, as other cases we recount indicate, young men who did not engage in the active pursuit of heterosexual relationships considered normal for adolescent boys often found themselves at a disadvantage in their dealings with peers and with authorities. In this chapter, then, we describe an emerging urban adolescent identity based on experimentation with "adult" forms of socializing and sexual behavior and rejection of such "adult" responsibilities as household and family formation.

The Road from Home

After accusing her fourteen-year-old daughter of being "incorrigible," "scandalous," "disobedient," "capricious," and a "drunk," Señora Dolores Rodríguez, a housekeeper who worked and resided at a social club for chauffeurs in Mexico City, told the Tribunal Administrativo para Menores in 1927 that she was incapable of "disciplining" her daughter, Estela, and asked that the institution assume custody of the girl until such time as she could learn to behave and demonstrate "filial love" for her mother. (All names have been changed.)

According to the social worker who investigated the conflicted family relationship, the problems between parent and adolescent had started when Rodríguez had discovered that Estela, who neither attended school nor held a job, had been spending her spare time with an older, married man, who earned a living selling pulque, the cheap fermented cactus juice popular among the city's lower classes. Señora Rodríguez had further learned that Estela took advantage of the times her mother left her alone in the house to sneak out and enjoy theater extravaganzas and movies with her boyfriend. Knowing the *pulquero* had a wife and children, Señora Rodríguez had indicated to her daughter that she disapproved of the relationship, but Estela had merely ignored her mother's warnings and continued to socialize with the married man. Worse, on her outings, Estela had made the acquaintance of women of "bad conduct" who lived in the neighborhood and spent their free time with the drivers who frequented the social club where the family lived. To prevent her daughter from falling into further disgrace, Rodríguez had demanded the girl join her on her errands on the afternoon of June 23 rather than stay at home unsupervised. However, the court documents reflect that the girl "refused to accompany the señora, creating a scandal in the street with her flagrant disobedience and capriciousness."

When the police intervened in the fight, Estela indicated that she preferred to go to the station with them rather than return home with her mother. Angry with her daughter for flouting her authority and for carrying on an ill-advised relationship, Rodríguez made the startling accusation that Estela had "abandoned the house to practice prostitution." For her part, Estela "denied firmly that she had ever abandoned the home" and justified her relationship with the pulquero by noting that her mother had recently brought a man who was not her husband to live with the family in their one-room abode. Rather than return to the small apartment to live with the strange man, her mother, and her siblings, Estela told the court that she would prefer to "work as a servant as soon as she [had] her liberty" so that she could pursue her own interests on and off the job.[17]

This conflict between Estela and Señora Rodríguez is interesting because it reveals the tensions between a mother and her daughter regarding the child's sexual behavior and hints at similar frustrations on Estela's part regarding her mother's disruption of domestic harmony by introducing a new man into the household. An uneducated girl who had failed to pass the second grade despite four years at school, Estela had perhaps felt isolated at home until her relationship with the pulquero opened her eyes to the city's wider entertainments and public diversions. The institutional documents fail to reveal how Estela met the pulquero or if it was ever determined whether she and the married man had actually been sexually involved. Despite her claims that Estela had become a prostitute, Señora Rodríguez admitted to investigators that in reality she believed the pulquero had "respected the minor." It may well be that by raising the issue of prostitution (in the mother's case) and domestic servitude (in Estela's), both Señora Rodríguez and her daughter strategically invoked language that they believed would resonate with court officials' perceptions of the occupations available to uneducated young women. It is clear that Estela identified domestic labor as a way to gain independence from her family and the freedom to socialize with whom she wished without having to embrace the adult responsibility of starting a new household; servitude, which generally involved living with a family and working in their home, would likely guarantee her food and lodging until such time as she chose to try a different occupation. Rather than find placement as a domestic servant, however, Estela spent three and a half years at the Escuela Correccional para Mujeres before being released to her mother's custody in January of 1931.

Freedom and financial independence were among the principal reasons young women cited for having run away from home, according to case files archived with the Consejo Tutelar para Menores Infractores. Social workers' notes also reflect a sense that many young women left their families to avoid unpleasant conflicts with, or unwanted attention from, older, unrelated men living with the family. In Estela's case, her mother's new companion may have created for the girl an uncomfortable situation in which she felt sexually vulnerable to his advances. By developing a relationship with the pulquero, she was able to escape the house and confirm that she preferred a life away from the Centro Social de Choferes. Like Estela, young women directed themselves, or were directed, toward domestic service because of the perception that the work would afford them protection, lodging in the employer's home, and an opportunity to earn an honorable wage.[18] Although they were ostensibly protected by their isolation in a domestic setting, young women took advantage of opportunities to meet other servants in the neighborhood or while undertaking errands for their employers, and to forge social connections and romantic attachments in the parks, plazas, and markets they frequented. A new slate of revolutionary laws, moreover, ensured a worker's right to a day of rest and mandated that employers allow servants time to pursue such interests as vocational training and education, as well.[19]

The domestic's placement as a servant living with a family that was not her own offered young women embarking on an independent life opportunities for friendship, romance, and cultural experimentation, combined with a measure of social protection. By contrast, market work offered young women the chance to earn money within an even less strictured, therefore less protected, environment than the servant's. Market vendors frequently hired girls to assist them in their stalls or, perhaps, to attract customers with their good looks and lively conversation.[20] Girls who worked in markets had to contend with their employers' oversight, but their opportunities for establishing friendships and romantic connections were more numerous than the limited excursions afforded domestic servants. Their access to products, including cosmetics and stockings, linked by advertisers to beauty and sex appeal, also gave them opportunities to copy and experiment with the diverse fashions and social behavior they saw embraced by older women of their acquaintance. The same freedoms that made the market a space for cultivating promising romance, however, also made it an unreliable source of job security, for adolescent flirtation frequently clashed with employers' priorities. Elena Quesada, an assistant in a clothing stall, lost her job after only one week because her employer complained that she preferred to spend her time applying makeup and chatting with her friends and boyfriend rather than attending to her duties.[21] When Felipa Arredondo was working in the Morelos Market, she began to flirt with an older man who owned the neighboring stall and was soon apprehended for stealing gifts for him to encourage his affection.[22]

Markets offered space outside the home for adolescent girls to wear makeup, don sexually provocative clothing, and meet potential romantic partners among the working boys or older men who frequented their worksites as merchants, deliverers, or customers. But it is not always clear what girls who flirted with men in these public settings were seeking—attention? romance? marriage? Social workers quick to dismiss flirtation as evidence of inherent bad tendencies employed language in their reports that often obscures girls' motivations in the sexually charged market milieu. The case of twelve-year-old

Figure 7.1.   Customer at a grocery stall in the market of La Merced, 1928. Source: Fondo Casasola, Fototeca Nacional, Instituto Nacional de Antropología e Historia.

Araceli Perdigon, who was interned at the correctional school run by the Mexico City Tribunal para Menores at her family's request in 1933, raises more questions than answers. According to her grandmother, the girl had dropped out of school and spent her time selling lottery tickets in the *zócalo* (main plaza) or on the streets near the Palacio de Hierro department store, where she occasionally picked pockets or cheated her clients out of change to supplement her income. Moreover, Araceli used her presence on the street to flirt with male pedestrians, taking the advice of a friend who told her to "dress well and find a rich man so she would never lack anything."[23]

Work associated with the street offered boys opportunities to practice adult masculine roles among their peers, to explore public entertainments, and to make sexual liaisons as well. Eduardo Luna's older siblings agreed that his tendency to stay out late, drink, and be disobedient dated from his employment as a driver's assistant. About six months previous, following in the footsteps of an older brother who worked as a driver, Eduardo had left his job as a mechanic's apprentice to work as an assistant to the driver of a privately owned automobile. He then began to spend his time with the other young drivers, who, officials noted, "generally have few scruples, they smoke, and they invite him to go out with them at night," the implication being that they were frequenting nightspots where they associated with women of dubious reputations. Under the influence of his new friends, Eduardo had become disrespectful and had begun coming home late. The family complained that he now spent his time drifting and loafing, *vagando*, with drivers.[24]

Alberto Reynoso's case demonstrates the extent to which one young man went in his efforts to establish an independent identity. Until the age of fifteen, Alberto had lived with his grandmother and had completed three years of school. A short apprenticeship with his uncle, a mechanic, ended after his father beat him for staying out all night. Alberto then left home and worked briefly as an assistant to a driver, who whetted the boy's taste for adventure by taking him on trips to Puebla, Toluca, and Chalco. By age sixteen, when he was arrested in 1927 for smoking marijuana with a group of boys who gathered to hang out at the Salto del Agua fountain, Alberto had been living on scant earnings from shining shoes, sleeping at friends' houses, in public dormitories, or on the street, and eating in the markets. The intervening authorities described the youth's friends as vagrant and perverse. In their company, Alberto had attended "diversions improper for his age, such as theaters of the lowest category, where he has seen immoral productions" and "developed a taste for cigarettes, cinema and plays in the immoral theater," as well as frequenting "houses of women of dissolute conduct."[25]

The prevalence of petty theft by teenage boys points to the importance of taking risks and flouting authority in defining urban adolescent masculinity, even among boys who earned enough to buy snacks, trinkets, or admission to the cinema. Mimicking a long tradition among *rateros*, career pickpockets and thieves, boys who worked and socialized on the street sometimes adopted aliases, such as "el Capitán" and "el Gallo," that projected their aspirations toward leadership and bravery.[26] Some boys like Guillermo Camacho, a twelve-year-old arrested in 1928 for taking a pineapple from a fruit stand, may have stolen because they were hungry or because they lacked money for favorite entertainments such as movies.[27] Other youths used the proceeds from stealing to fund more extensive activities. Ricardo Pacheco, eighteen years old, worked as an apprentice to an ironworker on the Calle de Mecánicos. His mother, a tortilla maker, described her son's friends as "bad company" and blamed them for Ricardo's turn to crime. An investigation revealed that Ricardo and his friends had stolen an automobile tire, women's cosmetics, thirty bottles of beer, one hundred cigars, and eighty boxes of cigarettes, some of which they may have wished to consume. Proceeds from the sale of the goods may have been intended for use in the brothels, which Ricardo confessed to frequenting. Although Ricardo earned a comparatively good wage, stealing represented an opportunity not only for proving his daring to his peers by flouting the law, but also the means to obtain additional spending money for entertainments such as smoking, drinking, and sex with prostitutes, that further demonstrated his masculinity to himself and to his friends.[28]

For many urban adolescents, the first steps along the road from home took them to venues where work and socializing mixed. Work offered a taste of financial independence and introduced them to leisure pursuits that had the potential to lead to sexual encounters. Young men like Ricardo Pacheco, the apprentice iron worker and petty thief, moved from the realm of family and respectable work to public spaces where he and his peers challenged authority by stealing and gained sexual experience with prostitutes. For Ricardo, as for many other urban youths, it was not his job but rather his diversions with friends his own age that defined his stance of independence from parents and public authorities and his claim to masculinity and sexual identity. Similarly, but from the perspective of intervening officials, what characterized Alberto Reynoso's behavior as perverse was less his vagrancy than his choice of friends and entertainments.

Like their male counterparts, young women actively pursued new entertainment options and sought venues to socialize with their own age group, but their activities were not without consequences. Even constraining employment like domestic service, representing for many girls a temporary compromise between parental supervision and independence, nevertheless opened the way to unsupervised leisure time, but the work's low wages also limited girls' access to the fashions and entertainments they enjoyed. Socializing at the expense of work cost Elena Quesada her market job and tempted Felipa Arredondo into theft in order to cultivate a budding romance. These adolescents cultivated social communities away from family in their work spaces, where they began to experiment with flirtation, romance, and sex without having to assume the responsibilities of family or household formation.

Dangerous Intersections

As early as the 1910s, dance halls, cabarets, *carpas,* and cantinas competed for the spending money and free time of Mexico City's growing population of men and women. Theaters had long provided entertainment to the city's well-to-do classes, and carpas, a kind of traveling theater or circus, offered a less expensive option for the city's working poor.[29] Of course, men and women gathered at establishments that sold pulque, beer, and other intoxicants as they had for hundreds of years. Since at least the middle of the nineteenth century, formal brothels of all classes had similarly been a staple of the urban cultural scene—at least for men. But in the aftermath of revolution and in response to trends in entertainment styles popular in the United States and Europe, cabarets, dance academies, and *salones de baile* proliferated. Inspired by revolutionary discourses regarding the state's duty to "redeem" the popular classes, the city council had sought to limit the lure of the brothel by instituting new

Figure 7.2.   **Women and men during a get-together at Salón México, ca. 1934.**
Source: Fondo Casasola, Fototeca Nacional, Instituto Nacional de Antropología e Historia.

sanitary regulations that prohibited brothels from selling liquor and restricted the hours during which proprietors could offer visiting clients musical enter-tainment. In response, patrons sought out the new cabarets and dance halls, which gained in popularity as sexually charged venues where men and women could meet to enjoy entertainment and perhaps a sexual encounter. With names such as the Palacio de Marmol, the Paris Cabaret, and the Crystal Cabaret, these venues sought to evoke a mature, cosmopolitan, European am-bience, but the clientele frequently included registered prostitutes, rural mi-grants, and day laborers, as well as working adolescents.[30]

However much these exotically styled sites were spaces for entertainment, they were also venues where young men and women earned a living and where sex and work frequently intersected. Whereas work in domestic service, in mar-kets, or on the street afforded young men and women a chance to experiment sexually, work in cantinas and cabarets frequently made work and sex one and the same. In the cases we describe, those adolescents who participated in sexu-ally oriented businesses appear to have experienced the same yearnings for sex-ual attention, frustrations with family life, and mixed desire for independence reflected in the cases of domestic servants and market vendors mentioned above. Others, however, responded to parental abandonment and abuse by turning to sexual commerce. Boys who sought occupational opportunities in the city's demimonde attracted police attention, not because it was illegal to work as a male prostitute or, for that matter, to have sexual relations with other males, but because authorities deemed such activity scandalous and deviant and sought to repress it on medical grounds. Adolescents who worked or engaged in sexual activities on the margins of the city's growing entertainment industries were frequently vulnerable to abuse on the part of authorities and their clients alike. For those youths who confronted the challenges of flouting acceptable social roles for adolescent girls and boys, including the rejection of their families, forming alternative communities of friendship and support became a way to navigate treacherous social and cultural terrain.

The participation of young women in sexual commerce was a phenomenon about which public authorities worried a great deal, but in many cases the line between formal exchange of sex for money and mere sexual experimentation and promiscuity was blurry at best. The apprehension and investigation of Rosa Lozano and Sofia Navarrete on April 27, 1928, illustrates how ideas about what constituted acceptable reasons for girls' sexual promiscuity shaded investigators' analyses of the case. Ages seventeen (Rosa) and fifteen (Sofia), the girls were stopped by police upon leaving the Lux dance hall and heading in the direction of a nearby hotel with three men at 1:40 a.m. Both girls were regulars at the Lux and at other dance venues in the capital, attending the festivities several nights a week, and they enjoyed going to the theater and cinema, as well. Neither girl had more than a few years of education, and both had experienced part-time, low-wage factory work. The two girls had become friends at the centrally located tenement house, La Bella Elena, where they both lived. The two acknowledged being sexually active as well.

But it was here that the similarities between Rosa and Sofia ended. A former domestic servant and part-time packer at the La Anfora ceramics factory, Rosa lived in the _vecindad_ (tenement house) with her mother, a seamstress who had a stall in the Merced market, and several siblings. She told the social worker who interviewed her that she had lost her virginity to a young man named Enrique Ocampo, whom she had met at the Lux, and admitted that since her deflowering some years earlier, she had "frequented that dance salon and the 'Goya,' having relations with various men." As she indicated to the social worker who interviewed her, she also met men when she frequented bawdy theaters, such as the María Guerrero, and cinemas, where she enjoyed viewing the latest romantic stories.[31] But, Rosa emphasized, she was not in the habit of receiving money in exchange for engaging in sexual activity with the men she met and insisted that she was not a prostitute. Indeed, she recounted that the men with whom she had sex always told her to "wait for them," but they never returned for her. In exchange for helping her mother embroider and sew, Rosa received small sums of money to spend on her entertainments; thus, as she told social workers, she did not need to make money from her activities and had sex with various men because she enjoyed it.[32]

At the time of her apprehension with Rosa, Sofia Navarrete lived in the same tenement but did not count on the support of a mother or siblings. Originally from the state of San Luis Potosí north of the Central Valley, Sofia had traveled to Mexico City with her father after her mother's death. Abandoned by her father at a convent in the capital, she eventually secured a series of placements as a domestic servant and then as a nanny before finding work at a textile factory, where she earned a peso a day. It was at the factory known as La Central that Sofia met the sixteen-year-old machinist Jorge Espinosa, with whom she claimed to have first had sexual relations when he took her to his parents' house and, according to Sofia, initiated the encounter without her permission. But, according to Rosa, Sofia had told her that a man had paid her forty pesos to "deflower" her. Whatever the circumstances surrounding her sexual debut, Sofia stated that ever since that occasion, she had dedicated herself to prostitution. At the time of her apprehension, Sofia claimed to be supported by a man named "Roberto," who gave her enough money to pay her rent to Dolores Zuñiga, the woman with whom she lived at the Bella Elena. There is little in Sofia's case to suggest whether, like Rosa, she claimed to enjoy the liberty to be sexually active or whether she found her means of making a living unpalatable; she did emphasize, however, that she had determined that prostitution was an easy way to earn money and was not a practice she would give up easily.[33]

The cases of Rosa and Sofia, both placed into the state's custody for being too young to practice prostitution, reveal the challenges young women faced when becoming sexually active in the metropolis. By her own account, Rosa enjoyed spending time at dances and theaters and relished the opportunity to socialize with the men of the popular classes whom she met there. She insisted she was not engaged in sexual commerce, and she rejected authorities' attempts to portray her as economically desperate by insisting that her mother gave her the money she needed for activities around the metropolis. Rosa's ambitious socializing came at a price, however, for she recounted her recurring disappointment when the men with whom she had sexual relations failed to return for her, and a medical exam revealed that Rosa suffered from gonorrhea, as well as other genital-area infections. Social workers then dismissed the girl as being sexually promiscuous "out of vicious tendencies" and noted that even at the reformatory she preferred to spend her time "putting on makeup with the sole object of flirting with as many men as possible."[34]

As for Sofia, it is difficult to know how she experienced her abandonment by her father, violent sexual debut, and turn to sexual commerce. On her own in the capital, she had discovered that work in which she could play up her youth, femininity, and physical attractiveness offered her greater independence and financial security, and she had easily found work as a bar waitress before dedicating herself to more formal work as a prostitute. Sofia had developed a community of friends at La Bella Elena, and going out to the dances with Rosa gave her the opportunity to search for customers to supplement the income she earned from Roberto, about whom the documents reveal little but with whom she was likely sexually involved.[35] Although social workers agreed that Sofia and Rosa had become sexually promiscuous for different reasons ("vicious tendencies" in Rosa's case, and because she had been economically abandoned in Sofia's), they prescribed similar remedies for their situations. Both girls were remanded to the Escuela Correccional para Mujeres, where Rosa spent a little over a year before being released as a domestic servant to a woman by whom she had previously been employed.[36] Sofia, too, found herself returning to a life of domestic servitude. In 1931 she was released to the custody of a woman who promised to feed her and pay her ten pesos a month in exchange for Sofia's work in the family home.[37]

The cases of Rosa and Sofia illustrate the physical and psychological vulnerability adolescent girls who actively participated in the city's sex and entertainment cultures faced, but young women were not the only ones to encounter insecurity due to their sexual activities. Young men who engaged in sexual behavior deemed "feminine," that is, having sex with other men, were exposed to police harassment and family conflict, as well. By October 1927, when police detained Fernando Miranda for public drunkenness and scandal, the fifteen-year-old had already been arrested numerous times for public behavior considered scandalous and for engaging in sex with men near the downtown gardens of the Alameda. Known as "La Israela," the boy was described by the social worker reporting to the juvenile court as "one of the leaders of his guild," referring to homosexuals. Since Fernando had left his mother's home and his job as a tailor's assistant four years previous, he had entered an extensive social and sexual community that included boys working on the street and sleeping in public parks, male prostitutes, and members of the city's professional classes. On the occasion of his latest arrest, the police extracted enough evidence from Fernando to round up more than sixty men and boys described as his *queridos*, or boyfriends. In addition to supporting himself by exchanging sex for money, the youth had also developed two relatively long-term relationships. As his mother refused to have any contact with him, and he and his friends were subject to constant harassment by authorities, an extended community that accepted Fernando, as well as his ability to establish close relationships, may have compensated for the high cost of his sexual expression.[38]

In all three cases we have just described, adolescent sexual behavior considered "unnatural" placed young men and women in the hands of the state. Rosa claimed to enjoy her outings to the public dances followed by dates at a local hotel. The facts that she actively sought sexual adventure and rejected the idea that she was either economically desperate or a victim of rape or violence flew in the face of conventional ideas about proper feminine behavior; thus, even though Rosa never sought to register as a prostitute, she was placed in the reformatory until such time as the institution could establish her as a domestic servant in a home the court was certain would offer her guidance and a moral example. Sofia's explanation that abandonment, rape, and economic desperation had driven her to sexual promiscuity fit more comfortably into accepted narratives about femininity and sexuality; in this logic, Sofia was a victim of economic circumstances, unlike Rosa, who had "vicious tendencies."

In Fernando's case, his behavior failed to fit into the mold of acceptable adolescent sexual experience. Reformers understood that young men would seek sexual adventure with prostitutes or among their peers, and some social workers even acknowledged that adolescent boys experimented sexually with each other. But the boy's identification as the feminine "La Israela" and his conscious choice of masculine associates and intimate partners contravened what reformers believed to be natural behavior, and he, too, was institutionalized. Adolescents who found themselves at the dangerous intersection of sex and work experienced considerable friction with parents and a reformist revolutionary state not yet prepared to reform traditional gender norms.

Wrong Turns

Adolescents' pursuit of romance and sexual experience challenged parental attempts to assert household discipline and aggravated officials' concerns over the revolutionary generation's long-term reproductive health and ability to make adult commitments to responsibility and productivity. Public officials and educators encouraged young women to prepare themselves for mature motherhood, but for the optimum health of both mother and child, they urged that girls delay childbearing until they had finished school and found a responsible partner. Nevertheless, motherhood came early to many. In 1921, more than seventy-eight hundred women under the age of twenty in the federal district were married, widowed, or divorced, and more than four thousand of them had children.[39] Although on a nationwide scale births to mothers under the age of nineteen decreased from a little more than 20 percent of the total in 1920 to closer to 16 percent in 1929, underage women participated in the national baby boom of the late 1920s and 1930s, and the actual number of births to that age group in 1929 was twenty-eight thousand higher than at the start of the decade.[40] Census counts in the federal district for 1940, moreover, revealed close to eleven thousand married women under the age of eighteen and more than forty-five hundred living in informal unions.[41] The fleeting snapshots of the census counts, however, fail to convey the fact that many of these relationships, whether married or not, may have been of short duration. Nor can statistics depict the pitfalls that young women encountered in initiating sexual relationships and seeking longer-term commitments. Juvenile court cases in which adolescent girls or their mothers brought charges of rape against evasive boyfriends reveal that frequenting the very dance halls where couples met could sabotage a young woman's hopes for a more enduring relationship and that even suits resulting in marriage could rest on uncomfortable or unstable compromises.

Officials' conviction that dances and movie houses fostered the exchange of sex for money put girls who sought entertainment and love in such public spaces at a disadvantage in negotiating the outcome of romantic relationships, as fifteen-year-old Teresa Morán found to her dismay. In May 1938 at the public dance hall Playa, Teresa began regular meetings with Pedro Salas, a self-supporting waiter of seventeen. After two months of dating, Pedro persuaded Teresa to accompany him to a hotel that rented rooms by the hour. Teresa understood the invitation in terms of the courtship convention that made the exchange of a girl's virginity for a boy's promise of marriage the basis for initiating sexual relations. But Pedro, careful to avoid the promise of marriage, told Teresa only that he would not abandon her, meaning, he later asserted, that he would keep seeing her. When Pedro would not set a date for marriage even after two more sexual encounters, Teresa accused her boyfriend of *estupro* (rape). To establish that she had been dishonored by Pedro, Teresa submitted to a medical exam to demonstrate that she had been a virgin prior to their meeting. But virginity was not solely rooted in physical evidence, Pedro contended, asserting that when they first had sex at the hotel, he did not know whether or not Teresa was a virgin but assumed that she was not, owing to her frequent attendance at public dances. Even so, he conceded, he was willing to marry her.[42]

Pedro's evasive tactics drew on tacit gender codes, but formal legal practices frequently supported young men's interpretations of sexual relationships also. In late December 1927, Francisco Barrera, aged sixteen and supporting himself with a steady job as an electrician in a garage, became involved with fourteen-year-old Elvira Briseño, resident of the same tenement. A few weeks into their relationship, they spent all night kissing in the gardens of Chapultepec. As dawn broke, Francisco told Elvira that he would soon be moving away and that they should probably break up. Elvira, however, did not want to end the relationship. The couple discussed going away to live together, and after Elvira had collected some clothing from home, they took up residence in a hotel room. When eight days had elapsed, Elvira's mother came looking for the couple and demanded that Francisco marry her daughter. He, in turn, accused Elvira of having lost her virginity to a previous boyfriend and demanded 150 pesos from the girl's family for a medical exam to determine the truth before he would promise to marry her. At this point, Elvira's mother turned to the authorities and accused Francisco of rape.[43]

As in the case of Pedro and Teresa, law and convention mandated that marriage would resolve the charge. But just as Francisco had used allegations of Elvira's immorality, specifically her previous loss of virginity, to exempt himself from the obligation of marriage, the juvenile court also based its ruling on the reputation or honor of the protagonists. The couple, the court sustained, had gone to the hotel by mutual consent, a serious strike against Elvira's morality. Francisco, the court argued, had shown himself to be a moral and hardworking young man with bright prospects, while Elvira had a reputation as a flirt and was not considered "completely honorable," even by members of her own community. Unless Elvira were pregnant by Francisco, the court absolved him from any obligation to marry her and ordered the two to cease contact. By late March, however, a medical exam confirmed that Elvira was indeed pregnant, with conception dating from her residence with Francisco.[44]

While Elvira, like her contemporary Teresa Morán, pursued legal charges in hopes of achieving marriage, Francisco's actions demonstrated that he viewed the relationship as temporary. Francisco had initially used his impending move to justify breaking up with Elvira, but her reluctance to end the relationship had led to their sojourn at the hotel. Like his male peers, Francisco drew on social understandings and legal definitions that allowed him to initiate sexual relations with the implicit promise of marriage. He then attempted to evade commitment by accusing his girlfriend of having lost her virginity to another, thus denying her the law's standard for "chastity, morality and honor." After over a week of cohabitation with Elvira, Francisco's demand for a prohibitively high sum of money for a medical exam suggests that he did not expect her to go to such lengths to prove her case. The juvenile court initially absolved Francisco of responsibility, favoring the masculine perspective and following the letter of the law to blame Elvira for her own predicament. Until a doctor confirmed Elvira's pregnancy, it must have seemed to Francisco that he was off the hook. Although ultimately the couple's encounter may have resulted in marriage, the incident points to the decided advantages held by adolescent males for keeping sexual relationships casual.

Marriage, however, could also serve as a means for young men to avoid further entanglement with women who gave them problems. For Delfina Betancourt, seventeen and originally from the mining community Real del Monte in Hidalgo, a two-year relationship with Epifanio Avila ended without the marriage he had promised. Delfina had come to Mexico City to work as a servant in a position recommended to her by a female relative. At the age of fifteen, she had entered a sexual relationship with Epifanio, and their involvement had become serious enough that most evenings she spent at his parents' house. Indeed, Epifanio's parents, realizing that Delfina's family was aware that he was the "author" of her deflowerment, suggested the two get married, but some time went by without the ceremony taking place. Thereafter, the couple encountered difficulties, and Epifanio left Delfina to marry his former girlfriend. After that, Delfina dedicated herself to prostitution, living with a waiter in a cantina and spending her free time getting drunk at the bar and, according to reports, committing "all kinds of scandals" or attending movies and public dances.[45]

A woman journalist writing with tongue in cheek in 1925 lamented the demise of masculine honor and chivalry and suggested that young women carry their own *caballero*, meaning a stout stick, to mete out appropriate responses to sexual taunts on the street. Men's perceptions of women's growing assertiveness in romantic relationships created anxieties reflected by a cartoon published the same year. As two women dressed in elegant flapper fashions lounged idly, one inquired, "Are you faithful to your boyfriend?" The other paused before asking, ". . . and you?" to which her friend replied, "Me either."[46] But for many young women, sexual assertiveness came at a price. While Delfina, Elena, and Teresa might have entered into relationships with young men as equals in their desire for romance, sexual experience, or simply adventure, they soon encountered steep social, legal, and economic gradients of power positioning them at a disadvantage for influencing both the short-term and long-term outcomes of their involvements. Simply frequenting public dances and amusements where young people mixed suggested that an adolescent girl was sexually available and undermined her claim to an honorable reputation, a key factor in her argument for eventual marriage. Additionally, young men not only enjoyed legal protections in cases turning on sexual relations gone awry but also manipulated the condemnation that respectable society reserved for "fallen" women to distance themselves from confining relationships and their potential consequences. In seeking companions and community tolerant of their sexual histories, young women who took low-waged jobs in cantinas often found exchanging sex for money after hours a tempting next step.

New Directions

As suggested by the ballad celebrating the devil-may-care chauffeur's mastery of the street and access to sexual adventure, excursions into financial independence, romantic relationships, and public diversions could transport adolescent men and women to different destinations. Although they worked in the same markets and mingled at the same entertainments, they experienced those environments through relations of gender and power that constrained their choices, but not always in the same ways. For young men, the rites of establishing an independent masculine identity frequently placed them in conflict with parental authority and could result in an early eviction from the home onto the street. Young working-class men who sought alternative sexual communities did so at the risk of cutting family ties and losing access to respectable employment. Despite adolescent girls' defiant stance of independence from their parents, the outcomes of girls' sexual adventures all too often fulfilled their elders' dire warnings, as well as reproduced and perpetuated the gender hierarchies of the older generation. For adolescent men and women alike, low-waged jobs and the privations of homelessness frequently erased the boundary between work and diversion, but, again, in gender-distinct ways. Young men often resorted to petty theft to fund their access to entertainments. For young women on their own, public dances and cabarets were transformed from sites for romantic assignations to places to exchange sex for money.

In this chapter we have examined adolescents' claims of independence from parental authority often based on the initiation of sexual activity, choice and the construction of communities of peers, and preference for social activities. We have drawn on the methods of social history to locate our subjects in their larger contexts and relations of class and community; on gender history to illustrate the diverse ways in which adolescents, their parents, and the other adults with whom they interacted understood the meanings of masculinity and femininity in an urban, popular setting; and on history of the family to consider issues of life-course and intimate relationships among relatives. We have centered our investigation on the ways in which adolescents used the opportunities provided by their insertion into a fluid urban environment to craft independent social and romantic lives for themselves in the city's public spaces. We have sought to identify normal social patterns outside of normative structures, including law, institutional practice, and reform movements. In exploring links between life stage and questions of identity, we have found that young men and women between the ages of eleven and eighteen in Mexico City began to experiment with sexual activity in the context of their broader participation in the city's work and entertainment spaces. And we propose, moreover, that this demographically significant generation of urban youth influenced the evolution of Mexico City's social life by linking adolescent sexuality to the entertainment venues where adolescents gathered with their peer communities of choice.

Thus, our chapter points to an emergent youth culture well before the eruption of student politics of the rock 'n' roll generation of 1968. The cases of adolescent-parent conflict and the interventions of public authority that we examine fail to demonstrate that this teen experimentation fundamentally altered or even collectively challenged established relations of gender and power, but perhaps it paved the way for future change. Significant reconsideration of gender norms would not happen until the heirs of the revolution, including the adolescents we study in this article, had given birth to and reared the next generation. Their own children, in turn, would be the driving force behind a movement that questioned traditional power relations in Mexico, ushered in a new era of social activism around gender relations and sexual rights, and sought to overturn the sexual double standard.

Notes

1. Bottom half of "La Despedida del Soldado," broadside, half sheet, zinc etching, Art Institute of Chicago, 1944, 985; reproduced in Ron Tyler, ed. _Posada's Mexico_ (Washington, DC: Library of Congress and Amon Carter Museum of Western Art, 1979), 253, figure 167.

2. For official concerns in the late colonial period, see Juan Pedro Viquiera Albán, _Propriety and Permissiveness in Bourbon Mexico_, trans. Sonya Lipsett-Rivera and Sergio Rivera Ayala (Wilmington, DE: Scholarly Resources, 1999), esp. ch. 3, "Disorder or Street Diversions." On late nineteenth-century measures to curb the participation of minors in sexual commerce in the capital, see Katherine Elaine Bliss, _Compromised Positions: Prostitution, Public Health, and Gender Politics in Revolutionary Mexico City_ (University Park: Pennsylvania State University Press, 2001), esp. ch. 1, "The Porfirians' City of Pleasure: Prostitutes, Patrons, and Sexual Propriety." For comparison, see also Judith R. Walkowitz, _City of Dreadful Delight: Narratives of Sexual Danger in Late Victorian London_ (London: Virago, 1992).

3. See the city council's debates regarding urban entertainment over the first few months of 1915: for example, Ordinary Session of the Ayuntamiento de la Ciudad de México, January 22, 1915, _Boletín Municipal_, April 30, 1915, 9–11; Ordinary Session of the Ayuntamiento de la Ciudad de México, February 19, 1915, _Boletín Municipal_, April 30, 1915, 17.

4. Estados Unidos Mexicanos, Departamento de la Estadística Nacional, _Censo General de Habitantes, Distrito Federal, 30 de Noviembre de 1921_. Distrito Federal (Mexico City: Talleres Gráficos de la Nación, 1925), 15–16.

5. Ordinary session of the Ayuntamiento de la Ciudad de México, January 15, 1918, _Boletín Municipal_, January 29, 1918, 57; Mexico, Archivo General de la Nación. Consejo Tutelar para Menores Infractores, various (hereafter AGN, CTMI).

6. For an early study using the concept of adolescence, see Auguste Lemaitre, _La vie mentale de l'adolescent et ses anomalies, avec 30 figures dans la texte_ (Saint-Blaise: Foyer Solidariste, 1910). On the development of the specialty of adolescent medicine in the United States, see Heather Munro Prescott, _A Doctor of Their Own: The History of Adolescent Medicine_ (Cambridge, MA: Harvard University Press, 1998). See also Ruth M. Alexander, _The Girl Problem: Female Sexual Delinquency in New York, 1900–1930_ (Ithaca, NY: Cornell University Press, 1995); Regina G. Kunzel, _Fallen Women, Problem Girls: Unmarried Mothers and the Professionalization of Social Work, 1890–1945_ (New Haven, CT: Yale University Press, 1993); Mary E. Odem, _Delinquent Daughters: Protecting and Policing Adolescent Female Sexuality in the United States, 1885–1920_ (Chapel Hill: University of North Carolina Press, 1995); Kathy Peiss, _Cheap Amusements: Working Women and Leisure in Turn-of-the-Century New York_, 2nd ed. (Philadelphia: Temple University Press, 1987); David M. Pomfret, "Representations of Adolescence in the Modern City: Voluntary Provision and Work in Nottingham and Saint-Etienne, 1890–1914," _Journal of Family History_ 26, no. 4 (October 2001): 455–79.

7. Antonio E. Méndez-Vigatá, "Politics and Architectural Language: Post-Revolutionary Regimes in Mexico and Their Influence on Mexican Public Architecture, 1921–1952," in _Moder-_

nity and the Architecture of Mexico, ed. Edward R. Burian (Austin: University of Texas Press, 1997); see also Adrian A. Bantjes, "Burning Saints, Molding Minds: Iconoclasm, Civic Ritual and the Failed Cultural Revolution," in *Rituals of Rule, Rituals of Resistance: Public Celebrations and Popular Culture in Mexico*, ed. William H. Beezley, Cheryl English Martin, and William E. French (Wilmington, DE: Scholarly Resources, 1994).

8. For a broad spectrum of Mexican reform programs involving adolescence, see Katherine Elaine Bliss, "The Science of Redemption: Syphilis, Sexual Promiscuity, and Reformism in Revolutionary Mexico City," *Hispanic American Historical Review* 79, no. 1 (1999): 1–40; Ann S. Blum, "Cleaning the Revolutionary Household: Domestic Servants and Public Welfare in Mexico City, 1900–1935," *Journal of Women's History* 15, no. 4 (2004): 67–90; Primer Congreso Mexicano del Niño, *Memoria del Primer Congreso Mexicano del Niño* (Mexico City: El Universal, 1921); Patience A. Schell, "Nationalizing Children through Schools and Hygiene: Porfirian and Revolutionary Mexico City," *The Americas* 60, no. 4 (2004): 559–87; Alexandra Minna Stern, "Responsible Mothers and Normal Children: Eugenics and Nationalism in Post-Revolutionary Mexico City, 1920–1940," *Journal of Historical Sociology* 12, no. 4 (1999): 369–97; Mary Kay Vaughan, *The State, Education, and Social Class in Mexico, 1880–1928* (DeKalb: Northern Illinois University Press, 1982).

9. "Madres, Vigilar a Vuestras Hijas," *Mujer: Para la Elevación Moral e Intelectual de la Mujer* 1, no. 1 (December 1926): 3.

10. "Para las jóvenes. Escucha, medita," *Eugenesia: Revista mensual para el estudio de los problemas de la herencia* 3 (November 1942): 9–10.

11. Carlos Melquizo, "Una historia de todos los días," *CROM* 1, no. 5 (May 1, 1925): 26.

12. Juan Soto, *La educación sexual en la escuela mexicana: Libro para los padres y los maestros* (Mexico City: Ediciones Patria, 1933).

13. "Las irregulares," *Detectives* 3, no. 107 (August 27, 1934): 13; Andrés Gómez, "Siete días en una casa de Venus, IV" *Detectives* 2, no. 95 (June 4, 1934): 15

14. Mary Kay Vaughan, *Cultural Politics in Revolution: Teachers, Peasants and Schools in Mexico, 1930–1940* (Tucson: University of Arizona Press, 1997); Patience A. Schell, *Church and State Education in Revolutionary Mexico City* (Tucson: University of Arizona Press, 2003); Gilbert M. Joseph and Daniel Nugent, eds., *Everyday Forms of State Formation: Revolution and the Negotiation of Rule in Modern Mexico* (Durham, NC: Duke University Press, 1994).

15. Carmen Madrigal, *Los menores delincuentes: Estudio sobre la situación de los Tribunales para Menores: Doctrina y realidad* (Mexico City: Ediciones Botas, 1938). The first juvenile court in Mexico was established in 1923 in the state of San Luis Potosí. Genia Marín Hernández, *Historia del tratamiento a los menores infractores en el Distrito Federal* (Mexico City: Comisión Nacional de Derechos Humanos, 1991), 21. For comparison, see Michael Willrich, *City of Courts: Socializing Justice in Progressive Era Chicago* (New York: Cambridge University Press, 2003).

16. See, for example, Louise White, *The Comforts of Home: Prostitution in Colonial Nairobi* (Chicago: University of Chicago Press, 1990), 7; see also Florencia Mallon, "The Promise and Dilemma of Subaltern Studies: Perspectives from Latin American History," *American Historical Review* 99 (1995).

17. AGN, CTMI, box 1, file 449, 1927.

18. For example, AGN, CTMI, box 2, files 1806 and 1807, 1928.

19. Title II, chap. 14, art. 130, nos. 3 and 4; Title II, chap. 3, art. 69, *The Federal Labor Law: United States of Mexico, Effective August 28, 1931*, English translation (Mexico City: American Chamber of Commerce of Mexico, 1931), 6, 13.

20. On issues concerning women in markets and women's economic assertiveness in late colonial Mexico City, see Steve J. Stern, *The Secret History of Gender: Women, Men, and Power in Late Colonial Mexico* (Chapel Hill: University of North Carolina Press, 1995), 258–63. On markets and gender ideology in late nineteenth-century Mexico City, see Susie S. Porter, *Working*

Women in Mexico City: Public Discourses and Material Conditions, 1879–1931 (Tucson: University of Arizona Press, 2003), esp. ch. 6, "'And That It Is Custom Makes It Law: *Vendedoras* in the Public Sphere."

21. AGN, CTMI, box 1, file 1093, 1927.

22. AGN, CTMI, box 7, file 3542, 1930.

23. AGN, CTMI, box 4, file 7667, 1933.

24. AGN, CTMI, box 1, file 1054, 1927.

25. AGN, CTMI, box 1, file 156, 1927.

26. AGN-CTMI, box 19, file 6116, 1933; box 66, file 17898, 1938. See also Pablo Piccato, *City of Suspects: Crime in Mexico City, 1900–1931* (Durham, NC: Duke University Press, 2001), 148–52; 183.

27. AGN, CTMI, box 1, file 1596, 1928.

28. AGN, CTMI, box 19, file 6116, 1933.

29. Pedro Granados, *Las carpas de México: Leyendas y anécdotas del teatro popular* (Mexico City: Editorial Universe, 1984).

30. Archivo Histórico de la Ciudad de México, "Diversiones Públicas—Bailes," vol. 823, file 4.

31. AGN, CTMI, box 2, file 1806, 1928.

32. AGN, CTMI, box 2, file 1806, 1928.

33. AGN, CTMI, box 1, file 1807, 1928. The sexual vulnerability of migrant women is a theme discussed in Rachel G. Fuchs and Leslie Page Moch, "Pregnant, Single and Far from Home: Migrant Women in Nineteenth-Century Paris," *American Historical Review* 95 (1999): 1007–31.

34. AGN, CTMI, box 1, file 1806, 1928.

35. AGN, CTMI, box 1, file 1807, 1928.

36. AGN, CTMI, box 1, file 1806, 1928.

37. AGN, CTMI, box 1, file 1807, 1928.

38. AGN, CTMI, box 1, file 429, 1927.

39. Estados Unidos Mexicanos, Departamento de la Estadística Nacional, *Censo general de habitantes, 20 de Noviembre de 1921: Distrito Federal* (Mexico City: Talleres Gráficos de la Nación, 1925), 27, table 2.

40. Estados Unidos Mexicanos, Secretaría de la Economía Nacional, *Anuario estadístico de los Estados Unidos Mexicanos* (Mexico City: Dirección General de Estadística, 1939), 72–73, table 32.

41. Estados Unidos Mexicanos, *6o censo de población: 1940* (Mexico City: Secretaría de la Economía Nacional, Dirección General de Estadística, 1943), 17–18.

42. AGN, CTMI, box 66, file 17987, 1938. On conventions of courtship, see William E. French, "'Te Amo Muncho': The Love Letters of Pedro and Enriqueta," in *The Human Tradition in Mexico*, ed. Jeffrey M. Pilcher (Wilmington, DE: Scholarly Resources, 2003): 123–35. On legal definitions of seduction and rape, see Piccato, *City of Suspects*, esp. ch. 5, "Violence against Women," 103–31.

43. AGN, CTMI, box 1, file 1242, 1928.

44. AGN, CTMI, box 1, file 1242, 1928.

45. AGN, CTMI, box 4, file 6754, 1933.

46. "Perlita," *CROM* 1, no. 5 (May 1, 1925): 62; "Los bastones y las mujeres," *CROM* 1, no. 17 (November 15, 1925): 31. On the flapper image and rhetorical deployment of the stereotype of the "chica moderna" to affirm more conservative models of propriety, see Anne Rubenstein, *Bad Language, Naked Ladies, and Other Threats to the Nation: A Political History of Comic Books in Mexico* (Durham, NC: Duke University Press, 1998), esp. ch. 2, "Home-Loving and without Vices: 'Modernity,' 'Tradition,' and the Comic Book Audience."

8

Doctoring the National Body: Gender, Race, Eugenics, and the "Invert" in Urban Brazil, ca. 1920–1945

James N. Green

IN 1928, DR. VIRIATO FERNANDES NUNES PRESENTED a keynote speech entitled "Sexual Perversions in Legal Medicine" to the São Paulo School of Law. In his presentation, he emphasized the increasing visibility of men who engaged in sexual activities with other men. Nunes further noted that "*invertidos* [inverts] come from all ages and classes" and that "this depravation is very prevalent and seems to become more and more widespread."[1] Inverts, he argued, could be easily identified by their appearance, dress, and the jobs that they chose. Nunes's comments reflected mainstream medical and legal thinking about people who had sexual desires for those of the same sex. The notion of the *invert*, a term coined by an Italian forensic doctor in the late nineteenth century, described individuals whose sexual instinct was supposedly erroneously directed.[2] Moreover, Nunes, like most of his colleagues, associated the male invert with effeminacy, implying a link between his "misdirected" sexual desires and nontraditionally gendered comportment.

In his presentation, Nunes referred to two widely publicized sex-crime cases of the previous year: the killing of three young boys by Febrônio Índio do Brasil and the slaying of four youth by Prêto Amaral. Both men were of African heritage, and both cases involved rape and the brutal murder of the victims. Linking homosexuality to sadism, Dr. Nunes emphasized the threat that homosexual "perversion" presented to society. Unable to control their sexual impulses, he argued, "degenerate" figures such as Índio do Brasil and Prêto Amaral, and by extension all homosexuals, posed a serious danger to Brazil's social fabric, to the family, and to the proper ordering of gendered relationships. The subtext of his speech also evoked the ominous image of dark,

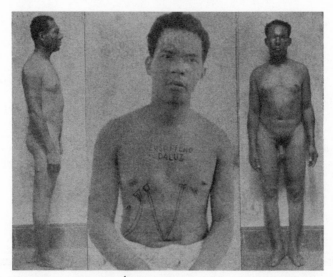

Figure 8.1.   Febrônio Índio do Brasil. Source: Leonídio Ribeiro,
Homossexualismo e Endocrinologia (Rio de Janeiro: Livraria
Francisco Alves, 1938).

sinister forces preying on the purity of innocent white Brazilian youth. His solution to containing homosexuality was to apply medical-legal knowledge and
science, which along with the assistance of courts and prisons, would contain,
control, and cure homosexuality, thereby assuring social tranquility.

In the next decade, more than a dozen additional doctors and criminologists
wrote more than thirty books, pamphlets, and articles about homosexuality,
relying heavily on European writings to shore up their home-grown ideas
about same-sex sexuality. Although Brazilian experts constantly cited European authors in their discussions about the origins, manifestations, and "treatment" of homosexuality, they tended to adapt the models they borrowed to
conform to prevalent Brazilian notions of sexuality and popular ideas about
same-sex sexual activity. Brazilian sexologists deemphasized the importance of
classifying homosexuals based on their sexual object choice, which was a key
component of the European medical construction of the homosexual by the
turn of the twentieth century. Instead, Brazilian writers focused more on specific gender-based behavior and hierarchical sexual roles in categorizing homosexuals. Thus, according to most European sexologists, a given man was a
homosexual if he had, or desired to have, sex with another man, regardless of
the specific fantasies or practices carried out in bed. Innate characteristics,
whether congenital or acquired, produced a unique being, the male homosexual, with a unique essence. In sexual intercourse, both the man penetrating the
other man and the person being penetrated were, therefore, considered homo-

sexuals. In interpreting European theories of homosexuality, Brazilian physicians and other observers reframed them along lines that conformed to popular assumptions that associated male homosexuality with effeminacy and passive sexual intercourse. Brazilian writers acknowledged the existence of "active," as well as "passive" individuals, but the emphasis was on the person who conformed more closely to traditional representations of women in Brazilian society, namely, the effeminate man who, to all appearances, was receptive in sexual intercourse. The "active" partner presumably possessed masculine characteristics and, therefore, did not have the same fixed homosexual essence typical of the effeminate man. This adaptation by Brazilian sexologists of European theories to local understandings of same-sex eroticism may explain why the model of the homosexual based on sexual object choice, which lumped all those who engaged in same-sex erotic activities into the same category, did not become a pervasive construct in Brazil in this period.[3]

Inverts (or "passive pederasts" as they were alternatively labeled) and effeminate men, indeed, were the main focus of these professionals' writings and research. In part, this was due to their greater visibility in the urban landscape of Rio de Janeiro and São Paulo, as well as their vulnerability to police harassment, arrest, and at times "scientific" research. With plucked eyebrows and rouged cheeks, they simply did not melt into the crowd. But the actual sexual practices of the alleged "passive pederasts" were more complicated than the models that the sexologists brought with them to their investigations. The fluidity in the sexual behavior of certain individuals and the slippage between "active" and "passive" sexual intercourse often defied the "Brazilian" paradigm that defined and categorized same-sex comportment.

Although most authors writing about the subject in the late 1920s and 1930s defined male homosexuality as somehow linked to effeminacy, they did not share a monolithic view about the origins, expressions, and possible cures of same-sex erotic behavior. Nevertheless, their overlapping training in law, medicine, psychiatry, and criminology suggests viewing their work as a whole within the broader interdisciplinary context of medicolegal investigations and discourses. Many held multiple positions as professors in universities and directors of government institutes or agencies, while maintaining private practices, all of which provided multiple income sources.[4] Their training in medicine or law, and sometimes in both fields, placed them among a small elite of middle- and upper-class professionals who relied on family ties, patronage, and personal loyalty to their mentors to establish and advance their careers.[5] This limited circle of physicians, lawyers, criminologists, and psychiatrists interacted in the same medical schools or professional organizations and published articles in the same handful of journals on subjects related to crime, sexuality, law, and medicine.[6] Their writings on homosexuality, while divergent in many details, were ultimately similar in their overall approach to the subject.

Among the most influential of this circle of professions was Dr. Leonídio Ribeiro, who at the beginning of President Getúlio Vargas's fifteen-year rule (1930–1945) served as the head of the National Institute for Identification attached to the Federal District Civil Police in Rio de Janeiro. In 1938, Ribeiro published *Homossexualismo e Endocrinologia*, in which he linked homosexuality to hormonal disorders.[7] Ribeiro had conducted morphological studies of the physical form and body structure of 195 homosexuals arrested by the Rio de Janeiro police in the mid-1930s in an attempt to identify characteristics that might indicate why certain men were homosexuals. In the results of his "research," he argued that there was a relationship between a defective endocrine system and this sexual "perversion." Ribeiro postulated that if the glands that excreted hormones into the bloodstream were malfunctional, they would cause homosexuality. Ribeiro insisted that scientists could identify the "disorder" by noting different, or "abnormal," manifestations in the body.

In the same year that Ribeiro's book on homosexuality came out, students from the São Paulo Institute of Criminology organized a project to study the "habits, customs and the living conditions of homosexuals in that city."[8] They visited the main areas in downtown São Paulo where homosexuals congregated and interviewed nine men. Their goal was to establish "the bases for a better understanding of homosexuality in all of its aspects through observing the phenomenon by scientific means and analyzing its repercussions in the social realm."[9] Gaining the confidence of their subjects, these medical students entered their apartments, took explicit pictures, recorded the details of their lives, and noted slang, dress, and daily habits. Dr. Edmur de Aguiar Whitaker, professor of psychology and juridical psychiatry at the Institute of Criminology and the director of the project, summarized the findings of the report: "With this [information], we are able to act with confidence in our fight against this abnormality. It is easier to ignore homosexuality than to remedy it since homosexuals' own attempts to correct themselves are not crowned with success. Thus, we look toward contributing to the solution of this problem which has assumed such serious proportions among us."[10]

This process of increased awareness of homosexuality within Brazilian society and the fear and anxieties about its ever more visible manifestations reached a peak in 1940. In that year, jurists in charge of rewriting the Brazilian criminal code of 1890 seriously considered introducing a provision that would punish homosexual acts between consenting adults with up to five years in prison.[11] (Sodomy had been decriminalized at the beginning of the nineteenth century as a part of reforms of Brazil's legal system inspired by the Napoleonic Code.)

Suddenly, in the late 1920s and 1930s, homosexuality became the object of scholarly studies. Why were physicians, criminologists, and jurists researching the links between same-sex erotic behavior and physical, mental, and social disorders? Why did medicolegal discourse about homosexuality contain a racial subtext? In short, why did homosexuality become a threat to the proper ordering of Brazilian society? The answer lies in part in the dramatic transformations that occurred in Brazil in the first half of the twentieth century. Between 1920 and 1945, Rio de Janeiro and São Paulo, the economic, political and cultural centers of Brazil, became the battlegrounds for contested notions of national identity and divergent visions of the country's political and economic future. The events that took place during this period and the disputed ideological and social constructions of nation, race, cultural identity, gender, and the body shaped and were shaped by a nascent urban homosexual subculture and a medicolegal discourse about it. This chapter examines the relationship between two related developments: the growing visibility of male homosexuality in Brazil's two most important urban centers and the increase in writings about same-sex eroticism by physicians, criminologists, and jurists, especially as they relate to the construction of race and homosexuality as two interrelated "perversions" of the "degenerated" Brazilian body.[12]

Economic, Political, Social, and Cultural Transformations

Modernization and industrialization after World War I had a tremendous impact on men, women, the family, and gender relations. Migration and immigration and the process of urbanization crowded hundreds of thousands of new people into the country's major cities. The population of Rio de Janeiro doubled between 1906 and 1940, jumping from 811,443 inhabitants to 1,764,141.[13] The increase for São Paulo was even more dramatic. In 1900, the city had 239,820 inhabitants. In 1920 that figure increased 140 percent to 579,033. In the next two decades, that is, from 1920 to 1940, the population increased another 120 percent to 1,326,261.[14] The traditional patriarchal family began to bend under modernization trends. Middle-class women entered the workforce in increasing numbers, joining working-class immigrant women and poor Brazilians in the double toils of being both housewives and breadwinners. Industrialization promoted a culture of consumption and brought women out of the cloistered domestic sphere. Hollywood films and women's magazines glamorized the "new woman" and promoted new cultural values that encouraged women to assume a more public profile. Changes in fashions triggered widespread unease about the apparent "masculinization" of women and "feminization" of men.

The modernization of Rio de Janeiro and São Paulo, which included transformations in the urban landscape, created new public social spaces, including new public plazas and parks, movie theaters, and train stations. Some of these new spaces were soon appropriated by homosexuals, who, like heterosexuals, flocked to Rio and São Paulo from small towns and rural areas throughout the country in search of work and a better life. Their growing visibility provoked further anxiety about properly gendered social roles.

Another plausible cause for the growing attention to homosexuality in the 1920s and 1930s was the general process of increased intervention by Brazilian physicians, jurists, and criminologists in social matters after World War I. Social and moral issues, these professionals argued, were not concerns for the police or the church but problems to be addressed by science and medicine. Eugenic theories, imported from Europe and the United States and adapted to the unique Brazilian circumstances, dominated the Brazilian League for Mental Hygiene as well as the thinking of leading criminologists and social anthropologists. Positivist ideology that emphasized the use of "scientific" knowledge to modernize the state and society had provided the theoretical underpinning for the 1889 overthrow of the monarchy and the establishment of a republican government. Like their European counterparts, Brazilian positivists also argued emphatically for the intervention of scientists and physicians in issues of daily life and considered that the state could play a positive role in improving society.

These two developments, namely, the growing visibility of homosexuality and the increased medicalization of the social issue, took place within a larger context of political instability that continued uninterrupted throughout the 1920s and 1930s. In 1917 and 1919, anarchists and socialists led two unsuccessful general strikes in São Paulo, the emerging industrial center of the nation. Throughout the 1920s, young army officers staged a series of unsuccessful revolts against the government and articulated a vague program in opposition to the ruling oligarchy and in favor of reforms in the electoral process. In 1930, the Brazilian economy went into a tailspin as coffee prices crashed with the onset of the Great Depression. That same year, the unsuccessful presidential candidate and former governor Getúlio Vargas headed a military revolt that catapulted him into the presidency and ended the thirty-five-year political hegemony of the states of São Paulo and Minas Gerais. The internal political conflicts that ensued—the rebellion of São Paulo against the central government in 1932, the failed communist insurrection of 1935, the aborted fascist coup d'etat in 1938—all increased anxieties about the stability of the entire political and social order.

Controlling and "Curing" Homosexuality

Within this context, homosexuality in the 1920s and 1930s represented sexuality that had not been contained and controlled. Just as the social body was out of control, so too was the physical body of the homosexual, whose malfunctioning hormonal systems caused immoral and degenerate behavior. The solution presented by some physicians, such as Professor Rocha Vaz of the Medical School in Rio de Janeiro, included a strategy of legal or criminal sanctions combined with medical treatment. In a paper presented at a conference of the Society of Medicine and Surgery of Rio de Janeiro held in 1933, he stated his position clearly: "Don't tolerate homosexuality, but cure it; the problem is resolved with the police and with the doctor."[15]

Other physicians and jurists argued that since homosexuality was caused by hormonal imbalances, it should be treated exclusively within the realm of medicine. Ribeiro, in his book *Homossexualismo e Endocrinologia*, argued, "The practices of sexual inversion can no longer be considered a sin, vice, or crime since in most cases it has been shown to involve sick or abnormal individuals who should be not punished since they need treatment and assistance above all else."[16]

The positivist tradition in Brazil, which supported the state's intervention in solving social ills, encouraged physicians, jurists, and criminologists to play a role in discovering, studying, and proposing cures for those sicknesses in the social body of an otherwise vigorous and healthy nation. This tradition served as a backdrop to debates about race, eugenics, the place of the women in Brazilian society, and the causes of homosexuals' sexual degeneration. According to some medical and legal experts, it was communists, fascists, criminals, degenerate blacks, and homosexuals who represented unhealthy elements. These social maladies had to be controlled and/or cured. The 1930s became a testing ground for how best to purify and heal these ailments of the Brazilian nation.

Social anxieties and medicolegal writings about homosexuality were not new inventions of the 1920s and 1930s. In fact, both a Brazilian homosexual subculture and medical writings about it date back to the 1860s, if not earlier. In 1872, Dr. Francisco Ferraz de Macedo published a study on prostitution in Rio de Janeiro that included a detailed account of same-sex erotic behavior practiced by "sodomites."[17] Twenty-two years later, in 1894, Francisco José Viveiros de Castro, a professor of criminal law at Rio de Janeiro's law school, wrote a volume entitled *Assaults on Decency: Studies on Sexual Aberrations* that described same-sex erotic activity in downtown Rio de Janeiro. He wrote, "They groomed themselves so that they could be easily recognized. They used very short jackets, silk scarves hanging from their pockets, very tight pants designed to fit the form of their thighs and buttocks. They approached the passers-by asking for a match to light a cigarette in a sweet voice with provocative and lascivious body movements."[18] In 1906, Dr. Pires de Almeida added to this literature. He published a treatise on homosexuality in Rio de Janeiro that confirmed the observations about a vibrant subculture described thirty-five years earlier.[19] According to the doctor, homosexuals could be found in "entrances of theaters, cafes, restaurants, billiard halls, doorways of convents, the stairways of the churches, the trees around Campo de Santana [a popular public park], the bath houses, and the basements of theaters." Almeida noted that they socialized in groups of two or three, or cruised the streets alone, dressed elegantly, hid their real age with the appropriate clothes, and used red ties as a coded indication of their sexual proclivities, a practice that seems to date back to the mid-nineteenth century in Brazil.

These three observers from the late nineteenth and early twentieth centuries documented a vibrant social scene where men met in public places and used clothing, slang, and gestures to attract sexual partners. These areas also became sites of cross-class and cross-racial mingling of different sectors of Brazil's rigidly stratified society.[20] What distinguished the 1920s and 1930s from the turn of the century, then, were not the forms of same-sex contact and the fact that physicians were documenting this activity but the intensities of both the subculture and the anxiety it provoked.

Borrowing and Adapting Theories

At the turn of the twentieth century, Viveiros de Castro and Pires de Almeida based their ideas about homosexuality on European medical literature. So too, the Brazilian physicians and criminologists who wrote on the subject between 1920 and 1945 summarized theories imported from France, Germany, England, Spain, and occasionally the United States to explain the nature of this "perversion." As historian Nancy Leys Stepan has noted, Latin Americans, including Brazilians, looked to European thinkers and "embraced science as a form of progressive knowledge, as an alternative to the religious view of reality and as a means of establishing a new form of cultural power."[21] These appropriations related to new research being conducted in Europe and the United States in endocrinology and hormonal functioning in the 1920s and 1930s, as well as general theories about eugenics, criminal behavior, and social deviancy.[22] Two international figures particularly stand out in this regard as exerting the most influence in shaping Brazilian notions about homosexuality and its relationship to race, gender, criminality, and the biological causes of homosexuality. They are Cesare Lombroso, the Italian criminologist, and Gregorio Marañón, a professor at the University of Madrid.

Cesare Lombroso (1836–1909), one of the pioneers in the field of criminal anthropology, defended the theory of the born criminal, *delinquente nato*, whose weakened nervous system predisposed him to engage in degenerate behavior, which included mutilation, torture, homosexuality, and the tattooing of the body.[23] Lombroso and his followers used phenotypes, that is, physical appearances, to determine criminal degeneracy. His work influenced Ribeiro, who employed Lombroso's anthropometric[24] techniques to measure the body parts of the 195 men arrested in Rio de Janeiro in 1932 in order to prove the link between hormonal imbalances and homosexuality.[25] Ribeiro received the Lombroso Prize in 1933 for his criminal-anthropological investigations, including his 1932 study of Carioca homosexuals.

The other influential international figure was Gregorio Marañón (1887–1960), a professor of medicine at the University of Madrid, who penned the introduction to Ribeiro's 1938 work *Homossexualismo e Endocrinologia*. In 1930 Marañón published *La evolución de la sexualidad e los estados intersexuales* in Spain.[26] He also wrote a summary of his theory about intersexuality for the Brazilian medicolegal journal *Arquivos de Medicina Legal e de Identificação*, where so many articles on homosexuality appeared in the late 1930s.[27] Arguing that homosexuals possessed both masculine and feminine characteristics due to a hormonal imbalance, Marañón offered a biological explanation for homosexuality. The term *intersexual* described this liminal positioning between the two sexes. Marañón, however, recognized that this condition was merely a predisposition toward homosexuality. Exogenous factors, such as religion and ethics, could moderate or annul it.[28] By suggesting that it was possible to change one's homosexual condition, Marañón created a space for the intervention of the church rather than medicine as a possible vehicle for the recuperation of the intersexual. In this respect, his theories, and those of many of his followers in Brazil, looked to science without abandoning more traditional notions of how to contain manifestations of deviant behavior. Although biology played a significant role in the making of the intersexual, morality, ethics, and sexual restraint might prove sufficient to overcome physiological deficiencies.

Marañón's ideas about the endocrine origins of homosexuality were adopted by most other Brazilian physicians and criminologists writing on the subject in the 1930s. Among them was Afrânio Peixoto, a leading forensic physician, who argued for another term, *missexual*, because of the mixture of the masculine and feminine he diagnosed in these "abnormal" and "degenerate" beings.[29] Peixoto and other physicians also agreed with Ribeiro and Marañón that external, nonbiological factors could affect homosexual behavior and even modify the sexual desires of a given individual. Nor were there actually any substantive differences in the various terms employed by these physicians to describe homosexuality. Both the intersexual and the missexual were people whose malfunctioning biological makeup had produced both masculine and feminine sexual characteristics with the resulting erotic desires for the same sex. Whereas the term *inversion* emphasized the sexual-object choice of the individual, *intersexual* and *missexual* focused on the biological causes of this disorder. The cure, while primarily biologically based, might also involve psychological and moral efforts, that is to say, physicians, psychologists, and the church.

The combination of these ideas, namely, the theory of the biologically degenerate nature of homosexuality and the notion that those who suffered from this organic defect possessed a mixed and undefined sexual identity, held disconcerting implications for physicians, who, in general, were members of Brazil's elite and defenders of the moral order.[30] As anthropologist Carlos Alberto Messeder Pereira has noted, "The categories of *missexualidade* or *intersexualidade*" point basically to the "mixture," "the confusion" of masculine and feminine characters, which should be separate. Even the category "sexual inversion" points to something that is "out of place," inverted. Thus, when the medicolegal profession employs these categories in the 1930s, their main concern is the need for a "correct ordering" or for "putting things in their correct places."[31]

The ambiguous nature of the intersexual or missexual's biological makeup and his inverted sexual desires also destabilized gender categories. Homosex-

Figure 8.2.   Woman studied by Antonio Carlos Pacheco e Silva, also published in the article entitled "A curious case of feminine homosexuality." Source: Antônio Carlos Pacheco e Silva, *Psiquiatria clínica e forense* (São Paulo: Companhia Editora Nacional, 1940).

uality, as conceived by the physicians and criminologists, upset notions of proper gender roles. Most of the individuals whom they observed had feminine behavior that was considered part and parcel of their disorder. These "passive pederasts," as they continued to be called, engaged in sexual acts associated with traditional notions of feminine "passivity." Understanding the exact causes of this biological degeneration and possibly finding a cure for this disorder would also mean the correction of improper comportment. Men behaving in womanly ways could once again be returned to appropriate masculinity.

Examining Bodies

Not satisfied with merely repeating European theories, Leonídio Ribeiro also attempted to verify them by conducting research on Brazilian subjects. The political and administrative requirements of the new regime headed by Getúlio Vargas facilitated his study of "deviant" behavior along the lines suggested by Lombroso and Marañón. This was partly the result of the reorganization of the federal police in the nation's capital, an element of Vargas's overall strategy of modernizing and centralizing governmental power, as well as controlling rebellious workers and the restless underclass. After 1930, government-issued identification cards and employment passbooks assisted employers and the police in keeping track of anarchist and socialist labor agitators, undisciplined employees, and vagrants.[32] Improved fingerprinting methods aided the accurate identification of citizens and immigrants alike. Perfecting blood-type tests and "discovering" the links between race and criminality offered more "scientific" means to contain and control an unruly urban population. The research conducted by Ribeiro, as the director of the Department of Identification of the Federal District Civil Police, was part of this effort. His study of the 195 homosexuals arrested by the Carioca police in 1932 used modern criminological methods to identify Brazilians with "pathological deviations" and cure their inappropriate, antisocial sexual activities. Whereas turn-of-the-century studies of same-sex erotic behavior in Rio de Janeiro had relied on the personal, anecdotal observations of physicians and jurists, Ribeiro used his position and the power of the police to obtain a sizeable sampling for his investigation.[33] The increased influence of the state in the 1930s aided his efforts to recognize, classify, and possibly cure these individuals.

Ribeiro never described the prototypic homosexual based on the results of his measuring efforts, but, from the data he collected, it would appear to have been an underweight young man of normal height with longer than normal arms and legs and a shortened thorax. Ribeiro also never explained the actual relationship between these characteristics and homosexuality. Presumably, bone development was linked to the endocrine system, yet Ribeiro failed to make this connection explicit. Ribeiro's scientific reasoning was itself more circular than linear. His logic was simple: these are the physical characteristics of almost two hundred declared homosexuals; the most common phenotype noted, therefore, represents the physical attributes of the typical homosexual.

To further link the physical characteristics he observed with the supposed endocrine imbalances in his subjects, Ribeiro also examined the distribution of body, pubic, and head hair, arguing that secondary sexual characteristics served as an excellent means of identifying hormonal malfunctions and, therefore, homosexuality.[34] According to Ribeiro, Marañón had found feminine hair distribution in 75 percent of the homosexuals he examined. Using Marañón's criteria, Ribeiro compared the shape of his subjects' pubic hair to that of what he considered to be ideal, masculine, hexagonal-shaped hair growth covering the stomach, thighs, and the area between the scrotum and the anus.[35] His findings, however, did not live up to those of his mentor. Most of the men Ribeiro studied had "normal" body hair distribution (60 percent) or no body hair at all (37 percent). A mere 3 percent had "abnormal or exaggerated" body hair. Moreover, only 18.46 percent had "feminine" triangulated pubic hair.

As if to compensate for inconclusive statistical findings, Ribeiro provided numerous lineup shots of nude men with captions that pointed to their "feminine forms and physiognomy, with pubic hair distributed in a triangular shape."[36] He also published photographs of subjects who lacked pubic hair, but then went on to point out that these men normally shaved it off. Ribeiro did not comment on why the men engaged in this practice, but it may be the reason why he found nearly 20 percent of the men with triangulated pubic hair. Perhaps some homosexuals in the 1930s shaped or shaved off the hair around their genitals to evoke the image of seductive women, just as they used a bit of rouge or makeup to suggest the feminine. Whereas this explanation points to the conscious construction of an effeminate persona through the use of physical markings associated with women, Ribeiro, nevertheless, suggested that the distribution of body hair represented an essential and inherent biological characteristic of the homosexual.

Without presenting any quantitative data to back up his conclusions, Ribeiro argued that other physical characteristics caused by endocrine malfunctioning were also linked to homosexuality. They included gynecomastia (the abnormal enlargement of the breast in a male), "feminine distribution of body fat," wide hips, and enlarged genitals. Ribeiro illustrated his assertions through a series of photographs, although in some cases his criteria and definitions drew no relationship to the point he was trying to make. For example, four photographs of male genitals were captioned as "different passive pederasts with exaggerated development of the penis." In another section of his work, the subjects of the same four photographs were described as "homosexuals showing the normal or exaggerated development of their external organs." One is at a loss to determine which of the four examples of male genitals is normal and which is exaggerated in size.[37] In addition to ignoring or falsely presenting his own empirical evidence, Ribeiro never addressed the contradiction in his argument that both feminine characteristics and "oversized" sexual organs, presumably due to some endocrinal excess, were signs of homosexuality.

The criminologist then presented another conclusion based on Marañón's work, again unsubstantiated by the data, to argue his thesis: "In two-thirds of the cases studied by us, there was at least one sign of disturbances of an endocrine nature, revealing alterations of the genital and adrenal glands."[38] In other words, homosexuality could be traced to biological abnormalities in a majority of the subjects observed. In another part of his study on homosexuality, he acknowledged other theories that pointed to exogenous factors. Failed love affairs, poor moral upbringing, separation of the sexes in schools, and overprotective mothers were among the psychological factors Ribeiro mentioned.[39] After recognizing these exogenous factors in the causation of homosexuality, Ribeiro quickly returned to his biological explanation: "Even though some of the arguments presented by the psychoanalyst are to a certain point acceptable, the theory which has gained more and more ground affirms that in the majority of cases of sexual inversion there is an organic cause or predisposition which can be provoked, favored or aggravated by environmental influences."[40] As this statement makes clear, Ribeiro was not a strict biological determinist. He recognized other factors that could cause homosexual behavior. The "essential" homosexual, however, was a man whose hormonal chemistry dictated his sexual desires. External factors might strengthen or attenuate homosexual tendencies, but the disordered body was the ultimate cause of this degeneration. Regardless of the fact that Ribeiro and others occasionally mentioned Sigmund Freud, psychoanalytical theories about homosexuality had little resonance among the group of physicians and criminologists who wrote about the subject in Brazil in the 1930s.

In short, other than the finding that 56 percent of the men examined had longer than "normal" arms and legs, Ribeiro's investigation provided little physical evidence of any links between hormones and homosexuality. Indeed, his entire research model was seriously flawed. He did not conduct a control study on two hundred declared heterosexuals to verify his results. Nor did Ribeiro provide adequate explanations as to why 34 percent of the men he measured showed no observable physiological manifestations of homosexuality. Nevertheless, over the next decade, more than a dozen physicians and criminologists cited Ribeiro's study without ever questioning his dubious statistical findings and inconsistent logic. His theories, research methods, and analysis became the model for other miniresearch projects conducted in Brazil, especially in São Paulo, which in turn influenced further thinking and writing about the subject.[41] One such study was conducted by Edmur de Aguiar Whitaker, a psychiatrist working for the Anthropology Laboratory of the São Paulo Police Department's Identification Service.[42] Following Ribeiro's methodological approach of using arrested subjects for his study, Whitaker examined eight homosexuals, again without a control group. All eight men were diagnosed with "secondary feminine sexual characteristics," such as triangulated pubic hair and a wide pelvic structure. Whitaker further reported that most were psychopaths (without explaining how he reached that conclusion) with limited or normal intelligence. He conceded, however, that "in addition to endogenous degenerative disorder, this abnormality can be, in its exogenous form, the result of an unbalanced personality [or] a poor adaptation to one's environment." Whitaker recommended a correctional medical cure without specifying what that might entail. In this regard, his views coincided with Dr. Viriato Fernandes Nunes, whose 1928 legal essay was mentioned at the beginning of this chapter.

Unlike Ribeiro and Antônio Carlos Pacheco e Silva, the director of the Juquery State Mental Hospital in São Paulo, Nunes did not argue that homosexuality was based on inherent biological factors. Rather he pointed to the social causes and impact of the behavior. Nunes acknowledged that "the punishments which in former times castigated perverts such as Prêto Amaral and Febrônio Índio do Brasil were excessively rigorous and without any scientific basis."[43] Comparing them to punishments of the day, Nunes assured his reader that progress had been achieved: "Society benefited very little from the elimination of these criminals. They should be removed and regenerated if possible. Today, with modern therapeutic processes, with the study of psychoanalysis, one can restore the psychiatric balance that these perverts lack. And when that is not achieved, the criminal will be detained but with comfort and humanity while unable to commit other offenses." On a practical level, Nunes pointed to the proposed establishment of São Paulo's Manicômio Judiciário, an asylum for the criminally insane, as the privileged place to achieve this goal. He argued that its location next to the Juquery State Mental Hospital, either as an independent hospital or as a dependency of the state hospital, would facilitate its objectives.[44] In other words, homosexuality, with proper treatment, could be medically and psychiatrically controlled and perhaps cured.

Race and (Homo)sexuality

The writings of the late 1920s and the 1930s never drew an explicit link between race and homosexuality, but the connection was embedded in the underlying themes of the text. The choice of certain figures to symbolize the extreme excesses of the "perversion" relied on pejorative cultural stereotypes about nonwhite Brazilians held by many in the medicolegal profession, as well as among sectors of the intellectual elite in general.[45] The work of Leonídio Ribeiro and Antônio Carlos Pacheco e Silva exemplify this approach. While Ribeiro only used a page or two to describe "effeminate men," he devoted an entire chapter of *Homossexualismo e endocrinologia* to the celebrated case of Febrônio Índio do Brasil.[46] Readers of his book could only extract an extremely limited vision of the lives of ordinary homosexuals in the 1930s, distorted as they may have been by the physician's own prejudices. But they received voluminous information about an alleged dark-skinned sadistic murderer and rapist of innocent children.

Ribeiro's interest in Febrônio Índio do Brasil was not merely didactic. He had a personal stake in the case. Ribeiro was one of three criminologists who had testified at the trial on behalf of the defense and argued that Febrônio was insane and therefore should be sentenced *ad vitam* to the Manicômio Judiciário in Rio de Janeiro. From Ribeiro's perspective, the case took on a broader significance as a study of how society should deal with homosexuality that degenerated into insanity. In an unusual twist, Ribeiro linked homosexuality and sadism and noted that "the known cases of sadism do not occur among excessively masculine individuals, as is the popular notion, but rather among those of effeminate organization, such as the Marquis de Sade."[47] Unlike most sexologists who associated sadism with extreme forms of masculine sexual energy, Ribeiro strangely enough feminized the infamous symbol of sadism to prove his point. Ribeiro then presented a detailed account of Febrônio's life, emphasizing his long arrest record. The physician culminated his account with the accusation that Febrônio had attracted several youth to deserted places where he tortured, sexually molested, and then killed them.

Ribeiro's description of Febrônio began by defining him racially: "Febrônio is a dark *mestiço* [mixed racial background] whose characteristics [are a result] of the crossing of *caboclo* [in this case Indian] with *prêto* [black]."[48] In the medical language of the 1920s and 1930s, influenced as it was by eugenics theories, Febrônio's racial mixture implied degeneration. Yet Ribeiro also relied on his theory of hormonal disorder to explain Febrônio's behavior. Three lineup photographs of Febrônio accompanying the chapter seem carefully placed in the volume to substantiate Ribeiro's theory of the link between homosexuality and a malfunctioning endocrine system that would cause degeneration. The caption reads, "Homosexual—sadist, Febrônio, author of three homicides by strangulation, besides other crimes, showing signs of endocrine disturbances."[49] Paradoxically, as in the lineup shots of the 195 homosexuals mentioned earlier, it is difficult for the observer to note any difference between Febrônio's appearance and that of any other average naked man of his age. To compensate for the inconclusive proof presented in the book's images, Ribeiro relies on captions to contradict his visual documentation.[50]

Antônio Carlos Pacheco e Silva similarly used images of race, crime, and sadism to create the specter of the homosexual as a danger to society.[51] In a chapter titled "Constitutional Psychopaths. Atypical States of Degeneration" in his 1940 award-winning book *Psiquiatria clínica e forense* (*Clinical Psychiatry and Forensics*), Pacheco e Silva outlined and defined an array of sexual perversions.[52] The eminent professor of clinical psychiatry at both the University of São Paulo and the Paulista Medical Schools listed these perversions as sadism, masochism, bestiality, exhibitionism, homosexuality, frigidity, nymphomania, necrophilia, and masturbation. To illustrate these degenerate behaviors, he provided four examples. One was a two-paragraph description of a man who molested the corpse of a six-year-old girl. A second example of sadism and necrophilia involved a thirty-two-year-old *pardo* (person of mixed racial background) who had sex with, and then strangled, a young boy.[53]

Two other cases received more prominent treatment in the chapter. One described a woman, photographed both in a dress and in men's clothes. Pointing out that Ribeiro's study of 195 homosexuals only referred to men, Pacheco e Silva explained how he and his colleagues discovered their subject: "A curious case of feminine homosexuality, which is the origin of this study, recently passed through the Psychiatric Clinic of the Medical School of the University of São Paulo. It is interesting in multiple ways. . . . It proves that cases of feminine sexual inversion also deserve to be explained in detail in light of modern endocrinological learning."[54]

On numerous occasions, the author stated that the subject, who was only referred to as E. R., was "sick." One gets the impression that his aversion to her was linked to the fact that she shamelessly cross-dressed, assumed a traditional masculine identity, and aggressively sought out female sexual partners. While E. R. was not accused of any criminal offense, the fact that she was black stood out. Her two portraits are prominently placed in the text, and she is described by reference to her race several times. We are told that she only sexually desired white women. As one of only a few examples of female homosexuality portrayed by medicolegal professionals in this period, the emphasis placed on her race conveyed a subtext that linked darker-skinned people to perversion.[55]

E. R. was not involved in criminal behavior, but Pacheco e Silva's fourth example, J. A. Amaral, was. He was the same figure that Nunes identified in his 1928 speech on "Sexual Perversions in Legal Medicine" to the São Paulo School of Law. The joint presentation by Pacheco e Silva of the two subjects offered a unified discourse: nonwhites were inclined to homosexuality, degeneracy, and even, at times, criminality. Throughout this case study, J. A. Amaral is referred to as "Prêto Amaral" (literally, "black Amaral"), a pejorative nickname that referred directly to his dark skin color. Amaral's first alleged victim was also discussed in racialized terms. "He was a white boy, fair, [with] green eyes, brown hair, looking fourteen years old."[56] The image was clear: a black man, a "prêto," had seduced, raped, and strangled an angelic boy. Two large mug shots captioned "O prêto Amaral," the black Amaral, accompanied the case study, as if to emphasize the point. The section on "hereditary background" stressed his African origins: "His parents were born in Africa—the father in the Congo and the mother in Mozambique. They came to Brazil as slaves and here were bought by the Viscount of Ouro Preto."[57] Pacheco e Silva's physical examination also highlighted Amaral's race: "This is an individual whose color is black, but is of a physiognomic type rare in his race. The nose, far from being flat, is aquiline and slightly curved."[58]

The author described the alleged seduction, murder, and molestation of four young victims. He then invoked European authorities to explain Amaral's sadistic and necrophilic behavior. Finally, Pacheco e Silva argued for isolation in a mental hospital rather than incarceration: "It is to the asylum and not to prison that these obsessive impulsive people should be sent, and the hideous character of the crimes committed by some of them should not be separated from the pathological nature of the act. It is rare for sexual perversion to be the only syndrome in these degenerates."[59] Like Nunes in 1928, Ribeiro and Pacheco e Silva a decade later argued for a "modern," scientific, and "humane" treatment of "perverts" who had committed other crimes. Ribeiro pointed to the homosexual acts of Febrônio as a way of linking homosexuality to criminality. Descriptions of his subjects suggested a similar relationship between race and degeneracy. Likewise, Pacheco e Silva connected sexual acts with murder and pathological behavior, and he too drew a connection between racial makeup and other disorders.

Why were the "scientific" observations and research results of Ribeiro, Pacheco e Silva, and other medicolegal professionals so readily accepted by their colleagues without any criticism of the methodology of their observations and the flawed logic of their arguments? In part, this had to do with the nature of the investigation related to race and crime taking place at the time. Many Brazilian intellectuals wholeheartedly embraced eugenic notions of the inferiority of certain races and the degenerate nature of certain social types, especially when the proponents of these theories were European. Moreover, the system of patronage and the hermetic character of this area of study discouraged criticism of mentors, sponsors, and colleagues. Rather than recognize and confront the inconsistency in European or Brazilian theories or research methods regarding crime, race, or homosexuality, this reduced number of intellectuals praised each other's work, wrote glowing introductions to each other's monographs, and cited each other's "findings." The culture engendered within this interlocking web of Brazilian professionals discouraged critical reflection on the results of research, whether it related to identifying "degeneracy" or offered an antidote for the sickness of homosexuality.

Retreating to the Margins

Paradoxically, there was a noted decline in writings about homosexuality by medicolegal professionals in the early 1940s, precisely at the moment when the Brazilian physical body under the President Getúlio Vargas's authoritarian *Estado Novo* (New State) of 1937 to 1945 was taking on such importance. Most historical works on the Estado Novo emphasize the centralization of political power and the restructuring of class relations during this period. Historians who have examined the regime's political ideology have shown how the Estado Novo relied on authoritarian practices that were part of Brazilian traditions, but were now modernized and incorporated as the regime's propaganda and educational vehicles for Vargas's policies. The growth of the state's power included the regulation of ordinary life from Carnival parades to trade unions.[60] Historian Alcir Lenharo has noted that "the broad project of the reordering of society—corporatism—was supported entirely in the image of the organic nature of the human body. The parts that composed society were thought of in the same way as the relationship among the organs of the body: integrated and without contradictions. The objective of the project, therefore, aimed at neutralizing the foci of social conflicts and making the classes (organs) in solidarity with each other."[61] Dissolving political parties, outlawing strikes, and maintaining strict press censorship were all part of the reordering of the political body.

The physical body itself was not left out of this reconstruction of the Brazilian nation. New magazines entered the market, emphasizing health, hygiene, and physical education. The government promoted a "new" masculinity that idealized strength, youth, and power. One physical education magazine summarized this ideal: "The new Physical Education should form a typical man who has the following characteristics: figure thinner than fuller, graceful muscles, flexibility, light-colored eyes, agile ... sweet, happy, virile ... sincere, honest, pure in acts and thoughts."[62] Schools and factories became sites of group exercises, sports, and marching. Brazil's entry into World War II in 1942 only accelerated this process as production became militarized. Vargas proclaimed on May Day that year to a crowd of industrial workers that "in the end, we are all soldiers of Brazil."[63]

Within this context, several hypotheses might explain the decrease in intellectual production about homosexuality under the Estado Novo. First of all, one must remember that most of the theoretical work about homosexuality had been borrowed from Europe and, to a much lesser extent, from the United

States. With the European continent in turmoil during the 1930s and the world at war in the 1940s, Brazilian intellectuals did not have easy access to new writings that could have added to the literature at hand or inspired new intellectual production. Second, no immediate medical cure accompanied the main endogenous medical explanation for homosexuality, namely hormonal imbalances. Testicle transplant therapy, a medical solution proposed by Leoní-dio Ribeiro, did not become a popular treatment; indeed, there appears no in-dication that Brazilian physicians ever attempted to test this possible remedy for homosexuality. The theories of Marañón and others on "intersexuality" and "missexuality," based on erroneous understandings of embryo develop-ment, had been discredited. Moreover, Brazilian physicians did not have the resources to establish laboratories to conduct their own research in en-docrinology or biochemistry.[64] Most reputable intellectuals began to abandon eugenic theories, especially those regarding racial issues, by the 1940s, par-tially because of the association of these ideas with Nazi Germany. Writers like Gilberto Freyre, who had emphasized the positive contributions of Africans to Brazilian culture, began to assume a prominent role in national intellectual debates, further discrediting racist-ridden eugenic ideas.[65] After a decade of intense discussion, writing, and "research," homosexuality as a topic of debate among medical and legal professionals retreated into the margins. Although the stated goal of many writers on the subject was to educate society about this social disease, much of their material was written in professional journals targeting the police, criminologists, and physicians. Their ideas about homo-sexuality certainly influenced the medical and legal professions, as well as criminologists, and thus had an impact on patterns of treatment by police, physicians, and psychiatrists. But, there is no indication that these publica-tions reached broad audiences. Thus, the effects of their writings on most ho-mosexuals was indirect at best.

This does not mean, however, that the writings of the medicolegal profes-sion on the subject became relegated to obscurity. The ideas and theories about homosexuality that were developed during the 1930s were popularized in the 1940s through sexual manuals, which reached broader sectors of Brazil-ian society. According to Celeste Zenha Guimarães, who researched the "myths" of homosexuality, "from the 1930s on, there was an expressive dis-semination of this kind of product [vulgarized sex manuals] which increased even more in the 1940s. These compendiums presented in accessible language . . . concepts . . . such as making the population fear engaging in certain acts as well as in having contact with the 'physical and moral types' described in the treatises of legal medicine and psychopathic forensics."[66]

Ultimately, the writings of physicians and other professionals of the 1930s dovetailed with these popular manuals on sex that reinforced long-held tra-ditional views about homosexuality. More widespread propagation of their theories and ideas through sexual education manuals tended to water down the enlightened elements in these professionals' proposals for the treatment of homosexuality. The new popular publications about sex often combined synthetic summaries of the theories of European and Brazilian sexologists with moralistic and religious statements that associated homosexuality with vice and corruption. One such book, *Psicoses de amor* by the prolific sexologist Hernâni de Irajá was already in its fourth edition in 1931, with four more editions out by 1954. Literary and scientific circles highly respected the work of this author. A front-page article in the popular magazine *Fon-Fon*, for example, heralded Irajá as one of the most important intellectuals of the day and the book as "a notable work about the subject of the pathology of love."[67] Like other Brazilian writers who treated the subject of homosexuality, Irajá borrowed heavily from new European theories about homosexuality, including the notion that both sexual partners should be considered homosexual. In spite of an approach to categorizing homosexuality that emphasized a person's object of desire rather than active/passive classifications, the widespread notions that homosexuals were effeminate men still prevailed over Irajá's definition.

Moreover, religious and moralistic metaphors continued to frame portraits of homosexuality. The illustration accompanying Irajá's chapter entitled "Homosexuality: Sexual Inversion" exemplifies the continuity in this presentation. An ink drawing of ghoulish figures whose fingernails and teeth dripped with blood set the tone of the text. Skeletal heads and suffering men crowded together to convey the message that homosexuality led straight to hell.[68] The author left no room for doubt about his views on the subject: "Homosexuality is love or the practice of sexual acts between individuals of the same sex. Morally and physically wasted individuals in the state of total corruption and decadence try to relive numbed sensations with new and strange pleasures. From hence comes the vice of pederasty."[69]

The medical, psychological, and criminal writings on homosexuality from Nunes in the 1920s to Irajá in the 1950s offered a varied approach to the study, classification, and considerations of same-sex desire. Although research and investigation on the subject began in the late nineteenth century, the consolidation of the role of the medical and legal professions under the republic (1889–1930) and during Vargas's rule (1930–1945) in relationship to the state facilitated the "medicalization" of the homosexual. Medicolegal professionals won the campaign to have more jurisdiction over the subject, although they had to share their authority with the police and the state. Under the Estado Novo, the governing elite decided not to establish a specific hospital to cure homosexuality or to pass a law explicitly naming homosexuals in crimes against public decency. It was not necessary. Metaphorically, the sick social body of the previous two decades was becoming robust through the interven-

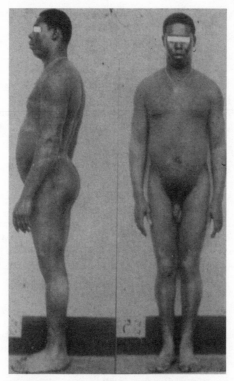

Figure 8.3.   One of the 195 arrested homosexuals used in Leonídio Ribeiro's study. Source: Leonídio Ribeiro, *Homossexualismo e Endocrinologia* (Rio de Janeiro: Livraria Francisco Alves, 1938).

tion of the state and the discipline of the new order. In this atmosphere, an emphasis was placed on a healthy, positive image of the Brazilian physical and social bodies, not on the notion of degeneration that had received such emphasis in the previous two decades. Regardless of the efforts of Ribeiro and others in the medicolegal profession to present a more "scientific" view of homosexuality, moralistic perspectives remained dominant in popular literature well into the 1970s.

Notes

1. Viriato Fernandes Nunes, "As perversões em medicina legal," Tese Inaugural da Faculdade de Direito de São Paulo (São Paulo: Irmãos Ferraz, 1928), 11.

2. Arrigo Tamassia invented the term *inversione dell'instinto sessuale*. Neurologists Jean-Martin Charcot and Valetin Magnan borrowed the concept to describe the case of a French man in 1882.

Vernon A. Rosario, *The Erotic Imagination: French Histories of Perversity* (New York: Oxford University Press, 1997), 70.

3. Talisman Ford, "Passion in the Eye of the Beholder: Sexuality as Seen by Brazilian Sexologists, 1900–1940" (PhD dissertation, Vanderbilt University, 1995), 162–70, 183–84.

4. For example, Leonídio Ribeiro, the most prolific of these authors, had a chair in legal medicine and criminology at the Flumenense Medical School. He also taught at the medical and law schools in Rio de Janeiro and simultaneously was the director of the Institute of Identification, linked to the Federal District Civil Police, and the head of the Laboratory of Infant Biology. Edmur de Aguiar Whitaker, second only to Ribeiro in the number of articles he published on the subject, was a psychiatric physician attached to the São Paulo police's Identification Service, as well as a professor of juridical psychology for the São Paulo Police Academy. Antônio Carlos Pacheco e Silva, another leading "expert" on homosexuality, was professor of clinical psychiatry at both the University of São Paulo and Paulista medical schools, as well as the director of the state-run Juquery Mental Asylum and the privately owned Pinel Sanatorium. Pacheco e Silva was also an active leader in the most important Brazilian eugenics association, the League of Mental Hygiene. Leonídio Ribeiro, *De médico a criminalista: Depoimentos ereminiscências* (Rio de Janeiro: Livraria São José, 1967), 1–5; Edmur de Aguiar Whitaker, *Manual de psicologia e psicopatiologia judiciárias* (São Paulo: Serviço Gráfico da Secretaria da Segurança Pública, 1958), 3; Antônio Carlos Pacheco e Silva, *Psiquiatria clínica e forense* (São Paulo: Companhia Editora Nacional, 1940), 354.

5. Ford, "Passion in the Eye of the Beholder," 32–48.

6. Among the publications that printed these men's articles on homosexuality were *Arquivos de polícia e identificação* (São Paulo), *Arquivos da polícia civil de São Paulo, Arquivos da sociedade de medicina legal e criminologia de São Paulo, Arquivos de medicina legal e de identificação* (Rio de Janeiro).

7. Leonídio Ribeiro, *Homossexualismo e endocrinologia,* with a foreword by Gregorio Marañón (Rio de Janeiro: Livraria Francisco Alves, 1938).

8. E. de Aguiar Whitaker, Eddi Kraus, Magino Roberto de Loliveira, Joel Botto Nogueira, and Ald Sinisgalli, "Estudo biográfico dos homossexuais (pederastas passivos) da capital de São Paulo. Aspectos da sua atividade social (costumes, hábitos, 'apelidos,' 'giria')," *Arquivos de polícia e identificação* 2, no. 1 (1938–1939): 244–62.

9. Whitaker et al., "Estudo biográfico dos homossexuais," 262.

10. Whitaker et al., "Estudo biográfico dos homossexuais," 262.

11. Leonídio Ribeiro, *O novo código penal e a medicina legal* (Rio de Janeiro: Jacintho, 1942).

12. For a more complete social history of male same-sex desire in twentieth-century Rio de Janeiro and São Paulo, see James N. Green, *Beyond Carnival: Male Homosexuality in Twentieth-Century Brazil* (Chicago: University of Chicago Press, 1999).

13. Instituto Brasileiro de Geografia e Estatística, *Recenseamento geral do Brasil [1º de setembro de 1940], Parte XVI-Distrito Federal* (Rio de Janeiro: Serviço Gráfico do Instituto Brasileiro de Geografia e Estatística, 1951), 1.

14. José Roberto de Araújo Filho, "A população paulistana," in *A evolução urbana,* ed. Aroldo de Azevedo, vol. 2 of *A cidade de São Paulo: Estudos de geografia urbana* (São Paulo: Editora Nacional, 1958), 169.

15. Rocha Vaz, "Aspectos clínicos da intersexualidade," *Arquivos de medicina legal e identificação* 3, no. 7 (August 1933): 200.

16. Ribeiro, *Homossexualismo e endocrinologia,* 27.

17. Francisco Ferraz de Macedo, "Da prostituição em geral e em particular em relação ao Rio de Janeiro" (medical thesis, Faculdade de Medicina da Universidade do Rio de Janeiro, 1872).

18. Francisco José Viveiros de Castro, *Atentados ao pudor: Estudos sobre as aberações do instinto sexual,* 3rd rev. and enl. ed. (Rio de Janeiro: Livraria Editora Freitas Bastos, 1934), 221–22.

19. Dr. José Ricardo Pires de Almeida, *Homossexualismo (A libertinagem no Rio de Janeiro): Estudo sobre as perversões do instincto genital* (Rio de Janeiro: Laemmert, 1906).

20. For a detailed historical account of the same-sex erotic subcultures of Rio de Janeiro and São Paulo, see Green, *Beyond Carnival.*

21. Nancy Stepan, *"The Hour of Eugenics": Race, Gender and Nation in Latin America* (Ithaca, NY: Cornell University Press, 1991), 41.

22. For a detailed description of the transmission of the eugenic theories to Brazilian physicians between the two world wars see Stepan, *The Hour of Eugenics,* and Jurandir Freire Costa, *História da psiquiatria no Brasil: Um corte ideológico* (Rio de Janeiro: Editora Documentário, 1976).

23. See Renzo Villa, *Il deviante e I suoi segni: Lombrosos e la nascita dell'antropologia criminale* (Milan: Angeli, 1985).

24. Anthropometrics is the measuring of the human body in terms of dimensions, proportions, and ratios. In the early twentieth century, many scientists used this technique to approach racial classifications and to compare humans to other primates.

25. From the historical records that we have, the legal basis for the arrests of the men that Ribeiro photographed and measured is not clear. Because same-sex activities between consenting adults did not constitute criminal behavior, the police likely arrested Ribeiro's subjects for vagrancy or public indecency, two vague categories that allowed public officials to detain individuals at will.

26. This work was also published in English in 1932.

27. Gregorio Marañón, "Una clasificación de los homosexuales desde el punto de vista médico-legal," *Arquivos de medicina legal e de identificação* 7, no. 15 (January 1937): 90–100.

28. Gregorio Marañón, "Prefácio," in Ribeiro, *Homossexualismo e endocrinologia,* 15.

29. Other physicians adopting Marañón's theories of endocrine imbalance included Afrânio Peixoto, "Missexualismo," *Arquivos de medicina legal e identificação* 3, no. 6 (February 1933): 67–73; Antônio Bello da Mota, "Homossexualismo em medicina legal," Tese de concurso à cátedra de Medicina Legal da Faculdade de Direito do Estado de Ceará (Rio de Janeiro: Typ. do Jornal do Comércio, 1937), 20–21; Edmur de Aguiar Whitaker, "Contribuição ao estudo dos homossexuais," *Arquivos de polícia e identificação* 2, no. 1 (1938–1939): 32–35; P. Moncau Jr., "Pesquisas endocrinológicas em criminosos," *Arquivos de polícia e identificação* 2 (1938–1939): 92–101; Pacheco e Silva, *Psiquiatria clínica e forense,* 354; Aldo Sinisgalli, "Consideraçãoes gerais sobre o homossexualismo," *Arquivos de polícia e identificação* 3 (1938–1940): 282–303; Silvio Marone, "Considerações em tôrno de uma nova classificação de missexuais," *Arquivos da polícia civil de São Paulo* 10 (December 1945): 103–36.

30. For an analysis of the social background and the professional ties among Brazilian sexologists, see ch. 2, "The Sexology Club: Background, Goals, and Motivations of Brazilian Sexologisits," in Ford, *Passion in the Eye of the Beholder,* 27–56.

31. Carlos Alberto Messeder Pereira, "O direito de curar: Homossexualidade e medicina legal no Brasil dos anos 30," in *A invenção do Brasil moderno: Medicina, educação e engenharia nos anos 20–30,* ed. Micael M. Herschmann and Carlos Alberto Messeder Pereira (Rio de Janeiro: Rocco, 1994), 109.

32. Efforts by the Brazilian government to control intractable workers began before Vargas came to power in 1930s. After the 1917 general strike in São Paulo and another strike movement in 1919, employers drew up a blacklist of "undesirable workers" and established the Department for Political and Social Order in 1924 to facilitate the repression of anarchists, socialists, and communists. Barbara Weinstein, *For Social Peace in Brazil: Industrialists and the Remaking of the Working Class in São Paulo, 1920–1964* (Chapel Hill: University of North Carolina Press, 1996), 53. For details about the growing police repression in Rio de Janeiro during the early years of Vargas's rule, see Michael L. Conniff, *Urban Politics in Brazil: The Rise of Populism, 1925–1945* (Pittsburgh: University of Pittsburgh Press, 1981), 138–42. For the impact of employment pass

books on workers, see also Warren Dean, *The Industrialization of São Paulo* (Austin: University of Texas Press, 1969), 186–92.

33. Ribeiro, *De médico a criminalista*, 237–43.

34. Ribeiro, *De médico a criminalista*, 108.

35. Ribeiro, *De médico a criminalista*, 41.

36. Ribeiro, *De médico a criminalista*, photographs between pp. 105 and 106.

37. Ribeiro, *De médico a criminalista*, photographs between pp. 104 and 105.

38. Ribeiro, *De médico a criminalista*, photographs between pp. 104 and 105.

39. Leonídio Ribeiro, "O problema médico-legal do homossexualismo sob o ponto de vista endocrinológico," *Revista jurídica* (Rio de Janeiro) 3 (1935): 146–47.

40. Ribeiro, *Homossexualismo e endocrinologia*, 36.

41. These studies included Moncau Jr.'s "Pesquisas endocrinológicas em criminosos," which examined eighty-six delinquents, including several "passive pederasts," to determine the endocrinological influences on them, as well as the research carried out by the students of the São Paulo Institute of Criminology under the direction of Whitaker.

42. Whitaker, "Contribuição ao estudo dos homossexuais," 32–35.

43. Whitaker, "Contribuição ao estudo dos homossexuais," 45–46.

44. Whitaker, "Contribuição ao estudo dos homossexuais," 46–47.

45. See the chapter titled "The Whitening Ideal after Scientific Racism," in *Black into White: Race and Nationality in Brazilian Thought* by Thomas E. Skidmore (Durham, NC: Duke University Press, 1993), 173–218.

46. For a detailed analysis of the role that Ribeiro played as a psychiatric adviser in the case and the ways in which the medicolegal profession constructed the link between sadism, homosexuality, spiritual prophecy, and insanity to justify his commitment to a mental institution instead of prison, see Peter Fry, "Febrônio Índio do Brasil: Onde cruzam a psiquiatria, a profecia, a homossexualidade e a lei," in *Caminhos cruzados: Linguagem, antropologia e ciências naturais*, ed. Alexandre Eulálio (São Paulo: Brasiliense, 1982), 65–80.

47. Ribeiro, *Homossexualismo e endocrinologia*, 116.

48. Ribeiro, *Homossexualismo e endocrinologia*, 123.

49. Ribeiro, *Homossexualismo e endocrinologia*, 123.

50. Nor was Ribeiro the only medicolegal expert to insist on the link between physical traits and criminality. Murillo de Campos, a psychiatrist who also served as a defense witnesses, echoed this perspective: "The psycho-sexual tendencies shown in Febrônio's crimes coincided with a physical constitution rich in developmental abnormalities of a eunuchoid nature (large pelvis, gynecomastia, no hair on the trunk or members, etc.) " (Ribeiro, *Homossexualismo e endocrinologia*, 130). The third member of the defense's expert panel, Heitor Carrilho, then the director of Rio de Janeiro's Hospital for the Criminally Insane, argued that Febrônio should be hospitalized for life instead of receiving the maximum sentence of thirty years for homicide. The judge agreed with him, and Febrônio remained in the Manicômio Judiciário for over fifty years. Fry, in his article "Febrônio Índio do Brasil," recounts a visit to the Hospital for the Criminally Insane to meet Febrônio in 1982 (Peter Fry, "Febrônio Índio do Brasil," 79).

51. The acclaimed psychiatrist publicly identified with the racial and eugenic notions that inferiorized nonwhites. He made a point of inserting his ideas into the political debate of the 1930s. Pacheco e Silva was elected to the Constituent Assembly that wrote the 1934 constitution. One of the issues vehemently discussed in the assembly was the relationship between race and immigration. Some representatives argued for restricting Asian and other nonwhite immigrants, due to the sharp increase in the number of Japanese immigrants that had entered Brazil in the 1920s. Pacheco e Silva spoke against nonwhite immigration, using psychoracial arguments to make his point. He declared emphatically that the "Japanese are extremely subject to certain mental disturbances and that, when mentally ill, they manifest accentuated tendencies to prac-

tice crimes" (quoted in Flávio Venâncio Luizetto, "Os constituintes em face da imigração" [master's thesis, Universidade de São Paulo, 1975], 27). Pacheco e Silva's speeches on race, eugenics, immigration, and the need to maintain the purity of the white race can be found in Antônio Carlos Pacheco e Silva, *Direito a saúde: Documentos de atividade parlamentar* (Brazil: n.p., 1934).

52. See "Psicopatias constitucionais: Estados atípicos de degeneração," in Pacheco e Silva, *Psiquiatria clínica e forense*, 346–81. The book won an award from the Medical School of the University of São Paulo and from the São Paulo Society of Legal Medicine and Criminology.

53. Pacheco e Silva, "Psicopatias constitucionais," 369–74.

54. Pacheco e Silva, "Psicopatias constitucionais," 374–81. The same case study appeared as an article, "Um interessante caso de homossexualismo feminino," *Arquivos da sociedade de medicina legal e criminologia de São Paulo* 10 (1939): 69–81. It was also reprinted by the São Paulo Society for Legal Medicine and Criminology as a pamphlet.

55. Sueann Caulfield has uncovered three other cases of women who dressed as men in her review of *Vida policial*, a weekly police journal from Rio de Janeiro. For her discussion of these "women-men," as they were called, see Sueann Caulfield, "Getting into Trouble: Dishonest Women, Modern Girls, and Women-Men in the Conceptual language of *Vida Policial*, 1925–1927," *Signs: Journal of Women in Culture and Society* 19, no. 11 (Autumn 1993): 172–74.

56. Pacheco e Silva, *Psiquiatria clínica e forense*, 361.

57. Pacheco e Silva, *Psiquiatria clínica e forense*, 361.

58. Pacheco e Silva, *Psiquiatria clínica e forense*, 365.

59. Pacheco e Silva, *Psiquiatria clínica e forense*, 369.

60. See Lúcia Lippi Oliveira, Mônica Pimenta Velloso, and Angela Maria de Castro Gomes, *Estado novo: Ideologia e poder* (Rio de Janeiro: Zahar, 1982).

61. Alcir Lenharo, *Sacralização da política* (Campinas: Papirus, 1986), 16–17.

62. *Educação física* 73 (1943): 11, quoted in Lenharo, *Sacralização da política*, 78–79.

63. *Educação física* 73 (1943): 11, quoted in Lenharo, *Sacralização da política*, 86.

64. Scientific investigation in Brazil was hampered by the fact that there were few institutions of higher education equipped to carry out such work. While the Instituto Oswaldo Cruz and similar entities conducted specific research projects in tropical medicine or in infectious diseases, they had limited resources. The University of São Paulo, the first modern university capable of conducting scientific research in the diverse fields of biology and chemistry, as well as the social sciences, was only founded in 1934. See Simon Schwartzman, *A Space for Science: The Development of the Scientific Community in Brazil* (University Park: Pennsylvania State University Press, 1991).

65. Stepan, *The Hour of Eugenics*, 167–70.

66. Celeste Zenha Guimarães, "Homossexualismo: Mitologias científicas" (PhD dissertation, Universidade Estadual de Campinas, 1994), 346–47.

67. "*Psicoses do amor* de Hernâni de Irajá," *Fon-Fon* (Rio de Janeiro) 6 (February 7, 1931): 1.

68. Hernâni Irajá, *Psicoses do amor: Estudos sobre as alterações do instinto sexual*, 9th ed. (Irmãos Pongetti: Rio de Janeiro, 1954), 185.

69. Irajá, *Psicoses do amor*, 185.

9

Masculinity, Primitivism, and Power: Gaucho, Tango, and the Shaping of Argentine National Identity

Eduardo P. Archetti

IN A NEWSPAPER CHRONICLE PUBLISHED IN 1932, Roberto Arlt, one of the greatest modern Argentine writers, protested against the extensive use of the image of the gaucho in everything that could be defined as Argentine: polo players with names like Miles, Lacey, Harrington, or Nelson; tango orchestras with musicians with names like Cattaruzzo, Nijisky, Dupont, or Müller; tango singers singing tangos that had nothing to do with rural scenarios; and football players who played with "creole courage" or "gaucho enthusiasm" or using "typical pampa technique." In his complaint, Arlt confirmed the successful dominance of "gaucho/mestizo imagery" as a model of transformation and hybridization that made it possible for millions of immigrants coming to Argentina from the 1880s to become "creolized" and converted symbolically into "gauchos" (Arlt 1994: 101–104). The gauchos were related to the past, to rural life, and, in a concrete way, to cultural roots (Montaldo 1999: 157). Football and polo were imported and global sport practices. Tango was also a contemporary creation. Thus, the leisure activities, dance, and sport that became popular were, in a sense, modern radical creations and models of change and, at the same time, means of promoting cultural continuity. The Argentine use of gaucho imagery illustrates how modernity embraced romanticism and tradition.

From 1900 to 1930, Argentina was changed under the impact of massive European immigration that provoked a remaking of national identity. In Argentina, the process of nation-state building concerned not only the effective extension of authority over a territory and a people but also the constitution of subjects as "national" beings, identifying with and accepting the claims the state might make on them. If the construction of the state is largely recognized as dependent on annexation, subjugation, and co-option, "nation" is its complement, making it possible to rally citizens, to generate subjective commitment and to elicit a sense of belonging (see Bertoni 2001). Issues of gender and ethnicity are central to the constitution of such "national" beings. In order to construct a masculine state based on wage-labor discipline and obligatory military service, populated, in other words, by virile subjects, the gaucho, in one of the major paradoxes of Argentine national imagining, was transformed into the male model of the nation at the very time he was disappearing from the Argentine countryside. Thus, the project of a nation masks heterogeneity and denies a space both to the communities that it submerges and to the alternative imageries that it displays.

This chapter is an illustration of these particular processes through the lens of the impact of gaucho imagery and dress in tango. We will see that gaucho dress and folk traditions were key components of a nationalist revival (see Goddard 2000). The connection between gaucho imagery and dress, in theory belonging to the past, also embraces tango, the modern dance and music created in Argentina in the 1880s and 1890s and exported to the world at the beginning of the twentieth century. The chapter examines the confluence of Argentine nationalism with European ideas of exoticism in defining a context in which tango could be referred to as gaucho music and dance. In this period, when Argentine elites were searching for national symbols, the accidental and convoluted relationships between the tango, an urban product, and gaucho clothes, associated with the rural past, offered a powerful temporary solution that brought together alternative images and ideas cut from past and present local cultural productions. It is not an accident that Europeans, particularly Parisians, saw tango as "gaucho dance and music." I assume here that through this dislocation, representations that are seemingly out of time and out of place are reinforced and "naturalized." Thus, symbolic power lies in the processes that serve to fix gaucho imagery while obscuring the ambiguities that underpin it (see Melhuus and Stølen 1996).

Marilyn Strathern has pointed out that "'tradition' is similar to, but not quite the same as and hence overlaps with, the idea of 'continuity'; it is continuity seen from the point of view of what is regarded as characteristic or typical about something" (Strathern 1992: 14). Tradition and primitivism, as we will see, are effective because they are defined and perceived by elites as ideological, political, and social mechanisms for the regulation of social order. Consequently, tradition can precede or be provoked by changes. In other words, the analysis of tradition makes possible a better understanding of cultural innovation. In this sense, some nationalist ideologies, a modern phenomenon, tend to be formulated and articulated in close relation to what is seen as traditional, as products of an idealized rural past. Carlos Alonso has called this ambiguous Latin American relationship with the project of modernity "the burden of modernity" (Alonso 1996). In this connection, cultural products created outside Europe will be codified by European cultural elites as "primitive." Primitivism is, thus, a constitutive part of the interaction between peripheries, like Argentina, and European centers.

The Social Decline of the Gaucho and Gauchesca Literature: The Question of National Language and Identity

From the end of the nineteenth century and through the first decades of the twentieth, Argentina became integrated into the global scene of massive world commodity exchange, vast international migrations, rapid urbanization, new forms of urban consumption, world sports competitions, and the circulation of mass cultural products. The main impulse had been foreign: foreign labor, foreign capital, and favorable foreign markets for its exports (meat and cereals). British investors possessed around 80 percent of the Argentine railway system, large tracts of its land, most of its tramways and urban utility companies, and some of the most important meat-packing plants and industries. Until World War I, no country in the world imported more goods per head of population than Argentina. Per capita incomes compared with those in Germany, Holland, and Belgium and were higher than those of Spain, Italy, and Sweden (Rock 1993).

Between 1890 and 1914, Argentina became one of the great immigrant nations in the modern world. In 1914, approximately one-third of Argentina's population of almost eight million, which the third census showed had increased more than fourfold since the first census of 1869, was foreign-born, the majority being Italian (39.4 percent) and Spanish (35.2 percent). Russian immigrants, primarily Jews escaping from political and ethnic persecution in the Russian Empire, formed the third largest group (4.1 percent). Syrians and Lebanese (2.7 percent) arrived after leaving another oppressive empire, the Ottoman. Immigrants also arrived from France, Germany, Denmark, and Austria-Hungary (mostly Serbo-Croatians and Friulans) (Solberg 1970: 38). The British formed a powerful minority. It is also important to point out that at least one-quarter of the population was composed of the descendants of immigrants from the past two generations.

Argentina received, between 1869 and 1930, more immigrants in relation to its native population than any other modern country. A mirror of this historical pattern exists in the growth and development of the capital city of Buenos Aires (the city of tango). The city grew rapidly from 180,000 inhabitants in 1869 to 1,576,000 in 1914. By 1930 the city had almost three million inhabitants, one-third of whom were immigrants (Ferrer 1972: 146), The proportions of foreigners were 13.8 percent in 1869, 24 percent in 1895, and 42.7 percent in 1914 (Vázquez Rial 1996: 24). A gender imbalance due to the arrival of a limited number of female immigrants, primarily among the younger population, meant that for long periods in the history of Buenos Aires, there was a predominance of males, creating, in urban settings, conditions for the growth of public arenas for excitement, like cabarets, and explicit sexual transactions, like brothels (see Guy 1991). Buenos Aires became a kind of cultural Babel, wherein English was the language of commerce and industry, French was the language of culture, and the tongues of daily life were a mixture of Spanish (and Galician), Italian (various dialects), and various Western and Eastern European languages. Buenos Aires in the 1920s, like New York, represented, in effect, a "truly global space of cultural connections and dissolutions" long before anthropology discovered global culture, diasporas, and multinational encounters (Clifford 1988: 4).

By the 1920s, a social and economic transformation of Argentina had been achieved and an incipient democracy consolidated. The country had "survived" the arrival of millions of immigrants and the changes provoked by new technologies, global connections, immersion in the world market, and massive urbanization (by 1930, 63 percent of the population of Argentina was urban). The country and the city of Buenos Aires were not only heterogeneous in the objective sense of being the product of ethnic and cultural mixings, but they were also *imagined* as such by intellectuals, writers, politicians, and, of course, the population in general (see Halperin Donghi 1987; Sarlo 1996; Bernand 1997). To imagine a homogeneous "imagined national community" in this historical setting was not easy. Much more imagination is required than is necessary when imagining the national in more ethnically homogenous societies with fewer dramatic demographic transformations. Ricardo Rojas, one of the most important nationalist writers of the period, considered the massive immigration and the lack of a clear educational policy oriented towards the integration of foreigners as a menace to cultural reproduction and national belonging (Rojas 1909: 89–90). Images of "invasion," language "corruption," and moral and sexual "chaos" represented by a massive presence of European prostitutes appear in his work and in the work of other writers like Leopoldo Lugones, Manuel Gálvez, Augusto Bunge, and Carlos Ibarguren. Even a modernist writer like Jorge Luis Borges in 1926 wrote about the city of Buenos Aires as a cosmopolitan fusion, contrasting the margins of Buenos Aires and its creole population with the center of the city, where the "babelic, the picturesque, the tearing off from the four points of the world, the Moor and the Jewish" dominated (Borges 1993: 24).

By World War I, the nationalists had found in the male gaucho—the free cowboy riding in the pampas, hunting, gathering, and working for a wage when needed—a symbol to represent the cultural heritage of the nation under "threat" by immigration (Solberg 1970; Slatta 1985; Prieto 1988; Delaney 1996). The liberal Argentine intelligentsia imagined that the arrival of immigrants from northern and central Europe would lead to the purification of the race and a radical improvement of the work ethic of the creole population. The result was not exactly as they expected. In place of northern Europeans, Italian, Spanish, Jewish, and Middle and Far Eastern immigrants prevailed (Schneider 1996). Undaunted, nationalists continued to claim the figure and cultural meaning of the gaucho as the primary symbolic type of Argentine nationality. Paradoxically, nationalist discourse revived the "barbaric" subject, the gaucho, who had been condemned to disappear through immigration, hybridization, and modernization. This reinvention of tradition was made possible by the privileged place that *literatura gauchesca* (gauchesque literature) occupied in popular urban and rural literary consumption beginning in the 1880s. The epic poem *Martín Fierro*, written by José Hernández in 1872 in a style reproducing gauchesque rural language, was a synthesis of the idealization of the gaucho (Borges 1980: 108). Its narrative of a gaucho struggling against state injustice in order to keep his freedom was transformed into a model for a "national literature." He was accompanied by other mythical figures, such as Santos Vega and Juan Moreira, both noble gauchos like himself, fighting for what they considered just and representing freedom and tradition (see Ludmer 1988; Rama 1996: 50–63). Adolfo Prieto has shown that gauchesque literature was also read in the cities, especially among European immigrants, to whom the colorful rural iconography was the only expression of something local and Argentine in the middle of the "generalized disorder produced by the cosmopolitan swallows," the term used to describe temporary immigrants who traveled between Europe and Argentina (Prieto 1988: 98–99). This literature created moral human types in situations of conflict and tension introduced by modernization and cosmopolitan values. These figures were brave and violent, but also elegant and polite when treated decently. They were men of honor and courage, symbolizing idealized aristocratic images. They were also important figures in other expressions of popular culture, like pantomime, circus, and Carnival (Chasteen 2000).

Argentina was a "new country" with a history in the making. Thus, tradition had to be imagined and, in many ways, recovered from the past. In a turbulent present much affected by the influx of foreigners and a rapid and chaotic growth of cities, nationalist writers believed that cosmopolitan Buenos Aires was not the place to look for new symbols of nationality. Instead, they found these symbols in the past, in the landscape, in the soil of the pampas, and in the imaginary reconstruction of a rural culture with its epic masculine figures in gauchesque literature. Borges observed in 1926, "Buenos Aires, in spite of being packed with two million individual destinies, will remain deserted and without a voice, until a symbol will inhabit her. The province is people: there are Santos Vega and the gaucho, Cruz and Martín Fierro, possibilities of gods. The city is still awaiting poeticization" (Borges 1993: 126).

This movement was not confined to literature and reading. "Societies of traditionalists," "creole centers," or "creole academies" were created with the mission of recreating the customs of the gaucho, which included music and dance. According to Carlos Vega, in the period from 1898 to 1914, hundreds of centers were established in the city of Buenos Aires and its suburban neighborhoods with names closely related to the mythical figures of gauchesque literature, such as Martín Fierro, Los perseguidos del Juez, Cruz, and Tradición de Santos Vega (Vega 1981: 13–57).[1] The recuperation of lost choreographies of traditional dances was one of the main aims of the associations. This effort was joined by the itinerant theater companies (*zarzuelas criollas*) and the so-called creole circus (*circo criollo*) playing gaucho dramas, which included live music and traditional dances as part of the performances. Dances like *cielitos*, *estilos*, *pericones*, *media cañas*, and *triunfos* were performed. Moreover, the incipient film industry was inspired by gaucho traditions, producing films with titles like *Alma Criolla, Tierra Argentina, El Gaucho* or *Romance Argentino*. In the record companies, labels like *criollo* and *nacional* were commonly used for people or groups singing folk songs or tenors singing classic opera, as well as for tango orchestras called *orquesta típica criolla* (typical creole orchestra). The two most important record companies were *Records Creole* and *Records National*. It is against this historical and cultural setting that the tango appears as representing, at the same time, the urban and the city of Buenos Aires as well as the creole and the national. The complexities of tango representation, then, are in subtle ways related to and legitimized by the revival of gaucho traditions. As for the gaucho himself, the processes of commoditization and modernization of Argentine rural production linked to the world market had drastic consequences. As private property expanded, the structural conditions that had produced an independent gaucho were dramatically changed. The transformation of the gaucho into the male model of the nation coincided with his disappearance from the pampa.

The Transformations of Tango: From Urban Dance and Music into a Gaucho Representation

The tango was born in the *arrabales* (the outskirts of the city) of Buenos Aires in the 1880s. Borges pointed out that tango was a typical suburban product and that in the arrabales, the rural presence was still important but did not radically influence the tango's development. He wrote that "the tango is not rural, it is *porteño* [meaning that it was from the port city of Buenos Aires]. Its fatherland is the pink corners of the streets of the outskirts, not the countryside;

its milieu the poor neighborhoods; its symbol, the weeping willows, never the *ombu* [the typical tree representing the pampas]" (Borges 1993: 103). One of the social figures in the arrabal was the *compadre*, a male character with roots in the rural areas, often employed in the slaughter houses that proliferated there. Simon Collier has vividly described him as follows:

> The free nomadic *gaucho* world had more or less vanished by the 1880s, yet the suburban *compadre* did perhaps inherit certain *gaucho* values: pride, independence, ostentatious masculinity, a propensity to settle matters of honour with knives. More numerous than the *compadres* were the young men of poor background who sought to imitate them and who were known as *compadritos*, street toughs well depicted in the literature of the time and easily identifiable by their contemporaries from their standard attire: slouch hat, loosely-knotted silk neckerchief, knife discreetly tucked into belt, high-heeled boots. (1992: 94–95)

The tango was thus populated by compadres and compadritos at a time when the gaucho heroes were important in popular culture and literature. Gauchos and compadritos, in a kind of unusual blending, became, during this period, representative characters in Carnival processions held in Buenos Aires (Chasteen 2000).

By 1890, a new style of couple dancing evolved that was called *baile de corte y quebradas* (cut-and-break dance), a name referring to its sudden stops and breaks. It was also known as *milonga*, a name that designated a rural dance. In the new form, the compadritos combined the milonga with the style and movement of the *candombe*, the popular dance of Afro-Argentines living in Buenos Aires, characterized by quebradas and cortes. The quebrada was an improvised, very athletic contortion, while the corte was a sudden pause, a break in the normal figures of the dance. In the candombe, the movements were done by women and men separately, while in the tango the quebradas and cortes were performed when the partners danced together. John Charles Chasteen correctly writes that "the characteristic profile of modern tango choreography finally emerged from an encounter between *candombe* moves and the closed-couple choreography of the international ballroom repertoire" (Chasteen 2000: 54). The candombe withered into a conventional courtship dance during the second half of the nineteenth century, joining popular dances like the polka, mazurka, and especially the *habanera*, the Spanish-Cuban rhythm that was very trendy in Latin America. Alejo Carpentier has observed that in the tango the Argentine black population, which had almost disappeared by the end of the nineteenth century, was recuperated in a kind of unexpected marriage with the European habanera more than with the Cuban *contradanza* (Carpentier 2001: 99). It is, thus, commonly accepted that the influence of candombe movements into the closed-couple choreography of habanera is the closest antecedent of tango. Simon Collier has perfectly summarized this creative process:

The tango . . . was just a fusion of disparate and convergent elements: the jerky, semi-athletic contortions of the *candombe*, the steps of the *milonga* and mazurka, the adapted rhythm and melody of the *habanera*. Europe, America, and Africa all met in the *arrabales* of Buenos Aires, and thus the tango was born—by improvisation, by trial and error, and by spontaneous popular creativity. (1992: 97)

Urban life in Buenos Aires was rapidly transformed during the first two decades of the twentieth century. Luxury hotels, restaurants, bistros, hundreds of cafés, a world-famous opera house, and theaters were built by European architects. This prompted changes in the use of leisure time and created a new environment outside the walls of privacy and home. The appearance of public arenas created new conditions for public participation and enjoyment where cultural life, sports, and sexual concerns dominated. Four institutions, where tango as dance was prominent, provided the public with new excitements and opportunities for the deployment of sexual fantasies and virility: the brothel, the dancing academies (*academias de baile*), "cafes with waitresses" (*café de camareras*), and the cabarets. These arenas provided a space for women, albeit of a special kind. The tango was directly related to these public contexts: in the last two decades of the nineteenth century, the brothel and the dancing academies were the places where the original tango dance was created. Later, at the beginning of the twentieth century, the cabaret became a privileged public space for dancing, playing, and singing. It has been assumed that originally the tango was only music and was mostly danced by male couples. However, the importance of the dancing academies as meeting places for men and "waitresses," or for couples, cannot be overlooked. The first period of tango, lasting from 1880 to 1920, has been called *la Guardia Vieja*, or "the old guard." Harp, flute, violin, and guitar dominated the orchestra until the 1920s, when the piano and bandoneon were gradually introduced. Because the main objective was to produce music for dancing, the style of playing was "oral," in the sense that musicians improvised all the time without performing real solos. The playing took the form of a kind of dialogue between the orchestra and the dancers in which musical improvisation was closely related to a rich and complex "erotic" choreography. At the beginning, then, the tango was for dancing and not for listening. The texts accompanying the music were direct, daring, insolent, and, in the opinion of many, reflected a kind of male primitive exhibitionism (see Romano 1991).

The new tango developed after the 1920s, and has been called the tango of *la Nueva Guardia,* or the New Guard (Ferrer 1960: 31–36). Both the musical composition of this period and the new orchestras drastically reduced the degree of improvisation, as the conductors became more concerned with details and nuances in the orchestration than with the performances of improvised solos. In this sense, the tango evolved in the opposite direction of jazz. The most important change, however, can be observed in the lyrics. The new authors of the tango told compressed, moving stories about characters and moral dilemmas that were easily understood and identified by a vast, heterogeneous, lower- and middle-class audience. Thus, the tango shifted from being first and foremost a musical expression to being primarily a narrative interpreted by a plethora of extraordinary singers, both male and female.

The tango gradually entered into the popular theater, the *sainete*, displacing the other music and dances that predominated during the creole theater (*zarzuelismo criollo*). The first appearance was in 1918 in the sainete Los Dientes del Perro (Dog's teeth), where Carlos Gardel sang "Mi noche triste" ("My Sad Night"), composed in 1917 by Pascual Contursi. In the mythology of tango, it was this tango that inaugurated the epoch of the New Guard. Since then, and during the 1920s, there were tangos, orchestras, and singers in the most popular sainetes, normally performed in cabarets, a typical urban arena.

The orchestras also entered the dancing halls and cabarets. The cabarets of Buenos Aires in the 1920s were generally elegant, but also dark and secretive, definitely not a place for family entertainment. The cabaret became both a real and an imagined arena for "timing out" and, for many women, for "stepping out," even though only a minority of women actually moved into its sphere. It was both an existing physical space and a dramatic fictional stage for many tango stories. In tango lyrics, the cabaret appears as a key place for erotic attraction and sexual freedom, a powerful image to contrast to the home, the local bar, and the *barrio* (neighborhood), which were regulated by moral concerns and duties. In this setting, as well in the different dancing arenas, the clothes were urban, modern, elegant, and sophisticated. Neither dancers nor orchestras nor singers used gaucho clothes, which were evidently considered out of place. Tango was thus disconnected from its rural origins, the mixed dress of the compadritos, and turned into the representation of a quintessential urban way of life.

The globalization of tango took place during this period with the help of modern technology, including radio, movies, and records. Some of the singers, as we will see in the next section with the case of Carlos Gardel, and the orchestras became famous worldwide. This very process of globalization served to invent a "tradition," a mirror in which Argentines could see themselves precisely because "others" began to see them. The narrative, the dance, and the music of tango became a key element in the creation of a "typical" Argentine cultural product. The texts as a written discourse became a sort of "popular poetics." However, the impact of the words without the power of the music would probably have been quite different. The forceful combination of text and music gave the written emotional stories a special dimension because they were both sung and danced. In Europe, in contrast, the music and the dance were more important than the lyrics. In this context, and especially when orchestras or dancers performed in cabarets and different types of shows, the gaucho costume, as a symbol of the typical Argentina, gained importance.

The tango as a dance arrived in Paris as early as the 1900s, where it was seen as equally as exotic as other musical genres: tropical Cuban music, flamenco, Russian and Hawaiian dances, and, later, North American jazz.[2] In Paris, the tango, that dance born in the city of Buenos Aires, came to be seen as the creation and very embodiment of the rural gaucho. The European gaze conditioned the evolution of the dance and the way the opposition between wild and sophisticated eroticism was presented. Dress was important in establishing symbolic frontiers between tango's authenticity and modernity. Moreover, in 1913, one could feel that almost everything in France was related to tango: tea-tango, champagne-tango, chocolate-tango, dinner-tango, and exhibition-tango (Zalko 1998: 72). The tango-color, an intense orange, was popular in the making of women's clothes. A popular drink, a mix of beer and grenadine still possible to get today in Paris, was called tango. The impact on women's dress was also important: tango cocktail dresses were designed, with the harem trouser-skirt and the tango corset being the most successful innovations. The latter was defined as revolutionary because it was flexible and led many women to abandon orthodox fixed corsetry (Savigliano 1995: 125).

The tango was experienced as different not only because it brought about the changes I mentioned but also because it was coming from a distant place, from a country with a vast pampa populated by gauchos that had attracted millions of European immigrants in the last few decades. Marta Savigliano has pointed out that the fascination of tango as a dance was not necessarily related to an instinctive sensuality, as in many "primitive" dances, but to what she calls the process of seduction, a couple dancing and keeping their erotic impulses under control, "measuring each other's powers" (Savigliano 1995: 110). However, tango was seen as an exotic dance coming from an exotic place with a flavor of primitivism. Andre de Fouquiéres, a dance pedagogue, wrote in 1913 that tango was "a dance of the famous gauchos, cattle herders in South America, rough men who evidently cannot enjoy the precious manners of our salons—their temperament goes from brutal courtship to a body-to-body that resembles a fight—the tango . . . cannot be directly imported. It must be stopped at customs for a serious inspection and should be subjected to serious modifications" (Fouquiéres 1913: 58). The role of European dance pedagogues, and not only Fouquiéres, was to domesticate and civilize what they imagined was the brutal gaucho style of dancing (see Veloz and Veloz 1937: 21–22). The result was the establishment of a distinction between a primal, manly dance and a sophisticated and more effeminate European one.

Primitivism was the imposition of a set of European expectations on others and their cultural products. Frances Connelly has described primitivism as "subverting the foundations of rational order in order to pursue the irrational for its own sake" (Connelly 1999: 14). As an artistic expression it was seen as rude, naive, expressing great feeling and great passion, lacking structured narrative, and putting a strong emphasis on extreme bodily exhibitions. In this sense, tango was perceived as being as "primitive" as African art. The postwar Parisian passion for *l'art negre* created an intense cult of exotic figures and masks of African art that fit with the European interest in cubist and surrealist aesthetics. Thus, the association with the wild life of the gauchos in the Argentine pampas was not an accident; it was central to modern visual art. The trope of primitivism created some key oppositions: passion/reason, body/mind, nature/culture, and primitive/civilized. These oppositions were also gendered and "raced." In the 1910s, Argentine dancers had problems finding jobs in Paris, and if they did find work, many of them were obliged to wear gaucho costumes. This communicated that the "wild" and "exotic" dance was being performed by authentic Argentine males. The same thing happened with touring orchestras and dancers all over Europe and the United States. Linda Nochlin has characterized this attitude as a way of defining the "other" in relation to a "peculiar elusive wild life" (Nochlin 1989: 50). Primitivism was a powerful ideology subsuming disparate manifestations into an aesthetic framework creating the exotic and, at the same time, incorporating a modified version of that very exoticism.

However, the fascination for primitivism in European representations of the tango was tinged with ambivalence because, in fact, the tango became a typical dance-hall and ballroom dance. The exotic, wild, and original choreography, developed by Argentine dancers, was transformed by French pedagogues into a stylistic and almost balletic dance. "Modern choreography" became a field in which the French dance pedagogues reigned. Fouquiéres suggested a kind of choreographic revolution, condensing the countless steps into just eight main figures. Savigliano observes that "these attempts to domesticate the tango were for the most part favourably received" (Savigliano 1995: 122). The influential North American dancers and pedagogues Irine and Vernon Castle observed that the original Argentine dance was extremely difficult; therefore, it was necessary to simplify and polish it. They suggested that, for dancing, learning six fundamental steps was enough (Castle and Castle 1914: 83–85). Yolanda and Frank Veloz, a world famous dance couple in the 1930s, imagined the original sensual, violent, and difficult figures as the product of men dancing in gaucho costume, high-top boots, and spurs (Veloz and Veloz 1937: 2). They related the lack of success of tango in the 1900s in London to its uncivilized and wild choreography. According to them, the French dancer M. de Rhynal codified and tamed the dance after weeks of trials at the Imperial Country Club in Nice in 1907. This version of the tango was finally accepted by the English in the summer of 1912 (Veloz and Veloz 1937: 21–21). Tango was thus transformed into a global dance, once a reduced choreographic grammar was produced. Borges commented on this transformation from sexual wildness to urban dance, pointing out that before the triumph in Paris, the tango was an "orgiastic devilry" and, after it, just "a way of walking" (1980: 89).

Adolfo Bioy Casares observed that the tango danced by Rudolf Valentino and Beatrice Domingues dressed in gaucho clothes in *The Four Horseman of the Apocalypse*, a 1921 Hollywood silent movie, anchored a kind of dominant aesthetic model identified with traditional Argentina (Bioy Casares 1970: 27). He concludes that gaucho dress, to a certain extent, was imposed by a kind of colonial gaze and that, for many *porteños*, this image was "false." In fact, the Argentine elite, many of whom thought of themselves as European, feared that in the world of global images, Valentino's clothes and attitudes would be identified with Argentine gauchos. The connection between Argentina, gauchos, primitivism, and tango was maintained for a long time. Even in the 1930s, as the great tango poet Enrique Santos Discépolo experienced, it was possible to find orchestras and dancers in Paris wearing gaucho clothes. Discépolo called them "incredible and inexplicable gauchos," and in the cabaret Le Lapin, he even saw a "gaucho sailor" (Zalko 1998: 138).

During the 1910s in Argentina, tango was clearly the most typical product of the cosmopolitan urban culture of Buenos Aires. In the provinces, folk dances and music were practiced in rural areas and were part of traditional rituals and ceremonies. I have pointed out the importance of the traditionalist movement in the provinces making up the pampa region. In the province of Santiago del Estero, located in a relatively poor area in northeastern Argentina, Andrés Chazarreta, a teacher and improvisational musician, started compiling folk songs and recovering the choreography of traditional dances in the 1910s. He acknowledged that his inspiration derived from the reading of gauchesque literature, attending performances of the creole circus, and the resistance against imported dances like the mazurka and polka that were still being danced in his province (Vega 1981: 102–103). In 1911 he formed a company with dancers and musicians and performed in Santiago del Estero with great impact.[3] They danced *chacareras, gatos, escondidos, palitos, huellas, bailecitos,* and *malambos*. The company, dressed in gaucho clothes, was called the Creole Dancing Company (*Compañía de Baile Criollo*). Visiting and performing in other cities in northern Argentina did not bring about the same success. Chazarreta's main aspiration, however, was to present his group in Buenos Aires. He waited ten years. In 1921, with a new group called the Company of Native Art (*Compañía de Arte Nativo*), Chazarreta presented a spectacle that conquered the public and received the critical acclaim of Buenos Aires. Such was the response that they performed to full audiences for one and a half months. Carlos Vega explained the triumph of folklore in Buenos Aires as an indication of the discovery by the "foreign and cosmopolitan" Buenos

Aires of the existence of the "other Argentina," with its marginalized native population and its traditions (Vega 1981: 141–43; see also Alen Lascano 1972). The press unanimously defined the success as an example of national revival.

It is also important to mention the strong revivalist movement that was initiated in 1926 in the town of San Antonio de Areco, in the province of Buenos Aires. Ricardo Güiraldes, author of *Don Segundo Sombra*, a masterpiece of gauchesque literature, received a tribute from a revivalist gaucho movement. Hundreds of people with gaucho clothes and horses visited him in his *estancia* (rural estate or ranch) "La Porteña": folk songs were played and danced; the *retreta del desierto*, military music played by the Argentine army, was performed; and traditional horse races were organized, culminating in a show displaying horse-handling skills. A local committee was formed with the aim of creating a national day of tradition. In 1939, the government of the province of Buenos Aires declared November 10 the Day of Tradition, as a commemoration of the birthday of the writer José Hernández, author of the epic gaucho poem *Martín Fierro*. Since 1939, the Day of Tradition has been celebrated in the town of San Antonio de Areco (see Blache 1979).

The tango, exotic and wild, was appropriated by Europe as a symbol and expression of Argentina. Global travel continued to have a great impact on other distant places like Japan, Egypt, and Turkey, and in this process a particular cultural product was generalized and seen as representing "the national." Obviously, tango was not the only music and dance of Argentina. The folklore presented by Chazarreta, also defined by Argentines as national, did not travel to the world, but remained rural, local, and particular. Paris recreated tango, while Buenos Aires discovered the hinterland of Argentina. In Argentina itself, the coexistence of folklore and tango was evident. Even before the New Guard period initiated in 1917, great singers cultivated the creole music of the pampa provinces before moving to the tango. The distance between these two genres was not so extreme. Some of the performers were transformed from "rural" into typically "urban" singers through the practice of tango. I will illustrate this transformation with examples drawn from the life of Carlos Gardel, the famous Argentine tango singer.

The Transformation of the Singer Carlos Gardel:
From Folk Songs to Tango

In the early 1910s, Gardel was a local bar singer in Buenos Aires (from El Abasto) with a certain fame in other neighborhoods (Barracas, Corrales, or Palermo). His repertoire was creole rural music (*estilo, cifra, triunfo, cielito, milonga, zamba, vals criollo*), songs that had a wide acceptance all over Argentina and were also very popular in Buenos Aires. In 1912 he joined Francisco Martino in a three-month tour along the West Railways Line, singing in all the small towns of the provinces of Buenos Aires and La Pampa. In 1913 he recorded some records for the Columbia label. Gardel, accompanying himself on guitar, recorded fifteen songs, fourteen of which were issued on seven double-sided records. Most of the songs were estilos, triunfos, and cifras. In the same year, José Razzano, a rather famous singer, joined Gardel and Martino. They toured the province of Buenos Aires from July to September, performing in social clubs, cinemas, bars, and, in some cases, infantry barracks. The local newspaper in Rojas commented that "the provincial airs, *estilos* and *vidalitas* executed last night by the trio . . . were heard with profound delight and went straight to the hearts of the few creoles who were at the performance" (an allusion to the fact that the majority of the audience comprised immigrants, not creoles, who were defined as Argentines born in Argentina). The newspapers in Bragado reported that the show was given by "professional singers" and not by local *payadores*. In General Viamonte, *La Tarde* reported a "delightful and agreeable evening" provided by "three creoles of purest breed" who "gave us pleasant hours of patriotic reminiscence, singing beautiful *estilos* and various other songs with the traditional feeling of the gauchos" (Collier 1986: 133). The connection between creole authenticity and traditional gaucho feelings was expressed in the music of Gardel, Martino, and Razzano. The nation was being reproduced through its music and dance.

Martino left the group and the famous Gardel-Razzano duo was born. Their formal debut was in the cabaret Armenonville in December 1915, where they shared the show with a tango orchestra comprising, among others, extraordinary musicians, like Roberto Firpo on piano, Eduardo Arolas on bandoneon, and David Roccatagliata on violin. As I have pointed out, the cultural scene in Buenos Aires during the 1910s was dominated by traditional forms of Argentine theater: sainete and criollo. By 1920, there were fifty theaters in the city. The theaters and the cinemas were important for Gardel and Razzano because during the intermezzos, live entertainment was offered. The duo toured other big cities in Argentina, including Rosario, Santa Fe, and Córdoba. Their repertoire of creole folk songs, or rather, popular songs composed in folk or countryside idiom, was coming to be recognized as original and distinctive. In 1916 they also started an international career, first in Uruguay and later in Brazil. The tour to Brazil was very important and consolidated the singers' fame. As always, they played in the intermezzos of the plays, sainetes, or criollos, interpreted by the Compañía Dramática Nacional. The Brazilian press presented Gardel and Razzano's music as regional, rural, and creole (as suffering creole songs). Creole folk songs were now completely established as part of the variety repertoire. Gardel and Razzano became unchallenged leaders in the field of popular music, with their style being extensively imitated by less talented artists. An important turn was Gardel's encounter with the famous theater actor José Alippi. His great success was the performing of the popular gaucho drama *Juan Moreira*, a favorite of Buenos Aires audiences ever since its first performance in 1886. In November 1915, a new and spectacular production of *Juan Moreira* was launched, with Alippi playing the part of Moreira, the unfortunate gaucho. Gardel and Razzano sang their songs in scene six, as part of a "grand country fiesta," and contributed in no small degree to the show's great success. Creole music was played in gaucho dress. The rural imagery was part of a show in which the gaucho lifestyle was portrayed in its different facets, including the gaucho's loves, his woman, his horse, his dances, and the everyday routines of his life. The gaucho's life was depicted in such a way that audiences were driven into admiration of, and concern for, the values of courage, virility, and freedom. The gaucho's love of freedom and autonomy was thus exaggerated.

In 1917–1918, Gardel encountered a new popular song, the tango, far removed from the normal folk repertoire of the duo. Collier writes that "these were the years when Gardel and the Argentine tango finally came together, the years when this superb artist began the gradual ascent to his ultimate, undisputed position as the supreme figure of the entire tango story" (1986: 54). Gardel entered into the world of tango and represented it until his sudden death in 1935. Even today, Gardel is remembered as the legend of tango. From 1925 to 1930, he had consolidated his fame touring in Europe and becoming a film star. Nevertheless, Gardel never gave up singing creole songs, introducing in 1921 and 1925 in his repertoire some of the compositions by Chazarreta (Grünewald 1994: 98, 105). He was still recording them in the 1920s and early 1930s. The careers of professional artists like Gardel and other musicians and singers illustrate the interface between different genres of music (see Vila 1991: 115). The musical landscape of Argentina was multifarious and reflected the complexities of a nation in the making. The distance, therefore, between gaucho representations and modernity was not so great. The gaucho male imagery and the tango embraced each other; consequently, the gaucho become central to a particular mode of being modern. It is the context of this connection between tango and creole folk songs that makes it easy to understand why tango musicians and singers accepted without resistance the European gaze defining them as "gauchos."

Conclusion

This chapter discusses the subtle ways in which dress, dance, and nation were expressed through tango and folklore. I have shown that the external (postcolonial) gaze creating tango and gaucho clothes as representations of the nation was important but that this connection had been latent in Argentina. The transition from creole folk songs to tango was, in many cases, without conflict or contradiction. The life of Carlos Gardel is an example of the transformation from folk songs and gaucho clothes to tango. Through time, gaucho dress came to be less identified with tango than with folk songs and traditionalist movements. The end of the story is clear: tango became a more universal dance, and in this process, gaucho clothes lost their meaning. However, the revival of folk songs in the 1940s and 1950s consolidated the gaucho dress as a symbol of a virile and masculine nation. Tango music and dance became, in many ways, universal and less national, while folk creole songs represented the "deep nation."

In a country of massive immigration, we can see national discourse, images, and performances as examples of dislocated identities; as a result of these dislocations, we can expect the meaning of "otherness" to shift as well. In more homogeneous societies, if such exist at all, I expect dislocation to be less apparent and the lack of an explicit model of transformation to be more evident: nationality is defined and experienced as more evident, as less problematic. In a society like that of Argentina, an accomplished national imagery will attempt to integrate the different "othernesses" because it needs all the fragments, all the dislocated and mismatched identities, and it relies on the changing character of the groups that inhabit a given territory. Argentina entered into modernity by producing a series of identities and culturally contradictory tendencies that impeded integration and containment in a single national imagery as envisaged by the nationalists and the representatives of traditionalist movements. My examples show that Argentine cultural identity was thus highly dependent upon multiplicity. Folklore encompassed tango and vice versa. Gardel was a folk singer as well as the quintessence of tango. Confronted with rapid changes, tradition—or what was defined as tradition—was perceived as a guarantee of cultural continuity, as a way of generating a sense of belonging. The idealization of gaucho masculinity provided a powerful cultural model relating maleness and Argentine identity as intrinsic aspects of a more encompassing national identity. Tango, perceived as gaucho dance in Europe, was an expression of an exotic primitivism in need of transformation. Dance pedagogues transformed it into a domesticated ballroom dance, while keeping gaucho dress in performances helped to maintain a sense of an authentic Argentine identity.

Notes

1. Ruben Oliven (1996) has shown how the gaucho traditionalist movement in contemporary Brazil has recreated regional and national identities. Many of his observations and empirical findings can be related to the ideology and objectives of the traditionalist movement in Argentina. His rich ethnography needs to be replicated in Argentina.

2. Elaine Brody has pointed out that the Great Expositions of 1867 and 1878 in Paris prepared the way for the great impact of exotic music in 1889. The organizing committee in 1889 envisaged music as one of the main attractions of the exposition. She writes that for "the first time at this exhibition, there were performances of 'exotic' music which were perceived as 'musical' performances" (1987: 94). She concludes saying that by 1889 "many Europeans showed a readiness to listen to music as a cultural universal, even if its origins were Cambodian or Sioux" (1987: 95) See Elaine Brody, *Paris: The Musical Kaleidoscope, 1870–1925* (New York: George Braziller, 1987).

3. Andres Chazarreta defined himself as a *folklorista*. He was not a member of the incipient group of people introducing the science of folklore to Argentina. By 1900, due to the work of Roberto Lehmann Nitsche, folklore as an approach to understanding traditions was accepted in intellectual circles in Buenos Aires. Ricardo Rojas, the nationalist writer, supported Chazarreta's work and saw himself as taking part in this movement of recovering the lost traditions of northeastern Argentina. In 1922, he founded the first section of folklore at the Institute of Literature, University of Buenos Aires (Vega 1981: 90).

Works Cited

Alen Lascano, Luis. 1972. *Andrés Chazarreta y el folklore.* Buenos Aires: Centro Editor de América Latina.

Alonso, Carlos J. 1996. The Burden of Modernity. *Modern Language Quarterly* 57:2227–35.

Arlt, Roberto. 1994. *Aguafuertes porteñas: cultura y política.* Buenos Aires: Losada.

Bernand, Carmen. 1997. *Histoire de Buenos Aires.* Paris: Fayard.

Bertoni, Lilia Ana. 2001. *Patriotas, cosmopolitas y nacionalistas. La construcción de la nacionalidad argentina a fines del siglo XIX.* Buenos Aires: Fondo de Cultura Económica.

Bioy Casares, Adolfo. 1970. *Memoria de la pampa y los gauchos.* Buenos Aires: Sur.

Blache, Martha. 1979. Dos aspectos de la tradición en San Antonio de Areco. *Folklore Americano* 27:163–94.

Borges, Jorge Luis. 1980. Discusión. In *Prosa completa.* Vol. 1. Barcelona. Bruguera.

———. 1993. *El idioma de los Argentinos.* Buenos Aires: Sudamericana.

Brody, Elaine. 1987. *Paris: the musical kaleidoscope, 1870–1925.* New York: George Braziller.

Carpentier, Alejo. 2001. *Music in Cuba.* Minneapolis: University of Minnesota Press.

Castle, Irine, and Vernon Castle. 1914. *Modern Dancing.* New York: Harper and Brothers Co.

Chasteen, John Charles. 2000. "Black Kings, Blackface Carnival, and Nineteenth-century Origins of the Tango." In *Latin American Popular Culture: An Introduction,* ed. William H. Beezley and Linda A. Curcio-Nagy. Wilmington, DE: SRBooks.

Clifford, James. 1988. *The Predicament of Culture.* Cambridge, MA: Harvard University Press.

Collier, Simon. 1986. *The Life, Music and Times of Carlos Gardel.* Pittsburgh: University of Pittsburgh Press.

———. 1992, The Popular Roots of the Argentine Tango. *History Workshop* 34:92–100.

Connelly, Frances S. 1999. *The Sleep of Reason: Primitivism in Modern European Art and Aesthetics.* University Park: Pennsylvania State University Press.

Delaney, Jeanne. 1996. Making Sense of Modernity: Changing Attitudes toward the Immigrant and the Gaucho in Turn-of-the-Century Argentina. *Comparative Studies in Society and History* 38(3):434–59.

Ferrer, Aldo. 1972. *La economía Argentina.* Buenos Aires: Fondo de Cultura Económica.

Ferrer, Horacio. 1960. *El tango. Su historia y evolución.* Buenos Aires: A. Peña Lillo.

Fouquiéres, Andre de. 1913. Les danses nouvelles: le tango. *Femina* 284:58–61.

Goddard, Victoria. 2000. The Virile Nation: Gender and Ethnicity in the Re-construction of Argentinian Pasts. *Goldsmiths Anthropology Research Papers* 4.

Grünewald, José L. 1994. *Carlos Gardel. Lunfardo e tango*. Rio de Janeiro: Editora Nova Fronteira.

Guy, Donna. 1991. *Sex and Danger in Buenos Aires: Prostitution, Family, and Nation in Argentina*. Lincoln: University of Nebraska Press.

Halperin Donghi, Tulio. 1987. *El espejo de la historia*. Buenos Aires: Sudamericana.

Ludmer, Josefina. 1988. *El género gauchesco. Un tratado sobre la patria*. Buenos Aires: Editorial Sudamericana.

Melhuus, Marit, and Kristi Anne Stølen. 1996. Introduction. In *Machos, Mistresses, Madonnas: Contesting the Power of the Latin American Gender Imagery*, ed. Marit Melhuus and Kristi Anne Stølen. London: Verso.

Montaldo, Graciela. 1999. *Ficciones culturales y fábulas de identidad en América Latina*. Rosario, Argentina: Beatriz Viterbo Editora.

Nochlin, Linda. 1989. *The Politics of Vision: Essays in Nineteenth-Century Art and Society*. New York: Harper & Row.

Oliven, Ruben. 1996. *Tradition Matters: Modern Gaucho Identity in Brazil*. New York. Columbia University Press.

Prieto, Adolfo. 1988. *El discurso criollista en la formación de la Argentina moderna*. Buenos Aires: Editorial Sudamericana.

Rama, Carlos M. 1996. *The Lettered City*. Durham, NC: Duke University Press,

Rock, David. 1993. "From the First World War to 1930." In *Argentina since Independence*, ed. Leslie Bethell. Cambridge: Cambridge University Press.

Rojas, Ricardo. 1909. *La restauración nacionalista*. Buenos Aires: Ediciones Centurion.

Romano, Eduardo. 1991. *Las letras del tango. Antología cronológica: 1900–1980*. Rosario, Argentina: Editorial Fundación Ros.

Sarlo, Beatriz. 1996. Modernidad y mezcla cultural. In *Buenos Aires 1880–1930: La capital de un imperio imaginario*, ed. Hector Vázquez Rial. Madrid: Alianza Editorial.

Savigliano, Marta. 1995. *Tango and the Political Economy of Passion*. Boulder, CO: Westview Press.

Schneider, Arnd. 1996. The Two Faces of Modernity: Concepts of the Melting Pot in Argentina. *Critique of Anthropology* 16(2):173–98.

Slatta, Richard. 1985. The Gaucho in Argentina's Quest for Identity. *Canadian Review of Studies in Nationalism* 12(1):23–38.

Solberg, Carl. 1970. *Immigration and Nationalism: Argentina and Chile, 1890–1914*. Austin: University of Texas Press.

Strathern, Marilyn. 1992. *After Nature: English Kinship in the Late Twentieth Century*. Cambridge: Cambridge University Press.

Vázques Rial, Héctor. 1996. Superpoblación y concentración urbana en un país desierto. In *Buenos Aires 1880–1930: La capital de un imperio imaginario*, ed. Héctor Vázquez Rial. Madrid: Alianza Editorial.

Vega, Carlos. 1981. *Apuntes para la historia del movimiento tradicionalista argentino*. Buenos Aires: Instituto Nacional de Musicología.

Veloz, Frank, and Yolanda Veloz. 1937. *Tango and Rumba. The Dances of Today and Tomorrow*. New York: Harper and Brothers Publishers.

Vila, Pablo. 1991. Tango to Folk: Hegemony Construction and Popular Identities in Argentina. *Studies in Latin American Popular Culture* 10:107–39.

Zalko, Nardo. 1998. *Un siècle de tango Paris-Buenos Aires*. Paris: Editions du Félin.

10

Gender, Sexuality, and Revolution: Making Histories and Cultural Politics in Nicaragua, 1979–2001

Cymene Howe

O N A SWELTERING AFTERNOON IN JUNE 2001, Miguel[1] and I sat together, sipping acutely sweet instant coffee and talking about his many years as a member of Nicaragua's revolutionary party, the Frente Sandinista de Liberación Nacional (FSLN), or Sandinistas. Miguel explained that he had been dismissed from the Sandinista army during the 1980s in the midst of the Contra war, a counterinsurgency supported by the United States, because his officers considered him "too broken-wristed," or, in North American terms, too "effeminate" for military service. In the years that followed, he became an advocate for, as he put it, "the rights of *los homosexuales*" in Nicaragua. Reflecting on his years of activism in a country where homosexuality is generally stigmatized or ridiculed, Miguel explained to me,

> We went to the media, we went to the written media, we went to the radio and the TV and we sat down and we said, we are homosexuals, we are lesbians; we want you to respect our rights, that you respect our human rights. We are all equal to whomever. We are good kids, we are good fathers, we are good mothers, we are good neighbors, we are good workers. Equal. There are bad ones too, like everyone. But we are humans, and here we are.

Miguel frames his bids for tolerance of sexuality as an issue of human rights—a set of discourses and international legal instruments that have had a significant impact on gender rights (Ahmend An-Na'Im 1992; Peters and Wolper 1995; Steiner and Alston 1996), and, more recently, on sexuality rights (Adam, Duyvendak, and Krouwel 1999; Altman 2001; Steiner and Alston 1996). This chapter explores the political and cultural maneuvers experienced by Miguel and other gender and sexuality activists, from the days of dictatorship to the present neoliberal era in Nicaragua. Doing so allows us to see the shifts in thinking that led many of these Nicaraguans from the tenets of *Sandinismo*—the revolutionary, socialist ideology that animated the revolution—to the framework of human rights and sexuality advocacy.[2]

The revolutionary period of the Sandinistas (1979–1990) radically transformed the political culture of Nicaragua. But Nicaraguan politics were also transformed in the aftermath of revolution by an influx of transnational discourses and identity politics. The experiences of living in a society undergoing a revolution, coupled with ideological exchanges with allies in the North, or so-called First World, shaped new social movements and conditioned cultural praxis in ways unique to Nicaragua. This chapter focuses on the shifting political relationships among gender, sexuality, and revolution in Nicaragua from 1979 to 2001. Through the lens of sexuality and gender politics, I focus in particular on feminism, women's rights organizing, and lesbian and homosexual activism to argue that activists' experiences and schooling in Sandinismo has generated a distinct kind of identity politics in postrevolutionary Nicaragua. While the terminology and political frameworks that activists use may differ from Sandinismo, the communitarian principles that structured the revolution continue to influence political expression and activism in the present. From this standpoint, it is less useful to think of neoliberal Nicaragua as "postrevolutionary" than it is to consider these political practices as part of a longer cultural and political tradition—these are new ways of establishing social justice in a country that is consistently one of the two poorest in the Western Hemisphere.

Making Histories: Ethnography and Political Pasts

The information presented here emerges from fieldwork observations, interviews, both formal and informal, and documents, official and unofficial, all of which were gathered during on-site interviews in Nicaragua from 1999 to 2001. The people I worked with and who are quoted here, like Miguel, were, and in many cases continue to be, involved in civil society (or non-state-oriented) politics in Nicaragua. They are members of lesbian and homosexual men's discussion groups, advocates of reproductive and gender rights, and employees of nongovernmental organizations (NGOs) based in Nicaragua that attempt to change the cultural perceptions and legal codes around gender and sexuality in Nicaragua.

Gender, the social and cultural expectations associated with being male or female, and sexuality, whether an adopted identity or an ascribed status affixed to one's sexual preference or orientation, are deeply related phenomena in Nicaragua. In the day-to-day politics of activists, the dynamics between sexuality and gender are intimately intertwined as activists struggle against both direct and diffuse power—exercised by the state through legislation or more obliquely by the populace through social norms and cultural conventions. The machinations of power are not always "top down," and many gender and sexuality activists struggle against injustice due to their marginalized place in Nicaragua's social hierarchy. Following the logic of those who live these politics, then, this discussion focuses on the intersecting concerns of both "women" as a political constituency, and "sexual minorities," or lesbians and homosexual men,[3] as a political constituency.

This analysis considers lesbian and homosexual men's activism (what I will call "sexuality activism"), along with women's rights and feminist activism (or "gender activism") for several reasons. On an ideological level, socialist revolutionary discourses often frame both sexual and gender identities as antithetical to the socioeconomic class-based tenets of classical Marxist thinking. While sexual minorities and women activists in Nicaragua did not always face exactly the same obstacles to equal status, each constituency was, for the most part, framed by the architects of Sandinismo as a distraction from the "true" goals of the revolutionary project. On a practical level, both of these identity-based activist constituencies were present and actively demanded their rights in different ways during the Sandinista era. Through the 1980s and 1990s, many of those who sought to draw attention to the particular obstacles faced by women and sexual minorities shared similar concerns.

Sexuality rights activists in Nicaragua have often understood their struggle for acceptance as partially blocked and impacted by the gender dynamics of machismo. In Nicaragua, machismo is an "emic" (or "insider") category describing a set of gender attributes that are culturally and historically specific. By preserving the term in context, I want to maintain the integrity of the ideas expressed by activists and others as they reflect on social dynamics. The term *machismo* is often used in Latin American and elsewhere to connote, and sometimes justify or excuse, some men's behaviors, including excessive drinking and fighting, womanizing, abandonment of responsibilities, cockiness, recklessness, displays of extreme jealousy, attempting to control women and subordinates, and demonstrations of physical prowess. Octavio Paz, the eminent Mexican author, poetically described machismo as "the masculine pole of life" that rotates around one axis: power. Machismo has also been understood, to a much lesser extent, to embody such masculine gender attributes as generosity, stoicism, courage, formalness, respectability, and pride (LeVine 1993: 80). Machismo, as a set of behaviors and a social concept, has become, in many settings, a kind of shorthand to designate "all things negative" about Latin American men (Gutmann 1996) both in and outside of Latin America.

As such, the concept of machismo can function to further marginalize Third World men, and Latinos and Chicano men in particular. The potential misuse of machismo in this sense must be cautioned against.

In the case of Nicaragua, machismo operates in political, social, and cultural processes as a day-to-day dynamic and, on a conceptual level, to inform the way people speak and think about masculinity, gender, and power. Nicaraguan women regularly exchange horrific experiences that they attribute to the machinations of machismo. Newspaper accounts of domestic violence in Nicaragua often suggest that machismo is the root cause of abuse. By the same token, many nonheterosexual men and women underscore the impact of machismo in their marginalization (Howe 2003; Lancaster 1992). In the same way that machismo draws a strict line between appropriate gender behavior for men and women, so too does machismo designate what constitutes correct "manliness" and sexual behavior as opposed to inappropriate behavior (Carrillo 2002: 24). Since at least the time of the Sandinistas, machismo has been singled out as a cultural hurdle and barrier to a more egalitarian society. Since the early 1990s and the beginning of Nicaragua's autonomous women's movement, machismo has been cited as something against which the movement must struggle.

From the point of view of sexuality activists, in a dualistic gender system, the privileging of men over women and of heterosexuality over homosexuality are related social phenomena, each of which reciprocally upholds the other. Many feminist activists also agree that the same dynamics of *heterosexismo* (heterosexism, or the privileging of heterosexuality) are related to gender inequalities, such as domestic violence, that limit women's ability to enjoy their full human rights. However, while there are clear connections between the dynamics of sexuality and gender, therefore a seemingly natural link between activists' goals, gender and sexuality are not coterminous. In Nicaragua, some women's rights activists have been wary of associating their goals of liberation too closely with those of gays and lesbians for fear of delegitimizing their cause.

Reading Histories: Sexuality and Gender

The lens of sexuality and gender activism reveals one of many possible readings of a complex political terrain. One of my intentions here is to unveil the constructed nature of the history I present in order to make explicit that history is as much a narrative construction about what happened as it is a recounting of what happened. However, history is not merely a text waiting to be deconstructed but rather a collection of events in which people have lived, died, suffered, and overcome hardships. In recounting this aspect of

Nicaraguan history from 1979 to 2001, I therefore present a much-abbreviated history of a nation-state that has been involved in global processes since at least the 1500s.

One of these global processes has been a troubled history of U.S. political, economic, and military intervention. On the streets of Managua, Nicaragua's capital city, there is a common refrain spoken in resignation: "Here in Nicaragua, we are so far from God and so close to the United States." In order to map the political relationships among gender, sexuality, and revolution, I first draw attention to the tangled history of Nicaragua and the United States. This history of U.S. intervention has led many contemporary gender and sexuality activists to approach ideologies from the North with caution; their activist strategies are not mere replicas of feminist and lesbian and gay rights movements in the United States.

Second, I describe the development of gender and sexuality political organizing in Nicaragua, making explicit the interconnections between Nicaragua and a larger global context. The rights struggles of lesbians, homosexual men, and women in Nicaragua have been generated out of multiple, combined discourses and historical events. An articulated process linking local knowledge with a global diffusion of information about homosexuality and women's rights movements—such as the distribution of condoms for AIDS prevention by North American health brigades in the 1980s and feminist discussion groups whose members included Nicaraguans as well as their international allies—has influenced identity politics in Nicaragua.

It was during the Sandinista era that sexuality activists achieved some room for maneuver, and women became political actors en masse. From 1979 to 1990, homosexuality was at times configured as a "northern import" and, as such, considered by many to be opposed to "traditional" Nicaraguan values. During these same years, women developed greater political participation, learning how to negotiate the bureaucratic and political nuances of the Nicaraguan state, as well as those of their international allies and the development agencies. In fact, discussions around gender during the Sandinista era would prefigure many debates in Nicaraguan politics at the beginning of the twenty-first century, including those about abortion, sexuality, and class status.

Socially conservative regimes since that time have similarly cast the struggle for homosexual and lesbian rights as the negative consequence of North American and European sexual revolutions and feminism, that is, as uninvited forms of modernity.[4] Such reasoning undoubtedly influenced lawmakers in the Nicaraguan National Assembly in 1992 when they passed legislation increasing the penalties for those found to have committed "sodomy," resulting in the most repressive antihomosexual penalties in all of Latin America. These more recent efforts to morally engineer the Nicaraguan state, however, have taken place in a world system where information about sexuality, liberation, and rainbow flags is abundant. By the 1990s, for example, virtually every urban center in Latin America, eastern Asia, and southern Africa had a number of lesbian and gay organizations (Adam, Duyvendak, and Krouwel 1999).

Gender and sexuality politics in Nicaragua are conditioned by the past in addition to this changing global landscape. Sandinismo, the philosophy of the revolution, continues to be evoked in the present. Although the Sandinista government is no longer institutionalized in the form of a revolutionary regime, those who were involved in the revolution, inspired by its commitment to socialist principles, nationalism, and progressive Christianity, continue to act, dissent, and critique in its spirit.[5]

From Colonial Outpost to Revolutionary Beacon:
Independence to Sandinismo, 1838–1979

Political, economic, and military domination by the United States has haunted Nicaragua since at least the middle of the nineteenth century. The U.S. government and industry have taken advantage of existing political rivalries and economic instability to leverage control and extract resources, human and natural, from Nicaragua. From outright interventions, installing dictators sympathetic to U.S. demands, and U.S. agents' making "voting recommendations" to the Nicaraguan populace, the relationship between the United States and Nicaragua has been one of very uneven, and very entangled, power dynamics. These interventions have altered the cultural, economic, and social structures in Nicaragua in significant ways, including maintaining inequalities of socioeconomic class, gender, and sexuality. The legacy of U.S. interventions and responses to them have not only shaped the revolutionary sentiments of the Sandinistas but also encouraged activists in the wake of revolution to draw their tactics from their own national heritage of social transformation.

Nicaragua has long been a politicized place, characterized by foreign intervention, like that of William Walker in the nineteenth century, and struggles to reinstate national sovereignty, especially those of Augusto Cesar Sandino against the U.S. Marine occupation in the 1920s and 1930s. Following Sandino's rebellion, the United States maintained a grip on Nicaragua, this time through a cozy relationship with the Somozas, a dictatorial regime that would rule the country for nearly half a century. Through successive dictatorships, the Somozas became a political institution in Nicaragua, characterized by liberal economic policies, political repression, nepotism, and labor and resource extraction, a philosophy and set of practices that came to be known as *Somocismo*.

Women under Somocismo had limited autonomy and political participation. While some women faithful to the regime benefited from employment and favors doled out by Somoza, Nicaragua's female majority—poor, rural women—lived at the bottom of a hierarchical system of exploitation. Women's inability to own property and earn wages signaled the difficult conditions suffered by underclass women during the dictatorship. Elite, and often socially conservative, women did organize politically and after a number of setbacks won suffrage in 1955 (González 2001). As dictator of a nominally democratic state, Somoza did promote a populist agenda, offering limited rights to women in exchange for their votes (González 2001; Gould 1990). Most Nicaraguan women had few political and economic tools with which to transform their status, and successive regimes showed little interest in the health, welfare, and rights of the disenfranchised female masses.

How the long Somoza years impacted homosexual men and women is less clear than in the case of women, but there is anecdotal evidence of both tolerance and repression. The Somoza regime maintained brothels with female prostitutes and purportedly allowed for male/male prostitution on the streets of Managua. A nightclub where men could gather and dance existed at different times during the Somoza era, and anecdotal reports in the 1990s suggested that the senior Somoza invited "homosexuals" to his parties. According to some sexuality activists, some of members of the National Guard frequented the gathering places of homosexual men in search of romantic liaisons. Other reports from the field, however, tell a different story. According to Enrique, "Somoza and La Guardia were the worst . . . they had it out for *cochones* (fags). Always!" At best, it seems that men's homosexual encounters were ignored or tolerated, and at worst, individual men were singled out for abuse. Lesbians, or women who had erotic and affective relationships with other women, do not figure in the rumors around homosexuality and Somocismo, and at present, their stories are unaccounted for in the historical record.

The mixed messages surrounding sexuality and Somocismo are an important dynamic foreshadowing the complexity of sexual and gender activism in contemporary Nicaragua. When the Sandinistas came to power, a concerted effort was made to tarnish the Somoza regime to its very core. Because of the sordid history of the regime—political repression, rape, torture, and the "disappearing" of dissidents—there was rightly much to vilify. However, the Sandinistas also placed a special focus upon sexuality in their claims against Somocismo. The Somozas and the National Guard had profited from prostitution, and brothels were the first buildings to be destroyed in the wake of the revolution; female prostitutes themselves became part of reeducation campaigns. Associating Somocismo with homosexuality and with sexual "deviance" generally, as in these anecdotes, may have been a way of further discrediting the dictatorship. The rumors that continue to circulate about Somocismo and the sexual "chaos" of the time are nearly always framed as "everybody knew it was true. . . . " The relationship between Somocismo, sexuality, exploitation, and "sexual deviance" is a complex web, with symbolic weight, in the minds of many Nicaraguans.

Reframing Somocismo in light of sexual and gendered perspectives allows for a deeper understanding of the Sandinista revolution that ultimately defeated the dictatorship. The minimal political gains made by elite women and the "tolerance" that may have been afforded to homosexual men under Somocismo were a far cry from the vast socialist engineering of the Sandinista era. These early political interventions were an equally distant prelude to the human rights demands made by nonheterosexual people in Nicaragua in the beginnings of the twenty-first century. First, however, there was a revolution to be had.

A Decade Draped in Red and Black, 1979–1990

In 1979, after almost twenty years in the making,[6] the FSLN marched triumphantly into the capital city of Managua carrying the Sandinista flag, and Tacho, the last of the Somoza family dictators, fled to more tolerant locales to the North. A momentary thaw in U.S. cold war policy during the Carter administration at the end of the 1970s allowed for what would become the victory of the Sandinista Revolution. But, as in all revolutions, a broad popular commitment to radical social change was fundamental to its success.

Ideologically, Sandinismo provided for the dissolution of all kinds of oppression, including, presumably, those based on gender and sexuality. However, the relationship among sexuality, gender, and revolution was a complex and often uneven set of practices in Sandinista Nicaragua. Women's involvement in the revolutionary effort was crucial, and women composed approximately 30 percent of the insurrectionary forces (Molyneaux 1985; Randall 1981). Women worked as combatants, field commanders, messengers, and keepers of safe houses and even commanded key military operations. As one woman put it, "We never entered into a lot of theoretical discussions about women's liberation. . . . In fact we never said that we were equal—we simply demonstrated it in the battlefields, on the barricades and in the mountains" (cited in Collinson 1990: 140). Despite the heroics of the revolution's "heroines," no woman was ever to be a part of the nine-man national directorate that ruled Sandinista Nicaragua; this limited women's formal participation in the political reconstruction of the country. Had women been more integral to the process, the politics of gender equality might have been debated sooner, and more profoundly.

The Sandinistas initiated social programs that provided the country with a more equitable distribution of power and wealth, including attention to rural peasants, the urban poor, women, and workers, historically disenfranchised sectors of the population. The FSLN's Agrarian Reform and Cooperative Laws

(1981) were the first in Latin America to recognize women's right to equal wages. Rural infrastructure was invigorated with new housing, health posts, public transportation, schools, electricity, safe water, vaccination campaigns, and a distribution network for basic foods. The Sandinistas also made remarkable gains in health and education, reducing national illiteracy from 50 percent to 13 percent within a few years of taking power and expanding preventive medicine to international acclaim (Americas Watch Committee 1985; Collinson 1990). Four weeks' paid maternity leave and legal rights for "illegitimate" children demonstrated the revolutionary commitment to uplifting those who had been marginalized (Molyneux 1985).

An explicitly feminist orientation was never embraced by the Sandinista ruling elite, but Sandinismo did benefit women generally. The FSLN party line placed women's rights within the provenance of "all forms of oppression and discrimination" described in this FSLN directive:

> We reject tendencies that promote the emancipation of women as the outcome of a struggle against men, or as an activity exclusively of women, for this type of position is divisive and distracts the people from their fundamental tasks. (Cited in Field 1999: 127)

The Sandinistas clearly suggest here a communitarian principle, one that embraces ideals of "the people" rather than the distinctions posed by gender inequality. Functioning as a feminine mouthpiece for the FSLN, Rosario Murillo, the first lady, mirrored this sentiment.

> I believe that in a revolution, a specific women's organization can't exist as it would be a way of perpetuating inequality. We don't talk about creating specific organizations for men and of men, in spite of their unequal situation vis-à-vis the exploited or oppressed in a class society. (Quoted in Collinson 1990: 143)

Sexual minorities, had they been given the same ideological attention here afforded to women, would have likely also fallen under the mantle of "false consciousness," a divisive identification distracting from the fundamental tasks of revolutionary endeavor.

The FSLN attempted to integrate women fully into the revolutionary project by forming the Asociación de Mujeres Nicaragüenses, Luisa Amanda Espinosa (AMNLAE). This women's branch of the party was intended to respond to "the woman question," which emerged in all twentieth-century Marxist projects. AMNLAE, an umbrella organization that appealed primarily to urban market women, housewives, and some teachers and nurses, insisted on a dialogue about family planning, domestic violence, and rape as policy concerns.[7] Through the 1980s, women's political participation in Nicaragua was higher than it had ever been, with women holding 40 percent of the seats in

**Figure 10.1.   In 2000, on the twenty-first anniversary
of the revolution, thousands continued to celebrate
the victory of the Sandinistas. Among the revelers
were two girls selling red and black bandanas (the
colors of the FSLN) to signify solidarity in an era of
free market capitalism. Source: author.**

Nicaragua's parliament. At the grassroots level, women commented on the
country's new constitution in 1985, outlining their economic concerns. In 1987
a landmark policy document on women's oppression, the *Proclama*, was released on International Women's Day. Urban women, often young university
students, were mobilized in literacy and health brigades that benefited rural
women; in some regions, women's illiteracy under Somoza was 100 percent
(compared to the national average of 50.35 percent) (Molyneaux 1985; Randall
1994: 12). While "feminism" may not have been the word used to describe these
interventions, clearly women's issues were not simply figments of middle-class
feminists' imagination but were of concern to poor and rural women as well.

Sandinista programs were generally beneficial to women as a constituency but did little to undo sexism. Rather, women were often refeminized as they were channeled into certain kinds of reproductive labor in accord with traditional gender roles. Women's sewing and food-processing cooperatives flourished across the country with support from the FSLN. While these projects focused on more traditional women's work, the cooperatives did foster solidarity among women and politicized women from diverse class backgrounds. An early Sandinista initiative banned the use of women's bodies in exploitative advertising, a move that both drew attention to the symbolic potency of the female form and critiqued the lascivious potential of market capitalism (Chinchilla 1994; Padilla, Murguialday, and Criquillon 1987).

The relationship between Sandinismo and women's political organizing during the 1980s was a complicated negotiation between two apparently contradictory ideological positions. Many Nicaraguans and scholars of the region credit the Sandinistas with providing for women's entrance into public debate as political actors. According to a long-time observer of the Sandinista Revolution,

> Young women, with their Spanish Catholic heritage of chastity and submission . . . [were brought] out into the arena of public struggle. A decade of revolutionary government promoted women's rights in health, education, labor, leadership, and more egalitarian legislation—some of it successful, some not. (Randall 1994: 34)

Sandinismo did raise the profile of women as political actors, but, as one scholar puts it, they "did not wage a campaign against sexism, or develop a comprehensive challenge to traditional gender roles" (Chuchryk 1991: 159). It was through Sandinismo that, for the first time in the history of Nicaragua, women achieved full legal equality and made important economic and social advances (Chinchilla 1990, 1994; Chuchryk 1991); it was also through Sandinismo that the ideological backdrop was laid for future identity-based political organizing. While less visible, the Sandinista era also provided "more room for maneuver" for those marginalized by their sexuality because it opened the door to discussions about, and engagements with, social justice (Thayer 1997: 399). These openings and the apparent heightened tolerance for identity-based concerns distinguishes Nicaragua's revolution from many other socialist projects around the world.

Challenges to Change

The women who formed the base of AMNLAE also faced their own internal conflicts around two especially salient issues, abortion and lesbian rights. Collectively, the women of AMNLAE questioned the association's goals: Was it to be an instrument of the Sandinista party or a women's organization that might challenge the party hierarchies? Some members of AMNLAE lobbied to take up the controversial issues; for others, recognition of sexual and repro-ductive rights—lesbian rights and abortion—was considered a troubling de-mand to make on the state. Abortion was illegal in Nicaragua prior to the San-dinistas' taking office, and although illegal abortion was the leading cause of death among women in Nicaragua, the Sandinistas never legalized the proce-dure. In part, the FSLN and AMNLAE feared alienating the conservative Catholic hierarchy—in a country that is overwhelming Catholic, abortion was a politically dangerous issue. The Contra war and heavy casualties on the front lines also propped up the state's pro-natalist stance.

Lesbian rights were considered by the socially conservative members of AMNLAE to be, likewise, politically risky vis-à-vis the church and of ques-tionable legitimacy to achieving women's rights overall. In the late 1980s, AMNLAE's director publicly stated that "lesbians march under their own ban-ner" (quoted in Collinson 1990: 25). They were, in other words, not welcome to raise their concerns with AMNLAE. This move clearly signaled that AMN-LAE, at least at the leadership level, wanted to distance itself from the con-tentious topic of homosexuality.[8] Again, the supposed moral rectitude of the revolutionary path allowed little room for sexuality diversity, at least at the po-litical and public level. The director of AMNLAE later recanted her statement, but the tensions surrounding issues like lesbianism, feminism, and women's rights were indicative of the complex processes being worked through in the context of the revolutionary state. In addition to distracting from the goals of "women" and "the people," lesbian rights were also often framed as foreign concerns, imported identities brought by European and North American women, as though there were no Nicaraguan women attracted to, or in rela-tionships with, other women. The tensions faced by AMNLAE in the 1980s foreshadow the ways in which issues of sexuality—and not only those con-cerned with reproduction—would later become part of a distinct trajectory in women's political organizing.

While the Sandinistas attempted to create a nation that would embrace a comprehensive and coherent revolutionary vision, the FSLN was also forced to contend with the United States in its "front yard." The Carter administra-tion reluctantly accepted the Sandinista government in 1979, but the Reagan regime took a decidedly different stance, contending that the Sandinistas were "destabilizing the hemisphere" (Rossett and Vandermeer 1986: 18–20). Under the auspices of preventing "Marxist-Leninist dictatorships" and "communist infiltration,"[9] the Reagan administration undertook, with the help of the CIA, a covert war against Nicaragua.[10] U.S. forces provided military training and economic support for the Contra (or counterrevolutionary) war, which cost

Nicaragua approximately thirty thousand lives and more than $12 billion in damages that bankrupted the economy.[11] A full-scale embargo, coupled with mandatory military service for Nicaraguan men, effectively hobbled the FSLN's base of support.

The war and ensuing draft also undoubtedly impacted the potential to transform gender relations in Nicaragua in significant ways. Women supported men on the front lines, many became organized as "mothers of heroes and martyrs" (Bayard de Volo 2001), and reproductive rights, abortion in particular, took on new significance as underpopulation and war depleted the country's human resources. The total effect of these wartime dynamics was to reinforce traditional gender roles rather than transform them. After nearly a decade of a soft-target counterinsurgency war and the social and economic wreckage it created, the Sandinistas were voted out of power in 1990.

The Sandinista Revolution generated a set of ideological principles and political strategies that continue to inform the work of contemporary activists. Nicaragua's revolutionary tenets have been described in various ways. According to a prominent Sandinista, a commitment to "Nationalism, Christian Values, Democracy and Social Justice" (Miguel D'Escoto in Rosset and Vandermeer 1986: 441) best captures the revolution's opposition to "domination, exploitation, and oppression" (Field 1999: 96–97). Sandinismo's promise was that a multiclass revolutionary effort would cause all other inequalities—including, for example, those based on race, gender, and ethnicity—to crumble. This goal, however, was more difficult to accomplish in practice than in theory. The FSLN's failure to attend to "identity" constituencies—such as indigenous people (Bourgois 1981; Field 1999; Hale 1996; Gould 1990, 1998), women (Babb 2001; Molyneux 1985; Randall 1994; Collinson 1990), and gays and lesbians (Adam 1989, 1993; Bolt González 1995; Randall 1993, 1994; Thayer 1997)—ultimately hindered the revolutionary vision of the Sandinistas. However, their successes were many, and the political advocacy strategies learned through Sandinismo would later prove invaluable in the struggle for identity-based rights.

Overall, the FSLN's position on feminism and women's rights was at times contradictory; Sandinista engagements with the "woman question" were not unlike the political practices found in other socialist states, such as Cuba, where policies generally benefited women's economic, legal, and social status. Women's roles as mothers, sexual commodities, and victims of machismo framed much of the FSLN's treatment of gender. But perhaps more important were the ideological effects of the Sandinista era—politicizing, in great numbers, women who had previously had little political experience or "voice." As Richard Stahler-Sholk (1995: 250) has suggested, the experiences of the 1980s, bringing many women into political action and gender debates, made social subjects out of those who were once mere objects of policy. The ability to discuss machismo, violence against women, and women's exclusion from positions of power in the party opened the door to new ways of thinking about, and acting upon, women's differential status in Nicaraguan society.[12] It is precisely this dynamic that foreshadows the construction of civil society activism around gender and sexuality that would become a part of Nicaragua's political landscape in the 1990s.

The Nicaraguan Gay Movement, Sandinistas, and la SIDA

During the 1980s, a contentious reworking of women's rights took place in Nicaragua, but the relationship between the Sandinista state and sexual minorities cannot be so easily summarized; nor did homosexuality receive the same visibility as gender. The Sandinista state did not overtly and systematically repress sexual minorities, but gay political organizing was "suppressed" (Babb 2001: 8). Thus, while the FSLN was out of the closet about the need to address women as a political constituency, the party did not apply this same logic to the rights of Nicaraguan lesbians and homosexual men. Indeed, one of the first acts of the Sandinista government in the early 1980s was to close gay bars and cordon off the gathering places of homosexual men because they were considered sites of "bourgeois decadence" (Randall 1993) and reminiscent of Somoza-era prostitution (Lancaster 1992), transgressive sexual behaviors that appeared antithetical to the revolution's "new man" ideals. The Sandinistas' initial responses toward homosexuality, however, would change over the course of the 1980s as the presumed incompatibility among sexuality, gender, and class-based struggles became less of an issue. Ultimately, it was through the Sandinista experiment that many lesbians and homosexual men in Nicaragua found their political "voice" and developed the political strategies and networks required to carry out their rights-based work in the 1990s.

In 1986 a clandestine group of gays and lesbians, calling themselves the Nicaraguan Gay Movement, began to meet and discuss the discrimination they faced as sexual minorities. The members of the movement were men and women, *internacionalistas* (foreigners in solidarity with the revolution), and Nicaraguans who identified as "lesbian," "gay," or "homosexual." Within months, the organization was infiltrated by Sandinista State Security and members were questioned—by some accounts, "interrogated"[13]—and told that their gatherings were "counterrevolutionary" because they were seen as an attempt to organize politically. The majority of the group had been, and continued to be, supporters of the revolutionary project; indeed, most were Sandinista Party members. According to some, Sandinista State Security was "embarrassed" about the intervention, and in the end, members of the gay movement in fact protected the revolutionary state by not disclosing publicly, particularly to the international media, what had occurred.

Sandinista State Security's decision to break up the meetings must be understood in context: Nicaragua was at war, and security precautions were at their height. The U.S. government's policy to topple the revolutionary regime "by any means necessary" was certainly on the mind of all Nicaraguans (Bretlinger 1995; Prevost and Vanden 1997). From this angle, any chink in the facade of revolutionary coherence was considered a breach of state security, and organizing outside of formal political structures was prohibited. The Sandinistas had already been criticized for their treatment of "minorities" (indigenous people in particular), which the White House claimed as evidence of "Communist repression" in classic cold war terms. The Nicaragua Gay Movement's meetings may have been halted because of wartime precautions, but the fact that sexual identity did not ally with the class-based ideals of the FSLN was undoubtedly a part of the equation as well. In either case, it is important to note that when they were asked to cease their meetings, members of the Nicaraguan Gay Movement agreed to do so, largely because they supported the revolutionary cause and did not want to endanger its success by providing more "repression" ammunition for the United States.

The politics of sexuality were stifled in the mid 1980s, but under the mantle of "health," activists found a nonthreatening way to advance their rights with the support of the Sandinista government. Preparing for a potential increase in HIV cases in the late 1980s,[14] lesbians organized in solidarity with gay men to disseminate information about the spread of the virus (Schreiber and Stephen 1989). The government's Ministry of Health (MINSA) spearheaded a significant shift in Sandinista policy toward homosexuals and lesbians when it initiated the Collective of Popular Educators Concerned with HIV/AIDS (CEP-SIDA). Then Health Minister Dora María Téllez invited informal discussion groups of lesbians and homosexual men to collaborate with MINSA on a new sex-education project. The coalition formed in 1988 and recruited two hundred people to conduct community health education and outreach. First, Téllez had to convince the revolutionary government that outreach workers should not be harassed by the police or other officials as they carried out their education work distributing pamphlets, condoms, and advice to homosexual men and female sex workers on the streets of Managua (Randall 1994: 294–75). The government agreed that the outreach work would be effective and was necessary; this marked the first "out" relationship between the Nicaraguan state and activists who defined themselves, in part, through their sexuality. This did not result in the government's wholeheartedly embracing sexual minorities as such, but it was an official shift in position and initiated a large-scale, productive relationship between Nicaraguan sexuality activists, their allies in the United States and Europe, and the Sandinista government.[15]

Figure 10.2. By the 1990s Nicaragua had a number of HIV/AIDS outreach and education campaigns. This poster reads, "Here, sex is safe" and advocates that men who have sex with men use a condom. Note the stained glass motif of the poster's artwork. Source: author.

Health *brigadistas* from U.S. and European cities arrived in Nicaragua to work in conjunction with local activists in the CEP-SIDA program. These solidarity brigades provided material support (such as condoms and popular education materials) for grassroots campaigns already underway in gay "cruising" areas and among female prostitutes. The specter of AIDS, with its potential to ravage the public health of the nation, functioned to usher in an age of relative cooperation between the Sandinistas and a nascent gay and lesbian rights movement. AIDS prevention programs, based on medical models of epidemic prevention, ultimately provided both a catalyst and a cover for lesbian and gay organizing. Importantly, it was during this time that concrete

activist coalitions were built between the United States and Nicaragua centering on sexuality, health, and rights. These same principles and political networks would continue to serve sexuality advocates in both the North and
Nicaragua after the revolutionary era ended.

Sandinista intrusions into organizations such as the Nicaraguan Gay Movement were far from exemplary, and the "official" stance of the Sandinista Party
did not include any mention of rights for nonheterosexual people. Sexuality
and policies aimed at alleviating the discrimination faced by homosexual men
and lesbians collectively were never a part of the Sandinista agenda. But neither did the Sandinistas practice heavy-handed persecution, detention, and
quarantine, as had been the case in Cuba (Argüelles and Rich 1984–1985;
Lumsden 1996).[16] On the one hand, suppressing the Nicaraguan Gay Movement and the initial attempts to "clean up" homosexual men's gathering places
served to marginalize sexual minorities further. On the other hand, the CEP-
SIDA coalition suggests a very different view of cooperation between the state
and sexuality activists. Scholars of lesbian and gay political organizing in
Nicaragua generally credit the Sandinistas with creating a political climate
that offered Nicaraguan lesbians and homosexual men greater autonomy, visibility, and political viability (Howe 2003; Thayer 1997). The Sandinistas' willingness to consider women's concerns likely offered a first step toward the organized work of self-identified "lesbians," "gays," and "homosexuals" because
it placed gender difference in the debate, allowing other forms of difference,
such as sexuality, to be brought to the fore.

Because many Nicaraguans who identified themselves as lesbian, gay, or homosexual were, like their neighbors, schooled in Sandinismo, their approach
to activism was distinct from the kinds of sexuality advocacy projects seen in
other parts of the world (Babb 2001; Lancaster 1992; Randall 1993, 1994;
Thayer 1997). Due to both ideological and economic circumstances,
Nicaraguan activists did not establish "gay ghettos" in which lesbians and gay
men populated particular urban neighborhoods. The enclave communities
that appeared in San José, Costa Rica, during the 1980s or in the United States
in 1950s had no analog in Nicaragua (Chauncey 1995; Kaiser 1998; Kennedy
and Davis 1994; D'Emilio and Freedman 1997). Economic hardship often prevented many homosexual Nicaraguans from leaving their natal homes, as
many were unable to afford their own separate living quarters. From a less
economically deterministic standpoint, some Nicaraguan lesbians and gay
men remained near their families of origin because of strong familial obligations. For heterosexual Nicaraguans, it is commonplace to reside with or very
near one's family of origin, even after marrying and beginning one's own family. Therefore, the lack of "gay ghettos" in Nicaragua was likely a product of
tradition, economics, and the influences of Sandinismo.

Many Nicaraguan sexuality activists were influenced and inspired by their revolutionary experience. Rather than focusing on political strategies that centered on individual needs and desires, Nicaraguan sexuality activists sought to revolutionize how Nicaraguan society conceived of sexuality more broadly. Instead of focusing their struggles upon the notion of a "sexual minority," they looked for broader and more inclusive mechanisms (Thayer 1997). One lesbian activist explained, for example,

> We realized that if we wanted to influence the population and promote respect and tolerance for sexual preference, we couldn't do it by staying in the ghetto. Gays and lesbians are not only those who are organized, but they are in all sectors; the majority are in the closet. So we broadened the groups we worked with. (Quoted in Thayer 1997: 394)

"Broadening the groups" with whom they worked not only involved reaching out to those in the closet, but it was in fact a distinct way of conceptualizing the constituency that sexuality activists hoped to reach. In and out of "the closet," activists aimed to spread their message to the larger Nicaraguan populace, not only to sexual minorities. Activists sought, in other words, to construct a political project where tolerance and respect for difference would be embraced by all Nicaraguans, not only those stigmatized by their sexual difference. This political orientation continues into the present in events such as the Sexuality Free from Prejudice events held in various Nicaraguan cities every June. Rather than designating these festivals as being about "gay pride," the dances, films, discussion panels, and other events are meant to encourage all Nicaraguans to embrace the ideal of tolerance of sexual difference. These tactics of inclusion demonstrate a marked difference from the identity-focused strategies of many lesbian and gay rights movements, both historic and contemporary, around the world (Adam, Duyvendak, and Krouwel 1999; Altman 2001; Donham 1998; Parker 1999; Warner 1999).[17]

Over the course of the 1980s, the Sandinista state reconfigured its relationship with sexuality activists from one of infiltration to one of cooperation. The organizing principles of sexuality activists appear to mirror the communitarian and socialist principles of Sandinismo, drawing more extensively from ideologies of "the people" than strict identity-based codes. Gay and lesbian activists from the United States and Europe brought their perspectives and political-organizing experiences with them, and exchanges between Nicaraguans and *sandalistas*[18] were a notable characteristic of the 1980s. The nascent struggle for sexuality rights cannot be fully understood without accounting for a larger international sphere. While contemporary identity politics in Nicaragua are linked to human rights groups, listserves, and international conferences and events such as the Gay Games, this information-economy form of politics had its early beginnings in, and is intimately tied to, Sandinismo.

Mothering the Nation: Neoliberalism and
Post-Sandinismo, 1990–2001

The electoral defeat of the Sandinistas in 1990 and the election of Violeta Barrios Chamorro signaled a profound change from state-based policies to a boom in civil society organizing. Chamorro was the first woman to be a head of state in Central America, but Chamorro's victory was not a boon to Nicaraguan women overall; nor was hers a feminist presidency. It was during Chamorro's reign that the Nicaraguan penal code was revised to persecute sexual minorities more rigorously, and services that were especially critical for women, like childcare and health services, were significantly reduced. However, in response to the stringent neoliberal reforms and more repressive antisodomy legislation of the Chamorro years, civil society organizations and activist groups were revitalized. Sandinista activists, now freed from political party obligations, and other gender and sexuality activists became motivated to struggle against the common enemy of the neoliberal and socially conservative state.

Chamorro's electoral victory in 1990 marked the end of revolution and the beginning of a series of socially conservative regimes. Comprising fourteen parties of disparate political orientation, Chamorro's Unified National Opposition (UNO) Party cannot be described as anything other than a concerted effort to disassemble Sandinista rule with the help of powerful allies.[19] Tens of millions of dollars were funneled to the UNO through the CIA and the National Endowment for Democracy (Walker and Armory 2000: 77). Backed by both U.S. and European interests, both financially and through written support—in the form of op-eds and advertisements in Nicaragua's national newspapers and the U.S. press—Chamorro's success was "a triumph for U.S. policy" (Prevost 1997: 3).[20]

Chamorro's regime demonstrated how sexuality and gender politics served as catalysts for debate, symbolic struggles, and a political reworking of "tradition." With a campaign that relied on antifeminist rhetoric, combined with socially conservative, antifeminist, and antigay legislation during her rule, Chamorro's presidency was more a "a perversion of feminism" than a feminist triumph (Lancaster 1992: 293). During both her campaign and as *la presidenta*, Chamorro was often clad in white, evoking both the Virgin Mary and a brand of feminine purity. Chamorro's political platform centered on the role she would play as a reconciling mother, loyal wife, and widow of the well-known Nicaraguan martyr Pedro Joaquín Chamorro.[21] In her own words, "I am not a feminist, nor do I wish to be one. I am a woman dedicated to my home, like Pedro taught me,"[22] Chamorro's objective to "mother" the nation was apparent in her promise to end the feud between what she called her "squabbling children," which were, of course, the two most prominent political parties themselves, the Liberals and the Sandinistas.[23] In her 1990 New Year's address to the nation, Chamorro promised that "the Nicaraguan family will return to unite with joy. . . . The people are going to choose our moral option and there will not be any more war nor misery nor hate because we will all be brothers."[24] While reconciliation and an end to the Contra war were certainly a high priority for most, if not every, Nicaraguan voting that year, Chamorro's attempts to be a "peacemaker" (Walker and Armory 2000: 78) can also be understood as an explicitly antifeminist stance as her rhetoric relied on traditional perceptions of women as mothering and naturally inclined to domestic pacification (Kampwirth 1998).

Chamorro's victory ultimately did little for women. Some of the first acts of her new government were to close the community-service, health, child-care, and welfare programs upon which many poor and middle-class women depended (Randall 1994: 222). Social services, health care, education, and housing facilities declined (Chavez Metoyer 1997: 115).[25] According to one Nicaraguan woman,

> the laws prevent us from deciding what to do with our own bodies with respect to how many children we want to have, and at the same time [the government] has canceled several maternal and child health programs and our children die from malnutrition and preventable and curable diseases. (Quoted in Wessel 1991: 542)

The social conservatism of the 1990s also changed sexuality and gender activism in Nicaragua. In response to the "common enemy" of the regime, new alliances were formed. Longtime activists and Sandinista women in particular found themselves freed from obligations to the party. With this, they channeled their efforts toward the "autonomous" women's movement, one that was also free from attachment to any political party, ideologically, financially, and in terms of leadership priorities.

The autonomous women's movement in Nicaragua, comprising NGOs, networks, and women's groups, adopted new strategies to enact gender politics, attempting to address the issues that the Sandinistas had not (Fernández Poncela 2001). This was the beginning of what many Nicaraguans refer to as the "boom" in civil society organizing, as opposed to state-based politics. These new political forms were spurred by increased democratization in Nicaragua as well as an influx of U.S. and European development funding for new social movements, providing some sexuality and gender activists with resources to respond to the conservative stance of the state. One commentator described the political depolarization and the relatively united front that followed.

> On the one hand, feminist movements everywhere [in the world] are gaining in strength. In Nicaragua, the fact that there's been a depolarization, politically speaking, has also opened up a space for this sort of struggle. And I think there's something else, which may be the most interesting reason of all: this government [UNO] and the political Right in general, have pushed a very conservative line on women. (Téllez quoted in Randall 1994: 259)

It was not long before the state's "very conservative line on women" would be crossed. In January 1991, eight hundred women gathered in Managua to convene a national forum on women's struggles under patriarchy. AMNLAE opposed the gathering as "inappropriate," but did ultimately send fifty delegates. The "52 Percent," as it was dubbed, marked a watershed moment in the development of the autonomous women's movement. Their resolutions included making violence against women a criminal offense; establishing networks to resolve problems rather than working under a verticalist, "umbrella organization" of the FSLN; commemorating International Women's Day; celebrating International Gay and Lesbian Day; and organizing a network of women journalists to found a radio station dedicated to women's issues (Agence France-Presse 1998). Lesbians at the Festival of the 52 Percent also held a public "coming out." Many participants formed alliances intent on critiquing and combating the erosion of sexuality and gender rights.

The implementation of a new penal code served as a key event to rally sexuality and gender activists around critical issues of privacy and individual rights. In 1992, the National Assembly revised the penal code and made Article 204, the "antisodomy law," more stringent. The new language was expansive, and the penalties were harsh.

> Anyone who induces, promotes, propagandizes or practices in scandalous form *concúbito* between persons of the same sex commits the crime of sodomy and shall incur one to three years imprisonment. (Bolt González 1995)[26]

Sandinista National Assembly members unanimously rejected the UNO-initiated reforms,[27] and sexuality and feminist activists launched a campaign emphasizing the reform's unconstitutionality and its violation of human rights. One lesbian and feminist leader explained,

> The lesbian and homosexual collectives have rejected Article 204 as unconstitutional and a violation of our human and civil rights. . . . The Nicaraguan Constitution protects all citizens from discrimination or persecution based on race, ideology, religion or sex and this latter point includes sexual preference. . . . The

ambiguous language of the article could be used against two same-sex people living together, were this deemed "scandalous" or to persecute journalists writing about homosexuals said to be "promoting" homosexuality. The public does not support Article 204. . . . It threatens everyone's right to keep the government out of the bedroom. (Hazel Fonseca quoted in Agence France Presse 1998)

The revised legislation not only took aim at sexual practices but could indict two people of the same sex living together "in sin." Importantly, the penal code came to implicate not only men who have sex with men, the usual province of antisodomy legislation, but women as well. The reach of the new code and its ambiguous language made it the kind of legal document that could easily be used as a tool of repression. In comparison to the dissolution of antisodomy laws in other Latin American states at the same time, Nicaragua's law was acutely retrograde.

Activists protested at the national and international levels, drawing from multiple layers of political pressure. They developed an educational outreach campaign regarding sexuality and sexual preference, produced flyers, and collected over four thousand signatures to support a presidential veto of the legislation (Bolt González 1995: 128). In addition to activating their base communities locally, activists contacted organizations such as Amnesty International and the International Gay and Lesbian Human Rights Coalition (IGLHRC), who readily condemned the legislation as antithetical to the human rights of all of Nicaragua's citizens. As a spokesperson for IGLHRC explained, "while other countries are making progress on human rights issues, the Nicaraguan government is moving backwards by making homosexual relations illegal. . . . [This is] Latin America's most repressive antisodomy legislation" (Panama 1992). The Nicaraguan Lesbian and Gay Pride Committee, along with twenty-five other organizations, hosted a series of events in order to campaign for a "Sexuality Free from Prejudice." Nonheterosexual and heterosexual people alike spoke at rallies to protest the reforms. Nevertheless, on July 8, 1992, President Chamorro ratified the series of reforms. On the heels of the signing, activists produced an analysis of Article 204 and protested at the National Assembly, and in 1994 an appeal was made to the Supreme Court—all efforts that were essentially ignored. Despite activists' protestations, the Chamorro government remained committed to state surveillance of sexuality.

While the antisodomy legislation was not overturned, the 1990s showed a fluorescence of gender and sexuality advocacy and the development of novel interventions to promote social change. In June 1991, a celebration for lesbians, homosexual men, and their allies was hosted publicly for the first time with films, music, and performances. Announcements were circulated around the country for this historic event.[28] While the Chamorro years showed a marked

Figure 10.3.   A protestor holds a sign declaring "No to Article 204," Nicaragua's anti-sodomy legislation. Source: author.

decline in social services for Nicaragua's underprivileged populations and a series of policy shifts that targeted the human rights and well-being of both women and sexual minorities, these years also marked the beginning of the autonomous women's movement and a public form of lesbian and gay activism. The Chamorro years proved but a prelude to the further economic restructuring, and also corruption, which would be the hallmarks of the Alemán era.

The election of Arnoldo Alemán in 1996 also resulted in new forms of social conservatism. Working closely with the United States Agency for International Development, the International Monetary Fund (IMF), and the World Bank, Alemán further downsized the public sector, restricted rural credit, privatized public-sector industries, and initiated legal changes that favored foreign investment. Alemán's policies reflected his neopopulist stance, one that relied on charisma, dramatic rhetoric, and garish public works projects—such as manicured traffic roundabouts and a towering statue of the Virgin Mary— aimed at impressing the impoverished masses. While reducing public expenditures and entreating the citizenry to *aguantar* (bear or suffer) neoliberal reforms, Alemán's personal fortune skyrocketed.

In addition to bloating his own bank accounts, Alemán developed new methods intended to inculcate the populace with a particular kind of sexual ethos. For example, new pedagogical materials were introduced into the public schools, venerating what the Nicaraguan Ministry of Education called

"Victorian morals." According to this state code of sexual ethics, "sex between people of the same sex, and sex with animals . . . are morally repugnant" (Ministerio de Educación y Deporte n.d.). By seamlessly equating bestiality with homosexuality, the Nicaraguan state furthered an agenda of moral engineering, marginalizing those who did not subscribe to heteronormativity.[29]

Re-Narrations

Development funding from northern nations, the ideals of committed activists, and the ongoing struggle for social equality continue to generate gender and sexuality activism in Nicaragua today. Prior to the 2001 presidential elections, I sat with a group of women activists as they lamented how they were constantly "putting out fires" on the political landscape. Their conversation then turned to the ongoing work of NGOs, advocacy groups, and women's health centers, which on a day-to-day basis provided for the needs of women and sexual minorities. Through consciousness-raising groups, education programs on HIV/AIDS, self-esteem workshops, and feminist and gay-positive TV and radio shows broadcast across Nicaragua, activists at various levels continue to make their messages heard. The Sexuality Free from Prejudice events continue to be held every June. Women protest on a weekly basis outside of Managua's megamall—a recent homage to neoliberal economics—where they demand the preservation of their reproductive rights.

Activism in Nicaragua continues, but it also continues to be threatened by the dire economic climate that is part and parcel of life in one of the Western Hemisphere's poorest nation-states. Miguel, whose sentiments began this chapter, spent many afternoons with me as we waited for the Managuan heat to subside, talking about remembered pasts and potential futures. His enthusiasm for the cause of sexuality rights in Nicaragua remains strong, though it weakens with each passing year that he is unable to find work in an economy that does not have nearly enough jobs for everyone, perhaps especially for sexual minorities. Miguel remains committed to the ideals of Sandinismo, citing the revolution, as so many others have, as perhaps the brightest moment in Nicaragua's history. From my perspective, Nicaragua continues to be a place where novel forms of advocacy are being created, though within a much transformed political and economic context.

Nicaragua's political cultures and advocacy strategies must be understood through the often imperial history between the United States and Nicaragua, as well as the sometimes allied relationship between Nicaraguan activists and supporters from the First World. Both of these relationships continue to impact both Nicaraguan state and civil society through the dissemination of monies and media images. Nicaragua's Sandinista era, its ideals, accomplishments, and unfulfilled promises, continue to engender unique forms of activism. Personal histories of militancy and social transformation compel many activists, who continue to be inspired by the passions and ideals of the revolutionary era. Nicaraguan activists articulate new demands linked to U.S. and European development projects, international human rights organizations, and identity-politics movements on a global scale. However, these seemingly new forms of politics should not be seen as wholly separate from the Sandinista revolution but, rather, as a novel articulation of many shared principles, even if the terms—the discourses and goals—are different. Advocates for sexuality and gender rights in contemporary Nicaragua draw from multiple sources, ranging from local Nicaraguan political histories to current transnational debates.

Political struggles based on gender and sexuality have been a long time in the making. Their past and their future must be seen within a larger framework that includes invasive politics and cultural hegemonies from the North, along with the political dissent that has characterized Nicaragua since colonialism. With this long view of history, it is clear that Nicaragua's status as "post" revolutionary is a matter of perspective. Particular politicized subjects—peasant revolutionaries at the beginning of the twentieth century, Marxist university students in the 1960s, and feminists in the 1990s—have all encountered tensions and triumphs in their struggles to build political movements. Likewise, the future of gender and sexuality activism in Nicaragua will continue to make use of the past in order to inform the present, drawing from global contexts in order to transform and resituate local meanings.

Notes

1. All names in this chapter have been changed to protect the identity of interviewees.

2. Nicaragua is a party to the Convention on the Elimination of All Forms of Discrimination against Women (CEDAW) and sent delegates to the United Nations fourth global conference on the status of women and children and the accompanying nongovernmental organization (NGO) conference in 1995. In contemporary Nicaragua, many activist materials and publications (such as *La Boletina* published by the feminist NGO *Puntos de Encuentro*) feature articles and points of action based on human rights principles. The Nicaraguan government has also initiated a federal office to monitor human rights offenses in that country, in addition to NGOs that provide legal counsel on human rights–related matters. Combined, the proliferation of human rights organizations, activism, and discourses suggests that many Nicaraguan activists and others have come to embrace human rights broadly as a basis for their political goals.

3. The term *gay* has not, until very recently by some, been widely used by Nicaraguans. I use the terms *homosexual* and *lesbian* to describe men and women who have sexual and affective relationships with people of the same sex, either exclusively or occasionally. *Lesbian* and *homosexual* are the recognized, nonderogatory terms, and my use of them here follows the anthropological convention of preserving local categories in cultural contexts. It is also important to point out that in Nicaragua, as in much of Latin America, there is often a distinction made between the "passive" and "active" partner in male/male sexual encounters. Historically, in Nicaragua, the active, or "mas-

culine," partner has not been stigmatized by his role in homosexual sex, while the passive, or "receiving," partner is marked as a *cochón* (loosely translated as "fag"). For a discussion of how varying degrees of stigma are apportioned and how they impact gender roles in Nicaragua, see Roger Lancaster, *Life Is Hard: Machismo, Danger, and the Intimacy of Power in Nicaragua* (1992).

4. There have likely always been women and men who have had affective, emotional, and/or sexual relationships with others of their same sex in Nicaragua, though they did not live under the mantle "lesbian," "homosexual," or "gay." The key here is that "tradition" is often counterposed against "modernity," particularly in discussions of sexuality, where morality and values often figure prominently.

5. The "spin" of the revolution, in other words, continues to exist, as do the transnational connections and allies that have come in the wake of revolution. In the minds of many Nicaraguans, the revolution continues to survive despite its failures and truncated history—as either nostalgic triumph or, conversely, a threat to the capitalist world order and the "new" Nicaragua and its neoliberal economic demands. In the speeches of activists and statesmen and in the policy decisions of lawmakers, the revolution continues to fuel the rhetoric of the nation at various levels, just as it continues to be a signature moment in Nicaragua's place in the world order. Although Nicaragua can no longer boast a socialist revolution (one of very few in the Americas), the nation-state continues, in the minds of many, to be a symbol of social justice rather than simply another underdeveloped Third World nation at the mercy of the IMF, World Bank, and United States. The continued popularity of former president Daniel Ortega and his significant electoral strength in consecutive elections (from 1990 to 2006) attest to the continued resonance of Sandinismo in Nicaragua.

6. The history and development of the FSLN is complex. It was founded in July 1961 by Carlos Fonseca, Tomás Borge, and Silvio Mayorga. In the ensuing months, other young would-be revolutionaries became involved, many of whom were students disenchanted with Nicaragua's more traditional Socialist Left. Fonseca was considered to be the primary architect of *Sandinismo* as he recrafted Sandino's original discourse for a new generation of revolutionaries (Palmer 1988). Mayorga was killed in an early guerilla battle in 1967. Fonseca was also killed in action in 1976; the story of his life and details of the early years of the FSLN are captured in Matilde Zimmerman's *Sandinista: Carlos Fonseca and the Nicaraguan Revolution* (2000). The FSLN underwent transformations and internal debates around military strategies and ideological priorities before successfully launching the cross-class and rural-urban coalition necessary to overthrow the entrenched dictatorship. A number of books examine the evolution of Sandinismo over time, from both analytic and first-person perspectives. These include Les W. Field's *The Grimace of Macho Ratón: Artisans, Identity and Nation in Late-Twentieth-Century Western Nicaragua* (1999), Peter Rossett and John Vandermeer's *The Nicaragua Reader: Documents of a Revolution under Fire*; Salman Rushdie's *The Jaguar Smile: A Nicaraguan Journey*; Margaret Randall's *Sandino's Daughters: Testimonies of Nicaraguan Women in Struggle* (1981); Rose J. Spalding's *The Political Economy of Revolutionary Nicaragua*; Thomas Walker's *Nicaragua: The Land of Sandino*; Katherine Hoyt's *The Many Faces of Sandinista Democracy*, and Roger N. Lancaster's *Thanks to God and the Revolution: Popular Religion and Class Consciousness in the New Nicaragua* (1988).

7. Prior to the revolution in July 1979, the Sandinistas had developed an organization to encourage women to participate in the struggle against the Somoza regime and denounce the human rights abuses of the administration. The Association of Women Confronting the National Problem (AMPRONAC) was founded in 1977 by the FSLN and began as a group of sixty women. By the time of the insurrection, its numbers had grown to more than eight thousand. AMPRONAC's strategies included demonstration, petitioning, occupation of churches, conveying messages from political prisoners to their families, and demanding that the government reveal the locations of those who had been "disappeared" through political repression.

8. Daniel Ortega echoed this sentiment at Managua's "Women and Law Conference" in 1988 when, in response to a question from a Costa Rican delegate about whether Nicaragua had a

policy of discrimination or denial of human rights in regard to homosexuals, Ortega replied, simply, no.

9. In his Presidential Address to a Joint Session of Congress, President Reagan opined, "The government of Nicaragua has treated us as an enemy. . . . [The minister of defense has] declared Marxism-Leninism [as a] guide. . . . Nicaragua's dictatorial junta . . . [e]ven worse than its predecessor . . . is helping Cuba and the Soviets to destabilize our hemisphere." For an extended excerpt of Reagan's speech, see Peter Rosset and John Vandermeer (1986: 18–22).

10. Operating out of military camps in Honduras, the Contra campaign of low-intensity warfare sought to destabilize the revolutionary regime by attacking soft targets, such as schools, health centers, and agricultural cooperatives sponsored by the FSLN. Earlier in the conflict, Contra propaganda campaigns intended to strengthen civilian opposition to the FSLN had the opposite of their intended effect and instead bolstered popular support for the revolution.

11. The neighboring countries of Mexico, Venezuela, Colombia, Panama, and Costa Rica, in support of Nicaragua, formed the "Contadora Group" in order to devise a peace plan. They were concerned with the destabilization of the region and U.S. hegemony and intervention. The Esquipulas Peace Accord was signed in August 1987 and signaled the military and diplomatic defeat of the Contras. However, Contra funding continued, as did their attacks. In 1988, Contra leaders and FSLN representatives agreed to sign the Sapoa Accord.

12. The Sandinista era also hosted a cultural renaissance, in particular among women, born of Nicaragua's longstanding poetic tradition. Literature and poetry by Nicaraguan women, drawing from their revolutionary experiences and their gendered perspectives, gained global popularity in the 1980s, and some Nicaraguan women authors continue to be read around the world. See for example, Gioconda Belli, *The Inhabited Woman* (1993) [*La Mujer Habitada* (1989)] and *The Country under My Skin: A Memoir of Love and War* (2002) and Daisy Zamora's book of poetry, *Riverbed of Memory* (1992).

13. During our interview, Marco, one of the members of the group originally rounded up by Sandinista State Security, explained that participants were "interrogated" and "treated badly." Others with whom I have spoken were surprised at how well they were treated by State Security, explaining that they were set free after only a few hours of discussion.

14. There were no known cases of AIDS in Nicaragua at this time. However, by January 1989, three deaths from AIDS and sixteen cases of HIV had been reported.

15. If the Nicaraguan state was less than exemplary in allowing political dissent of sexual minorities within its ranks, Nicaraguan officials' response to the threat of AIDS stands in stark contrast to the silence surrounding the epidemic in the United States in the 1980s.

16. Cuba purged homosexuals in the mid-1960s on the grounds that their sexuality was a symptom of bourgeois decadence (Young, cited in Collinson [1990: 24]). Further, early AIDS policy in Cuba mandated that those infected with HIV be quarantined. Policies of homosexual exclusion and persecution in revolutionary Cuba have been critiqued by the international community, often by North American lesbian and gay activists. Ian Lumsden (1996) argues that Cuban policies toward homosexuals must be understood within the context of colonialism and U.S. hemispheric domination. In his analysis of Cuban homosexuality from the sixteenth century to the present, Lumsden concludes that the potential for gay liberation in Cuba is conditioned by Cuba's economic marginality (especially after the collapse of the Soviet Union and continuing U.S. trade embargo) and location in a "broad political and historical context" (Lumsden 1996: xxi). Sandinista Nicaragua, in contrast, had no official policies of homosexual repression.

17. While identity-focused strategies have been productive and therefore have proliferated as political tactics around the world, a minoritizing identity is not the only rubric under which sexuality struggles operate. As Roger Lancaster points out for the United States, there is often a productive tension between two schools of thought: a "minoritizing" or "rights-oriented" approach that favors understanding homosexuality as innate/inborn versus a "universalist" or "liberation-

oriented" approach that views same-sex desires as part of a continuum of human desire—a kind of "everyone is a little bit gay" approach that effectively broadens homosexuality and implicates a broader swath of self-interest for the sexual politics at hand (Lacaster 2003: 274–80).

18. Les W. Field describes that "thousands of foreigners, especially North Americans and Western Europeans, flocked to Nicaragua following the triumph of the Sandinista Front on July 19, 1979, [and these] foreigners were officially accorded a semi-insider status as *internacionalistas* [foreigners in solidarity with the revolutionary process]" (Field 1999: 12). These international allies were also sometimes referred to themselves as "sandalistas."

19. Indeed, the only point of agreement between the various constituencies of the UNO was a desire to defeat the FSLN. The counterinsurgency war was escalated prior to the election, and Chamorro received 55 percent of the vote (Walker 2000).

20. Or, in the words of a State Department official during the first Bush administration, Chamorro's victory would suggest the successful "micromanag[ing of] the opposition" (*Time* 1990).

21. Violeta Barrios Chamorro is the widow of Pedro Joaquín Chamorro, who, during the Somoza dictatorship, was the editor of *La Prensa*. It was, according to many observers, Pedro Joaquín Chamorro's assassination that sparked the coalition rebellion required for the success of the Sandinista Revolution. In this way, Chamorro's story is akin to that of Eva Perón in Argentina, where a politically powerful husband provides the foundation for his wife's entry into public office.

22. Scarlet Cuadra, "Electorado Femenino por la Revolución," *Barricada* (Managua, January 13, 1990.

23. Chamorro promised reconciliation in the political sphere, an end to the war, and a "normalization" of relations with the United States. The war did end, as Chamorro's presidency had U.S. support. Her regime saw an increase in neoliberal economic reforms and external debt-management schemes. Increased economic pressures and emotional strains levied a toll on many women, especially those who were already economically marginalized. However, Chamorro's good relationship with the United States also resulted in increased development funding to the country.

24. *La Prensa* (Managua), January 5, 1990.

25. The U.S. Congress approved a $300 million aid package following Chamorro's victory. Her administration, however, did not continue to have the unqualified "blessings" of the United States. The UNO, a multiparty coalition, fractured over property rights. Chamorro refused to displace 120,000 peasant families who were occupying land that the *Frente* had confiscated. Senator Jesse Helms (R-NC), spearheaded the effort in the U.S. Congress to return confiscated property to U.S. citizens, viewing Nicaraguan property rights as a precedent for a post-Castro Cuba. Conflicts over property resulted in temporary aid freezes during the presidentisl administrations of both the first Bush and Clinton.

26. The complete wording of the code is as follows: "Comete delito de sodomía el que induzca, promueva, propagandice o practique en forma escandalosa el concúbito entre personas del mismo sexo. Sufrirá la pena de uno a tres años de prisión. Cuando uno de los que lo practican, aún en privado tuviere sobre el otro poder disciplinario o de mando, como ascendiente, guardador, maestro, jefe, guardian, o en cualquier otro concepto que implique influencia de autoridad o de dirección moral, se le aplicará la pena de la seducción ilegítima, como único responsable." The word *concúbito* is ambiguous in this context. It likely derives from *concubinato*, which literally means "living together," but more accurately translates to "living in sin," as it is associated with concubinage or extramarital sexual relationships. In the context of a legal document, this word choice is particularly ambiguous, suggesting sexual relations and the sharing of living space (between two people of the same sex and presumably thought to be homosexual) and "sodomy."

27. For a description of the assembly's voting process and the issues raised, see the interview with Doris Tijerino in Randall (1994: 226–27).

28. The first official display of public lesbian and gay identity, an activist protest rather than the celebratory format of the 1991 events, was in 1989 when a group of approximately thirty lesbian and gay Nicaraguans wore black T-shirts emblazoned with pink triangles to the anniversary of the revolution celebration held in Managua's Plaza of the Revolution.

29. The Alemán regime's particular rendering of Victorian "morality" is bedfellow to a growing social conservatism in Nicaraguan politics. Founded, on the one hand, on economic restructuring and neoliberal reforms, the conservative tract that characterized Nicaragua throughout the 1990s has been fed by transnational religious movements and a related backlash against reproductive rights. The nation's tide of moral engineering has been sustained by the conservatism of the national Catholic Church, led by Cardinal Obando y Bravo, as well as wider global initiatives by both Catholic and Protestant Church groups. Alemán's discriminatory pedagogy is part of a wider swath of moral engineering that has taken root in Nicaragua and elsewhere, making the political cultures in Nicaragua far from pristine, isolated, or discrete.

Works Cited

Adam, Barry D. 1993. In Nicaragua: Homosexuality without a Gay World. *Journal of Homosexuality* 24:171–81.

———. 1989. Pasivos y Activos en Nicaragua: Homosexuality without a Gay World. *Out/Look* (winter): 74–82.

Adam, Barry D., Jan Willem Duyvendak, and André Krouwel, eds. 1999. *The Global Emergence of Gay and Lesbian Politics: National Imprints of a Worldwide Movement.* Philadelphia: Temple University Press.

Agence France-Presse. 1998. Nicaragua: Forum on Women's Issues, at http://ladb.unm.edu/cgibin/SFgate (accessed October 12, 1998).

Ahmend An-Na'Im, Abdullah, ed. 1992. *Human Rights in Cross cultural Perspectives: A Quest for Consensus.* Philadelphia: University of Pennsylvania Press.

Altman, Dennis. 2001. *Global Sex.* Chicago: University of Chicago Press.

Americas Watch Committee. 1985. Human Rights in Nicaragua: Reagan, Rhetoric, and Reality. In *Nicaragua, Unfinished Revolution: The New Nicaragua Reader*, ed. P. Rosset and J. Vandermeer. New York: Grove Press.

Arguelles, Lourdes, and B. Ruby Rich. 1984. Homosexuality, Homophobia, and Revolution: Notes toward an Understanding of the Cuban Lesbian and Gay Male Experience, Part 1. *Signs* 9 (4): 683–99.

Babb, Florence. 2001. *After Revolution: Mapping Gender and Cultural Politics in Neoliberal Nicaragua.* Austin: University of Texas Press.

Bayard de Volo, Lorraine. 2001. *Mothers of Heroes and Martyrs—Gender Identity Politics in Nicaragua, 1979–1999.* Baltimore: Johns Hopkins University Press.

Belli, Gioconda. 2002. *The Country under My Skin: A Memoir of Love and War*, trans. Kristin Cordero. New York: Knopf.

Bolt González, Maria. 1995. Nicaragua. In *Unspoken Rules: Sexual Orientation and Women's Human rights*, ed. R. Rosenbloom. London: Cassell.

Bourgois, Phillipe. 1981. Class, Ethnicity, and the State among the Miskitu Amerindians of Northeastern Nicaragua. *Latin American Perspectives* 8 (2): 22–39.

Bretlinger, John. 1995. *The Best of What We Are: Reflections on the Nicaraguan Revolution.* Amherst: University of Massachusetts Press.

Carrillo, Héctor. 2002. *The Night Is Young: Sexuality in Mexico in the Time of AIDS.* Chicago: University of Chicago Press.

Chauncey, George. 1994. *Gay New York: Gender, Urban Culture, and the Making of the Gay Male World, 1890–1940*. New York: Basic Books.

Chavez Metoyer, Cynthia. 1997. Nicaragua's Transition of State Power: Through Feminist Lenses. In *The Undermining of the Sandinista Revolution*, ed. Gary Prevost and Harry E. Vanden. New York: St. Martins.

Chinchilla, Norma. 1994. Feminism, Revolution and Democratic Transitions in Nicaragua. In *The Women's Movement in Latin America*, ed. Jane Jaquette, 177–97, 2nd ed. Boulder, CO: Westview Press.

———. 1990. Revolutionary Popular Feminism in Nicaragua: Articulating Class, Gender and National Sovereignty. *Gender and Society* 4 (September): 370–97.

Chuchryk, Patricia. 1991. Women in the Revolution. In *Revolution and Counterrevolution in Nicaragua*, ed. Thomas Walker. Boulder, CO: Westview.

Collinson, Helen. 1990. *Women and Revolution*. London: Zed Books.

D'Emilio, John, and Estelle B. Freedman. 1997. *Intimate Matters: A History of Sexuality in America*. Chicago: University of Chicago Press.

Donham, Donald D. 1998. Freeing South Africa: The "Modernization" of Male-Male Sexuality in Soweto. *Cultural Anthropology* 13 (1): 3–21.

Fernández Poncela, Anna M. 2001. *Mujeres, revolución y cambio cultural: transformaciones sociales versus modelos culturales persistentes*. Barcelona: Anthropos Research & Publications.

Field, Les W. 1999. *The Grimace of Macho Ratón: Artisans, Identity and Nation in Late-Twentieth-Century Western Nicaragua*. Durham, NC: Duke University Press.

González, Victoria. 2001. Somocista Women, Right-Wing Politics, and Feminism in Nicaragua, 1936–1979. In *Radical Women in Latin America: Left and Right*, ed. Victoria González and Karen Kampwirth. University Park: Pennsylvania State University Press.

Gould, Jeffrey L. 1990. *To Lead as Equals: Rural Protest and Political Consciousness in Chinandega, Nicaragua, 1912–1979*. Chapel Hill: University of North Carolina Press.

———. 1998. *To Die in This Way: Nicaraguan Indians and the Myth of Mestizaje, 1880–1965*. Durham, NC: Duke University Press.

Gutmann, Matthew. 1996. *The Meanings of Macho: Being a Man in Mexico City*. Berkeley: University of California Press.

Hale, Charles. 1996. *Resistance and Contradiction: Miskitu Indians and the Nicaraguan State, 1894–1987*. Palo Alto, CA: Stanford University Press.

Howe, A. Cymene. 2003. Strategizing Sexualities, Re-imagining Gender, and Televisionary Tactics: The Cultural Politics of Social Struggle in Neoliberal Nicaragua. PhD diss., Department of Anthropology, University of New Mexico.

Kaiser, Charles. 1998. *The Gay Metropolis*. New York: Harvest Books.

Kampwirth, Karen. 1998. Feminism, Antifeminism, and Electoral Politics in Postwar Nicaragua and El Salvador. *Political Science Quarterly* 13 (2): 259–80.

———. 1996. Confronting Adversity with Experience: The Emergence of Feminism in Nicaragua. *Social Politics* (summer–fall): 136–58.

Kennedy, Elizabeth Lapovsky, and Madeline D. Davis. 1994. *Boots of Leather, Slippers of Gold: The History of a Lesbian Community*. New York: Penguin Books.

Lancaster, Roger. 2003. *The Trouble with Nature: Sex in Science and Popular Culture*. Berkeley: University of California Press.

———. 1992. *Life Is Hard: Machismo, Danger, and the Intimacy of Power in Nicaragua*. Berkeley: University of California Press.

———. 1988. *Thanks to God and the Revolution: Popular Religion and Class Consciousness in the New Nicaragua*. New York: Columbia University Press.

LeVine, Sarah. 1993. *Dolor y Alegría: Women and Social Change in Urban Mexico*. Madison: University of Wisconsin Press.

Lumsden, Ian. 1996. *Machos, Maricones, and Gays: Cuba and Homosexuality.* Philadelphia: Temple University Press.

Molyneux, Maxine. 1985. Mobilization without Emancipation? Women's Interests, the State, and Revolution in Nicaragua. *Feminist Studies* 11 (summer 1985): 227–54.

Padilla, Martha Luz, Clara Murguialday, and Ana Criquillon. 1987. Impact of the Sandinista Agrarian Reform on Rural Women's Subordination. In *Rural Women and State Policy: Feminist Perspectives on Latin American Agricultural Development,* ed. Carmen Diana Deere and Magdalena León, 124–41. Boulder, CO: Westview Press.

Palmer, Steven. 1988. Carlos Fonseca and the Construction of Sandinismo in Nicaragua. *Latin American Research Review* 23 (1) (1988): 92–121.

Panama. 1992. Nicaragua: Controversial Reforms to Penal Code Ratified by President, at http://ladb.unm.edu/cgi-binSFgate (accessed October 12, 1998).

Parker, Richard. 1999. *Beneath the Equator: Cultures of Desire, Male Homosexuality, and Emerging Gay Communities in Brazil.* New York: Routledge.

Peters, Julie Stone, and Andrea Wolper, eds. 1995. *Women's Rights, Human Rights: International Feminist Perspectives.* New York: Routledge.

Prevost, Gary, and Harry E. Vanden, eds. 1997. *The Undermining of the Sandinista Revolution.* New York: St. Martin's Press.

Randall, Margaret. 1993. To Change Our Own Reality and the World: A Conversation with Lesbians in Nicaragua. *Signs* 18 (4): 907–24.

———. 1994. *Sandino's Daughters Revisited: Feminism in Nicaragua.* New Brunswick, NJ: Rutgers University Press.

Randall, Margaret, and Lynda Yang. 1981. *Sandino's Daughters: Testimonies of Nicaraguan Women in Struggle.* Vancouver, BC: New Star Books.

Rich, B. Ruby, and Lourdes Arguelles. 1985. Homosexuality, Homophobia, and Revolution: Notes toward an Understanding of the Cuban Lesbian and Gay Male Experience, Part II. *Signs* 11 (1): 120–36.

Rosset, Peter, and John Vandermeer, eds. 1986. *Nicaragua, Unfinished Revolution: The New Nicaragua Reader.* New York: Grove Press.

Sandinista de Liberación Nacional. 1998. Nicaragua: Resignations Exacerbate Crisis in the *Frente,* at http://ladb.unm.edu/ (accessed October 12, 1998).

Schreiber, Tatiana, and Lynn Stephen. 1989. AIDS education—Nicaraguan Style. *Out/Look* (winter): 78–80.

Stahler-Sholk, Richard. 1995. Sandinista Social and Economic Policy: The Mixed Blessings of Hindsight. *Latin American Research Review* 30 (2): 245–69.

Steiner, Henry J., and Philip Alston. 1996. *International Human Rights in Context: Law, Politics, Morals.* Oxford: Clarendon Press.

Thayer, Millie. 1997. Identity, Revolution and Democracy: Lesbian Movements in Central America. *Social Problems* 44 (3): 386–406.

Trouillot, Michel Rolph. 1995. *Silencing the Past: Power and the Production of History.* Boston: Beacon Press.

Walker, Thomas W. 2000. Nicaragua: Transition through Revolution. In *Repression, Resistance, and Democratic Transition in Central America,* ed. Thomas W. Walker and Ariel C. Armony, 67–99. Wilmington, DE: Scholarly Resources.

Warner, Michael. 1999. *The Trouble with Normal: Sex, Politics, and the Ethics of Queer Life.* New York: Free Press.

Wessel, Lois. 1991. Reproductive Rights in Nicaragua: From the Sandinistas to the Government of Violeta Chamorro. *Feminist Studies* 17 (3): 537–45.

Zimmerman, Matilde. 2000. *Sandinista: Carlos Fonseca and the Nicaraguan Revolution.* Durham, NC: Duke University Press.

11

Gendering the Space of Death: Memory, Democratization, and the Domestic

Lessie Jo Frazier

CONTESTS FOR POLITICAL POWER in transitions to democracy entail struggles over memory, the interpretive power to define the relationship between present and past. My own intervention in that contested field begins with my fieldwork in the gendered politics of the therapeutic project undertaken by the Chilean postdictatorship government to treat and then reintegrate survivors of state violence. In their efforts to contain the ramifications of terror, the mental-health services of the Chilean postdictatorship state inadvertently feminized their patients. In addition, by the time of the second civilian presidency in 1994, the entire mental-health system had been gendered, a process that resulted in the privileging of women and children as nonpolitical victims. This left intact the gendered politics of the military regime, a politics premised upon the supposed need to discipline and domesticate the unruly national body through a process of depoliticization. In transitions to democracy, failure to recognize what Michael Taussig has called the "space of death," the sphere of interaction between the oppressor and the oppressed where the making and unmaking of order takes place, means that political efforts to dissipate this space of death may, even inadvertently, allow it further to permeate and structure civil society.[1] Memory becomes important to this process as it can serve both as the means through which the space of death gets perpetuated and as a possible tool for dismantling that space.

The concept of the space of death emphasizes that the powerful experience of torture and repression is shared between the violator and the violated, creating a perverse kind of intimacy. It is referred to as death because it is a kind of social death that can include the removal of the person from his or her social context, the attempt to dismantle his or her sense of personhood, the dismantling and reshaping of subjectivity, and the threat of complete annihilation. In authoritarian regimes of state terror, the space of death is a patriarchal, bourgeois, and domestic space. By not interrogating the space of death brought into being during the period of state terror, postdictatorship societies cannot dismantle the legacies of authoritarian rule, including the ongoing subterranean power of military sectors and their backers. One of these legacies has been the widespread absorption of militaries' rhetoric of antipolitics such that being political continues to be considered suspect and dirty. If being a political actor is bad, then what hope is there for building viable democracies where people can exercise citizenship, especially in societies in which the tortured and torturers share the same streets? Civilian government policies that pretend that this is not an issue, or at best hope to avoid it or diffuse the question by promoting "reconciliation," underestimate the power of that prior moment to continue to shape political and social dynamics.

Gender can become a key for untangling this bind, because paying attention to both the domestic sphere and the gendering of agency and of political rhetorics enables us to see the ways in which authoritarianism fundamentally penetrated and pervaded daily life and continues to do so. During the military dictatorship, feminist activists in Chile had argued that authoritarianism in the public sphere was linked to that in the private. For example, the group Women for Life (Mujeres por la Vida) took to the streets demanding democracy in the street and in the home. These activists increasingly recognized a connection between military rule and the struggle over patrimony, or the rule of the father. In doing so, they drew on the work of fellow Chilean feminist Julieta Kirkwood, who developed a theory of domestic authoritarianism in which she insightfully pointed to the ways in which the ideologies of the left, center, and right confined women to the sphere of the "domestic private" and reduced the "feminine problem" to "the dispute over the defense of the family (Chilean or proletarian)." For Kirkwood and others, these ideologies shared the fact that they left unmentioned all that the delimiting of the "feminine problem" to the private sphere engendered and perpetuated, especially "hierarchical interior networks that included rigid and authoritarian forms of discipline."[2] Under the military, this feature of Chilean political culture was used to the military's advantage; Kirkwood argued that in order to impose its authoritarianism, the military not only called upon the power of the armed forces but also on the brutal "underlying authoritarianism in civil society," resulting in the "total imposition of a patrimonialist State."[3] For Kirkwood, then, authoritarianism and its violent methods could not be understood without a gendered theory of politics. Kirkwood saw the domestic and the public as mutually constituting realms and realized that fighting an authoritarian state requires the dismantling of authoritarian structures across those spaces.

In this chapter, I argue that due to the degree to which this work of dismantling authoritarian structures has yet to take place in Chile's regime transition from military to civilian rule, the space of death continues to permeate social relations at all levels. This process occurred not only in Chile but also in other South American countries, including Argentina, Uruguay, and Brazil. Though the oppressions in each country reflected specific national dynamics, they shared common ideological frameworks, most significantly, ideas about ways to combat what the militaries perceived to be threats to national security. As the space of death also results in the production of perverted, or monstrously embodied, subjectivities, the dominant narrow definition of democracy has limited the range of possibilities for political subjectivity in contemporary Chile. To better understand the Chilean case, I draw on the work of Argentine author Luisa Valenzuela, who compellingly analyzes the intertwining of domestic and state violence under military rule. I focus on her short story *Other Weapons* (1985),[4] telling of the moment of recognition, of knowledge, in the space of death as generating possibilities for new subjectivities.

Blood and Memory: State Terror as Transformative Violence under Military Rule

In order to understand the predicament of postdictatorship societies, we must first specify the space of death as constituted under military rule. South American military regimes of the 1970s and 1980s justified their brutal dictatorships with a rhetoric imbued with metaphors of the body; military metaphors of disease depicted monstrous bodies, contaminated by political ideology, attacking the integrity of the national body defended only by the blood of its soldiers:

> In our reflections, we must remember our dead, because the blood shed here has no price; it is because of the memory of this loss that we will never accept anything that will ruin or pervert the military victory or make us forget its clear and tremendous cost.[5]

In this 1980 speech, Argentine general Leopoldo Galtieri summoned the specter of the soldier, a largely mythological figure of sacrifice given the minimal scale of the opposition by armed guerrilla movements, martyred for *his* nation. The general conveyed a specifically gendered sense of ownership and gaze onto the nation, a totalizing masculinist gaze. The mythical blood spilled "here" demarcated the space of the nation, displacing from national memory the bodies of the disappeared and tortured civilians; such delimiting of who belongs and who does not, usually through gendered and racialized categories, has been central to the process of nation making.[6] What the general promises never to forget is a reign of state terror under military rule in Argentina lasting from 1976 until 1983; in Chile, a similar regime existed from 1973 until 1990.

Military regimes operated under the rubric of "National Security Doctrine," a cold war strategy to fight communist subversion and to assert order within the space of the nation that prescribed the kidnapping, detention, torture, exile, execution, and disappearance of thousands of citizens, often youths, union leaders, and most other organized sectors of society. Under this doctrine, anyone involved in politics became suspect, and political practice was cast as inherently dangerous, even perverting to the nation, as expressed by the general in the passage above. Militaries claimed to defend the nation as its apolitical guardians who followed National Security Doctrine in a spatially organized process of identifying, locating, and eradicating those it defined as the national enemy. Moreover, the doctrine became a blueprint to carve up national landscapes into administrative police-state units as the military restructured national economies around neoliberal, free market principles, inscribing in the memory of both the subjugated and the supportive populace a particular landscape of state terror glorifying militarism, the nation, and the authoritarian state. Paramilitary and military personnel were anointed the new vanguards of the homeland and indoctrinated into the role of torturer. The act of torture instantiated a cult of masculinity, and security personnel who refused to torture were themselves interrogated about their (homo)sexuality and allegiance to the fatherland.[7] Military regimes engaged and maintained a specific construction of the relationship between heterosexual masculinity and violence premised upon and supporting the primacy of patrimony, wherein the promise of security of the house and security of the nation were mutually constituted.

Under National Security Doctrine, the military saw the nation-state as an organism vulnerable to contamination by subversive forces depicted as monstrous, diseased bodies, as Argentine foreign minister Admiral César Guzetti elaborated in August 1976:

> When the social body of the country has been contaminated by a disease that corrodes its entrails, it forms antibodies. These antibodies cannot be considered in the same way as microbes. As the government controls and destroys the guerrilla, the action of the antibody will disappear, as is already happening. It is only a natural reaction to a sick body.[8]

The nation as body, the military as antibody, and the guerrilla as a diseased, monstrous body: these comprised the organizing metaphors of National Security Doctrine. Purging the subversive disease from the national body became the overriding task, worth the cost of civilian lives. A former vicar of the Argentine Army, Monseñor Victorio Bonamin had a revealing method for healing the national body: "When blood spills there is redemption; God is redeeming, through the Argentine Army, the Argentine nation."[9] Both the contaminated and the innocent blood of the nation would be let to cleanse the body of the nation. For the generals, blood is memory, fluid and permeating, let to remember and let to forget. Through the flow of national blood as memory, redemption would reach across the *patria* (fatherland), the national patrimony encompassing the feminized space of the motherland as culture, affect, and social reproduction, together with more masculine realms of political institutions, economic resources, and the frontiers to be defended from encroachment. Thus, the patria served as a place encompassing state and civil society, *la plaza mayor* (the principle square and center of governmental power) and *la casa* (the house), in which this nationalist redemption took place.

In subsuming the realm of the public, militaries relegated collective memory to private spaces where it "fed fear."[10] The space of death transcended public/private dichotomies, yet, at the same time, allowed the domestic to be a refuge from repression and a sanctuary for resistant memory, thus placing and displacing the space of death. While we cannot "know" the space of death because it is social death, a gendered analysis of the shape of the space of death reveals the ways in which military investment in the defense of national patrimony transcended boundaries of public and private interests and justified violent incursions into the domestic for the forging and policing of particular kinds of subjectivities.

If the architects of National Security Doctrine located the security of the home as a foundational justification, then by depicting the space of death as a domestic space, Luisa Valenzuela's short story domesticates the Dirty War, pushing back at prevailing politics by concealing the dangerous political story beneath the sexualized plot. In this sense, the tale is the inverse of a more standard narrative in which political intrigue alludes to illicit sexual encounters, an ironic inversion of forbidden spaces within the narrative. It depicts the historical irony of the military regime's rhetoric about the sacredness of the realm of the family juxtaposed against its own violation of that sanctum through the invasion and appropriation of commonplace spaces and objects of the home. Feminist analyses of the domestic romance can provide invaluable insight into the gendered dimensions of state violence because the domestic romance and the political history of the nation in Latin America have been inextricably linked in an "erotics of politics."[11] As we shall see, *Other Weapons* can be read as mocking dreams of domestic and national bliss as it moves beyond depicting the domestic as solely a space for the enactment of political allegory to show the ways in which national and domestic spaces are mutually constituted. Erotic scenes approximate the place of the military as a locus for desire in Argentine and Chilean political cultures (a complex of sectors: hegemonic, counterhegemonic, nominally apolitical), a locus of desire that human rights activists continue to struggle to decenter. In relocating the terrain of the political, a story of extreme state violence can reveal the ubiquitous quotidian nature of domestic violence against women as state terror magnifies patriarchal despotism in contemporary societies, requiring us analytically to break down the oppositions of domestic and state terror in order to recognize the ways in which state terror perpetuated "microdespotisms."[12]

To think further about the domestication of state violence, Chile's mode of transition to democracy provides a particularly interesting case in that the inadvertent gendering of reparations projects reinforced the intertwined dynamic of domestic violence and state terror. Politicians leading the constrained transitions to civilian rule in the late 1980s and 1990s trod a narrow path between the human rights movements' outrage and desire to prosecute abuses, on the one hand, and the militaries' ongoing ability to forestall and circumvent such attempts forcefully, on the other. Negotiating these conflicting interests to forge a space for civil society, civilian leaders tried to reinscribe boundaries of public and private by circumscribing past conflict under the rubric of so-called political violence. In an effort to contain and bring to an end the era of state terror, civilian politicians cordoned off the temporal and spatial limits of political violence and human rights, their actions and rhetoric acting like yellow tape around a crime scene.

Perpetuating the Space of Death in Transitions to Free Market Democracy: The Chilean Case

The central problem in Chile over the years since the end of formal military rule has been the inability to address human rights violations of the past (in terms of reparations or prosecutions of perpetrators), especially the problem of survivors of torture, detention, and internal and external exile (except for the health program, state reparations policies overwhelmingly privileged the immediate families of people who had been killed, and the civilian government's official "Truth and Reconciliation" report only documented cases ending in death). This is why the shift in the state-health reparations program away from human rights issues to intrafamilial violence is so disturbing. The premise was that, after a certain amount of time, those affected most directly by state violence should "get over it" and reintegrate into society. This is the obvious problem with the policy shift, but there are deeper, more disturbing implications. Feminist movements have taught us that "the personal is political," but here we have an example of bringing in something defined as "domestic," that is, violence within families, as a way of depoliticizing issues defined as "political." After feminism, we have to explore the linkages between these forms of violence, as they are all "political."

Chile's transition from military to civilian rule began in the early 1980s when the worldwide recession undermined the legitimacy of the military regime's neoliberal economic policies of privatization, incentives for foreign investment in the export sector, and the reduction of government social programs. In the midst of the recession, numerous social movements began to stage large-scale public demonstrations against the military. Leading this movement were shantytown associations, collective soup kitchens, human rights groups, and other organizations in which a large proportion of militants and leaders were women; among these groups were feminist organizations, such as Women for Life, who explicitly articulated the need for democracy both "on the street and in the home."[13] The military had attempted to formalize its rule with a new constitution stipulating a plebiscite to choose between civilian or military rule by the end of the decade; however, through this 1989 plebiscite and subsequent presidential election, approximately 60 percent of Chileans managed to vote the military and its most vehement supporters out of power, and civilian rule resumed in 1990.

In order to mark the transition from military to civilian rule, the new civilian government established a commission to undertake a very limited investigation of human rights abuses under military rule. Because the investigations were limited to cases resulting in death, the full extent of the torture was never fully documented. The Truth and Reconciliation Commission made a number of recommendations to the civilian government to facilitate its objective of historical closure, including recommendations for reparations to victims of state violence. Most of these reparations were directed toward the immediate families of those who had died, although some housing and small-business loan programs were extended to ex-political prisoners and those returning from exile. The farthest-reaching and most fiscally significant reparations project was the establishment of the Mental Health and Human Rights Program that extended comprehensive health care, with an emphasis on psychosocial services, to families of the executed and disappeared, returned exiles, and ex–political prisoners.

The mental-health reparations program grew out of two decades of work by mental health care professionals in using psychosocial therapy for human rights victims as a form of political activism. The Mental Health and Human Rights Movement in Latin America crafted a type of political psychology that refused to pathologize the troubles of those damaged by human rights abuses (understood as a collectivity) and instead insisted that the social, political, and economic structures that generated state violence required dismantling.[14] The institutionalization of this movement by the new civilian government changed its political emphasis and, in fact, caused deep divisions between those professionals who decided to work with the civilian government and those who questioned the government program's organizing presuppositions. Reviewing the published reports of the state's mental-health program and interviewing program officials, health care professionals, social workers, and patients, made it clear to me that while the program was designed in a spirit of advocacy for those abused by the state, ultimately, it was intended as a temporary measure to help reintegrate human rights victims into a reemerging civil society. As such, it complemented the notion of a transition to democracy as a defined, liminal, spaciotemporal configuration between the time of the military dictatorship and a period termed democracy. In this liminal space, state psychiatrists, psychologists, and social workers would delimit and resolve individual and familial memories of state violence. Political leaders argued that the delicacy of Chile's shift from military to civilian rule limited their ability to bring military officials to justice because, while the military had retired from complete control of the government (except for military-designated senators-for-life), pro-military personnel staffed both the courts and government lower-level administrative and clerical offices; the military's institutional structure remained completely intact, with the former dictator as supreme commander.[15] The civilian state's pragmatist politics meant that one of its most significant efforts to address the legacies of the past worked through a health program directed at taming the memories of those most directly scarred by that history of state violence. Still, this program provided vital—though limited by scarce resources—health services to that sector of society in a context of the commodification of health care and the near total privatization of state health services (thus lack of affordable health care) begun under the military and intensified by the civilian government.[16]

In 1994, presidential elections and the peaceful transition from the first civilian presidency to a second prompted the state's declaration that the transition to democracy in Chile had been completed (though this statement was later retracted). Supposedly no longer needed to deal with victims of state aggression, the Mental Health and Human Rights Program was incorporated into the Ministry of Health as the Mental Health and Violence Program, with its main emphasis on domestic violence against children, women, and the elderly, all defined as apolitical. Relegating issues of political violence to the past, the civilian government also refused, at that point, to recognize ongoing human rights abuses in Chile, especially in the area of police violence against political protesters, common criminals, and, primarily, drug-related offenders, as well as ongoing legacies of state terror. State policy shifted from a project of treating subordinate memory as pathology to the erasure of those memories as anachronistic. Moreover, the shift in the program's emphasis entailed the domestication of human rights and violence, thus shifting human rights out of the realm of the political and public and seeing violence as a product of culturally and socially backwards, dysfunctional (i.e., anomalous) individuals in the domestic sphere or of cultural and social backwardness in general.

The undercurrents in the initial mental health and human rights program had already resulted in an inadvertent gendering of program politics, a pattern more overtly exacerbated by the program's shift in emphasis to intrafamilial violence. The domestic violence program was oriented around the treatment and advocacy of so-called victims defined as nonmasculine: nonadults (children and elderly) and women defined as subject to abuse and thus deemed worthy of state intervention. This feminization of the state's clientele extended the implicit gendering of the prior mental-health and human rights program that had worked primarily through patterns of treatment. Because men generally were more reticent to engage in psychotherapy, there was an overrepresentation of women who actually used the full range of resources (though in practice, very little systematic therapy seems to have been conducted due to very limited resources). The men tended only to go for regular medical care; men were also much more likely to protest against the paternalistic structuring of health-care delivery relations. Many men resented the underlying assumption that the program's staff knew the answers and that the patients were the problem, as well as the refusal by some staff members to believe men's stories of torture or to see any connection between torture and current physical problems. The program staff, according to my interviews and to the project's official report, also experienced a disproportionately high turnover of male professionals who seemed less willing to tolerate the stressful working conditions and the relative lack of infrastructural support from the central government.[17]

In thinking about how the implicit gendering of the program affected its shift to an emphasis on domestic violence, I base the following discussion of the program on a key text, the program's 1998 technical manual. I am interested, for purposes of this chapter, in the ways in which state actors framed the problem of violence and human rights during the crucial first decade after military rule. How programs actually work in practice is another matter, as we saw in the case of the domestic violence program's predecessor, the Mental Health and Human Rights Program; for the purpose of focusing on the politics of memory in periods of democratization, I am focusing on this articulation of state policy to understand the first decade of civilian rule when the civilian government formulated crucial strategies for a political transition from military rule.[18]

To the program officers' credit, the manual reveals that they were clearly cognizant of the need to think about women's rights as human rights and of the state's responsibility to protect human rights.[19] Undoubtedly this was at least partially related to trends in international funding for public-health and social-services projects, as "women's rights as human rights" was an important theme for 1990s international organizations. For example, they discussed the problem of obligatory or coerced maternity;[20] they openly confronted the abuse of power in the home; and furthermore, the program recognized women as agents of their own lives[21] and used gender, which they defined as culture plus biology[22] (a term against which right-wing senators had launched a political diatribe a few years earlier), as a way of thinking about relations of power. As the manual states, "Violent conduct is understood as an effective form of 'control over the other.'"[23]

While the program represented an enormous step in state policies toward women and the family, I see two key limiting elements in this framework. First, in the manual there was almost no use of the term *men* to specify the predominant agents of intrafamilial violence, let alone *patriarchy* as an operative concept. As in the sentence quoted above, discussion of violent actions is generally phrased in the passive voice, refusing to specify the perpetrator. Similarly, the discussion of coerced maternity skirts the issue of patriarchal investment in women's bodies as instruments of reproduction. One of the program's concrete strategies for "promoting healthy family relations" was to provide information to the public about the benefits of a more "flexible distribution of the roles associated with the genders,"[24] but such a strategy promises to have little impact if it never confronts men's investment in not flexibly redistributing gender roles (note the prevalence of neoliberal vocabulary). While the manual notes the "gradual democratization of the family" as a component of the current social structure, it does not espouse the democratization of family dynamics as an ultimate goal; rather, this is noted as a stress factor that results in violence.[25] While the program's explanation of its mission points to men's abuse of power as the problem, it never questions their right to that power, implying that the alternative to abusing power is the benevolent exercise of that power. Without confronting men's stake in unequal gender definitions, it is understandable that almost all of the program's interventions were still directed toward the "victim," rather than challenging power directly. In this strategy, the program to treat mental-health problems resulting from "domestic" violence replicated the politics of its "political" violence predecessor.

On a more profound level—this is my second major concern with the program's framework—the two phases of the program also similarly expressed a relatively depoliticized understanding of the politics of violence. The analysis of intrafamilial violence located this violence in the realm of "cultural beliefs,"[26] echoing the state's recent project of "cultural modernization" and the early-twentieth-century rhetoric of the "social question" (alcohol and other vices, for example) as the source of social conflict (as opposed to class exploitation). When describing the factors contributing to stress within families, the program noted increasing "external pressures" and "growing instability" without specifying the political and economic changes that had created these conditions. While correctly pointing to the stresses of poverty for children, women, and the elderly,[27] the program neglected to mention that these conditions hold for a great percentage of Chilean families, and by leaving this observation at the level of general phenomena, the state naturalized poverty[28] and its concomitant layers of brutality. For example, in blaming cultural ignorance, the program made public education a core component of its strategy.[29] Left out of this call for education is the context of the collapse of Chile's education system with privatizations begun under the military and continued under civilian rule. Grounded in modernist compartmentalizations of human life, violence was displaced from the realm of political economy and relocated to the realms of society and culture, divisions overlapping the gendered distinction between public and private. In sum, domestic violence, in the state's conception, was thoroughly domestic.

Attempting to foreground the domestic, international activists have worked to ensure that universalistic discussions of human rights address the particular problems of subordinate groups, such as women and children, as political problems. However, we are seeing that this discourse is vulnerable to readings from the opposite direction: subjects from the domestic sphere can be used to depoliticize questions of violence and human rights. In spite of the limitations of the Mental Health and Human Rights Program, it had constituted an important effort that explicitly recognized human rights abuses under the military, albeit in a patronizing manner from the point of view of many patients, and created a certain official space for those most directly impacted by military rule. The civilian government virtually abandoned a program that explicitly recognized human rights abuses under the military. In its place, the state positioned itself paternalistically as advocate and protector of sectors of society perceived as vulnerable and "voiceless."[30]

In the neoliberal restructuring of Chile around the logic of the market, debates about state policies toward the domestic/the family may have been more about the commodification of patrimony and the concomitant redefinition of the relationship between state patriarchy and the prerogatives of the local patriarch than about the interests of patriarchy's most subordinate sectors, especially women, children, and the elderly. To illustrate this process of redefinition, I conclude this section with an example of relevant legislative action. In 1998, I attended a session of the Chilean Congress with a number of women's organizations because scheduled to appear on the legislative docket that day was a bill to increase penalties against women who had abortions; women's groups wanted to form a presence in the chamber to protest the measure.

While the abortion bill never actually came up, the most important legislation tackled that day was, ironically, a bill to remove the oldest piece of social legislation in Chile, the law distinguishing legitimate from illegitimate children.[31] The debate ranged from opinions offered by senators of the ruling coalition parties to senators from the pro-military parties; even Senator-for-Life Augusto Pinochet spoke, his feeble voice nearly drowned out by cries of indignation from the women observing from the gallery. The general insisted that without a law to regulate inheritance based on legitimacy, the family, thus the nation, would be endangered. The only senator to bring the concerns of women and children to the table and to point to the problem of negligent patriarchs was conservative Evelyn Mattai, daughter of a prominent military officer, who pointed to the rampant neglect of children and the need for more responsible fathers. What the rest of the Congress debated, in effect, across ostensible political lines, was the relationship of social laws defining legitimacy to the problem of national patrimony, understood as the regulation of the inheritance of private property.[32] When the former dictator defended the nineteenth-century law as a safeguard of national security, he further underlined the link in military logic between National Security Doctrine and patriarchy; in other words, he located national patrimony in the domestic. Thus, those who favored abrogating the law in this congressional debate were deregulating inheritance and thus pushing neoliberal logic far beyond the point where the military had been willing to go, to subsume the domestic as national patrimony within the space of the market.

To explore the question of what kinds of subjectivities might challenge the integrity of the space of death, we will retrace our steps in the political chronology of the region to think more about the constitution of that space under military rule through Luisa Valenzuela's Argentine tale *Other Weapons*. Though Valenzuela's analysis comes mostly out of her own experiences as an Argentine, the kinds of dynamics she portrays emerge from Dirty War military ideologies shared across the region. The story thus provides an apt framework for thinking through the Chilean case in my conclusions. Before we begin, let me be clear: I do not read the erotics of this story as representing the desires of people subjected to torture but rather as allegorically depicting the problem of hegemony (a political project for rule configured by the negotiation of coercion and consent) in the nation-state under state terror.[33]

Other Weapons: The Intimate Economies of
Violence in Market States

In this story, Valenzuela depicts the ways in which the Dirty War structured both memory and amnesia and traces the process of remembering in which the body, pleasure, and pain form the core of the intimacy between the victimizer and the victim. In the course of the story, the amnesiac learns to put names to objects, to the man, and to herself (in that order), thus to know a domestic space whose significance has been presented to her as naturalized. The space of death takes form in the bourgeois respectability of the modern apartment, complete with servants and domestic artifacts. The infusion of the uncanny and of evil into the domestic is reminiscent of a gothic space in which the modernist project of distinguishing between the monster and the hero is revealed and questioned.

The action takes place in a modern, urban apartment with windows facing a concrete wall, a bedroom of mirrors, a locked door with a two-way peephole and a key on the ledge above, and a framed wedding picture. Its inhabitants include the bride in the picture, Laura, who suffers from amnesia; a housekeeper, Martina; and the groom, a military officer who visits periodically, always accompanied by two men who remain just outside the door. The woman knows only of her desire for the man whose name she can't remember (so she addresses him by a varying litany of names). When she's alone, she spends a lot of time looking at her body in the mirrors and noticing her nose, which has been broken and healed and the long scar snaking down her back: "Sometimes her head aches, and that pain is the only thing that really belongs to her and that she can communicate to the man. Then he gets worried, both hoping and fearing that she'll remember something specific."[34] From here on, the narrative is punctuated by subtitles (the array of weapons) and incidents. I've chosen a few of these titled sections, summarized them, and divided them into three groups following the plotline: (1) seemingly innocuous objects of the home; (2) more sinister objects that don't quite fit into a model of domestic contentment and entail issues of doubt, violence, and intimacy; and (3) a grouping that relates to secrets, revelations, and resolution.

The Photograph: The wedding picture she doesn't recall and her desire for the man she can't remember.

The Plant: Laura requests a plant. The housekeeper relays the message to the man. He agrees as long as it "isn't too wild. Something nice and urban. Buy it from a good flower-shop."[35]

The Mirrors: He forces her to watch herself as her body responds to his lovemaking: "He shouts 'Open your eyes. . . . Open your eyes, spit it out, tell me who sent you, who gave the order,' and she shouts such an intense, deep NO that her answer is silent in the space they're in and he doesn't hear it."[36] And she whispers his real name, Roque, for the first time.

The Window: She stares out the window, and as her mind wanders, she thinks about a weapon, a time bomb waiting to explode as he comes down the street. Then, she thinks of her need for his caresses as the only way she can feel alive, or when he threatens because his voice tells her about being somewhere else: "There's that dark area of her memory which also keeps to itself and not precisely because it wants to."[37]

The bourgeois house filled with domestic commodities reminds us of the willingness of sectors of the Argentine and Chilean public to support the military takeover in the name of establishing the order necessary for capitalist prosperity. The domestic objects are misrecognized as signs of security, when instead they give material form to the violent social relations that supply luxurious security for elite sectors at the expense of the chronic instability of everyday forms of violence enacted against the majority of the population through direct state violence and through the daily chaos of structural adjustments of the economy. The coveted space of the "Market" has become "the agony of the open market."[38]

This first group of objects indelibly connects issues of desire, violence, and memory as physically inscribed on her body. In this sense, memory has less to do with self-consciousness than with experience and sensation. In the next group, as Valenzuela lays out her plot, we see emergent doubts and recollections, as well as growing proximity to the truth of her identity.

The Well: She feels that the only moments that are truly hers are when they have sex. She imagines a well within herself that contains all that she really is but doesn't know.

The Whip: One day, in the bedroom, he brings out a whip. She begins to scream uncontrollably. He puts it away, and suddenly she remembers the sensation of true love for one who is dead: "Then she feels that she's been so close to the revelation, to the explanation. But it's not worth getting to the explanation through pain. . . . It's a soft, protective cloud she has to try to keep there so as not to collapse and suddenly fall into memory."[39]

The Peephole: She knows that by not helping her, he actually enables her to open her inner doors; he gives her a chance to see herself in the mirrors and then he gives her a chance to see herself through the eyes of others—by raping her in the living room with the peephole open.

Space shapes the way in which Laura comes to desire and accommodate the man, and she must turn that space inside out as she struggles to regain control over meaning—of the body, pleasure, pain, and so forth—at times through remembering, and at other times through a refusal of memory. Forgetting is structured and habituated. The story presents the pain of not remembering along with the pleasure and comfort of forgetting; resistance cannot be completely separated from accommodation; rather, these form a continuum along which memories mingle with inchoate suspicions. Forgetting involves the fragmentation and reconstitution of the autonomous subject, in this case, Laura's already uncertain and rapidly disintegrating sense of her position in the household, the inverse of the domestic narrative of transition from bride to housewife. Laura must piece together her own identity in terms of her body and her elusive particular history, even as the tortured body had condensed all that the military regimes had tried to negate in national politics. Similarly, Argentina and Chile were confronted with their histories as Latin American nations after pretensions to European "civilization" had been brutally torn apart, much as the respectable wedding photograph masks social relations of rape and imprisonment.

This contradictory process of needing to remember, yet recognizing the safety and comfort of forgetting, also could describe the ways in which new civilian presidents positioned themselves as opposition figures to the military, yet remained susceptible to intimidation by the military not to pursue full, formal, public recognition through judicial proceedings and the public naming of torturers (one possible political significance of Valenzuela's naming of her male military character). We could look to Laura's rape in front of the peephole as mirroring the voyeuristic participation of other nation-states in state terror— for example, the collaborative actions of Latin American militaries, such as the coordinated effort to eliminate political enemies in exile known as Operation Condor—and the military's need to demonstrate its ability to tame any internal opposition. All of this gets juxtaposed with the gazes of other kinds of international organizations and networks, such as Amnesty International and Human Rights Watch, that were attempting to foreground human rights issues in world politics.

The second grouping gives us a sense of the intimacy of the space of death and the potential satiation of Laura's desire through a recovery of "the truth." The peephole allows her to see herself through the disembodied eyes of an other looking at her tortured body. In the final sections of the story, we see the arrogance with which the man perceives his relation to the ideological truth in both a sense of impunity and a belief in the destructive force of this truth. But if truth, in its various forms, is to be the ultimate weapon, it is a prop in search of an agent and a meaning, connecting the recuperation of one's own history and the ability to act. Both the gun and the truth remain the unspoken weapons (i.e., Valenzuela does not use them as subtitles), signaling the interplay between the word and violence against the body as weapons that may work for either party.

The Secrets: After a long absence (due to an attempted coup within the military), he returns wishing to resolve everything by telling her the truth (which she doesn't want to hear). He hands her a loaded gun, which he says is the weapon with which she (along with her male partner who was immediately killed) attempted to assassinate him (but he is sure she no longer wants to): "Nothing can be perfect if you stay out there, on the other side of things, if you refuse to know. I saved your life, do you know that?"[40]

The Revelation: He tells her that he saved her by beating her and breaking her will and forcing her to love him. He tells her, "I've got my weapons, too."

The Ending: She responds by asking him to come to bed. He tells her that the experiment is over, he's leaving, and she's free to go too: "She sees his back move away and feels like the fog is beginning to clear. She starts to understand a few things—what that black instrument is for, that thing he calls a gun. She lifts it and aims."[41]

How can we relate the centrality of gender in Valenzuela's story to the history of Argentine and Chilean politics? This issue becomes clearer if we see the ways in which Valenzuela emphasizes the power of "other weapons" as potentially successful, yet contradictory, avenues of resistance. Perhaps the locked door with the fake key represents a drive toward complete rebellion that would prove fruitless, whereas the real fissures susceptible to resistance come from within the contradictions of the system itself (for example, when the man forces Laura to look in the mirror and thus exposes her to her scarred body). Also, it is significant that the officer (the embodiment of male power) sees a woman as sufficiently less threatening (than the male companion whom he kills immediately) and as malleable. Having cast the guerrilla as the monster who threatens civilization, the military excised the monster from the national (feminine) body as the scars on Laura's back mark the military's blundering attempt to suture the nation back together. In this story, we can read traces of the gothic narrative of the monster misrecognized—it is so often the monster's creator who has stepped beyond the edge of common humanity.[42] In assuming that the woman (read nation) can be remade, the military officer recognizes neither his own monstrosity nor the danger of her weapons.

While critics have rightly questioned the nature of these as so-called female weapons and the limits of change within the domestic space,[43] I argue that Valenzuela's story entails many possible readings of the link between state violence and domestic violence. In torture, the space of death invokes and then defiles the sense of security embodied in signs of the domestic. In Elaine Scarry's words, these signs of the domestic mark "the location of the human being's most expansive potential"; the intentional use of a domestic vocabulary and domestic objects as violent artifacts "demonstrates that everything is a weapon," such that the objects and civilization along with them are "annihilated."[44] This dismantling of the domestic might be particularly effective in the torture of female prisoners, since the woman's ostensibly sacred domain becomes the site of her undoing. However, if we step outside of this bourgeois logic of the domestic and look instead at these domestic artifacts as the locus of bourgeois patrimony/property and combine this with the omnipresence of everyday forms of domestic violence, then we are forced to question a reading of the domestic as a necessarily safe and nurturing space.

Other Weapons can be read as mocking the military's romanticization of the domestic, as seen in its rendition of the Dirty War as a national romance featuring the military as the heroic defender of national honor. Feminist scholars have urged us to question the notion that a sharp distinction exists between sexual violence and normative heterosexual intercourse; rather than a distinction, these form part of a continuum of power relations, a difference of degree rather than of kind. These scholars have also shown that the specific eroticism of heterosexual romance lies in the latent force of that passion[45] as illustrated by the fact that romantic fiction typically narrates the aggression and subsequent repentance of the hero and the redemption of the heroine's virtue by the romantic plot,[46] a plot disturbingly echoed in the civil legislation of many Latin American countries that dropped rape charges against rapists who would agree to marry the raped woman. In Chile, this legislation was overturned only in 1999.

As helpful as these insights are for deromanticizing heterosexualist narratives, they leave intact the normative casting of protagonists as male and female actors in the most conventional senses, thus offer little transformative potential. Judith Halberstam does this work in her analysis of gothic horror and the technology of monsters when she mobilizes queer theory to posit the emergence of a subjectivity that transcends the modernist dichotomy of human/monster to assume new forms of agency. This is the figure of the "last girl" in horror films who emerges, scarred from previous attacks, to appropriate the (phallic) weapons previously used against her and becomes a queered subject able to transcend the violent scenario that threatened her annihilation.[47] Here, I think that the concept of "being queered" can be useful for indicating not just a transgendered positionality but, moreover, a capacity to act that is emergent from, yet does not make sense within, or in fact transcends, dominant cultural and political frameworks for agency.[48] Valenzuela shapes just such a character in Laura, who is able to look in the mirror to assemble the pieces of her memories, reconnect them with her scarred body, unpack the structure of domestic discipline and the story imposed upon her, and ultimately, by recognizing the gun, reclaim the capacity to act. Hence, a queered reading (in this sense, I am adopting Halberstam's claims for a queer methodology for reading against the grain to interrogate gendered characterizations of subjectivity) of *Other Weapons* transcends the disciplinary framework of the love story to tackle the problem of power.

Yet, access to power might itself be distorting. Franz Fanon explored the contradictions he saw as inherent in the use of force; he worried that anticolonial revolutionaries were so distorted by the legacies of colonialism that their use of force to achieve political transformation could become a crude weapon of indiscriminate violence. Paolo Freire similarly argued that power itself must be rethought and retaught if oppressed sectors were to avoid reenacting arbitrary dominance. Both Fanon and Freire cautioned against the danger of arbitrary violence in the anti-imperialist movements of the 1960s, their crucial analyses of power understandably shaped by the twin colonial imaginaries of civilization (the measured use of force) and barbarism (the indiscriminate use of force).[49] In the face of this problem, nonviolence as a political practice provided an often effective strategy, especially in the heightened militarism of the cold war; yet, nonviolence skirted the problem of the dominant framing of the use of force, even while strategically deploying that frame (for example, in the movements of the mothers of the disappeared). Feminisms since this period have contributed to the postcolonial theorizing of power by attempting to rethink the parameters of emancipatory subjectivities, and queer theory pushes these insights further by refusing to sanitize subaltern subjectivities. Here I expand on Kirkwood's idea that knowledge based on alterity, by which she means a position of subordinate difference, is perverting. Any hope for an exit from the space of death may lie in the critical, mnemonic revalorization of perverse subjectivities, that is, in this instance, in the unpacking of the modernist mistaking of master and monster that shaped the terms of the Dirty War. It is these perverse subjectivities that have the potential to become a basis for political agency, defined as the capacity to act in contests for power, in the twenty-first century.

Locating the Space of Death in the Time of Reconciliation

> Reconciliation constitutes a difficult beginning of an era of maturity and responsibility realistically assumed by everyone. The scars represent not only a painful memory, but also the foundation of a strong democracy, of a united and free people, a people who learned that subversion and terrorism constitute the inexorable death of liberty.
>
> —Argentine Military Junta[50]

In the shift from military to civilian rule, the Argentine and Chilean states shared the rhetoric of reconciliation as "healing," a means adopted by civilian leaders for coping with the political challenges posed by collective memories of state violence. These cases have become templates for regime transitions in other parts of the world, such as Africa and Eastern Europe. Reconciliation as healing has been a trope adopted by not only civilian political leaders but also by military leaders, as the quote above by the Argentine military junta demonstrates. Healing metaphors inadvertently perpetuated the military narrative of the nation as a body subject to intervention; from this perspective, reconciliation became the suturing together of the national body on which the rhetorical "scars" served as a reminder of the "liberating" necessity of the violence of military rule, a justification often invoked to defend the greater good of (particularly in the Chilean case) economic neoliberal restructuring. This rationale remained within the familiar modernist foundational narrative of surgically, scientifically shaping human society, of distinguishing the human ("a united and free people") from the monstrous ("terrorism and subversion"). The militaries (as in the quote above) then rightly implicated "everyone" in this project. The relevant transition, the restructuring of the Argentine and Chilean economies around a market ethic, had already happened well before redemocratization; thus, patrimony, as construed in the patriarchal intervention of the military, had already been safeguarded.

South American militaries' rhetoric of their own agency as apolitical melded handily with discourses of "the end of history" more generally in the post–cold war era.[51] We see the power of this valorization of the apolitical and the demonization of political actors in recent public assaults on activists, most notably Rigoberta Menchu, for being "political" actors rather than appropriately "innocent" victims of human rights abuses. Unfortunately, human rights movements often implicitly echoed this rhetoric in their defense of prisoners-of-conscience as privileged over those implicated in, or advocating the use of, force (classically defined as politics by other means). As a consequence, those actors defined as having been political, and especially those whose scarred bodies mark their prior involvement, operate within an increasingly constrained public space.

The Chilean case, in particular, has become a paradigmatic and precedent-setting one for the pursuit of justice in the aftermath of state terror. The efforts of a Spanish judge to extradite General Pinochet from England (where he had traveled for minor surgery) on charges of crimes against humanity opened up new possibilities in the international politics of justice. The British House of Lords ruled that, indeed, General Pinochet could be extradited to Spain for trial for the crime of torture, and the testimony of torture survivors was critical to the House of Lords' decision, one the Chilean (civilian) state sent government officials to argue against in the name of national sovereignty. In the end, the general was not extradited on grounds of ill health and was returned to Chile with the agreement that the Chilean judicial system would pursue prosecution of these human rights crimes. However, subsequent judicial investigations in Chile have not dealt with cases of torture but rather with disappearances (the covert seizing of people whose existence is thereafter denied and whose bodies have never been recovered) legally interpreted as kidnapping and with illegal executions. Simultaneous civil cases have sought reparations from the Chilean state for families of the executed and disappeared. While torture had constituted the central grounds for the pursuit of justice in Britain, by and large, cases of torture survivors have been silenced in the Chilean public discourse on justice, on the part of the civilian state, the military, and human rights lawyers. It is precisely this silence that marks the degree to which the space of death continues to permeate Chilean society today.

Much of my fieldwork in Chile during the first decade after military rule focused on ex–political prisoners as they contended with the shifting of the democratizing state's reparations health program from so-called political violence to so-called domestic violence. In March 2001, I accompanied an ex–political prisoner, Miguel Rojas (not his real name), to the public hospital emergency room three days in a row, where he claimed his right to health care as a reparations program beneficiary. As a nurse attempted to draw blood, making two unsuccessful punctures in his arm, Miguel explained that she would have more luck getting the needle in if she switched to his other side as that arm had suffered multiple fractures as a result of torture sessions. As she jabbed the needle under his skin, she said, "Well, you must have been political [hence interrogated for a reason]. What party were you in?" Today, to claim agency as a political actor is to be labeled suspect (a scarred monstrous body subject to emasculating penetration by the state); to insist on pursuing transformative, emancipatory politics is to embrace perverted subjectivities.

Analyses of memories of state violence that accept the periodization implicit under the rubric of so-called transitions to democracy mistakenly accept the space of death. Human rights discourses that insist on redeeming political activists, cast by the military as monsters, as passive victims of a monstrous state, perpetuate the same dichotomies operationalized by military regimes. In the struggle for a truly transformative change to *other weapons*, looking at the scars through the mirror of critical theory may point to new emancipatory subjectivities that can appropriate and transcend the gendered, violent rhetoric of the modernist nation-state.

Notes

Parts of this chapter were previously published in "Medicalizing Human Rights and Domesticating Violence in Postdictatorship Market-States," in *Violence and the Body: Race, Gender and the State*, ed. Arturo J. Aldama (Bloomington: Indiana University Press, 2003). Reprinted with permission.

1. Michael Taussig defines the space of death as a "threshold," neither inherently repressive nor emancipatory but about the making and unmaking of order, a paradigm of the Latin American experience, revealing the entanglement of social relations within a culture of terror. For me, it is the location of the destruction and production of subjectivities, of producing appropriate bourgeois citizens for the nation in the case of the "Dirty War." For the military, those who could not be salvaged had to be destroyed. See Michael Taussig, "Culture of Terror—Space of Death. Roger Casement's Putumayo Report and the Explanation of Torture," *Comparative Studies in Society and History* 26 (July 1984): 467–68. The space of death is also discussed in Michael Taussig, *Shamanism, Colonialism, and the Wild Man: A Study in Terror and Healing* (Chicago: University of Chicago Press, 1987).

2. Julieta Kirkwood, *Feminarios*, ed. Sonia Montecino (Santiago: Ediciones Documentales, 1987), 121.

3. Kirkwood, *Feminarios*, 117–19.

4. Luisa Valenzuela, *Other Weapons*, trans. Deborah Bonner (Hanover, U.K.: Ediciones del Norte, 1985). Originally published in Spanish as *Cambio de armas* (Hanover, U.K.: Ediciones del Norte, 1982).

5. Leopoldo Galtieri's speech is found in Brian Loveman and Thomas M. Davies Jr., eds., *The Politics of Antipolitics: The Military in Latin America* (Lincoln: University of Nebraska Press, 1989), 203.

6. See Mary Louise Pratt, "Overwriting Pinochet: Undoing the Culture of Fear in Chile," in *The Places of History: Regionalism Revisited in Latin America*, ed. Doris Sommer (Durham, NC: Duke University Press, 1999).

7. On this, see Frank Graziano, *Divine Violence: Spectacle, Psychosexuality, and Radical Christianity in the Argentine "Dirty War"* (Boulder, CO: Westview Press, 1992), and Marguerite Feitlowitz, *A Lexicon of Terror: Argentina and the Legacies of Torture* (New York: Oxford University Press, 1998).

8. Lawyers Committee for International Human Rights, *Violations of Human Rights in Argentina: 1976–1979* (Geneva: United Nations Commission on Human Rights, 1979), 3–4.

9. Steven Gregory and Daniel Timerman, "Rituals of the Modern State: The Case of Torture in Argentina," *Dialectical Anthropology* 11 (1986): 70.

10. Michael Taussig, "Violence and Resistance in the Americas: The Legacy of the Conquest, in *The Nervous System*, by Michael Taussig (New York: Routledge, 1992), 48.

11. Doris Sommer, "Irresistible Romance: The Foundational Fictions of Latin America," in *Nation and Narration*, ed. Homi K. Bhabha (London: Routledge, 1990), 6–7.

12. Fernando Reati, "Argentine Political Violence and Artistic Representation in Films of the 1980s," *Latin American Literary Review* (July–December 1989): 35.

13. See Jean Franco, "Going Public: Reinhabiting the Private," in *Critical Passions*, ed. Mary Louise Pratt and Kathleen Newman (Durham, NC: Duke University Press, 1999), 48–65; Ann Matear, "'Desde la protesta a la propuesta': The Institutionalization of the Women's Movement in Chile," in *Gender Politics in Latin America: Debates in Theory and Practice*, ed. Elizabeth Dore (New York: Monthly Review Press, 1997), 84–100; and Pratt, Overwriting Pinochet," 21–33.

14. Nancy Hollander Caro, *Liberation Psychology* (New Brunswick, NJ: Rutgers, 1997).

15. Ariel Dorfman portrays the terrible intimacy between a woman survivor and her torturer and, although rejecting vengeance, refuses to resolve conflicting memories of state violence in the paradigm of forgiveness. See Ariel Dorfman, *Death and the Maiden* (New York: Penguin, 1991).

16. Julia Paley, *Marketing Democracy: Power and Social Movements in Post-Dictatorship Chile* (Berkeley: University of California Press, 2001).

17. Rosario Domínguez V. et al., *Salud y derechos humanos: Una experiencia desde el sistema público chileno 1991–1993* (Santiago: Programa de Reparación y Atención Integral de Salud y Derechos Humanos, Ministerio de Salud [PRAIS], 1994).

18. By 2000, the Ministry of Health had begun to disarticulate the so-called political and domestic components of the program, due in large part to the increased demand for services by the "political" clients and their mobilization in a national federation of program beneficiaries.

19. Ministerio de Salud, *Manual de apoyo técnico para las acciones de salud en violencia intrafamiliar* (Santiago: Publicaciones de Salud Mental, 1998), 30.

20. Ministerio de Salud, *Manual de apoyo técnico*, 58–59.

21. Ministerio de Salud, *Manual de apoyo técnico*, 70 and 75.

22. Ministerio de Salud, *Manual de apoyo técnico*, 19.

23. Ministerio de Salud, *Manual de apoyo técnico*, 30.

24. Ministerio de Salud, *Manual de apoyo técnico*, 46.

25. Ministerio de Salud, *Manual de apoyo técnico*, 20.

26. Ministerio de Salud, *Manual de apoyo técnico*, 30.

27. Ministerio de Salud, *Manual de apoyo técnico*, 39.

28. Ministerio de Salud, *Manual de apoyo técnico*, 46.

29. Ministerio de Salud, *Manual de apoyo técnico*, 42.

30. On the infantilizing paradigm for late-modern citizenship, see Lauren Berlant, "America, 'Fat,' the Fetus," in *Gendered Agents: Women and Institutional Knowledge*, ed. Paul A. Boyle and Silvestra Mariniella (Durham, NC: Duke University Press, 1998). On market citizenship in Chile, see Veronica Schild, "Neo-Liberalism's New Gendered Market Citizens: The 'Civilizing' Dimension of Social Programmes in Chile," *Citizenship Studies* 4, no. 3 (2000): 275–305.

31. Some senators noted during the legislative debate that it was odd to penalize illegitimate children when key founders of the Chilean nation-state, especially Bernardo O'Higgins, were themselves illegitimate. On the foundling in Chilean national identity, see Sonia Montecino, *Madres y huachos* (Santiago: Cuarto Propio, 1991).

32. Nineteenth-century liberal efforts to loosen strictures of gender-differentiated inheritance were not based on notions of greater equity but, rather, on the need to relocate more resources to the realm of the market; see Silvia Arrom, "Changes in Family Law in the Nineteenth Century: The Civil Codes of 1870 and 1884," *Journal of Family History* (fall 1985): 305–17.

33. Ximena Bunster-Burotto, "Surviving beyond Fear: Women and Torture in Latin America," in *Women and Change in Latin America*, ed. June Nash and Helen Safa (South Hadley: Bergin and Garvey, 1986).

34. Valenzuela, *Other Weapons*, 107.

35. Valenzuela, *Other Weapons*, 113.

36. Valenzuela, *Other Weapons*, 115.

37. Valenzuela, *Other Weapons*, 117.

38. Paul H. Lewis, *The Crisis of Argentine Capitalism* (Chapel Hill: University of North Carolina Press, 1990).

39. Valenzuela, *Other Weapons*, 123.

40. Valenzuela, *Other Weapons*, 133.

41. Valenzuela, *Other Weapons*, 135.

42. Judith Halberstam, *Skin Shows: Gothic Horror and the Technology of Monsters* (Durham, NC: Duke University Press, 1995).

43. María-Inés Lagos-Pope, "Mujer y política en Cambio de Armas de Luisa Valenzuela," in *Hispamérica* (1987): 46–47, and Diana Taylor, *Disappearing Acts: Spectacles of Gender and Nationalism in Argentina's "Dirty War"* (Durham, NC: Duke University Press, 1997).

44. Elaine Scarry, *The Body in Pain: The Making and Unmaking of the World* (New York: Oxford University Press, 1985), 38–40.

45. On this, see Catherine MacKinnon, *Sex Equality: Rape Law* (New York: Foundation Press, 2001), and Penelope Harvey and Peter Gow, eds., *Sex and Violence: Issues in Representation and Experience* (London: Routledge, 1994).

46. Janice Radway, *Reading the Romance: Women, Patriarchy, and Popular Literature* (Chapel Hill: University of North Carolina Press, 1991).

47. Halberstam, *Skin Shows*.

48. Emilie Bergmann and Paul Julian Smith, eds., *¿Entiendes? Queer Readings, Hispanic Writings* (Durham, NC: Duke University Press, 1995).

49. Julie Skurski, "The Ambiguities of Authenticity in Latin America: Doña Barbara and the Construction of National Identity," in *Becoming National: A Reader*, ed. Geoff Eley and Ronald Suny (New York: Oxford University Press, 1996).

50. Quoted in Loveman and Davies, *The Politics of Antipolitics*, 211.

51. Tomás Moulian, "A Time of Forgetting: The Myths of the Chilean Transition," NACLA 22, no. 2 (September–October 1998): 22.

Appendix:
Mexican Internet Sites for
Gender and Sexuality

Wendy A. Vogt

THE RAPID EXPANSION OF MEDIA TECHNOLOGIES, particularly the Internet, has revolutionized the ways in which people interact, as well as how they imagine and negotiate social relations. The Internet allows individuals instantly to access information, communicate with friends and strangers, and participate in online political and social organizing. Moreover, the anonymous nature of cyberspace creates the potential for humans to transcend their bodies and socially constructed identities (i.e., race, gender, ethnicity, sexuality), as well as to develop, perform, embrace, or test out alternate identities.[1] Online, as most interactions currently occur without physical or verbal contact (although the increasing use of Web cams and Internet telephone services do enable visual and verbal contact), individuals may evade the judgments imposed upon them in face-to-face exchanges. Thus, cyberspace becomes a site where fixed and essentialized constructions of identity, as well as normative ideas of sex and sexuality based on physical appearance, sexual organs, traditional gender roles, or a combination thereof, are challenged. As such, it offers a particularly critical site for the study of gender, sexuality, representation, and social processes in and outside of Mexico.[2]

Growing numbers of Mexicans are now affected by access to the Internet, whether they actively create websites or blogs, "surf" the Web at home or in the Internet cafes cropping up across the country, or desire access that they do not have because of geographical, financial, or social barriers.[3] The proliferation of websites and blogs created by and for Mexicans provides evidence of an emerging cybercommunity unique to Mexico, as well as of Mexicans' growing participation in global cyberspace.[4] Given the power of electronic mediation to enable the imagining of alternative selves and entire worlds, for some Mexicans, identities premised upon nationality may be replaced by identification with more global networks of people based on common interests, identities, or both.[5] Although the Internet transcends national and geographical boundaries and identifications, people often use it for explicitly local purposes; thus, we can identify certain clusters of websites as products of particular social and cultural environments. Cyberspace offers a new space for the expression, (re)negotiation, and (re)invention of individual and collective identities, experiences, and perceptions of gender and sexuality.

Theoretically, the Internet allows anyone to share information via the Web. Marginalized groups certainly have had a presence there, perhaps best epitomized by Subcomandante Marcos's online manifestos during and since the Zapatista rebellion beginning in 1994. In addition, connecting people to the Internet has been a national project in Mexico since 2001, when President Vicente Fox initiated the e-Mexico program that seeks to provide Internet access to a wider range of the Mexican population. However, in reality, factors such as illiteracy, limited time and financial resources, and unequal gender relations still prevent many people from taking advantage of new technologies. Surfing the Web in Mexico today remains largely a middle- to upper-class activity, and the content of many websites reflects the sensibilities and activities of this social segment. Despite much rhetoric touting its democratic nature, cyberspace mirrors existing power structures based on race, class, gender, and sexuality.

Reflecting on these inequalities, feminist discussions of cyberculture center on the ways in which gender and sexuality can be politicized or depoliticized by the use of technology. Debates surrounding subjectivity and representation are central to the rich feminist literature on the intersections among gender, technology, and science, which spans the areas of reproductive and biological technologies, biomedicine, cyberculture, and science fiction.[6] This scholarship seeks to break down dichotomies between mind/body, machine/human, sex/gender, and male/female, highlighting issues of subjectivity and power in the highly contested arenas of science and technology. Much of the feminist literature questions whether we are living in a posthuman and/or postgender landscape. Donna Haraway's concept of the cyborg, for example, calls into question the boundary between human and machine by insisting that the two are inextricably linked and that one being can embody both the human and the machine simultaneously. The cyborg challenges traditional notions of subjectivity and helps us to understand the multiple ways individuals construct their identities.

The wealth of online information produced by women's groups, gay rights groups, dating services, individuals, and agencies offers a portal not only into the ways people construct their own and others' identities but also how they negotiate relations between genders.[7] While some Mexican websites challenge heteronormative dichotomies related to gender and sexuality, especially those that focus on lesbian, gay, bisexual, and transgender issues, it appears that essentialist gender distinctions remain prevalent on other websites, although there exists considerable disagreement on what the "characteristics," "rights," or "roles" of genders should be. For example, representations of Mexican women on dating sites as naturally loyal and nurturing and as good dancers prove markedly different from discussions of fluid and diverse sexual identities on a website like www.saldelcloset.com (Spanish for "coming out of the closet," or openly identifying as homosexual). Scholars of queer studies have already noted that the medium itself, much more than print culture, facilitates the person-to-person exchange of information and the creation and sharing of personal histories.[8]

In another interesting example, Colectivo de Hombres por Relaciones Igualitarias A.C. (CORIAC), a men's group, seeks to end violence aimed at women and children by men who exhibit *machista* characteristics; the fact that men are envisioned as capable of transforming themselves in order to respect and treat women as equals reveals that machismo, according to CORIAC, is not necessarily an inherent but a socially constructed quality. Clearly, this position still maintains the dichotomy of male/female, but it breaks down dominant associations of gender identities and rejects the notion of fixed identities. For many of the groups with avowedly political agendas, gender categories reflect both outward activism and inward reflection. This trend undermines the binary between strategic essentialism and constructionist conceptions of identity; contemporary groups can construct fluid and diverse understandings of gender identities, desires, and practices while simultaneously finding space to advance social change.

This appendix provides a sample of the diversity of online resources generated in Mexico that touch upon the above issues and thus offers an introduction to some of the various ways that Mexicans construct gender and identity. It includes websites from governmental, nongovernmental, and corporate organizations and projects. Several are purely Web-based informational or network-building sites, important in both feminist and gay rights movements. Other sites represent specific community centers or organizations disseminating information about services, sharing art and music, or hosting online discussion forums. Several of the websites listed below represent political initiatives designed to advance human rights, combat discrimination and gender violence, and provide a safe space to learn about sexuality, reproduction, and health concerns. This list is by no means exhaustive but is meant to provide an overview of the resources available and the creative ways people are using new technologies.

Websites and Sources

Amnistía Internacional Sección Mexicana
www.amnistia.org.mx
The website for the Mexican section of Amnesty International covers a wide range of issues from domestic violence to sex slavery to gay rights, and it gives special attention to the murdered and disappeared women of Ciudad Juárez, sponsoring an online petition. It is a valuable resource for information on current issues, Amnesty International's mission, and how to get involved.

Cimacnoticias
www.cimacnoticias.com
CIMAC's news website, www.cimacnoticias.com, "Journalism with a gendered perspective," received Yahoo! Mexico's 2001 award for best mass media site. Most of Cimacnoticias's articles feature themes relating to Mexican and Latin American women, with particular attention to violence and poverty.

Colectivo de Hombres por Relaciones Igualitarias A.C.
www.coriac.org.mx
CORIAC, a men's organization founded in 1993, dedicates its efforts to transforming unequal gender relations in Mexico. It strives to improve family relations with special emphasis on fatherhood, conflict resolution, gender, and sexuality. The website is rich in information for men wishing to participate in CORIAC or to conduct further research on themes of gender and sexuality.

Comité del Orgullo LGBT México
www.orgullomexico.org
This is the official website for the gay, lesbian, bisexual, and transgender pride movement in Mexico. The site includes educational information, news of current events, including annual gay pride marches in Mexico City, links to other sites, related articles, and information about how to get involved with the group.

Comunicación e Información de la Mujer (CIMAC)
www.cimac.org.mx
CIMAC promotes communication for equality, democracy, and social justice. Founded in 1988, the group builds networks between organizations and journalists dedicated to social justice through various media outlets, most recently the Internet. CIMAC strives to ensure that the social condition of women receives proper representation in the mass media.

Creatividad Feminista
www.creatividadfeminista.org

Creatividad Feminista is a multimedia website dedicated to supporting female artists, musicians, activists, and scholars working on a variety of themes related to gender, sexuality, and justice. With links to art, music, articles, e-books, and an online store, not only can women learn about, listen to, and view the work of others, but they can also upload their own work to share with others. The site is of Mexican origin and in Spanish, but it appeals to a larger audience. For example, the radio section features Chinese- and Arabic-language rock music.

Fraternidad Gay de la Ciudad de México
http://fraternidadgay.tripod.com
The website for Fraternidad Gay provides information about the organization and community resources and services for gay men in Mexico City. It includes book and movie recommendations, poetry, photographs, online chat rooms, games, and information on current events. The website also includes a discussion of the difference between being homosexual and being gay.

GDL Gay Radio
www.gdlgayradio.com
GDL Gay Radio is an online radio station based in Guadalajara, Mexico. Users can listen to various programs and music online as well as participate in online forums and read related news.

Grupo de Información en Reproducción Elegida (GIRE)
www.gire.org.mx
GIRE was founded in 1991 and strives to provide balanced and factual information concerning abortion and reproductive rights in Mexico. The website offers detailed information concerning these topics, with special attention to women who believe they may be pregnant.

Instituto de las Mujeres del Distrito Federal
www.inmujer.df.gob.mx
The official website for the Institute for Women in the federal district offers information and articles on health, employment, education, and women's rights. It also provides information on the institute's events and activities and links to other sites.

Instituto Nacional de las Mujeres, México
www.inmujeres.gob.mx
The official website for the National Institute for Women provides information on programs, news, and events, as well as links to women's networks. The organization is dedicated to promoting gender equality in Mexico.

La Neta
www.laneta.apc.org
La Neta (*la neta* is Mexican slang for "truth") is the Mexican branch of the larger electronic communications organization, Association for the Progress of Communications (APC), which works in twenty-five countries around the world. The goal of APC and La Neta is to foster communication between nongovernmental civil organizations and movements dedicated to social change and justice.

MejorAmor D. de R. L. de C.V.
www.mejoramor.com
Founded in 2001, Mejor Amor is an online dating service geared toward Latinos in Latin America and abroad. The company has offices in the United States and Mexico.

Mexican Matchmakers
www.mexicanmatchmakers.com
Located in Guadalajara, Mexican Matchmakers provides online introduction services between Mexican women and foreign men looking to marry. The site displays photos of women, and men can purchase e-mail addresses, send flowers, and arrange for personal introductions to Mexican women.

Modemmujer.org
www.modemmujer.org
Modemmujer.org offers online networking for women at the grassroots level. It connects more than fifteen hundred women's organizations and activists in dialogue about issues affecting women. Modemmujer.org users share information on a variety of themes, from the dates of conferences to theoretical articles. Modemmujer.org also hosts the website for Equidad de Género, Ciudadanía, Trabajo y Familia A.C., an organization dedicated to gender equality.

MujerArte A.C.
www.mujerarte.org
MujerArte is a women's organization devoted to using art to express the social condition of women in Mexico and promote equality and social justice. The website offers information about the group's current events and its featured artists.

Mujereshoy.com
www.mujereshoy.com
Self-described as the *portal de las latinoamericanas*, Mujereshoy.com serves as a starting point for navigating the Web and strives to provide women with in-

formation not found through traditional media sources. It provides articles, information, and online forums on issues of health, environment, gender, culture, cooking, and so forth. Mujereshoy.com is the Latin American branch for the Spanish-language Internet site Isis International, which focuses on women's issues and networks in a global context.

Nuestras Hijas de Regreso a Casa A.C.
www.mujeresdejuarez.org
This website provides information about the murdered and disappeared women of Ciudad Juarez, offering photographs and news of the victims in five languages. Crafted for an international audience, the website provides articles and information on how to get involved in efforts to prevent further violence.

Planet Out, Inc.
www.mx.gay.com
This is a general website geared toward the gay community in Mexico. It hosts chat rooms, personal ads, and information on vacations, fitness, shopping, and the like. It is the Mexican branch of www.gay.com.

Saldelcloset
www.saldelcloset.com
Perhaps one of the more explicit websites to deal with issues of sexual identity and "coming out of the closet," Saldelcloset offers articles and other resources aimed at educating individuals and encouraging them to express their sexual identities.

Sexología Educativa Integral A.C.
www.sexualidadonline.com
In July 2004, the website www.sexualidadonline.com celebrated its first anniversary. As Mexico's first Web page providing sex education, sexualidadonline.com uses professional and academic sources to educate men, women, and adolescents. It engages in discussions of subjects as diverse as female mutilation, Internet dating, and homosexuality. Sexualidadonline.com uses scientific, objective, and ethical sources to create a balanced source for individuals to learn about dangers, opinions, and options in relation to their sexuality.

Todamujer.com
www.todamujer.com
Todamujer.com provides information for women on topics ranging from sexuality and contraceptives to gourmet cooking and daily horoscopes. It focuses on improving life for women on an individual level, in the home and at the workplace, and in romantic relations.

Notes

I would like to thank the editors of this volume, William E. French and Katherine Elaine Bliss, as well as William H. Beezley for encouraging the research for this appendix. I would also like to thank Sarah E. Rubin for reading an earlier draft of this work.

1. For a discussion on postmodern fluidity and multiplicity of the self in computer-mediated worlds, see Sherry Turkle, *Life on the Screen: Identity in the Age of the Internet* (New York: Simon & Schuster, 1995). For an article on virtual gender swapping and its more experimental nature, see Lynne D. Roberts and Malcolm R. Parks, "The Social Geography of Gender-Switching in Virtual Environments on the Internet," in *Virtual Gender: Technology, Consumption and Identity*, ed. Eileen Green and Alison Adam (London: Routledge, 2001).

2. Although not specifically about gender, two excellent volumes that address the intersections among society, media, and technology are Kelly Askew and Richard R. Wilk, eds., *The Anthropology of Media: A Reader* (Malden MA: Blackwell, 2002), and Faye Ginsburg, Lila Abu-Lughod, and Brian Larkin, eds., *Media Worlds: Anthropology on New Terrain* (Berkeley: University of California Press, 2002).

3. Weblogs, or "blogs," are online journals that can be created for free and require no knowledge of writing computer code. The diverse content of blogs ranges from personal diaries to philosophical and political writings to homemade pornography.

4. For works dealing with the concept of a global civil society or global public sphere, see Dale F. Eikelman and Jon W. Anderson, eds., *New Media in the Muslim World: The Emerging Public Sphere*, 2nd ed. (Bloomington, IN: Indiana University Press, 2003), and Ginsburg, Abu-Lughod, and Larkin, *Media Worlds*.

5. Arjun Appadurai, *Modernity at Large: Cultural Dimensions of Globalization* (Minneapolis: University of Minnesota Press, 1996).

6. For works on biological and reproduction technologies, see Anne Fausto-Sterling, *Sexing the Body: Gender Politics and the Construction of Sexuality* (New York: Basic Books, 2000), and Rayna Rapp, *Testing Women, Testing the Fetus: The Social Impact of Amniocentesis in America* (New York: Routledge, 2000). For other works that address the intersections among gender, feminism, science, and technology, see Mary Flanagan and Austin Booth, *Reload: Rethinking Women + Cyberspace* (Cambridge, MA: MIT Press, 2002); Keith Grint and Rosalind Gill, eds., *The Gender-Technology Relation: Contemporary Theory and Research* (London, U.K.: Taylor & Francis Inc., 1995); Donna Haraway, *The Haraway Reader* (New York: Routledge, 2004); Gill Kirkup, Linda Janes, Kath Woodward, and Fione Hovenden, eds., *The Gendered Cyborg: A Reader* (London: Routledge, 2000); Nina Lykke and Rosi Braidotti, *Between Monsters, Goddesses and Cyborgs: Feminist Confrontations with Science, Medicine and Cyberspace* (London: Zed Books, 1996).

7. In a discussion of women's movements, Lynn Stephen calls upon scholars not only to focus on women as participants but also to look at the self-analysis and description women have produced. See Lynn Stephen, "Women's Rights Are Human Rights: The Merging of Feminine and Feminist Interests among El Salvador's Mothers of the Disappeared (CO-MADRES)," *American Ethnologist* 22, no. (4) (1995): 807–27.

8. See, for example, David William Foster, "Afterword," in *Latin American Literature and Mass Media*, ed. Edmundo Paz-Soldán and Debra A. Castillo (New York: Garland, 2001), 311.

Bibliography

Aguirre, Carlos A., and Robert Buffington, eds. *Reconstructing Criminality in Latin America.* Wilmington, DE: Scholarly Resources, 2000.

Alonso, Ana María. *Thread of Blood: Colonialism, Revolution, and Gender on Mexico's Northern Frontier.* Tucson: University of Arizona Press, 1995.

Altman, Dennis. *Global Sex.* Chicago: University of Chicago Press, 2001.

Appelbaum, Nancy P., Anne S. Macpherson, and Karin Alejandra Rosemblatt, eds. *Race and Nation in Modern Latin America.* Chapel Hill: University of North Carolina Press, 2003.

Archetti, Eduardo P. "Estilos y virtudes masculinas en El Gráfico: La creación del imaginario del fútbol argentino." *Desarrollo Económico* 139 (1995).

———. *Masculinities: Football, Polo and the Tango in Argentina.* Oxford, UK: Berg, 1999.

———. *El potrero, la pista, y el ring: Las patrias del deporte argentino.* Buenos Aires: Fondo de Cultura Económica, 2001.

Babb, Florence E. *After Revolution: Mapping Gender and Cultural Politics in Neoliberal Nicaragua.* Austin: University of Texas Press, 2001.

Balderston, Daniel, and Donna J. Guy, eds. *Sex and Sexuality in Latin America.* New York: New York University Press, 1997.

Bayard de Volo, Lorraine. *Mothers of Heroes and Martyrs—Gender Identity Politics in Nicaragua, 1979–1999.* Baltimore: Johns Hopkins University Press, 2001.

Beattie, Peter M. *The Tribute of Blood: Army, Honor, Race, and Nation in Brazil, 1864–1945.* Durham, NC: Duke University Press, 2001.

Beezley, William H., and Linda Curcio-Nagy, eds. *Latin American Popular Culture: An Introduction.* Wilmington, DE: Scholarly Resources, 2000.

Beezley, William H., Cheryl English Martin, and William E. French, eds. *Rituals of Rule, Rituals of Resistance: Public Celebrations and Popular Culture in Mexico.* Wilmington, DE: Scholarly Resources, 1994.

Bergmann, Emilie L., and Paul Julian Smith, eds. *¿Entiendes? Queer Readings, Hispanic Writings.* Durham, NC: Duke University Press, 1995.

Bertoni, Lilia Ana. *Patriotas, cosmopolitas y nacionalistas: La construcción de la nacionalidad argentina a fines del siglo XIX.* 1st ed. Buenos Aires: Fondo de Cultura Económica, 2001.

Besse, Susan K. *Restructuring Patriarchy: The Modernization of Gender Inequality in Brazil, 1914–1940.* Chapel Hill: University of North Carolina Press, 1996.

Bliss, Katherine Elaine. "The Science of Redemption: Syphilis, Sexual Promiscuity, and Reformism in Revolutionary Mexico City." *Hispanic American Historical Review* 79, no. 1 (1999): 1–40.

———. *Compromised Positions: Prostitution, Public Health, and Gender Politics in Revolutionary Mexico City.* University Park: Pennsylvania State University Press, 2001.

Blum, Ann S. "Cleaning the Revolutionary Household: Domestic Servants and Public Welfare in Mexico City, 1900–1935." *Journal of Women's History* 15, no. 4 (2004): 67–90.

Bronfman, Alejandra. "En Plena Libertad y Democracia: Negros Brujos and the Social Question in Cuba, 1904–1919." *Hispanic American Historical Review* 82, no. 3 (2002): 549–87.

———. *Measures of Equality: Social Science, Citizenship, and Race in Cuba, 1902–1940.* Chapel Hill: University of North Carolina Press, 2004.

Buffington, Robert. *Criminal and Citizen in Modern Mexico.* Lincoln: University of Nebraska Press, 2000.

Buffington, Robert, and Pablo Piccato. "Tales of Two Women: The Narrative Construal of Porfirian Reality." *The Americas* 55, no. 3 (1999): 391–424.

Butler, Judith P. *Bodies That Matter: On the Discursive Limits of "Sex."* New York: Routledge, 1993.

Cano, Gabriela, and Georgette José Valenzuela, eds. *Cuatro estudios de género en el México urbano del siglo XIX.* Mexico City: Programa Universitario de Estudios de Género, UNAM, 2001.

Carpentier, Alejo. *Music in Cuba.* Minneapolis: University of Minnesota Press, 2001.

Carrancá y Rivas, Raúl. *Derecho penitenciario. Cárcel y penas en México.* Mexico City: Editorial Porrúa, 1986.

Carrillo, Héctor. *The Night Is Young: Sexuality in Mexico in the Time of AIDS.* Chicago: University of Chicago Press, 2002.

Caulfield, Sueann. *In Defense of Honor: Sexual Morality, Modernity, and Nation in Early-Twentieth-Century Brazil.* Durham, NC: Duke University Press, 2000.

———. "The History of Gender in the Historiography of Latin America." *Hispanic American Historical Review* 81, no. 3 (2001): 451–90.

Chambers, Sarah C. *From Subjects to Citizens: Honor, Gender, and Politics in Arequipa, Peru, 1780–1854.* University Park: Pennsylvania State University Press, 1999.

———. "To the Company of Men Like My Husband, No Law Can Compel Me: The Limits of Sanctions against Wife Beating in Arequipa, Peru, 1780–1850." *Journal of Women's History* 11, no. 1 (1999): 31–52.

Chauncey, George. *Gay New York: Gender, Urban Culture, and the Makings of the Gay Male World, 1890–1940.* New York: Basic Books, 1994.

Chomsky, Aviva. *West Indian Workers and the United Fruit Company in Costa Rica, 1870–1940.* Baton Rouge: Louisiana State University Press, 1996.

Chomsky, Aviva, and Aldo Lauria-Santiago, eds. *Identity and Struggle at the Margins of the Nation-State: The Laboring Peoples of Central America and the Hispanic Caribbean.* Durham, NC: Duke University Press, 1998.

Connell, R. W. *Masculinities.* Cambridge, UK: Polity Press, 1995.

Cott, Nancy F. *Public Vows: A History of Marriage and the Nation.* Cambridge, MA: Harvard University Press, 2000.

de Abreu Esteves, Martha. *Meninas perdidas: Os populares e o cotidiano no amor no Rio de Janeiro da Belle Epoque.* Rio de Janeiro: Paz e Terra, 1989.

D'Emilio, John, and Estelle B. Freedman. *Intimate Matters: A History of Sexuality in America.* Chicago: University of Chicago Press, 1997.

de la Fuente, Alejandro. *A Nation for All: Race, Inequality, and Politics in Twentieth-Century Cuba.* Chapel Hill: University of North Carolina Press, 2001.

Del Priore, Mary, ed. *História da criança no Brasil*. São Paulo: Contexto, 1991.

———. *Ao sul do corpo: Condição feminina, maternidade e mentalidades no Brasil colonial*. Rio de Janeiro: José Olympio and Edune, 1993.

———. "História das mulheres: As vozes do silencio." In *Historiografia brasileira em perspectiva*, ed. Marcos Cesar de Freitas. São Paulo: Contexto, 1998.

———, ed. *História das crianças no Brasil*. Rio de Janeiro: Editora Contexto, 2000.

de Oliveira Costa, Albertina, and Cristina Bruschini, eds. *Entre o virtude e o pecado*. São Paulo: Fundação Carlos Chagas, 1992.

Díaz, Arlene J. "Gender Conflicts in the Courts of the Early Venezuelan Republic, Caracas, 1811–1840." *Crime, Histoire et Sociétés/Crime, History and Society* 2, no. 2 (1998): 35–53.

———. *Female Citizens, Patriarchs, and the Law in Venezuela, 1786–1904*. Lincoln: University of Nebraska Press, 2004.

Dore, Elizabeth, and Maxine Molyneux, eds. *Hidden Histories of Gender and the State in Latin America*. Durham, NC: Duke University Press, 2000.

Duden, Barbara. *The Woman beneath the Skin: A Doctor's Patients in Eighteenth-Century Germany*. Cambridge, MA: Harvard University Press, 1991.

Engel, Magali G. *Meretrizes e doutores: Saber médico e prostituição no Rio de Janeiro*. São Paulo: Brasiliense, 1989.

Euraque, Darío A. *Reinterpreting the Banana Republic: Region and State in Honduras, 1870–1972*. Chapel Hill: University of North Carolina Press, 1996.

Fausto-Sterling, Anne. *Sexing the Body: Gender Politics and the Construction of Sexuality*. 1st ed. New York: Basic Books, 2000.

Feitlowitz, Marguerite. *A Lexicon of Terror: Argentina and the Legacies of Torture*. New York: Oxford University Press, 1998.

Field, Les W. *The Grimace of Macho Ratón: Artisans, Identity, and Nation in Late-Twentieth-Century Western Nicaragua*. Durham, NC: Duke University Press, 1999.

Ford, Talisman. "Passion in the Eye of the Beholder: Sexuality as Seen by Brazilian Sexologists, 1900–1940." PhD dissertation, Vanderbilt University, 1995.

Foucault, Michel. *The History of Sexuality*. 1st ed. New York: Vintage Books, 1980.

———. *Microfísica del poder*, trans. and ed. Julia Varela and Fernando Alvarez-Uria. Madrid: La Piqueta, 1980.

Fraga Filho, Walter. *Mendigos, moleques e vadios na Bahia do século XIX*. São Paulo: Editora Hucitec, 1996.

French, William E. "Prostitutes and Guardian Angels: Women, Work and the Family in Porfirian Mexico." *Hispanic American Historical Review* 72, no. 4 (1992): 529–53.

———. "Imagining and the Cultural History of Nineteenth-Century Mexico." *Hispanic American Historical Review* 79, no. 2 (1999): 249–67.

———. "'Te Amo Muncho': The Love Letters of Pedro and Enriqueta." In *The Human Tradition in Mexico*, ed. Jeffrey M. Pilcher, 123–35. Wilmington, DE: Scholarly Resources, 2003.

García, Ana Lidia. *Problemas metodológicos de la historia de las mujeres: La historiografía dedicada al siglo XIX mexicano*. Mexico City: Universidad Nacional Autónoma de México, 1994.

García González, Armando, and Raquel Alvarez Peláez. *En busca de la raza perfecta: Eugenesia e higiene en Cuba (1898–1958)*. Madrid: Consejo Superior de Investigaciones Científicas, 1999.

González Vásquez, Fernando, and Elías Zeledón Cartín, eds. *Crónicas y relatos para la historia de Puerto Limón*. San José: Ministerio de Cultura, Juventud y Deportes, Centro de Investigación Conservación del Patrimonio Cultural, 1999.

Gordon, Edmund Tayloe. *Disparate Diasporas: Identity and Politics in an African Nicaraguan Community*. 1st ed. Austin: University of Texas Press, Austin, Institute of Latin American Studies, 1998.

Gould, Jeffrey L. *To Lead as Equals: Rural Protest and Political Consciousness in Chinandega, Nicaragua, 1912–1979*. Chapel Hill: University of North Carolina Press, 1990.

——. *To Die in This Way: Nicaraguan Indians and the Myth of Mestizaje, 1880–1965.* Durham, NC: Duke University Press, 1998.

Graziano, Frank. *Divine Violence: Spectacle, Psychosexuality, and Radical Christianity in the Argentine "Dirty War."* Boulder, CO: Westview Press, 1992.

Green, James Naylor. *Beyond Carnival: Male Homosexuality in Twentieth-Century Brazil.* Chicago: University of Chicago Press, 1999.

Green, James Naylor, and Florence E. Babb, eds. "Gender and Same-Sex Desire in Latin America." *Latin American Perspectives* 29, no. 2 (2002).

Gutmann, Matthew C. *The Meanings of Macho: Being a Man in Mexico City.* Berkeley: University of California Press, 1996.

——, ed. *Changing Men and Masculinities in Latin America.* Durham, NC: Duke University Press, 2003.

Guy, Donna J. *Sex and Danger in Buenos Aires: Prostitution, Family, and Nation in Argentina.* Lincoln: University of Nebraska Press, 1991.

——. *White Slavery and Mothers Alive and Dead: The Troubled Meeting of Sex, Gender, Public Health, and Progress in Latin America.* Lincoln: University of Nebraska Press, 2000.

Halberstam, Judith. *Skin Shows: Gothic Horror and the Technology of Monsters.* Durham, NC: Duke University Press, 1995.

Hall, Stuart, and Paul du Gay, eds. *Questions of Cultural Identity.* London: Sage, 1996.

Halperin, David M. "Is There a History of Sexuality?" *History Theory* 28, no. 3 (1989).

——. *How to Do the History of Homosexuality.* Chicago: University of Chicago Press, 2002.

Harvey, Penelope, and Peter Gow, eds. *Sex and Violence: Issues in Representation and Experience.* London: Routledge, 1994.

Herschmann, Micael M., and Carlos Alberto Messeder Pereira, eds. *A invenção do Brasil moderno: Medicina, educação e engenharia nos anos 20–30.* Rio de Janeiro: Rocco, 1994.

Howe, A. Cymene. "Strategizing Sexualities, Re-Imagining Gender, and Televisionary Tactics: The Cultural Politics of Social Struggle in Neoliberal Nicaragua." PhD dissertation, University of New Mexico, 2003.

Htun, Mala. *Sex and the State: Abortion, Divorce, and the Family under Latin American Dictatorships and Democracies.* Cambridge: Cambridge University Press, 2003.

Hunefeldt, Christine. *Liberalism in the Bedroom: Quarreling Spouses in Nineteenth-Century Lima.* University Park: Pennsylvania State University Press, 2000.

Irwin, Robert McKee, Edward J. McCaughan, and Michelle Rocio Nasser, eds. *The Famous 41: Sexuality and Social Control in Mexico, c. 1901.* 1st ed. New York: Palgrave Macmillan, 2003.

Iznaga, Diana. *Transculturación en Fernando Ortiz.* Havana: Editorial de Ciencias Sociales, 1989.

James, Daniel. *Doña María's Story: Life History, Memory, and Political Identity.* Durham, NC: Duke University Press, 2000.

Johnson, Lyman L., and Sonya Lipsett-Rivera, eds. *The Faces of Honor: Sex, Shame, and Violence in Colonial Latin America.* 1st ed. Albuquerque: University of New Mexico Press, 1998.

Joseph, Gilbert M., Catherine LeGrand, and Ricardo D. Salvatore, eds. *Close Encounters of Empire: Writing the Cultural History of U.S.–Latin American Relations.* Durham, NC: Duke University Press, 1998.

Kennedy, Elizabeth Lapovsky, and Madeline D. Davis. *Boots of Leather, Slippers of Gold: The History of a Lesbian Community.* New York: Penguin Books, 1994.

Klubock, Thomas Miller. "Writing the History of Women and Gender in Twentieth-Century Chile." *Hispanic American Historical Review* 81, nos. 3–4 (2001): 493–96.

Krouwel, André, Jan Willem Duyvendak, and Barry D. Adam, eds. *The Global Emergence of Gay and Lesbian Politics: National Imprints of a Worldwide Movement.* Philadelphia: Temple University Press, 1999.

Lancaster, Roger N. *Thanks to God and the Revolution: Popular Religion and Class Consciousness in the New Nicaragua.* New York: Columbia University Press, 1988.

——. *Life Is Hard: Machismo, Danger, and the Intimacy of Power in Nicaragua.* Berkeley: University of California Press, 1992.

——. *The Trouble with Nature: Sex in Science and Popular Culture.* Berkeley: University of California Press, 2003.

Lancaster, Roger N., and Micaela de Leonardo, eds. *The Gender and Sexuality Reader: Culture, History, Political Economy.* New York: Routledge, 1997.

Laqueur, Thomas Walter. *Making Sex: Body and Gender from the Greeks to Freud.* Cambridge, MA: Harvard University Press, 1990.

Lavrin, Asunción. *Women, Feminism, and Social Change in Argentina, Chile, and Uruguay, 1890–1940.* Lincoln: University of Nebraska Press, 1995.

Ludmer, Josefina. *El género gauchesco. Un tratado sobre la patria.* Buenos Aires: Editorial Sudamericana, 1988.

Lumsden, Ian. *Machos, Maricones, and Gays: Cuba and Homosexuality.* Philadelphia: Temple University Press, 1996.

MacGregor Campusano, Javier. "Historiografía sobre criminalidad y sistema penitenciario." *Secuencia: Revista de historia y ciencias sociales* 22 (1992): 221–57.

MacKinnon, Catherine. *Sex Equality: Rape Law.* New York: Foundation Press, 2001.

Marquardt, Steve. "'Green Havoc': Panama Disease, Environmental Change, and Labor Process in the Central American Banana Industry." *American Historical Review* 106, no. 1 (2001): 49–80.

——. "Pesticides, Parakeets, and Unions in the Costa Rican Banana Industry, 1938–1962." *Latin American Research Review* 37, no. 2 (2002): 3–36.

Melhuus, Marit, and Kristi Anne Stølen, eds. *Machos, Mistresses, Madonnas: Contesting the Power of Latin American Gender Imagery.* London: Verso, 1996.

Melossi, Dario, and Massimo Pavarini. *Cárcel y fábrica. Los orígenes del sistema penitenciario (siglos XVI–XIX).* Mexico City: Siglo Veintiuno, 1980.

Moberg, Mark. *Myths of Ethnicity and Nation: Immigration, Work, and Identity in the Belize Banana Industry.* 1st ed. Knoxville: University of Tennessee Press, 1997.

Molloy, Sylvia, and Robert McKee Irwin, eds. *Hispanisms and Homosexualities.* Durham, NC: Duke University Press, 1998.

Montaldo, Graciela R. *Ficciones culturales y fábulas de identidad en América Latina.* 1st ed. Rosario, Argentina: B. Viterbo Editora, 1999.

Montecino, Sonia. *Madres y huachos.* Santiago: Cuarto Propio, 1991.

Montoya, Rosario, Lessie Jo Frazier, and Janise Hurtig, eds. *Gender's Place: Feminist Anthropologies of Latin America.* New York: Palgrave Macmillan, 2002.

Mosse, George L. *Nationalism and Sexuality: Respectability and Abnormal Sexuality in Modern Europe.* 1st ed. New York: H. Fertig, 1985.

Naranjo Orovio, Consuelo, and Armando Garciá González. *Medicina y racismo en Cuba: La ciencia ante la inmigración canaria en el siglo XX.* Tenerife: Centro de la Cultura Popular Canaria, 1996.

Nelson, Diane M. *A Finger in the Wound: Body Politics in Quincentennial Guatemala.* Berkeley: University of California Press, 1999.

Nesvig, Martin. "The Lure of the Perverse: Moral Negotiation of Pederasty in Porfirian Mexico." *Mexican Studies/Estudios Mexicanos* 16, no. 1 (2000): 1–37.

——. "The Complicated Terrain of Latin American Homosexuality." *Hispanic American Historical Review* 81, nos. 3–4 (2001).

Nye, Robert A. *Masculinity and Male Codes of Honor in Modern France.* New York: Oxford University Press, 1993.

Oliven, Ruben George. *Tradition Matters: Modern Gaucho Identity in Brazil*. New York: Columbia University Press, 1996.

Padilla Arroyo, Antonio. "Criminalidad, cárceles y sistema penitenciario en México, 1876–1910." PhD dissertation, El Colegio de México, 1995.

Paley, Julia. *Marketing Democracy: Power and Social Movements in Post-Dictatorship Chile*. Berkeley: University of California Press, 2001.

Palmié, Stephan. "Fernando Ortiz and the Cooking of History." *Ibero-Amerikanisches Archiv* 24 (1998): 1–21.

———. *Wizards and Scientists: Explorations in Afro-Cuban Modernity and Tradition*. Durham, NC: Duke University Press, 2002.

Parker, David S. "Law, Honor, and Impunity in Spanish America: The Debate over Dueling, 1870–1920." *Law and History Review* 19, no. 2 (2001): 326–28.

Parker, Richard G. *Beneath the Equator: Cultures of Desire, Male Homosexuality, and Emerging Gay Communities in Brazil*. New York: Routledge, 1999.

Peard, Julyan. *Race, Place, and Medicine: The Idea of the Tropics in Nineteenth-Century Brazilian Medicine*. Durham, NC: Duke University Press, 1999.

Pedro, Joana Maria, ed. *Práticas proibidas: Práticas costumeiras de aborto e infantícidio no século XX*. Florianópolis, Brazil: Cidade Futura, 2003.

Penyak, Lee Michael. "Criminal Sexuality in Central Mexico, 1750–1850." PhD dissertation, University of Connecticut, 1993.

Piccato, Pablo. "Politics and the Technology of Honor: Dueling in Turn-of-the-Century Mexico." *Journal of Social History* 33, no. 2 (1999): 331–54.

———. *City of Suspects: Crime in Mexico City, 1900–1931*. Durham, NC: Duke University Press, 2001.

———. "'El Chalequero' or 'the Mexican Jack the Ripper': The Meanings of Sexual Violence in Turn-of-the-Century Mexico City." *Hispanic American Historical Review* 81, no. 3 (2001): 623.

———. "Interpretations of Sexuality in Mexico City Prisons: A Critical Version of Roumagnac." In *The Famous 41: Sexuality and Social Control in Mexico, c. 1901*, ed. Robert McKee Irwin, Edward J. McCaughan, and Michelle Rocio Nasser. New York: Palgrave Macmillan, 2003.

Pino Iturrieta, Elías. *Las ideas de los primeros venezolanos*. Caracas: Fondo Editorial Tropykos, 1987.

———. *La mentalidad venezolana de la emancipación*. 2nd ed. Caracas: Ediciones Eldorado, 1991.

———. *Contra lujuria, castidad: Historias de pecado en el siglo XVIII venezolano*. Caracas: Alfadil Ediciones, 1992.

———. *Ventaneras y castas, diabólicas y honestas*. Caracas: Editorial Planeta, 1993.

———. *Fueros, civilización y cuidadanía: Estudio sobre el siglo XIX en Venezuela*. Caracas: Universidad Católica Andrés Bello, 2000.

Pino Iturrieta, Elías, and Frédérique Lange. *Quimeras de amor, honor y pecado en el siglo XVIII venezolano*. Caracas, Venezuela: Editorial Planeta Venezolana, 1994.

Porter, Susie S. *Working Women in Mexico City: Public Discourses and Material Conditions, 1879–1931*. Tucson: University of Arizona Press, 2003.

Pratt, Mary Louise, and Kathleen Newman, eds. *Critical Passions*. Durham, NC: Duke University Press, 1999.

Prescott, Heather Munro. *A Doctor of Their Own: The History of Adolescent Medicine*. Cambridge, MA: Harvard University Press, 1998.

Prieto, Adolfo. *El discurso criollista en la formación de la Argentina moderna*. Buenos Aires: Editorial Sudamericana, 1988.

Prieur, Annick. *Mema's House, Mexico City: On Transvestites, Queens, and Machos*. Chicago: University of Chicago Press, 1998.

Putnam, Lara. *The Company They Kept: Migrants and the Politics of Gender in Caribbean Costa Rica, 1870–1960.* Chapel Hill: University of North Carolina Press, 2002.

Putnam, Lara Elizabeth. "Parentesco y producción: La organización social de la agricultura de exportación en la provincia de Limón, Costa Rica, 1920–1960." *Revista de Historia* 44 (2001): 121–58.

Quiza Moreno, Ricardo. "Fernando Ortíz y su hampa afrocubana." In *Diez nuevas miradas de historia de Cuba*, ed. José Piqueras Arenas. Castelló de la Plana: Universitat Jaume I, 1998.

Ramos Escandón, Carmen, ed. *Género e historia: La historiografía sobre la mujer.* Mexico City: Universidad Autónoma Metropolitana, 1992.

Randall, Margaret. *Sandino's Daughters Revisited: Feminism in Nicaragua.* New Brunswick, NJ: Rutgers University Press, 1994.

Randall, Margaret, and Lynda Yanz. *Sandino's Daughters: Testimonies of Nicaraguan Women in Struggle.* Vancouver, BC: New Star Books, 1981.

Rodríguez, Julia. "Encoding the Criminal: Criminology and the Science of 'Social Defense' in Modernizing Argentina (1880–1921)." PhD dissertation, Columbia University, New York, 1999.

Rodríguez S., Eugenia. "Género, historia y política en Centroamérica." In *Conferencias internacionales: Primer encuentro mesoamericano de estudios de género*, ed. Marcela Lararde, Guadalupe Espinoza, Margarita Pisano, Soledad González M., Eugenia Rodríguez S., and Graciela Hierro. La Antigua, Guatemala: FLACSO, 2001.

Romano, Eduardo. *Las letras del tango: Antología cronológica: 1900–1980.* Rosario, Argentina: Editorial Fundación Ros, 1991.

Rosemblatt, Karin Alejandra. *Gendered Compromises: Political Cultures and the State in Chile, 1920–1950.* Chapel Hill: University of North Carolina Press, 2000.

Rubenstein, Anne. *Bad Language, Naked Ladies, and Other Threats to the Nation: A Political History of Comic Books in Mexico.* Durham, NC: Duke University Press, 1998.

Ruggiero, Guido, and Edward Muir, eds. *Sex and Gender in Historical Perspective.* Baltimore: Johns Hopkins University Press, 1991.

Ruggiero, Kristen. "Honor, Maternity, and the Disciplining of Women: Infanticide in Late-Nineteenth-Century Buenos Aires." *Hispanic American Historical Review* 72, no. 3 (1992).

Sacristán, Cristina, and Pablo Piccato, eds. *Actores, espacios y debates en la historia de la esfera pública en la ciudad de México.* Mexico City: UNAM, Instituto de Investagaciones Históricas; Instituto Mora, 2005.

Sagredo, Rafael. *María Villa, (a) La Chiquita, no. 4002.* Mexico City: Cal y Arena, 1996.

Salessi, Jorge. *Médicos, maleantes y maricas: Higiene, criminología y homosexualidad en la construcción de la nación Argentina (Buenos Aires 1871–1914).* Rosario, Argentina: Beatriz Viterbo, 1995.

Salvatore, Ricardo D., and Carlos Aguirre, eds. *The Birth of the Penitentiary in Latin America: Essays on Criminology, Prison Reform and Social Control, 1830–1940.* Austin: University of Texas Press, 1996.

Salvatore, Ricardo D., Carlos Aguirre, and Gilbert M. Joseph, eds. *Crime and Punishment in Latin America: Law and Society since Late Colonial Times.* Durham, NC: Duke University Press, 2001.

Samper Kutschbach, Mario. *Generations of Settlers: Rural Households and Markets on the Costa Rican Frontier, 1850–1935.* Boulder, CO: Westview Press, 1990.

Sarlo, Beatriz. "Modernidad y mezcla cultural." In *Buenos Aires 1880–1930: La capital de un imperio imaginario*, ed. Héctor Vázquez Rial. Madrid: Alianza Editorial, 1996.

Savigliano, Marta. *Tango and the Political Economy of Passion.* Boulder, CO: Westview Press, 1995.

Scarry, Elaine. *The Body in Pain: The Making and Unmaking of the World.* New York: Oxford University Press, 1985.

Schell, Patience A. *Church and State Education in Revolutionary Mexico City.* Tucson: University of Arizona Press, 2003.

Scott, Joan Wallach. "Gender as a Useful Category of Historical Analysis." *American Historical Review* 91, no. 5 (1986).

———. *Gender and the Politics of History, Gender and Culture.* New York: Columbia University Press, 1999.

———, ed. *Feminism and History, Oxford Readings in Feminism.* New York: Oxford University Press, 1996.

Skurski, Julie. "The 'Leader' and the 'People': Representing the Nation in Postcolonial Venezuela." PhD dissertation, University of Chicago, Chicago, Illinois, 1993.

———. "The Ambiguities of Authenticity in Latin America: Doña Bárbara and the Construction of National Identity." In *Becoming National: A Reader,* ed. Geoff Eley and Ronald Suny. New York: Oxford University Press, 1996.

Soluri, John. "People, Plants, and Pathogens: The Eco-Social Dynamics of Export Banana Production in Honduras, 1875–1950." *Hispanic American Historical Review* 80, no. 3 (2000): 463–501.

———. "Consumo de masas, biodiversidad y fitomejoramiento del banano de exportación, 1920 a 1980." *Revista de Historia* 44 (2001): 33–66.

Sommer, Doris. "Irresistible Romance: The Foundational Fictions of Latin America." In *Nation and Narration,* ed. Homi K. Bhabha. London: Routledge, 1990.

———. *Foundational Fictions: The National Romances of Latin America.* Berkeley: University of California Press, 1991.

———, ed. *The Places of History: Regionalism Revisted in Latin America.* Durham, NC: Duke University Press, 1999.

Speckman, Elisa. *Crimen y castigo: Legislación penal, interpretaciones de la criminalidad y administración de justicia (Ciudad de México, 1872–1910).* Mexico City: El Colegio de México, 2002.

Stepan, Nancy Leys. *"The Hour of Eugenics:" Race, Gender and Nation in Latin America.* Ithaca, NY: Cornell University Press, 1991.

Stern, Alexandra Minna. "Buildings, Boundaries and Blood: Medicalization and Nation-Building on the U.S.-Mexico Border, 1910–1930." *Hispanic American Historical Review* 79, no. 1 (1999): 41–81.

———. "Responsible Mothers and Normal Children: Eugenics and Nationalism in Post-Revolutionary Mexico City, 1920–1940." *Journal of Historical Sociology* 12, no. 4 (1999): 369–97.

Stern, Steve J. *The Secret History of Gender: Women, Men and Power in Late Colonial Mexico.* Chapel Hill: University of North Carolina Press, 1995.

Stoner, K. Lynn. *From the House to the Streets: The Cuban Woman's Movement for Legal Reform, 1898–1940.* Durham, NC: Duke University Press, 1991.

Striffler, Steve. *In the Shadows of State and Capital: The United Fruit Company, Popular Struggle, and Agrarian Restructuring in Ecuador, 1900–1995.* Durham, NC: Duke University Press, 2002.

Suárez Findlay, Eileen J. *Imposing Decency: The Politics of Sexuality and Race in Puerto Rico, 1870–1920.* Durham, NC: Duke University Press, 1999.

Taussig, Michael T. *Shamanism, Colonialism, and the Wild Man: A Study in Terror and Healing.* Chicago: University of Chicago Press, 1986.

———. *The Nervous System.* New York: Routledge, 1992.

Taylor, Diana. *Disappearing Acts: Spectacles of Gender and Nationalism in Argentina's "Dirty War."* Durham, NC: Duke University Press, 1997.

Tinsman, Heidi. "Good Wives and Unfaithful Men: Gender Negotiations and Sexual Conflicts in the Chilean Agrarian Reform, 1964–1973." *Hispanic American Historical Review* 81, no. 3–4 (2001): 587–619.

———. *Partners in Conflict: The Politics of Gender, Sexuality, and Labor in the Chilean Agrarian Reform, 1950–1973.* Durham, NC: Duke University Press, 2002.

Vaughan, Mary Kay. *Cultural Politics in Revolution: Teachers, Peasants and Schools in Mexico, 1930–1940.* Tucson: University of Arizona Press, 1997.

Vázquez Rial, Héctor, ed. *Buenos Aires 1880–1930: La capital de un imperio imaginario.* Madrid: Alianza Editorial, 1996.

Vega, Carlos. *Apuntes para la historia del movimiento tradicionalista argentino.* Buenos Aires: Instituto Nacional de Musicología, 1981.

Viales Hurtado, Ronny J. *Después del enclave: Un estudio de la región atlántica costarricense, 1927–1950.* San José: Editorial de la Universidad de Costa Rica, 1998.

———. "Los liberales y la colonización de las áreas de frontera no cafetaleras. El caso de la región Atlántica (Caribe) costarricense entre 1870 y 1930." PhD dissertation, Universitat Autónoma de Barcelona, Barcelona, Spain, 2000.

Walker, Thomas, ed. *Revolution and Counterrevolution in Nicaragua.* Boulder, CO: Westview, 1991.

Walkowitz, Judith R. *City of Dreadful Delight: Narratives of Sexual Danger in Late Victorian London.* London: Virago, 1992.

Warner, Michael. *The Trouble with Normal: Sex, Politics and the Ethics of Queer Life.* New York: Free Press, 1999.

Weeks, Jeffrey. *Making Sexual History.* Cambridge, UK: Polity Press, 2000.

Whitney, Robert. *State and Revolution in Cuba: Mass Mobilization and Political Change, 1920–1940.* Chapel Hill: University of North Carolina Press, 2001.

Zeledón Cartín, Elías. *Viajes por la República de Costa Rica.* Vol. 2. San José: Ministerio de Cultura, Juventud y Deportes, 1997.

Index

Academy of Medicine (Brazil): Durocher's induction into, 68n13; Durocher's writings and, 63–64; speeches to, 52, 59–60

adolescents: crafting an independent identity among, 172–74, 183; crafting a sexual culture and, 167–69, 174; discursive category of, 13; emergence of category of, 166; gendered gradients of power and, 182–83; male same-sex relations and, 178–79; Mexican Revolution and, 166–67; modern fashion and, 167–68; pregnancy and, 179–81; sexuality and, 168–70, 176–79; spaces for entertainment and, 174–75; work and, 171–73, 175–76

Aguiar Whitaker, Dr. Edmur de, 190, 200

Alemán, Arnoldo, 252–53, 258n29

Asociación de Mujeres Nicaragüenses, Luisa Amanda Espinosa (AMNLAE): formation of, 238; internal conflicts in, 240–41; post-1990 regimes in Nicaragua and, 250

bananas: expansion of estates, 138–41

Batlle y Ordóñez, José: polemic with leaders of rival party, 119; president of Uruguay, 110, 118, 119–22

Belem prison: economic activities in, 93–94; establishing hierarchy among prisoners in, 92–93; establishment of, 91, 105n25; minor's department in, 93, 96, 98; sexual and affective relations in, 94–96; structure of vigilance in, 91–92; violence and, 91–92, 95–100; women's section of, 98–101

body: atavism as a theory and, 89; classification according to "race," 79; criminality and, 79–80, 83–84; "degenerated" Brazilian and, 191; Estado Novo and, 204, 206–7; gendering of, 87–88; historical construction of, 14–17; Internet and, 283; mapping of in Cuba, 76; military regimes and, 261; monstrous and, 263–65; relationship of social and physical and, 192–93; trope of healing and, 278–79

About the Contributors

Eduardo P. Archetti was a social anthropologist and professor at the University of Oslo, Norway. His work on popular culture in Argentina focused on football, polo, and male identity. His most recent monograph, *El potrero, la pista, y el ring: las patrias del deporte argentino*, was published in 2001 by the Fondo de Cultura Económica in Buenos Aires. Archetti passed away in June 2005.

Katherine Elaine Bliss is a visiting scholar at the Georgetown University Center for Latin American Studies. She is the author of *Compromised Positions: Prostitution, Public Health and Gender Politics in Revolutionary Mexico City* and has published articles related to gender, law, and public health in the *Hispanic American Historical Review, Latin American Research Review, Journal of Family History, Law and History Review*, and *Journal of Women's History*, in addition to book chapters and essays in edited collections.

Ann S. Blum has a PhD in Latin American history from the University of California, Berkeley, and teaches at the University of Massachusetts, Boston. She is currently completing a book titled *Domestic Economies*, which examines economically marginal urban families and domestic labor during Mexico's period of revolutionary reform. Her research on child abandonment, adoption, maternal-child health, and domestic service has appeared in the *Journal of Family History, The Americas*, and *Journal of Women's History*, as well as in anthologies on disease and medicine in Latin America and women's and gender history in postrevolutionary Mexico.

Alejandra Bronfman is assistant professor of Latin American and Caribbean history at the University of British Columbia, Vancouver, Canada. She received her PhD at Princeton University and has taught at the University of Florida and Yale University. She is the author of *Measures of Equality: Social Science, Citizenship and Race in Cuba, 1902–1940,* as well as of articles in the *Hispanic American Historical Review, Temas, Gender and History,* and *Journal of Social History.*

Arlene J. Díaz is associate professor of history at Indiana University, Bloomington, and the author of *Female Citizens, Patriarchs and the Law in Venezuela, 1786–1904.*

Lessie Jo Frazier is a historian and anthropologist in gender studies at Indiana University. She works on questions of political culture, human rights, sexuality, and gender. The chapter in this collection is part of her work in progress, *Desired States: Gender, Sexuality, and Political Culture in Chile.* Her first book, *Salt in the Sand: Memory, Violence and the Nation-State in Chile, 1890–Present,* is forthcoming. She is coeditor of *Gender's Place: Feminist Anthropologies of Latin America.*

William E. French is associate professor of history at the University of British Columbia, Vancouver, Canada. He is the author of *A Peaceful and Working People: Manners, Morals, and Class Formation in Northern Mexico* and coeditor of *Rituals of Rule, Rituals of Resistance: Public Celebrations and Popular Culture in Mexico.* He has published articles in the *Hispanic American Historical Review* and contributed to the *Oxford History of Mexico.* He is currently working on a book about love letters, diaries, and courtship in nineteenth- and twentieth-century Mexico.

James N. Green is associate professor of Brazilian history and culture at Brown University and the director of the Center for Latin American Studies. He is the author of *Beyond Carnival: Male Homosexuality in Twentieth-Century Brazil* and *"We Cannot Remain Silent": Opposition to the Brazilian Military Dictatorship in the U.S., 1964–1985* (forthcoming). Green is the past president of the Brazilian Studies Association and chair of the Committee on the Future of Brazilian Studies in the United States.

Cymene Howe holds a Mellon postdoctoral fellowship in the Department of Anthropology at Cornell University. Her work on new social movements and analyses of gender and sexuality in a transnational context takes a broad comparative perspective of global processes and their role in transforming sexuality and gender in the contemporary era. In the United States and Latin America, her research analyzes how meanings surrounding masculinity, femininity, and homosexuality are reshaped through local advocacy strategies and globally circulated concepts of rights, creating what she terms an "erotiscape." Her research has appeared in publications such as *Cultural Anthropology, City and Society,* and the collection *Life in America.*

David S. Parker is associate professor of history at Queen's University, Kingston, Ontario, Canada. He is author of *The Idea of the Middle Class: White-Collar Workers and Peruvian Society, 1900–1950,* and articles on labor, class formation, social policy, and the law in nineteenth- and early-twentieth-century Latin America.

Pablo Piccato is associate professor with the Department of History, Columbia University. He received his BA from the Universidad Nacional Autónoma de México and his MA and PhD from the University of Texas, Austin. His published work includes *City of Suspects: Crime in Mexico City, 1900–1931, Congreso y revolución: El parlamentarismo en la XXVI legislatura;* he is editor of *El poder legislativo en las décadas revolucionarias,* and, with Cristina Sacristán, *Actores, espacios y debates en la historia de la esfera pública en la ciudad de México* (2005), in addition to authoring articles and chapters in journals and edited collections.

Lara E. Putnam is associate professor of history at the University of Pittsburgh. She received her PhD from the University of Michigan, Ann Arbor. Putnam is the author of *The Company They Kept: Migrants and the Politics of Gender in Caribbean Costa Rica, 1870–1960* and coeditor of *Honor, Status and the Law in Modern Latin America.* Her current research focuses on issues related to migration, youth, and empire in the British Caribbean.

Wendy A. Vogt is a graduate student in the Department of Anthropology at the University of Arizona in Tucson. Her work focuses on gender, family relations, and women's networks in contemporary Mexico. She is currently working with indigenous migrants living in the U.S.-Mexico border region.

Erica M. Windler received her PhD from the University of Miami. Her work focuses on the history of childhood, gender, and family in nineteenth-century Brazil. She is currently on the faculty at Michigan State University, where she teaches in the Department of History.